Angel Sanctuary™

story and art by Kaori Yuki

vol.8

Angel Sanctuary

Vol. 8
Shôjo Edition

STORY AND ART BY KAORI YUKI

Translation/Alexis Kirsch
English Adaptation/Matt Segale
Touch-up & Lettering/James Hudnall
Cover, Graphics & Design/Izumi Evers
Editor/Pancha Diaz

Managing Editor/Annette Roman
Director of Production/Noboru Watanabe
Vice President of Publishing/Alvin Lu
Sr. Director of Acquisitions/Rika Inouye
VP of Sales & Marketing/Liza Coppola
Publisher/Hyoe Narita

Tenshi Kinryou Ku by Kaori Yuki © Kaori Yuki 1996
All rights reserved. First published in Japan in 1997 by HAKUSENSHA, Inc., Tokyo.
English language rights in America and Canada arranged with HAKUSENSHA, Inc.,
Tokyo. New and adapted artwork and text © 2005 VIZ, LLC.
All rights reserved.
The ANGEL SANCTUARY logo is a trademark of VIZ, LLC.
The stories, characters and incidents mentioned in this publication are entirely fictional.

Printed in Canada.

Published by VIZ, LLC
P.O. Box 77010
San Francisco, CA 94107

Shôjo Edition
10 9 8 7 6 5 4 3 2 1
First printing, May 2005

www.viz.com   store.viz.com

Angel Sanctuary

story and art by **Kaori Yuki** vol.8

The Story Thus Far

High school boy Setsuna Mudo's life is hellish. He's always been a troublemaker, but his worst sin was falling incestuously in love with his beautiful sister Sara. However, his troubles are preordained—he is the reincarnation of the Lady Alexiel, an angel who rebelled against Heaven and led the demons of Hell in a revolt. Her punishment was to be reborn into tragic life after tragic life. This time, her life is as Setsuna.

Setsuna's body, left behind on Earth while he searched Hell for his beloved Sara's soul, has died. When he returned from Hell along the Meidou path of reincarnation, he reemerged on Earth in the body of the Angel Alexiel. Now Setusna is determined to brave the gates of Heaven in order to retrieve his sister.

Meanwhile, Setsuna's friends have troubles of their own. Kira reveals the dark truth behind his history as the sword Nanatsusaya, and his seeming devotion to Alexiel. The demon Belial entices Kurai with the information that the "anti-soul" spell can return Setsuna's original body to life. Kurai can't get to Heaven to ask the physician Angel Raphael to perform the spell...but Lucifer also has the necessary power, and will resurrect Setsuna if Kurai becomes his bride.

And in Heaven, Sevothtarte chafes at having to abdicate his power to the mad Angel Rosiel, while the Great Angels Raphael and Michael begin to look into the fates of their brethren, and the rumors of a Savior resurrected among the Evils of Hell.

Contents

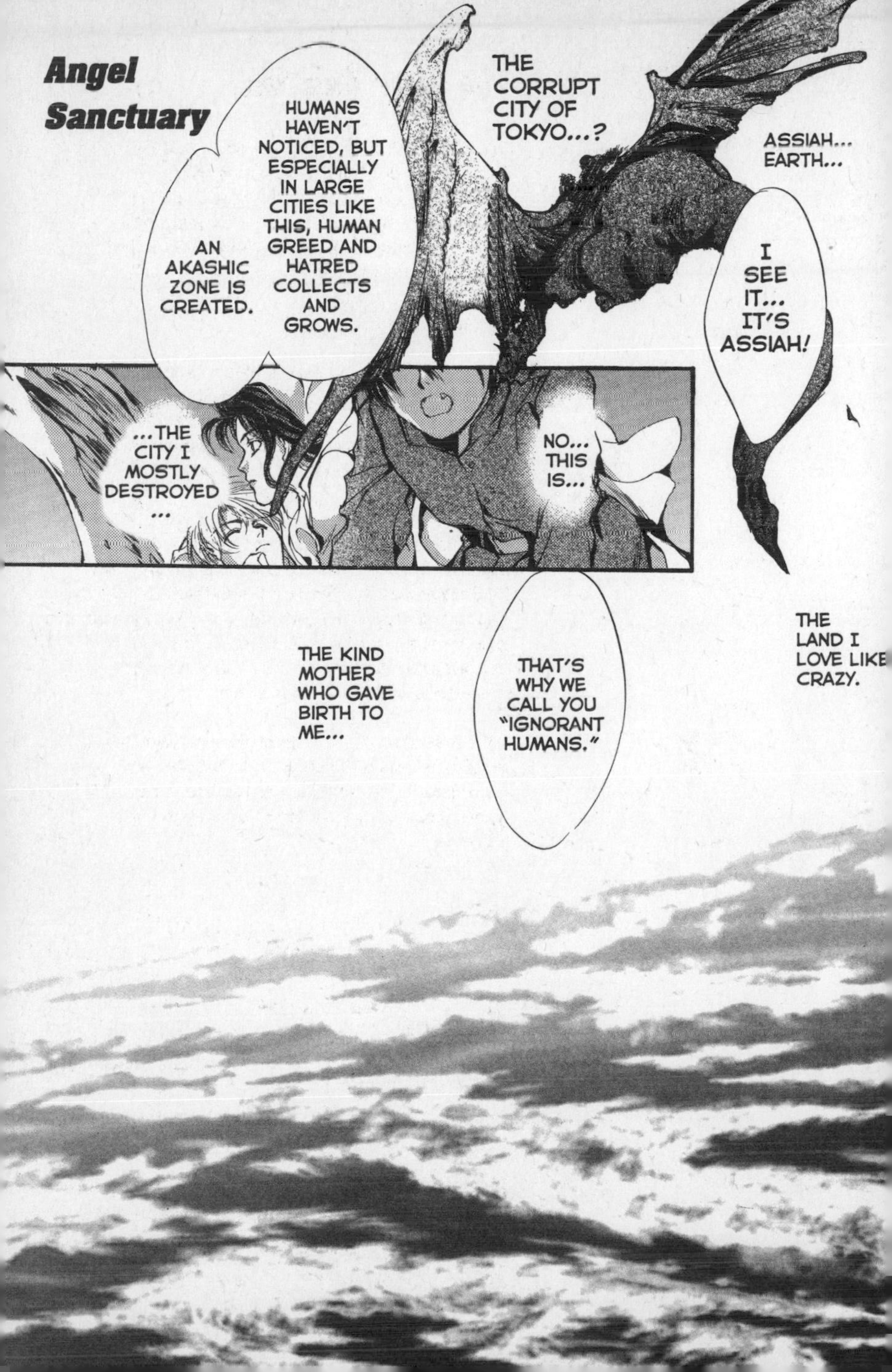
ASSIAH... EARTH...
I SEE IT... IT'S ASSIAH!
THE CORRUPT CITY OF TOKYO...?
HUMANS HAVEN'T NOTICED, BUT ESPECIALLY IN LARGE CITIES LIKE THIS, HUMAN GREED AND HATRED COLLECTS AND GROWS.
AN AKASHIC ZONE IS CREATED.
NO... THIS IS...
...THE CITY I MOSTLY DESTROYED ...
THE LAND I LOVE LIKE CRAZY.
THAT'S WHY WE CALL YOU "IGNORANT HUMANS."
THE KIND MOTHER WHO GAVE BIRTH TO ME...

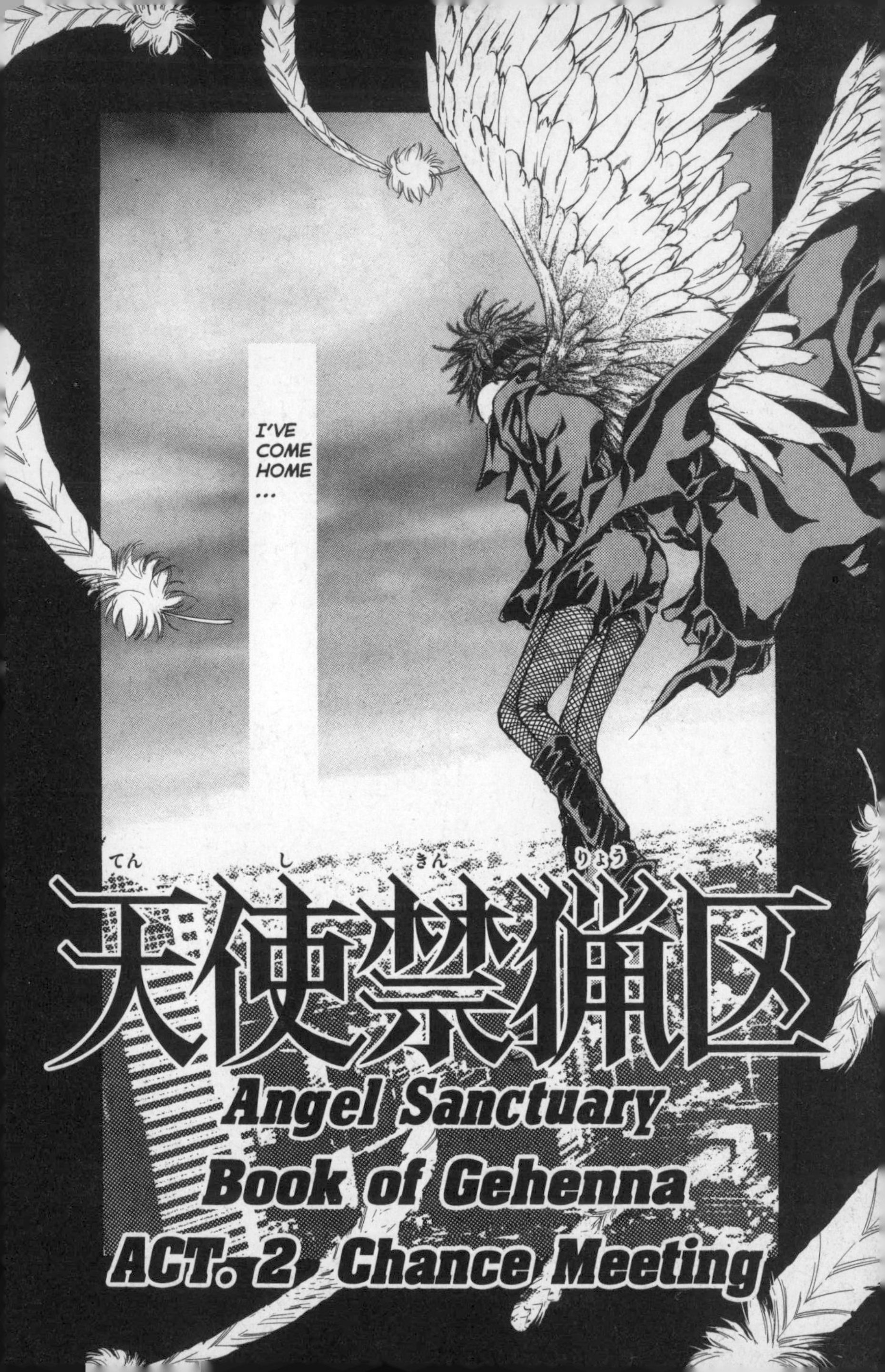
I'VE COME HOME ...
てん し きん りょう く
天使禁猟区
Angel Sanctuary
Book of Gehenna
ACT. 2 Chance Meeting

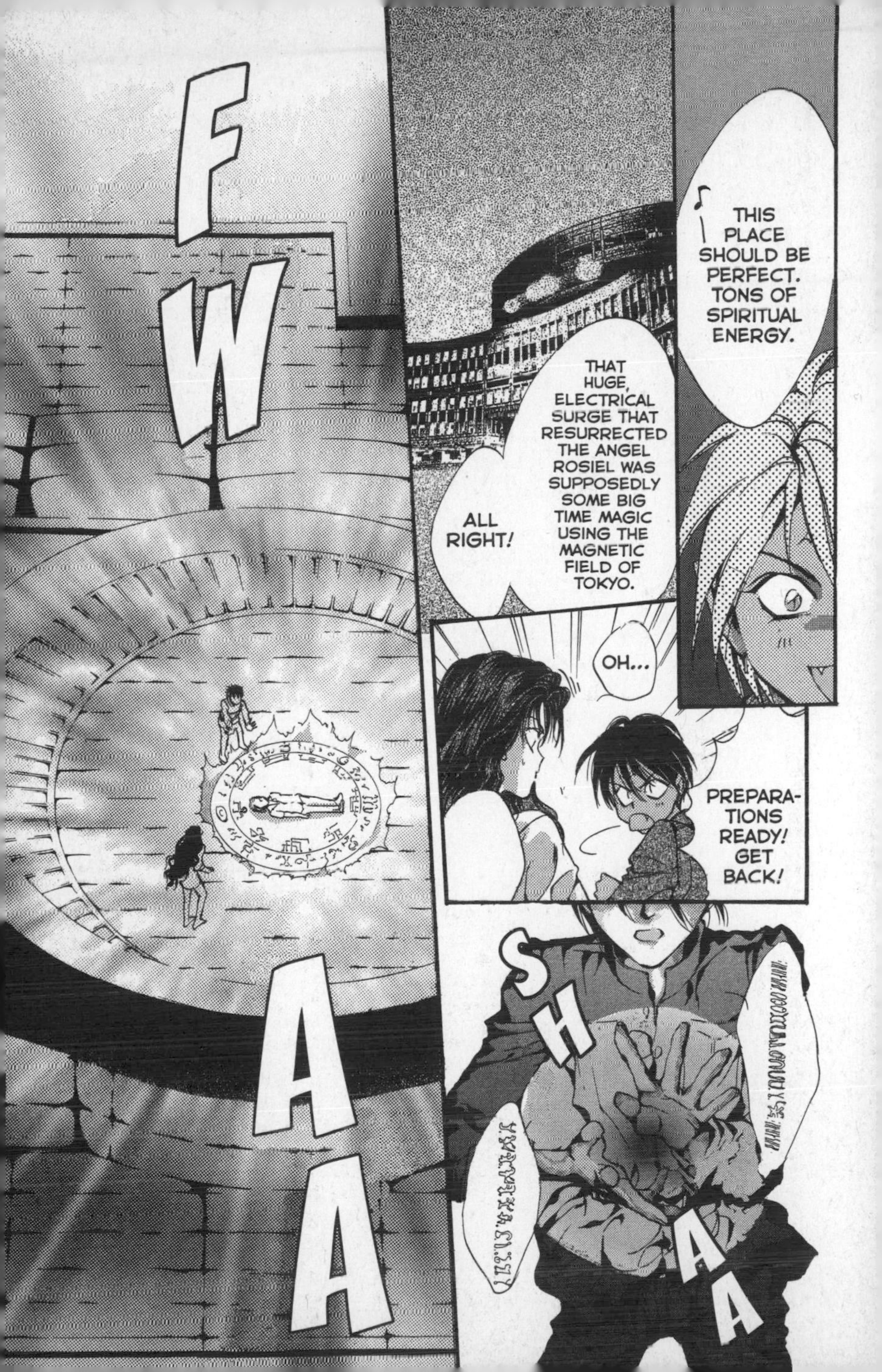
THIS PLACE SHOULD BE PERFECT. TONS OF SPIRITUAL ENERGY.
THAT HUGE, ELECTRICAL SURGE THAT RESURRECTED THE ANGEL ROSIEL WAS SUPPOSEDLY SOME BIG TIME MAGIC USING THE MAGNETIC FIELD OF TOKYO.
ALL RIGHT!
OH...
PREPARATIONS READY! GET BACK!
SHAAA
FWAAA

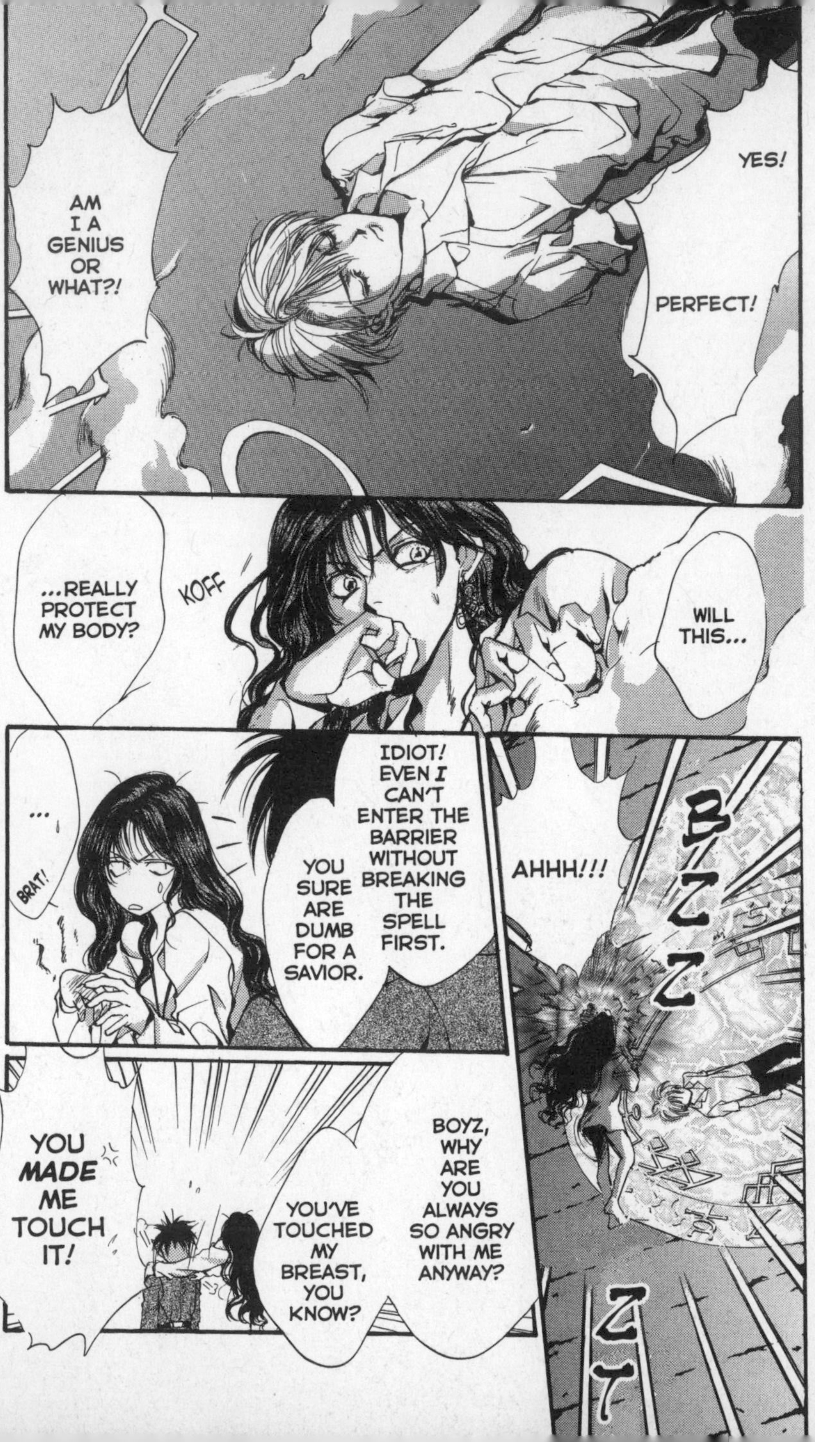
YES!
PERFECT!
AM I A GENIUS OR WHAT?!
WILL THIS...
KOFF
...REALLY PROTECT MY BODY?
BZZ
AHHH!!!
ZZT
IDIOT! EVEN I CAN'T ENTER THE BARRIER WITHOUT BREAKING THE SPELL FIRST.
YOU SURE ARE DUMB FOR A SAVIOR.
...
BRAT!
BOYZ, WHY ARE YOU ALWAYS SO ANGRY WITH ME ANYWAY?
YOU'VE TOUCHED MY BREAST, YOU KNOW?
YOU MADE ME TOUCH IT!

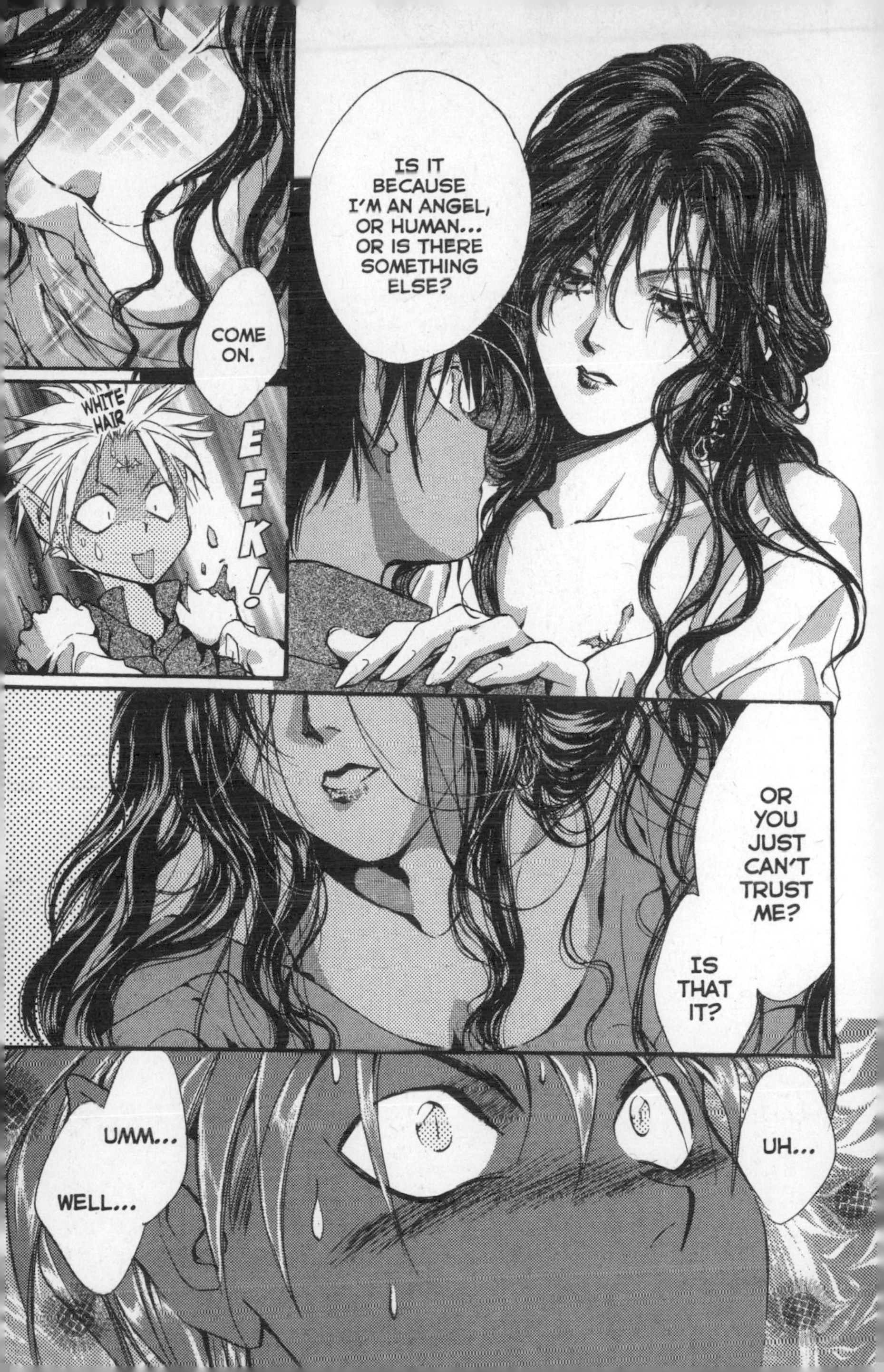
IS IT BECAUSE I'M AN ANGEL, OR HUMAN... OR IS THERE SOMETHING ELSE?
COME ON.
WHITE HAIR
EEK!
OR YOU JUST CAN'T TRUST ME?
IS THAT IT?
UH...
UMM...
WELL...

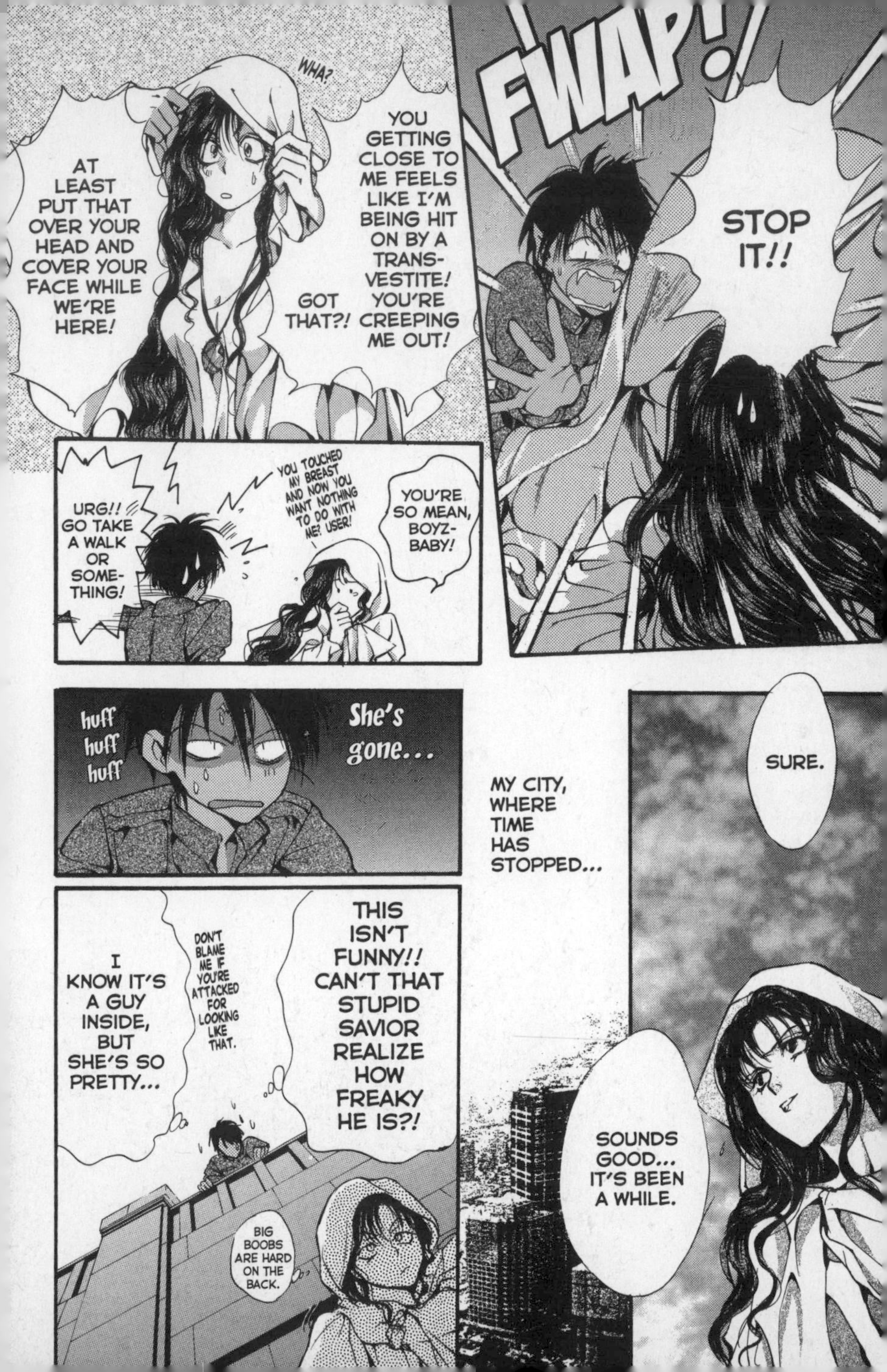
FWAP!
STOP IT!!
WHA?
YOU GETTING CLOSE TO ME FEELS LIKE I'M BEING HIT ON BY A TRANS-VESTITE! YOU'RE CREEPING ME OUT!
AT LEAST PUT THAT OVER YOUR HEAD AND COVER YOUR FACE WHILE WE'RE HERE!
GOT THAT?!
YOU'RE SO MEAN, BOYZ-BABY!
YOU TOUCHED MY BREAST AND NOW YOU WANT NOTHING TO DO WITH ME? USER!
URG!! GO TAKE A WALK OR SOME-THING!
SURE.
MY CITY, WHERE TIME HAS STOPPED...
SOUNDS GOOD... IT'S BEEN A WHILE.
She's gone...
huff huff huff
THIS ISN'T FUNNY!! CAN'T THAT STUPID SAVIOR REALIZE HOW FREAKY HE IS?!
DON'T BLAME ME IF YOU'RE ATTACKED FOR LOOKING LIKE THAT.
I KNOW IT'S A GUY INSIDE, BUT SHE'S SO PRETTY...
BIG BOOBS ARE HARD ON THE BACK.

It's Angel Sanctuary Book 8! Yeah, sorry for always starting these in the same way. Yes, like always I don't have much free time. It's always the same kind of problems. Things are so hectic, but I try my best. Umm...My working area changed! I moved in January, and the new space is larger so I'm much happier. It's like a dream, everything is so organized (compared to before). I even have enough desks for everyone now. The TV is huge and, there's a private room. No more problems with closets that are hard to open and showers with no hot water. No more problems!! Well... That's not true... There's always something.

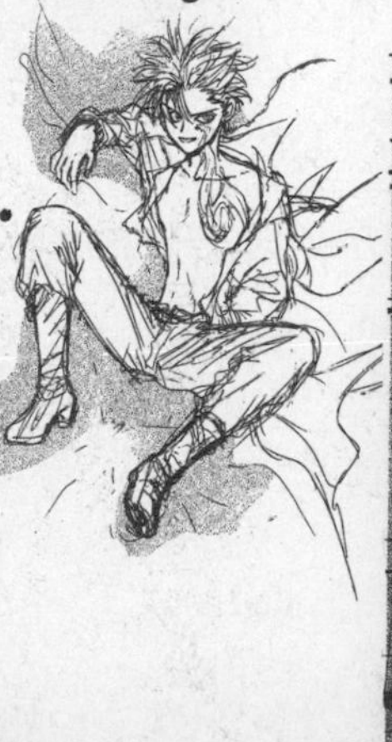

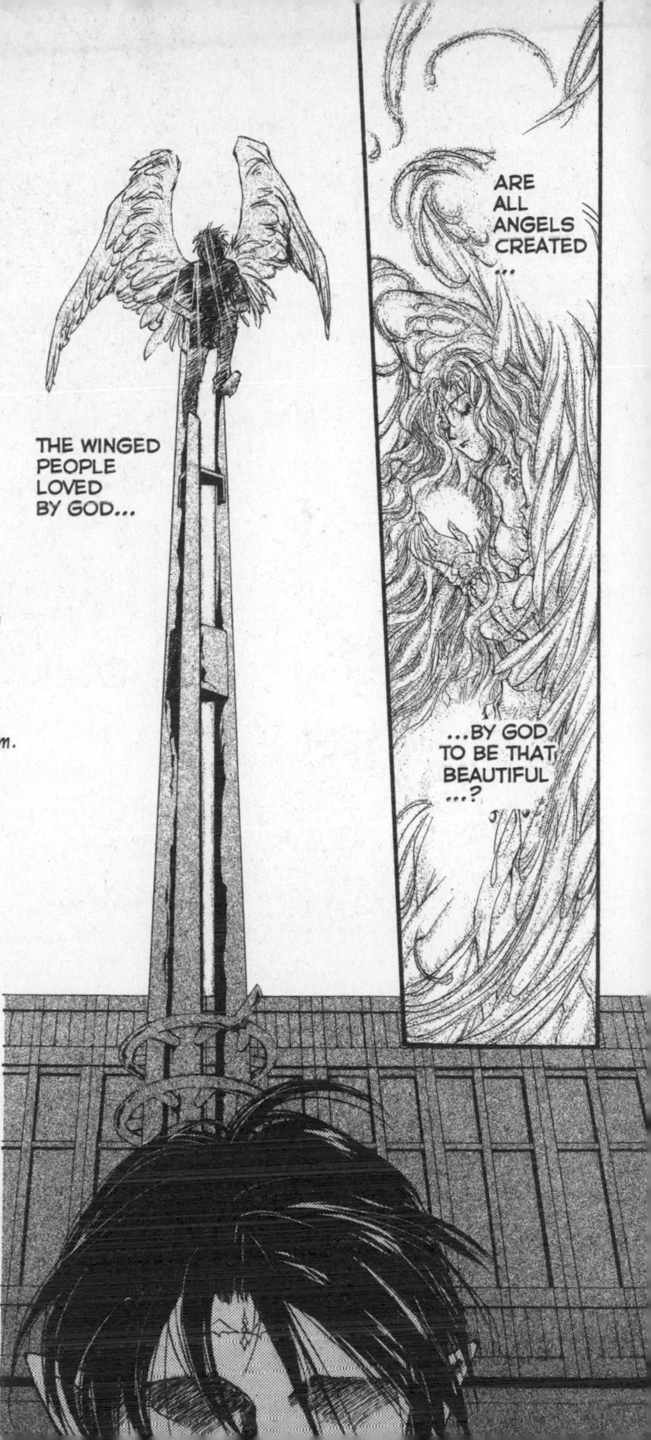
ARE ALL ANGELS CREATED ...
...BY GOD TO BE THAT BEAUTIFUL ...?
THE WINGED PEOPLE LOVED BY GOD...

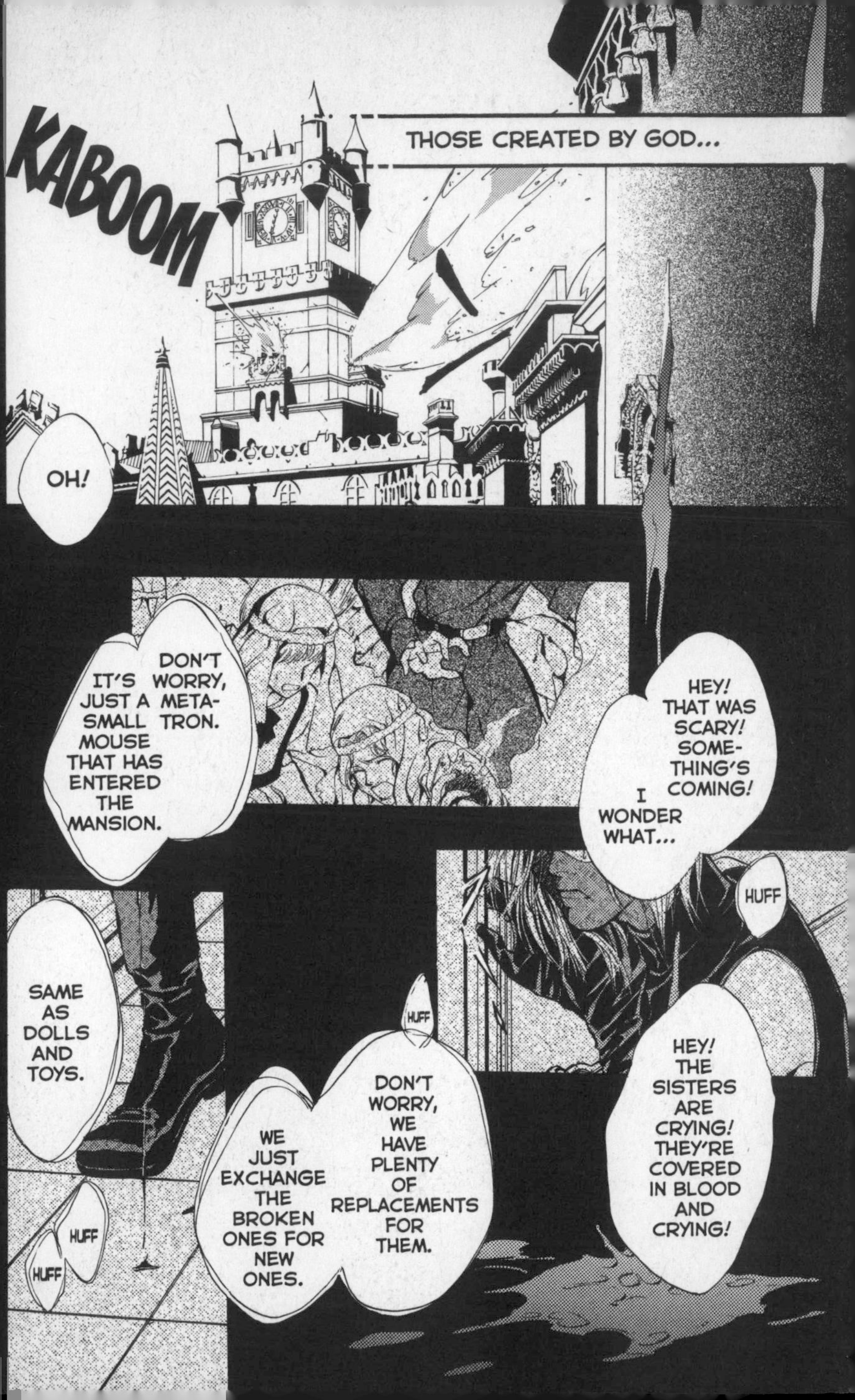
THOSE CREATED BY GOD...
KABOOM
OH!
HEY! THAT WAS SCARY! SOMETHING'S COMING! I WONDER WHAT...
DON'T WORRY, METATRON.
IT'S JUST A SMALL MOUSE THAT HAS ENTERED THE MANSION.
HUFF
HEY! THE SISTERS ARE CRYING! THEY'RE COVERED IN BLOOD AND CRYING!
HUFF
DON'T WORRY, WE HAVE PLENTY OF REPLACEMENTS FOR THEM.
WE JUST EXCHANGE THE BROKEN ONES FOR NEW ONES.
SAME AS DOLLS AND TOYS.
HUFF
HUFF

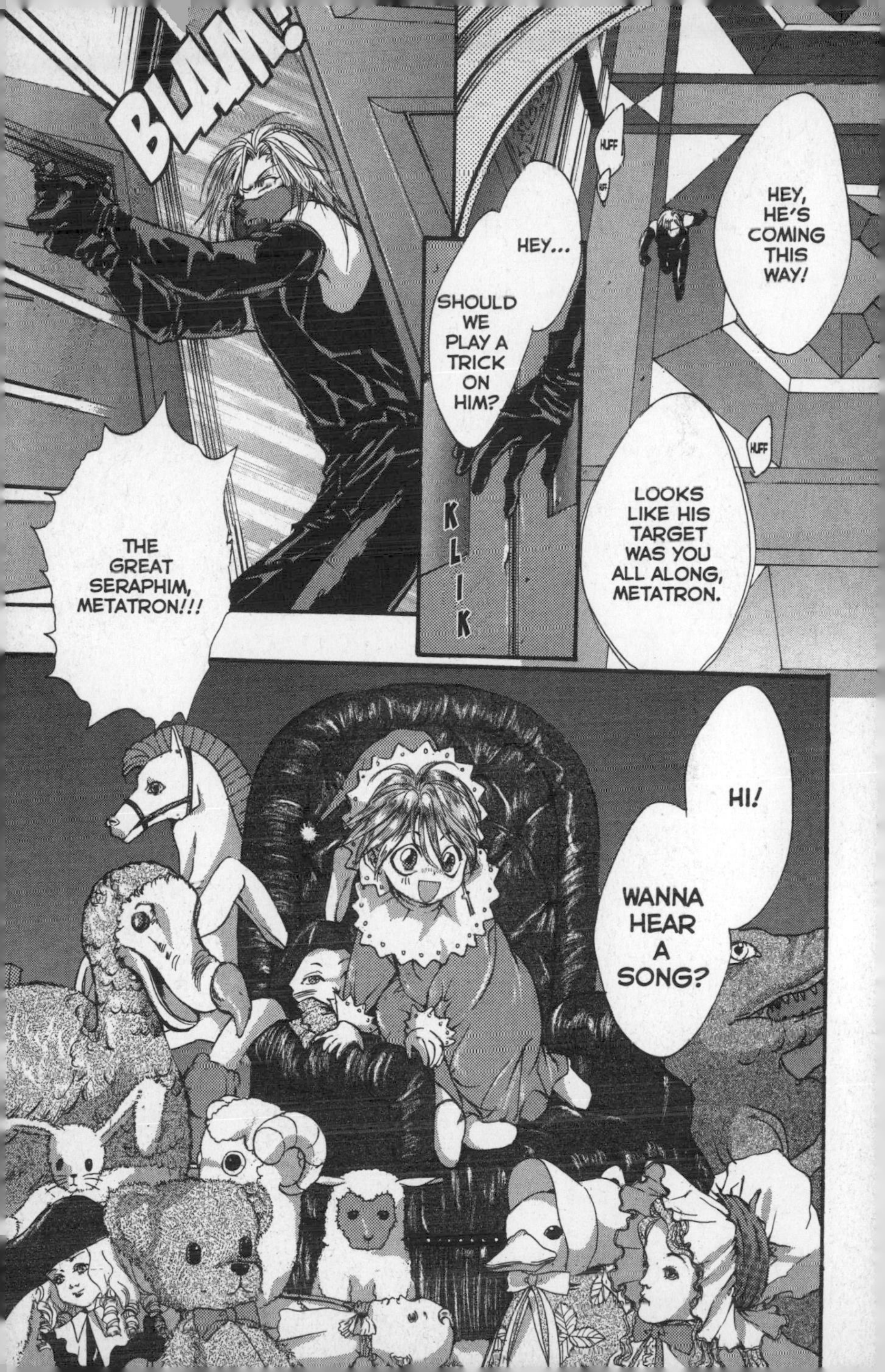
HEY, HE'S COMING THIS WAY!
HUFF
HUFF
HUFF
LOOKS LIKE HIS TARGET WAS YOU ALL ALONG, METATRON.
HEY...
SHOULD WE PLAY A TRICK ON HIM?
KLIK
BLAM!
THE GREAT SERAPHIM, METATRON!!!
HI!
WANNA HEAR A SONG?

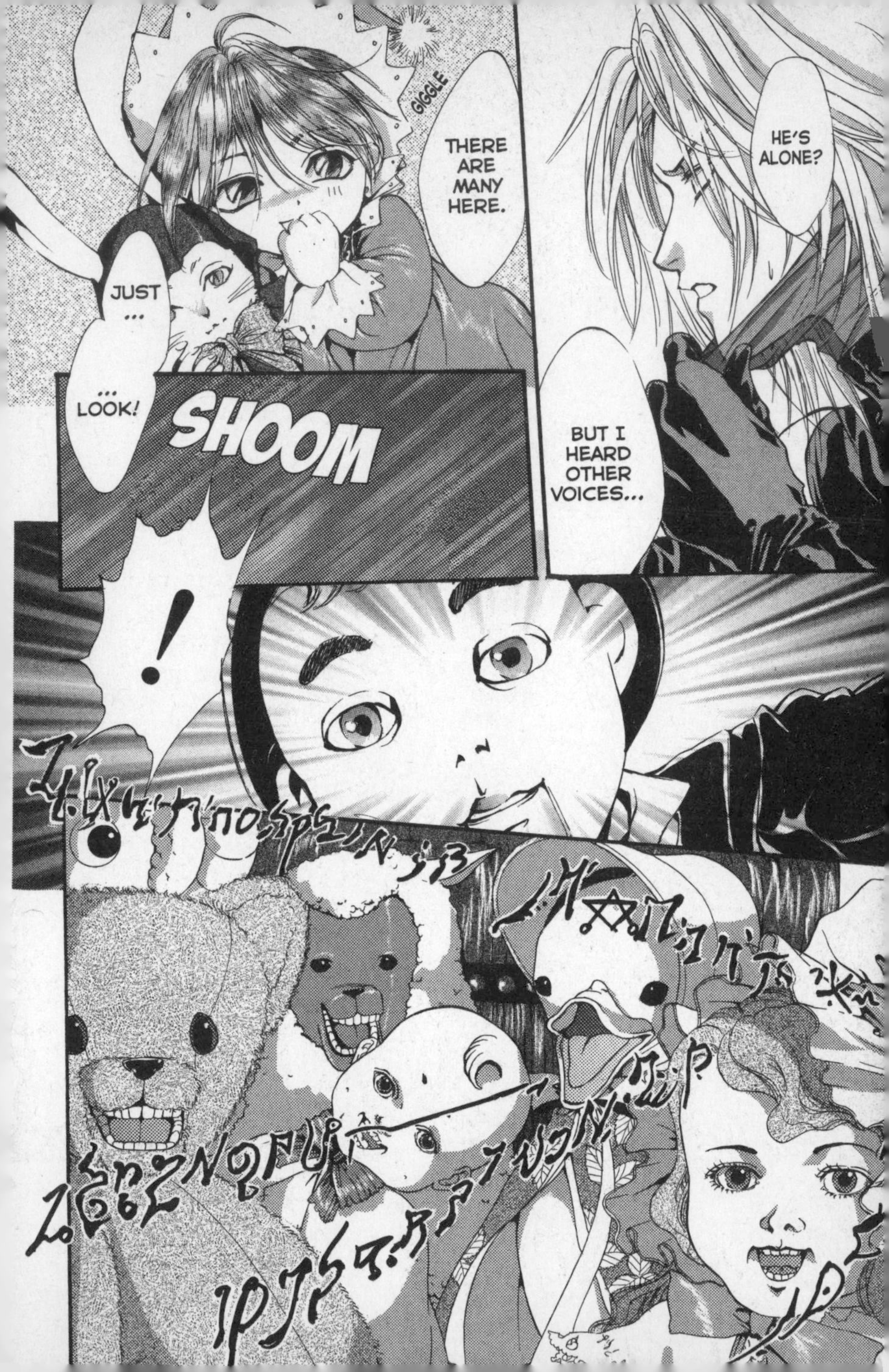
HE'S ALONE?
BUT I HEARD OTHER VOICES...
GIGGLE
THERE ARE MANY HERE.
JUST ...
... LOOK!
SHOOM
!

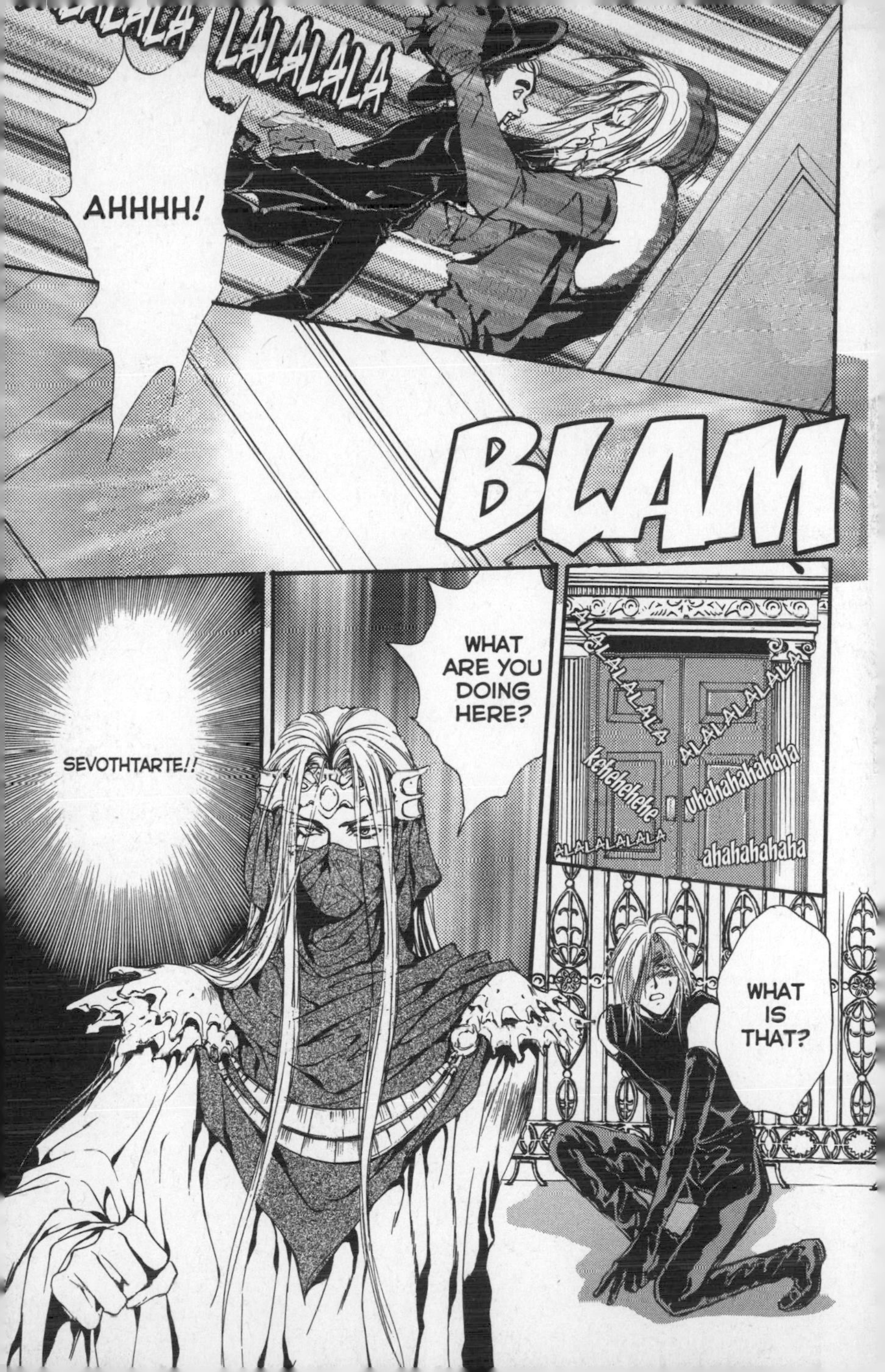
LALALALA
LALALA
AHHHH!
BLAM
ALALALALALALA
ALALALALALALA
uhahahahahaha
kehehehehe
ahahahahaha
ALALALALALA
WHAT ARE YOU DOING HERE?
SEVOTHTARTE!!
WHAT IS THAT?

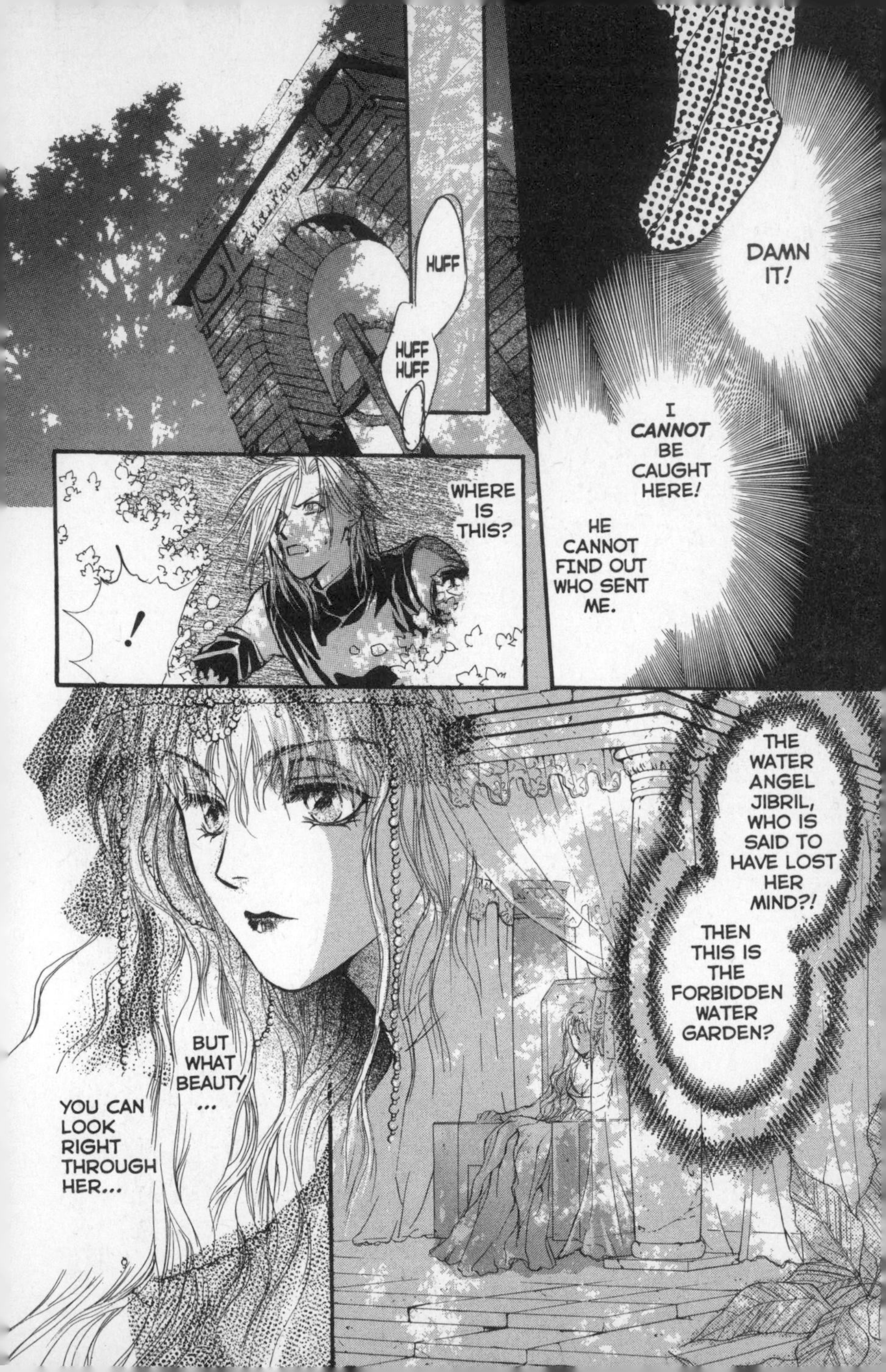
DAMN IT!
I *CANNOT* BE CAUGHT HERE!
HE CANNOT FIND OUT WHO SENT ME.
HUFF
HUFF HUFF
WHERE IS THIS?
!
THE WATER ANGEL JIBRIL, WHO IS SAID TO HAVE LOST HER MIND?!
THEN THIS IS THE FORBIDDEN WATER GARDEN?
BUT WHAT BEAUTY...
YOU CAN LOOK RIGHT THROUGH HER...

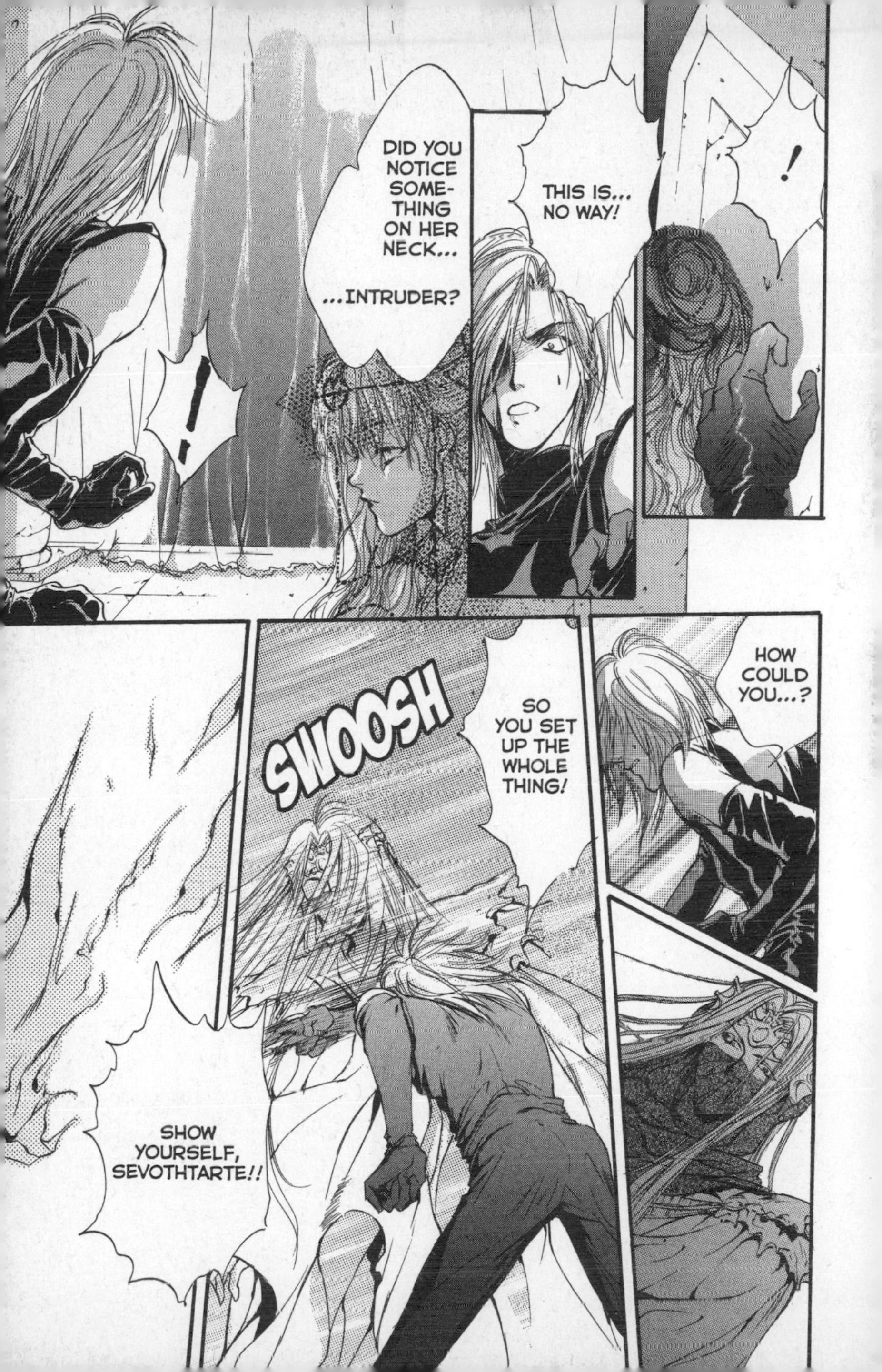
!
THIS IS... NO WAY!
DID YOU NOTICE SOME-THING ON HER NECK...
...INTRUDER?
!
HOW COULD YOU...?
SO YOU SET UP THE WHOLE THING!
SWOOSH
SHOW YOURSELF, SEVOTHTARTE!!

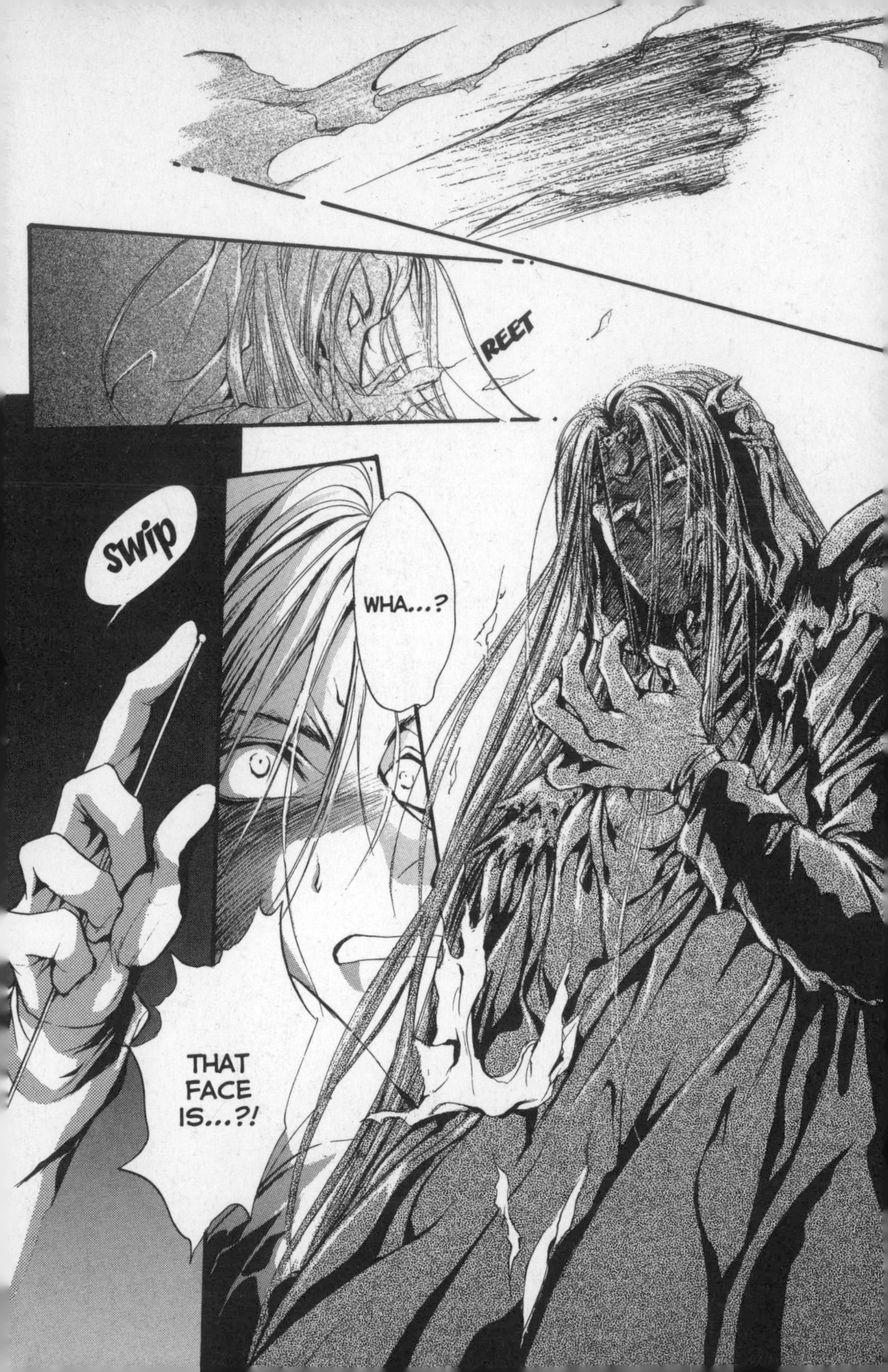
REET
WHA...?
swip
THAT FACE IS...?!

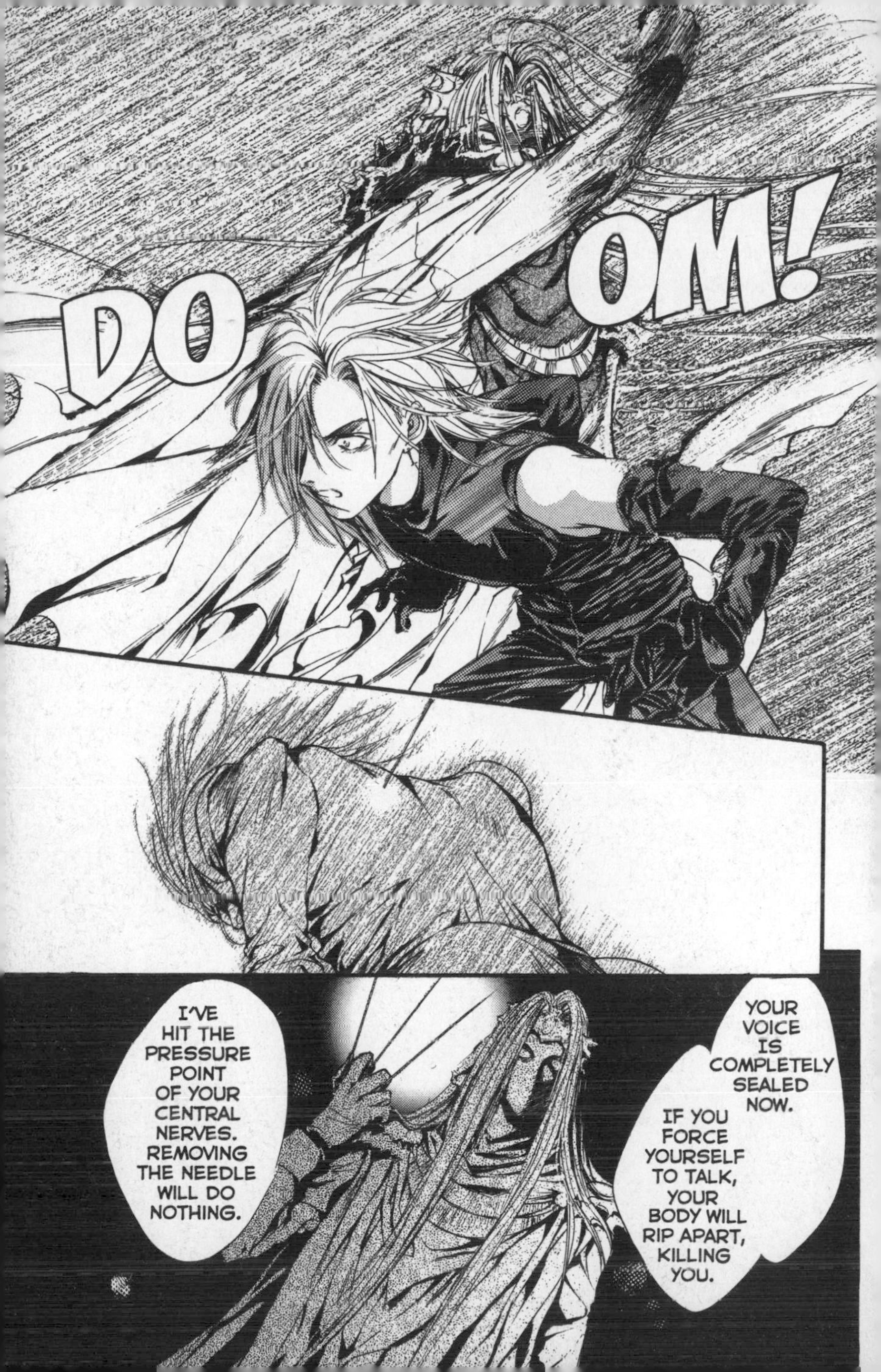
DOOM!
YOUR VOICE IS COMPLETELY SEALED NOW.
I'VE HIT THE PRESSURE POINT OF YOUR CENTRAL NERVES. REMOVING THE NEEDLE WILL DO NOTHING.
IF YOU FORCE YOURSELF TO TALK, YOUR BODY WILL RIP APART, KILLING YOU.

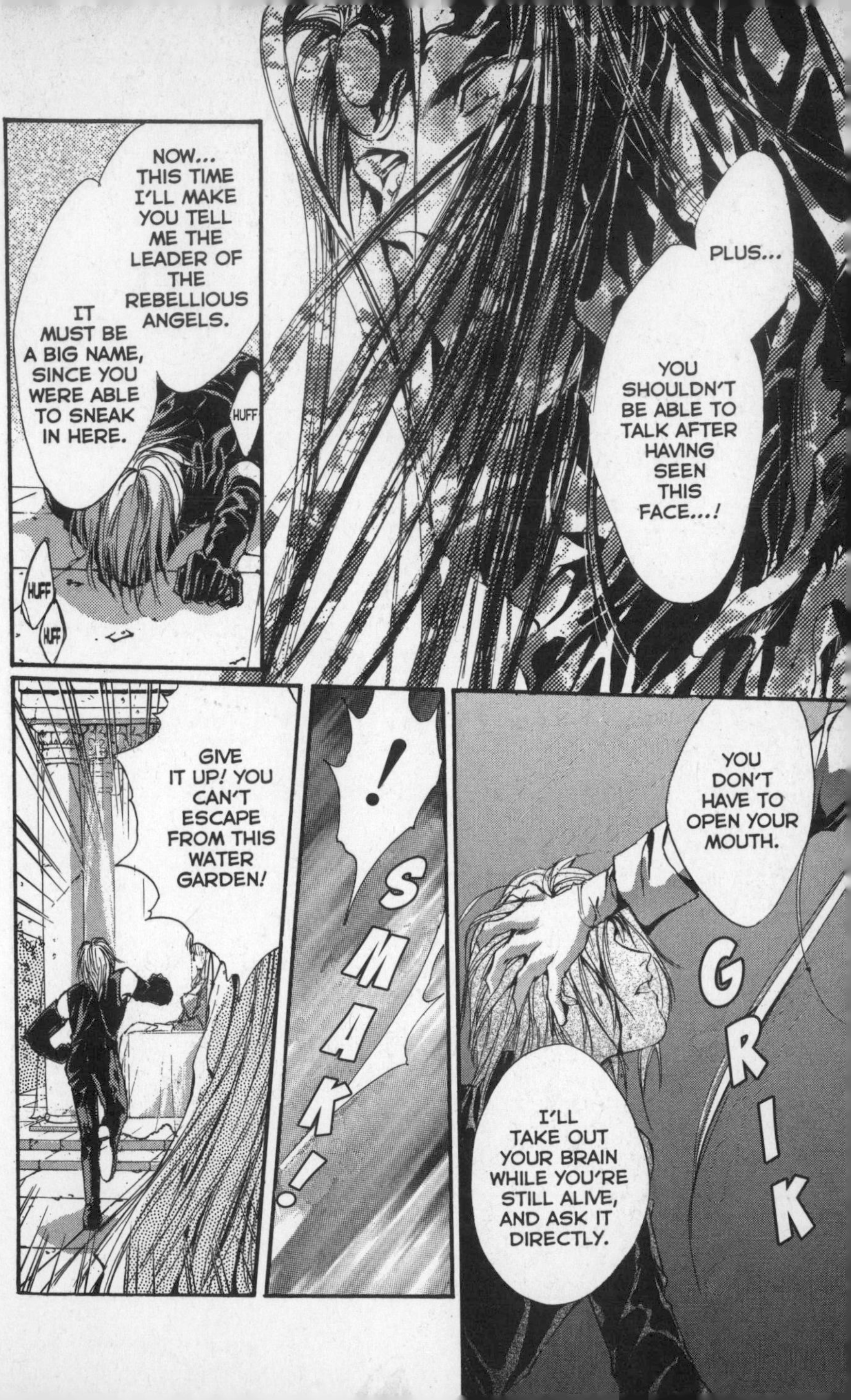
PLUS...
YOU SHOULDN'T BE ABLE TO TALK AFTER HAVING SEEN THIS FACE...!
NOW... THIS TIME I'LL MAKE YOU TELL ME THE LEADER OF THE REBELLIOUS ANGELS.
IT MUST BE A BIG NAME, SINCE YOU WERE ABLE TO SNEAK IN HERE.
HUFF
HUFF
HUFF
YOU DON'T HAVE TO OPEN YOUR MOUTH.
GRIK
I'LL TAKE OUT YOUR BRAIN WHILE YOU'RE STILL ALIVE, AND ASK IT DIRECTLY.
!
SMAK!
GIVE IT UP! YOU CAN'T ESCAPE FROM THIS WATER GARDEN!

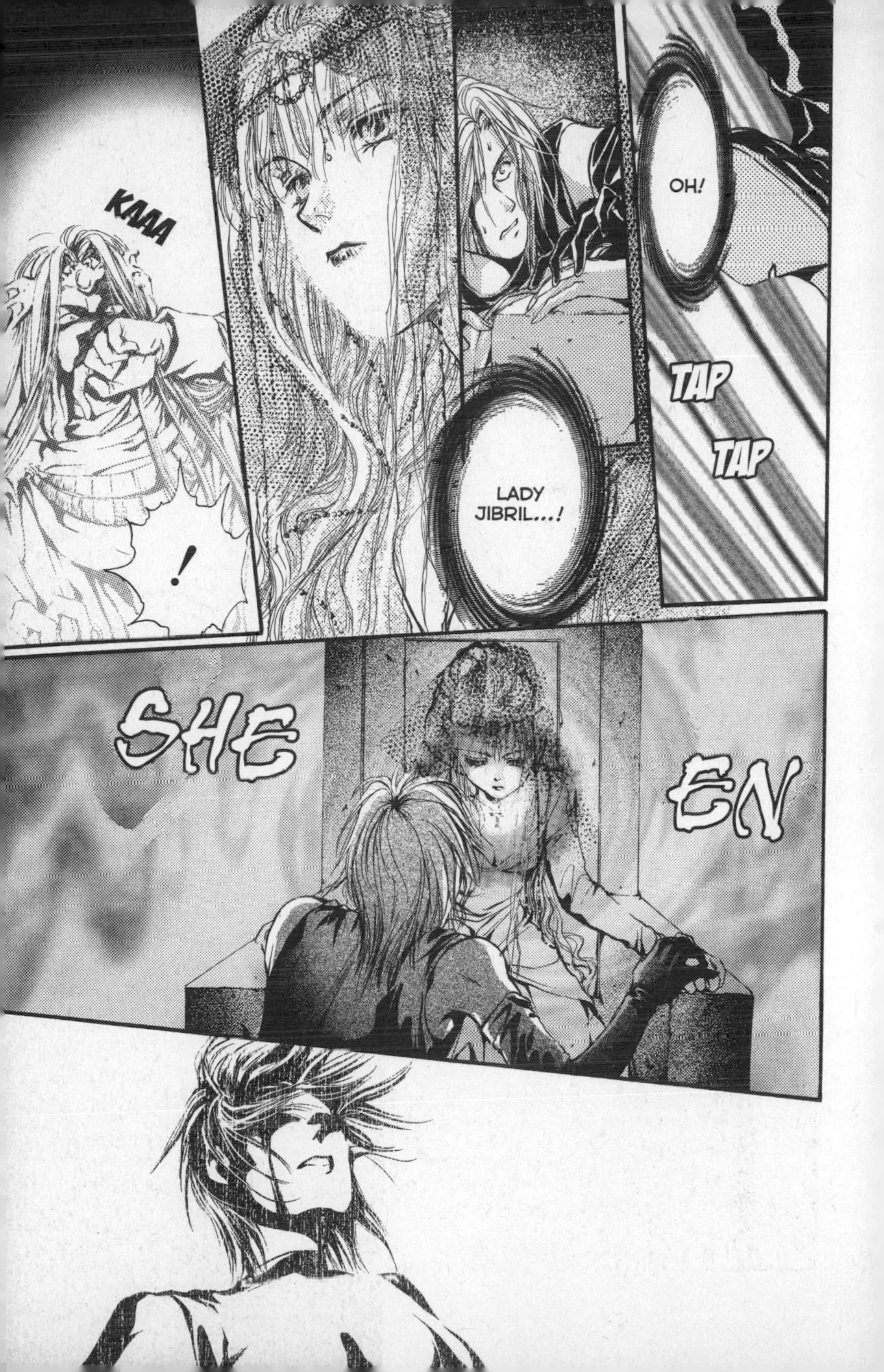
OH!
TAP
TAP
LADY JIBRIL...!
KAAA
!
SHE
EN

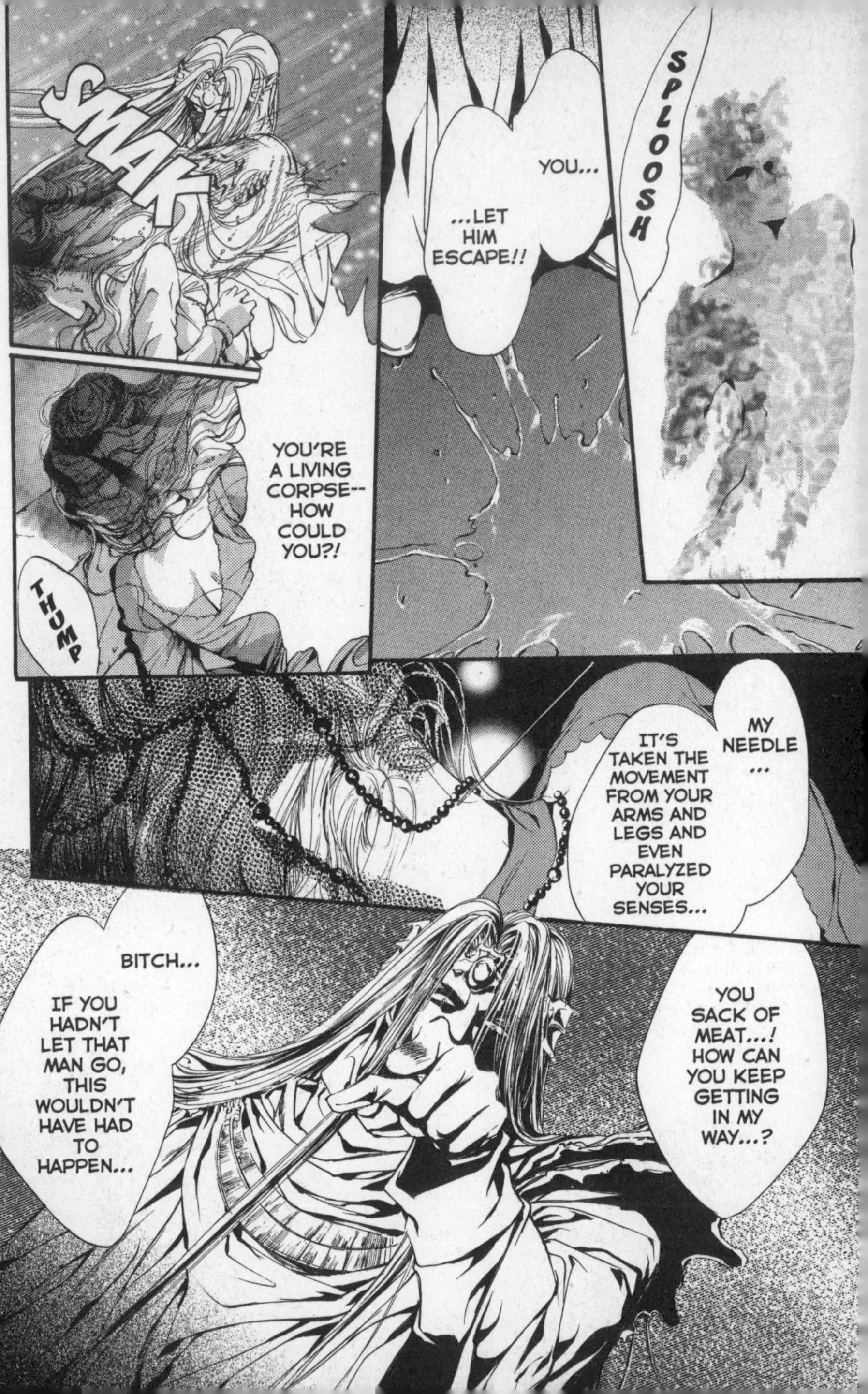
SPLOOSH
YOU...
...LET HIM ESCAPE!!
SMAK
YOU'RE A LIVING CORPSE-- HOW COULD YOU?!
THUMP
MY NEEDLE...
IT'S TAKEN THE MOVEMENT FROM YOUR ARMS AND LEGS AND EVEN PARALYZED YOUR SENSES...
YOU SACK OF MEAT...! HOW CAN YOU KEEP GETTING IN MY WAY...?
BITCH...
IF YOU HADN'T LET THAT MAN GO, THIS WOULDN'T HAVE HAD TO HAPPEN...

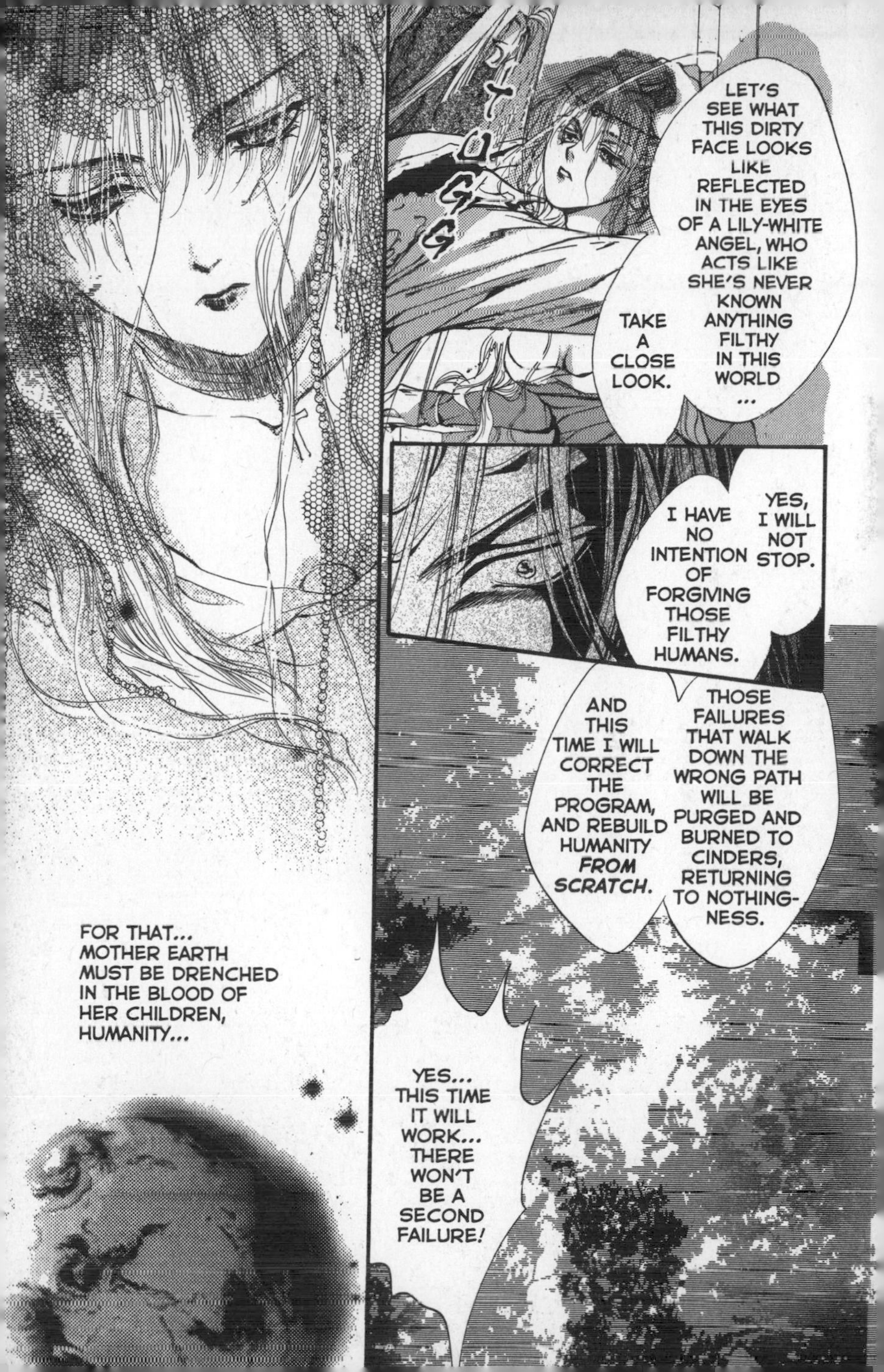
LET'S SEE WHAT THIS DIRTY FACE LOOKS LIKE REFLECTED IN THE EYES OF A LILY-WHITE ANGEL, WHO ACTS LIKE SHE'S NEVER KNOWN ANYTHING FILTHY IN THIS WORLD ...
TAKE A CLOSE LOOK.
YES, I WILL NOT STOP.
I HAVE NO INTENTION OF FORGIVING THOSE FILTHY HUMANS.
THOSE FAILURES THAT WALK DOWN THE WRONG PATH WILL BE PURGED AND BURNED TO CINDERS, RETURNING TO NOTHING-NESS.
AND THIS TIME I WILL CORRECT THE PROGRAM, AND REBUILD HUMANITY *FROM SCRATCH*.
YES... THIS TIME IT WILL WORK... THERE WON'T BE A SECOND FAILURE!
FOR THAT... MOTHER EARTH MUST BE DRENCHED IN THE BLOOD OF HER CHILDREN, HUMANITY...

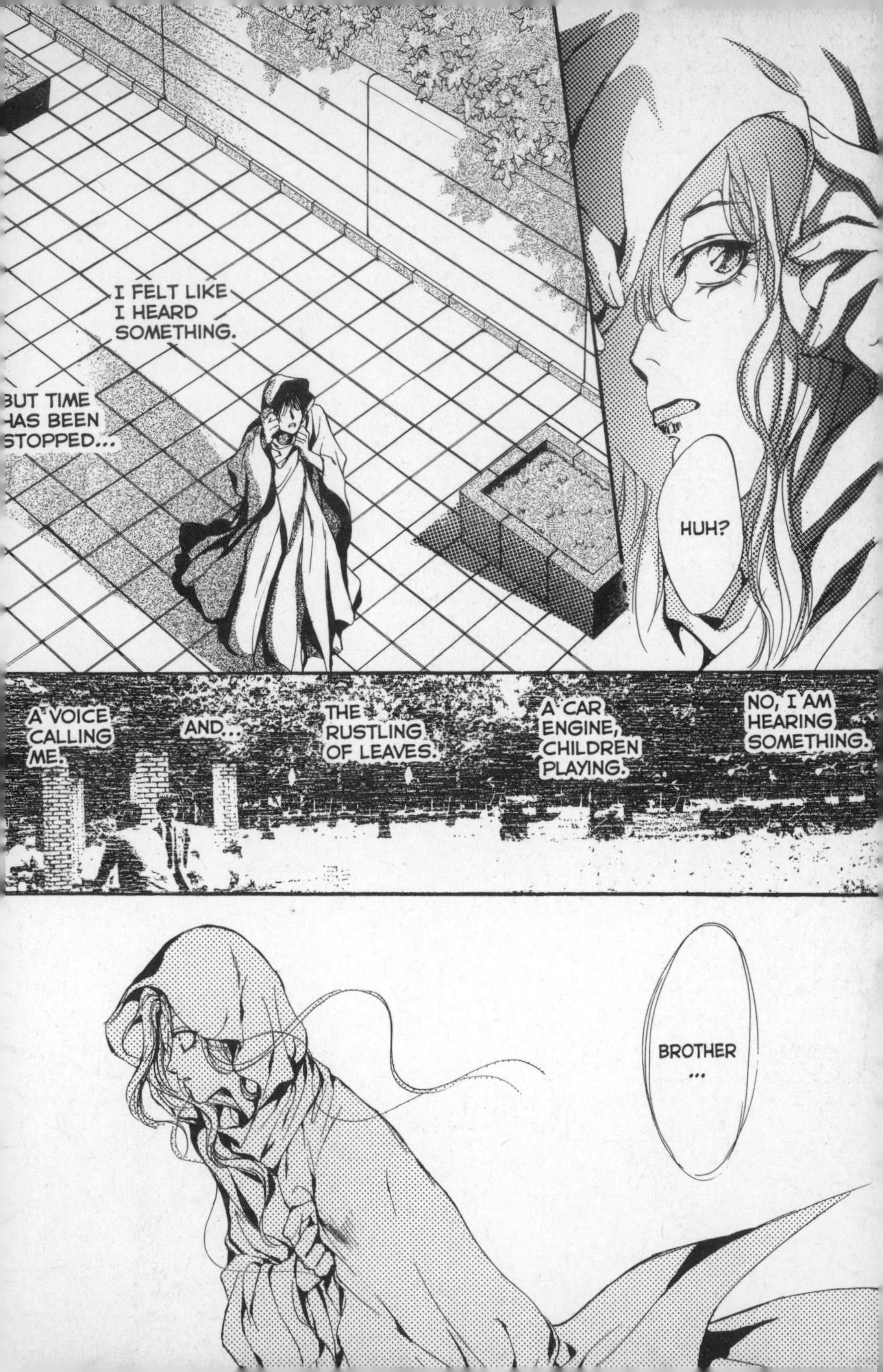
HUH?
I FELT LIKE I HEARD SOMETHING.
BUT TIME HAS BEEN STOPPED...
NO, I AM HEARING SOMETHING.
A CAR ENGINE, CHILDREN PLAYING.
THE RUSTLING OF LEAVES.
AND...
A VOICE CALLING ME.
BROTHER ...

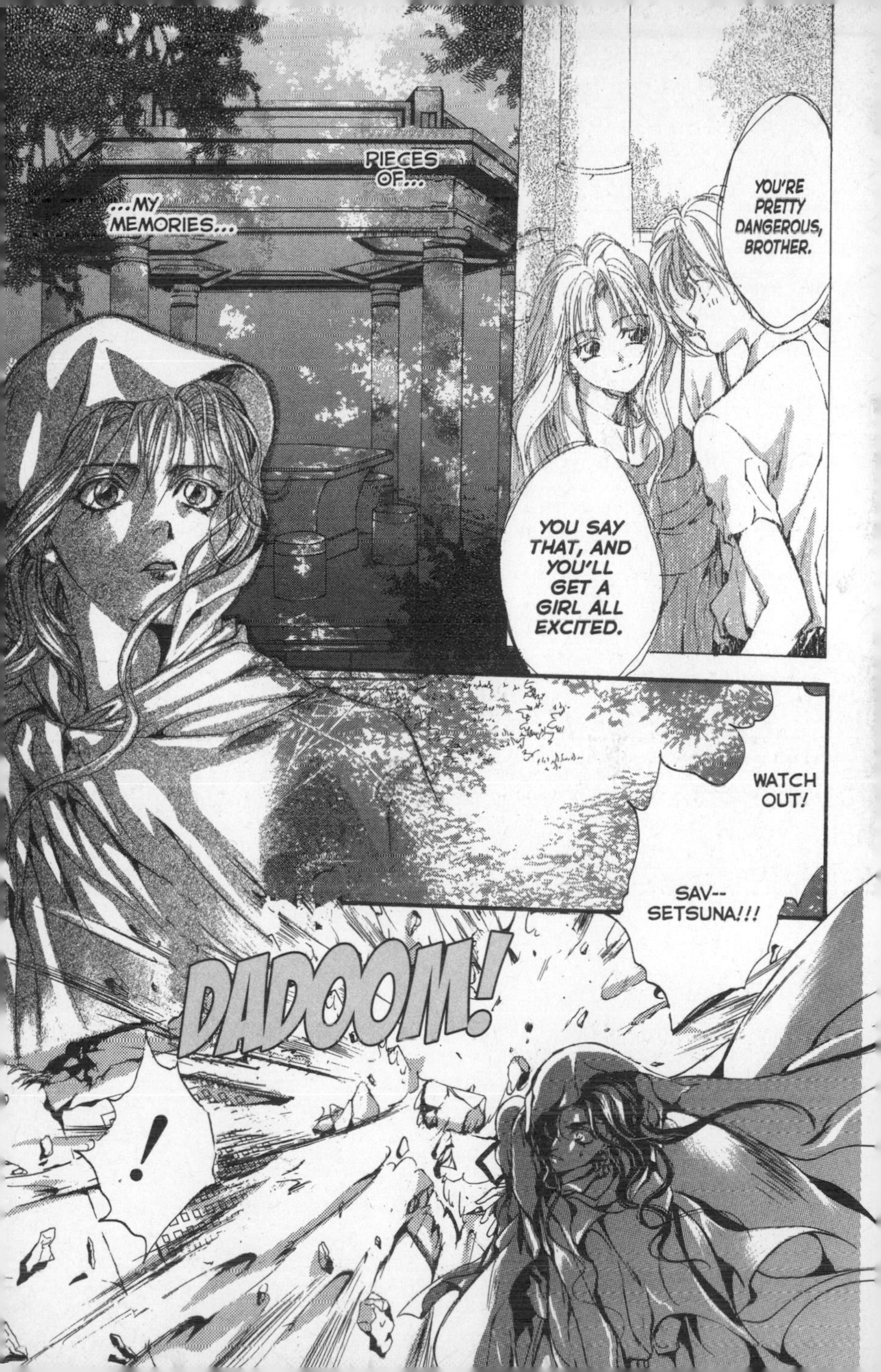
YOU'RE PRETTY DANGEROUS, BROTHER.
YOU SAY THAT, AND YOU'LL GET A GIRL ALL EXCITED.
PIECES OF...
...MY MEMORIES...
WATCH OUT!
SAV-- SETSUNA!!!
DADOOM!
!

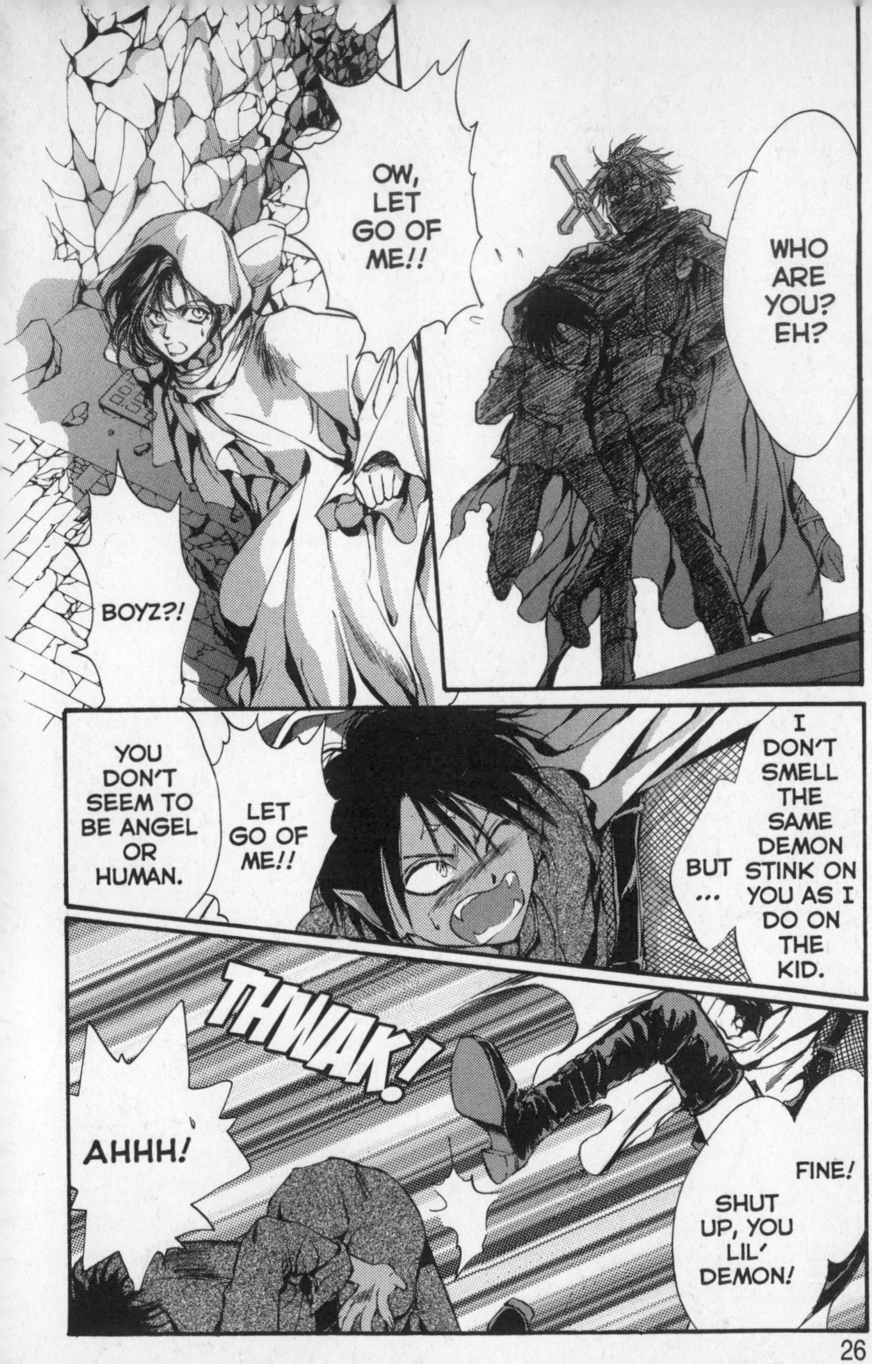
WHO ARE YOU? EH?
OW, LET GO OF ME!!
BOYZ?!
I DON'T SMELL THE SAME DEMON STINK ON YOU AS I DO ON THE KID.
BUT ...
LET GO OF ME!!
YOU DON'T SEEM TO BE ANGEL OR HUMAN.
FINE!
SHUT UP, YOU LIL' DEMON!
THWAK!
AHHH!

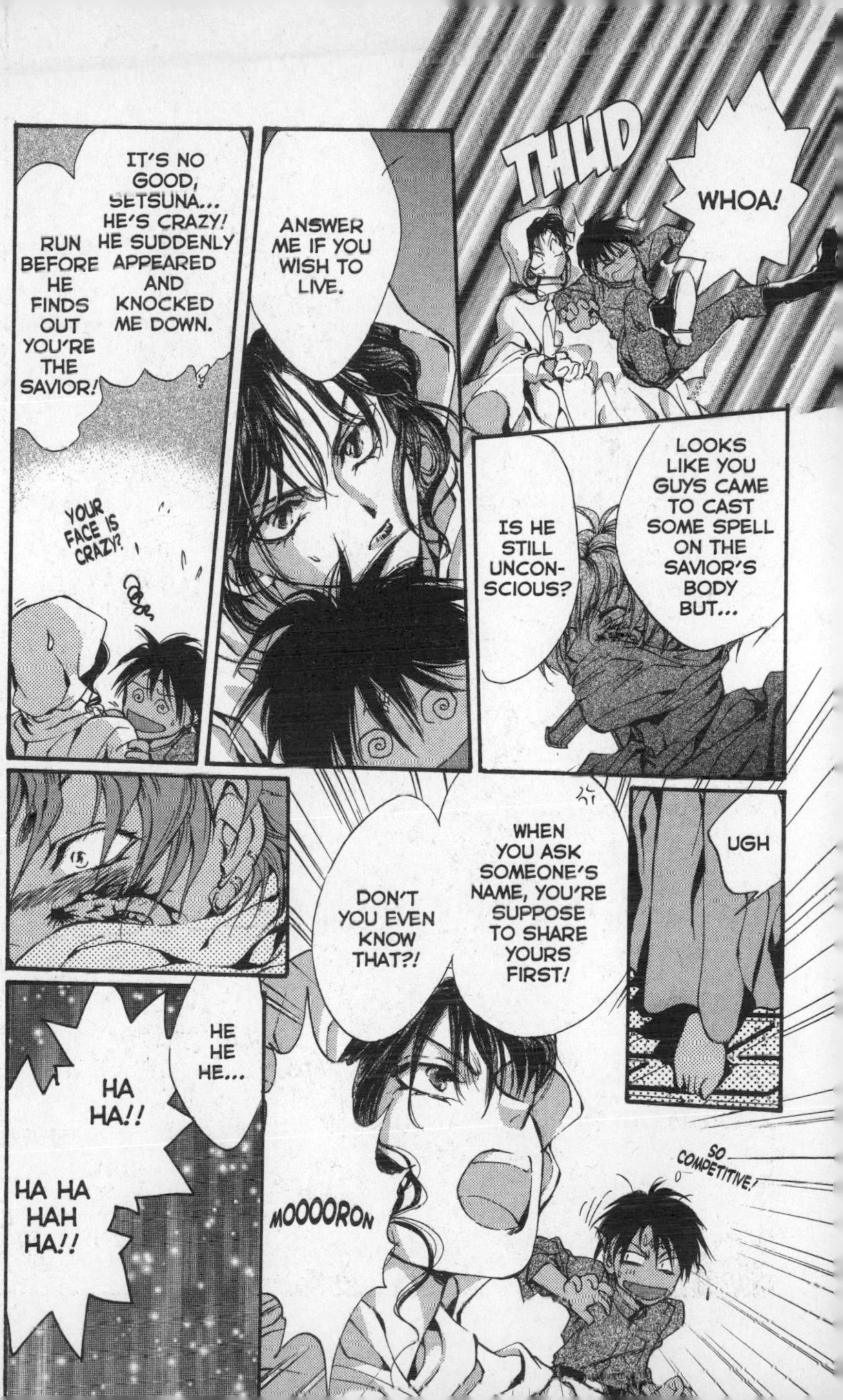
THUD
WHOA!
LOOKS LIKE YOU GUYS CAME TO CAST SOME SPELL ON THE SAVIOR'S BODY BUT...
IS HE STILL UNCONSCIOUS?
ANSWER ME IF YOU WISH TO LIVE.
IT'S NO GOOD, SETSUNA... HE'S CRAZY! HE SUDDENLY APPEARED AND KNOCKED ME DOWN.
RUN BEFORE HE FINDS OUT YOU'RE THE SAVIOR!
YOUR FACE IS CRAZY?
UGH
WHEN YOU ASK SOMEONE'S NAME, YOU'RE SUPPOSE TO SHARE YOURS FIRST!
DON'T YOU EVEN KNOW THAT?!
SO COMPETITIVE!
MOOOORON
HE HE HE...
HA HA!!
HA HA HAH HA!!

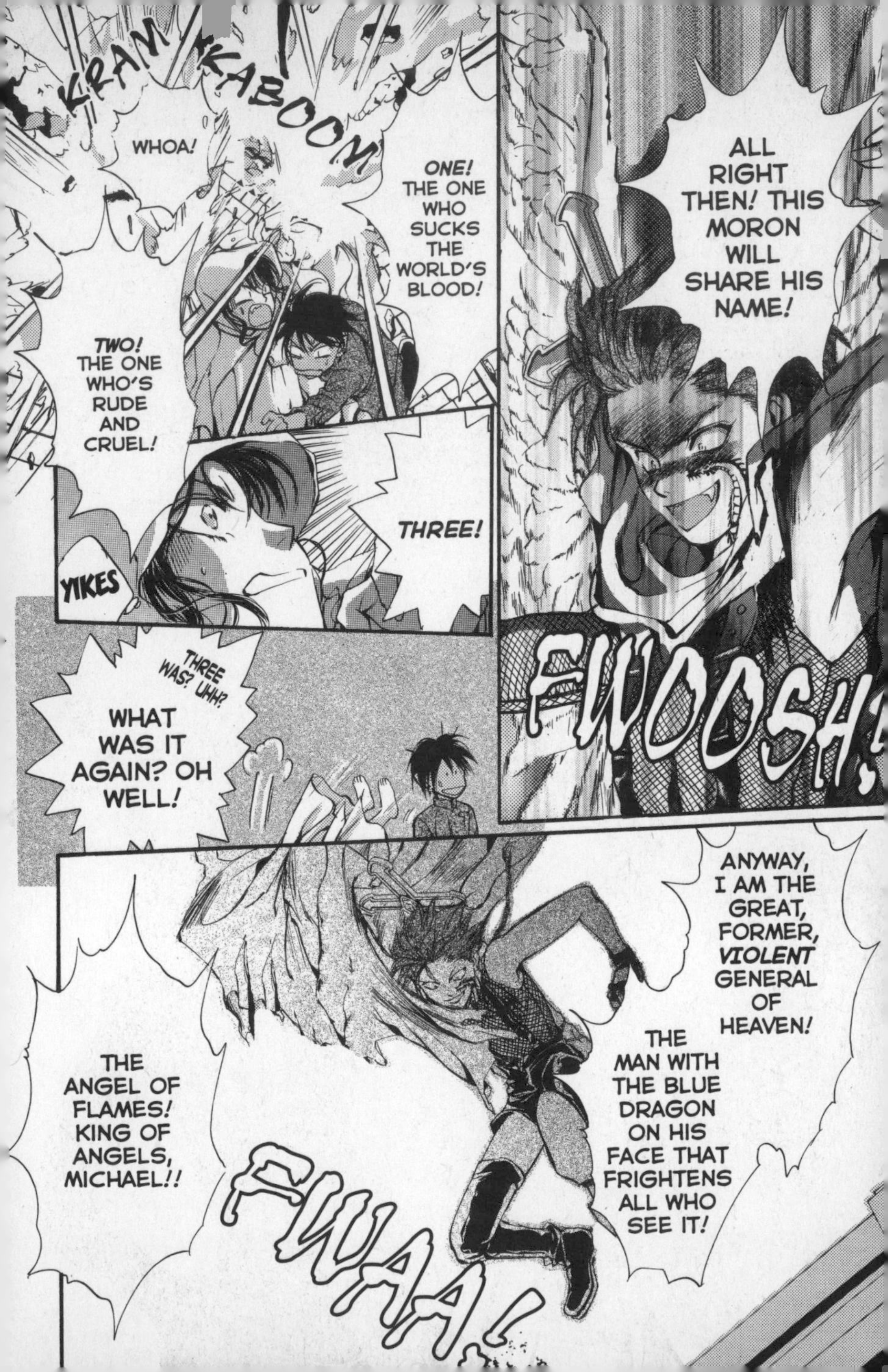
ALL RIGHT THEN! THIS MORON WILL SHARE HIS NAME!
FWOOSH!
KRAM KABOOM
ONE! THE ONE WHO SUCKS THE WORLD'S BLOOD!
WHOA!
TWO! THE ONE WHO'S RUDE AND CRUEL!
THREE!
YIKES
THREE WAS? UHH?
WHAT WAS IT AGAIN? OH WELL!
ANYWAY, I AM THE GREAT, FORMER, VIOLENT GENERAL OF HEAVEN!
THE MAN WITH THE BLUE DRAGON ON HIS FACE THAT FRIGHTENS ALL WHO SEE IT!
THE ANGEL OF FLAMES! KING OF ANGELS, MICHAEL!!
FWAA!

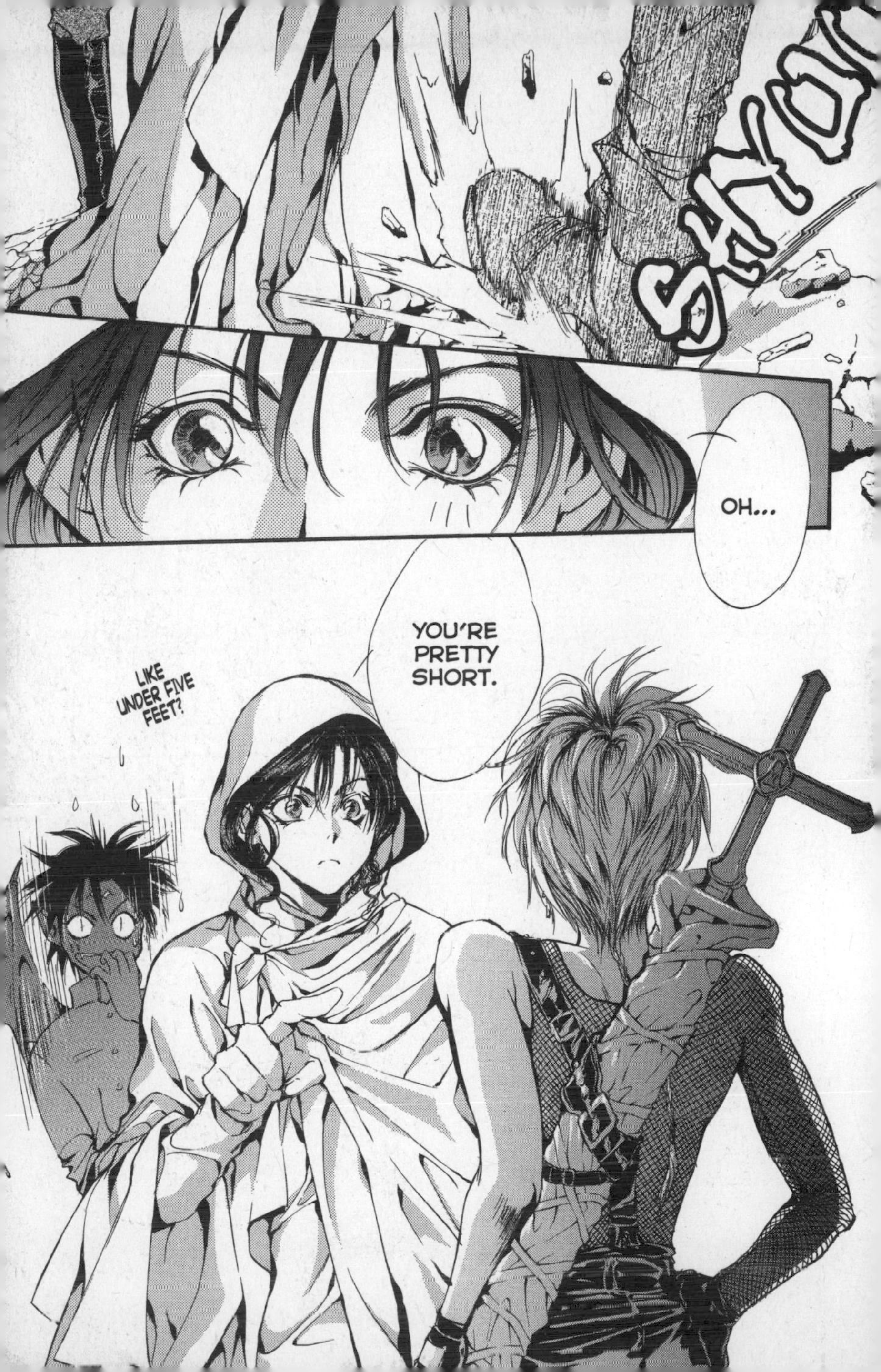
SHYO
OH...
YOU'RE PRETTY SHORT.
LIKE UNDER FIVE FEET?

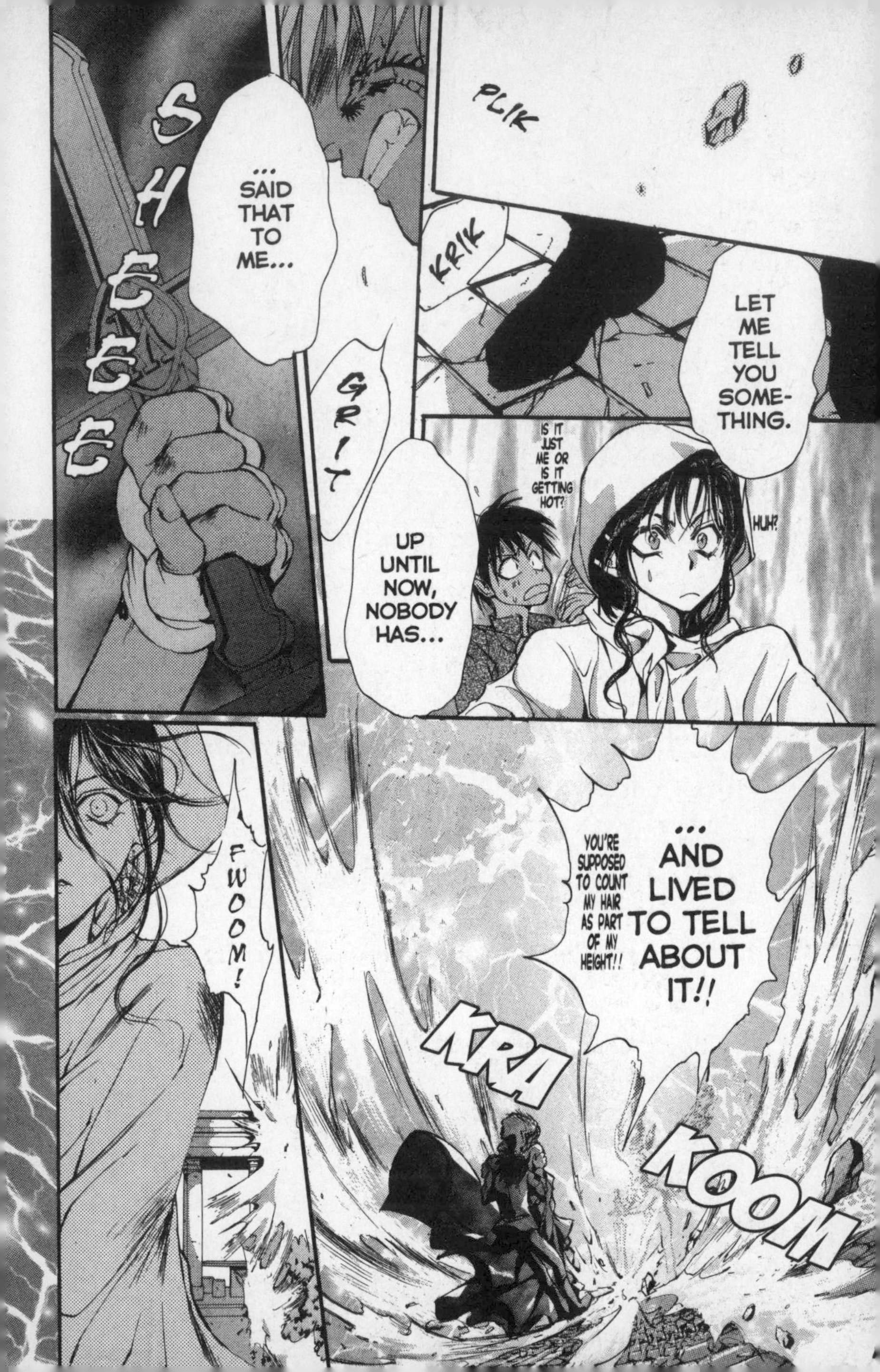
PLIK
KRIK
LET ME TELL YOU SOME-THING.
IS IT JUST ME OR IS IT GETTING HOT?
HUH?
SHEEEE
...SAID THAT TO ME...
GRIT
UP UNTIL NOW, NOBODY HAS...
...AND LIVED TO TELL ABOUT IT!!
YOU'RE SUPPOSED TO COUNT MY HAIR AS PART OF MY HEIGHT!!
KRA
KOOM
FWOOM!

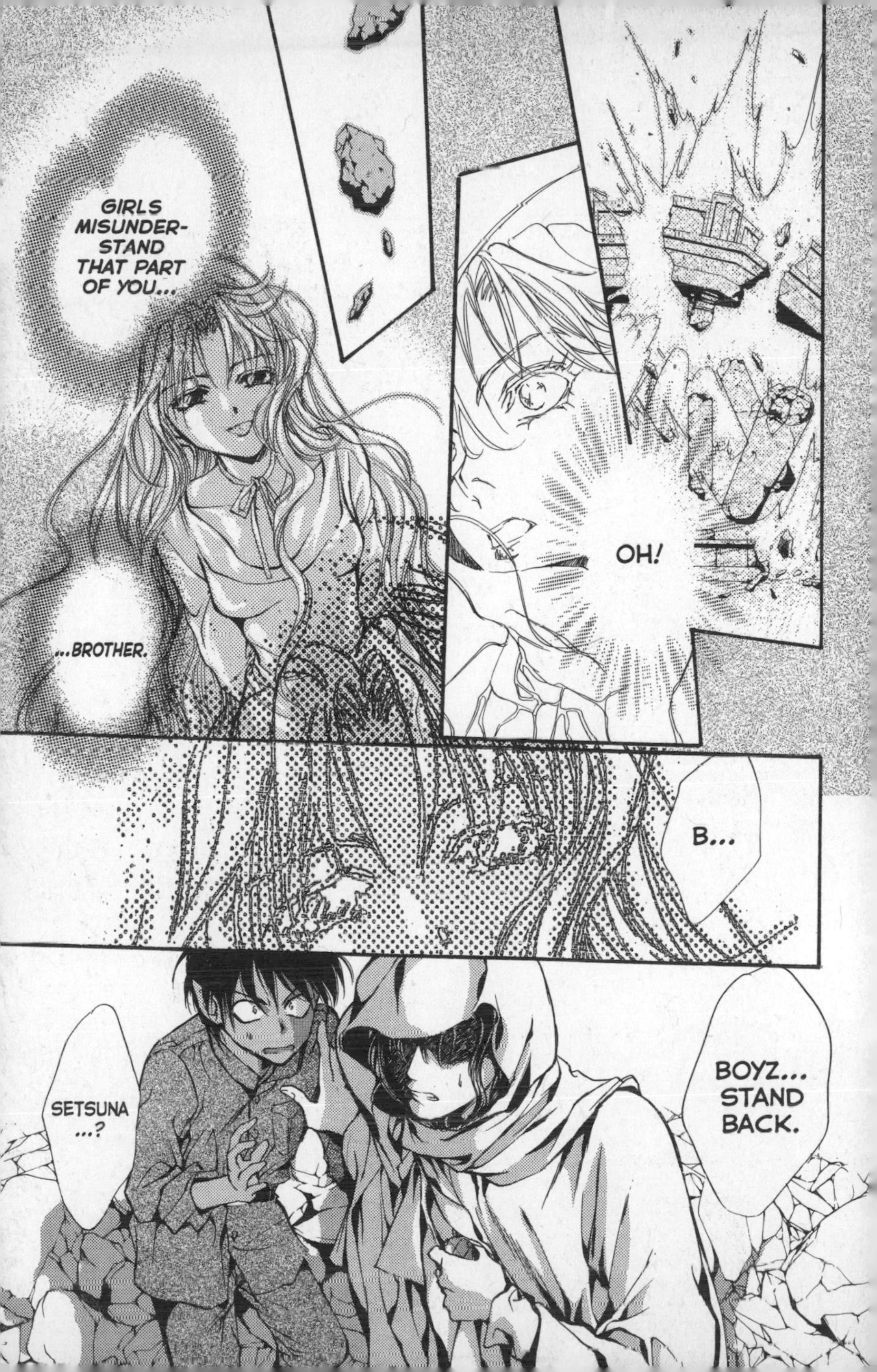
OH!
GIRLS MISUNDER-STAND THAT PART OF YOU...
...BROTHER.
B...
BOYZ... STAND BACK.
SETSUNA ...?

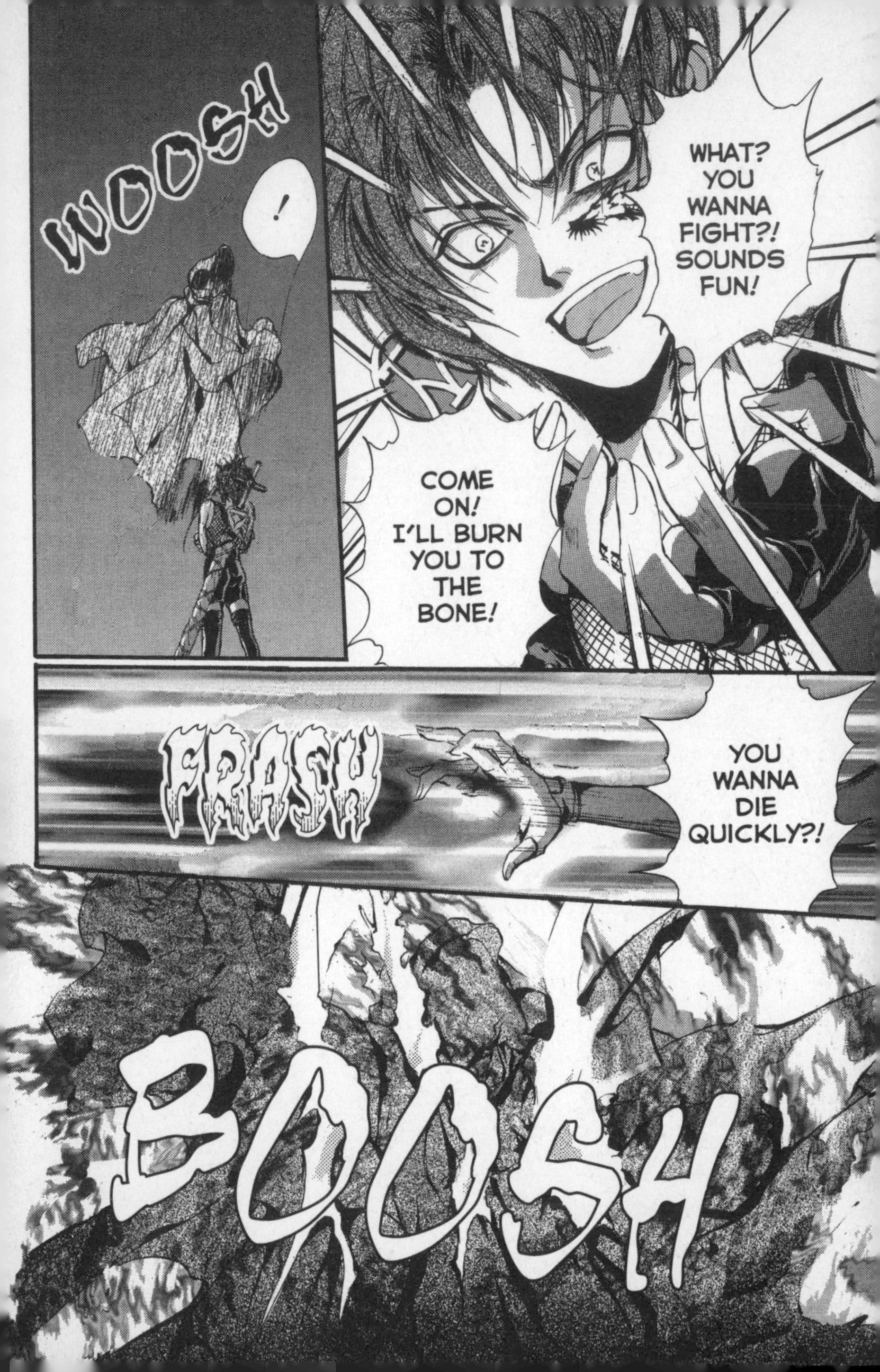

WHAT? YOU WANNA FIGHT?! SOUNDS FUN!
COME ON! I'LL BURN YOU TO THE BONE!
WOOSH
!
YOU WANNA DIE QUICKLY?!
FRASH
BOOSH

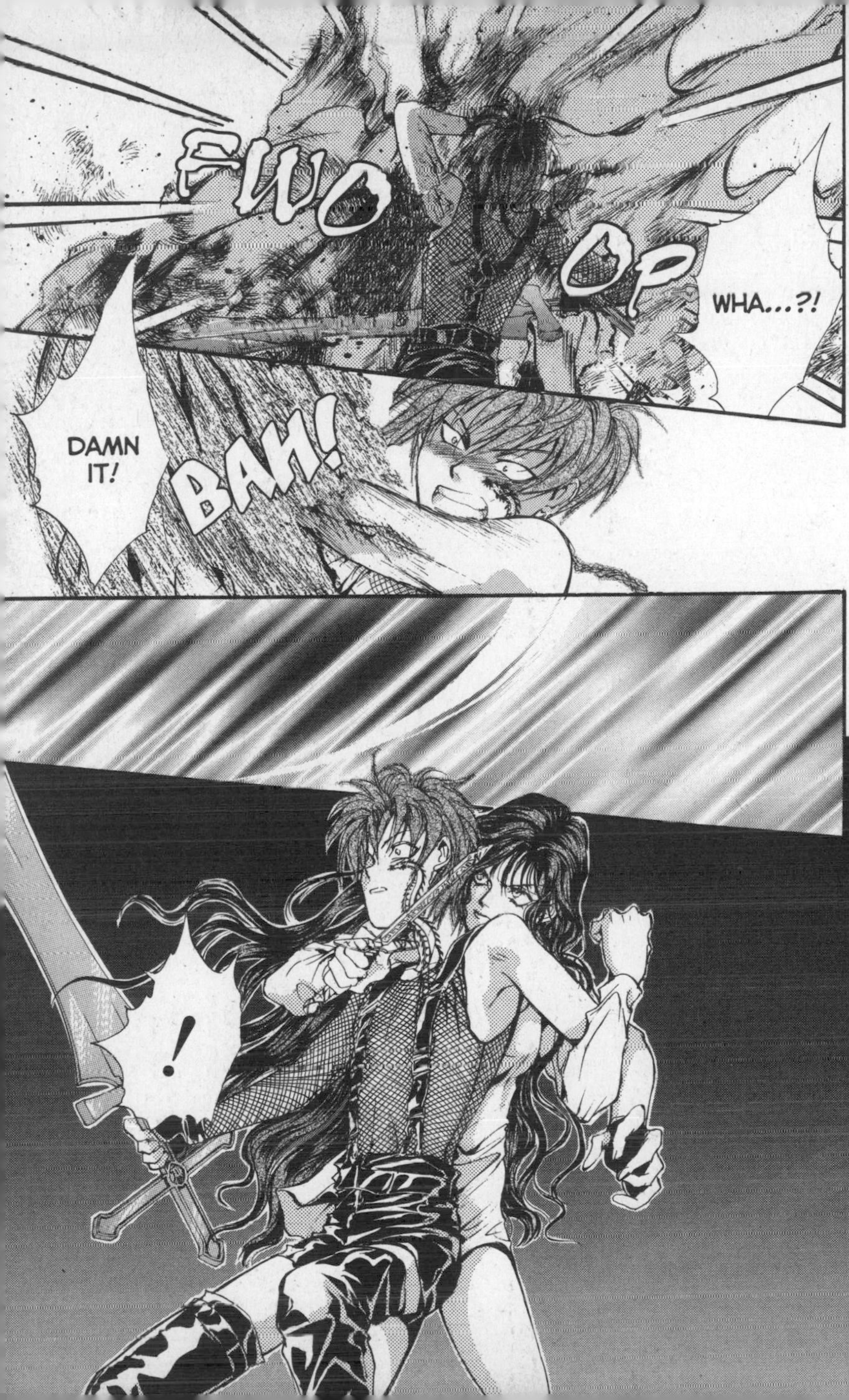
FWOOP
WHA...?!
BAH!
DAMN IT!
!

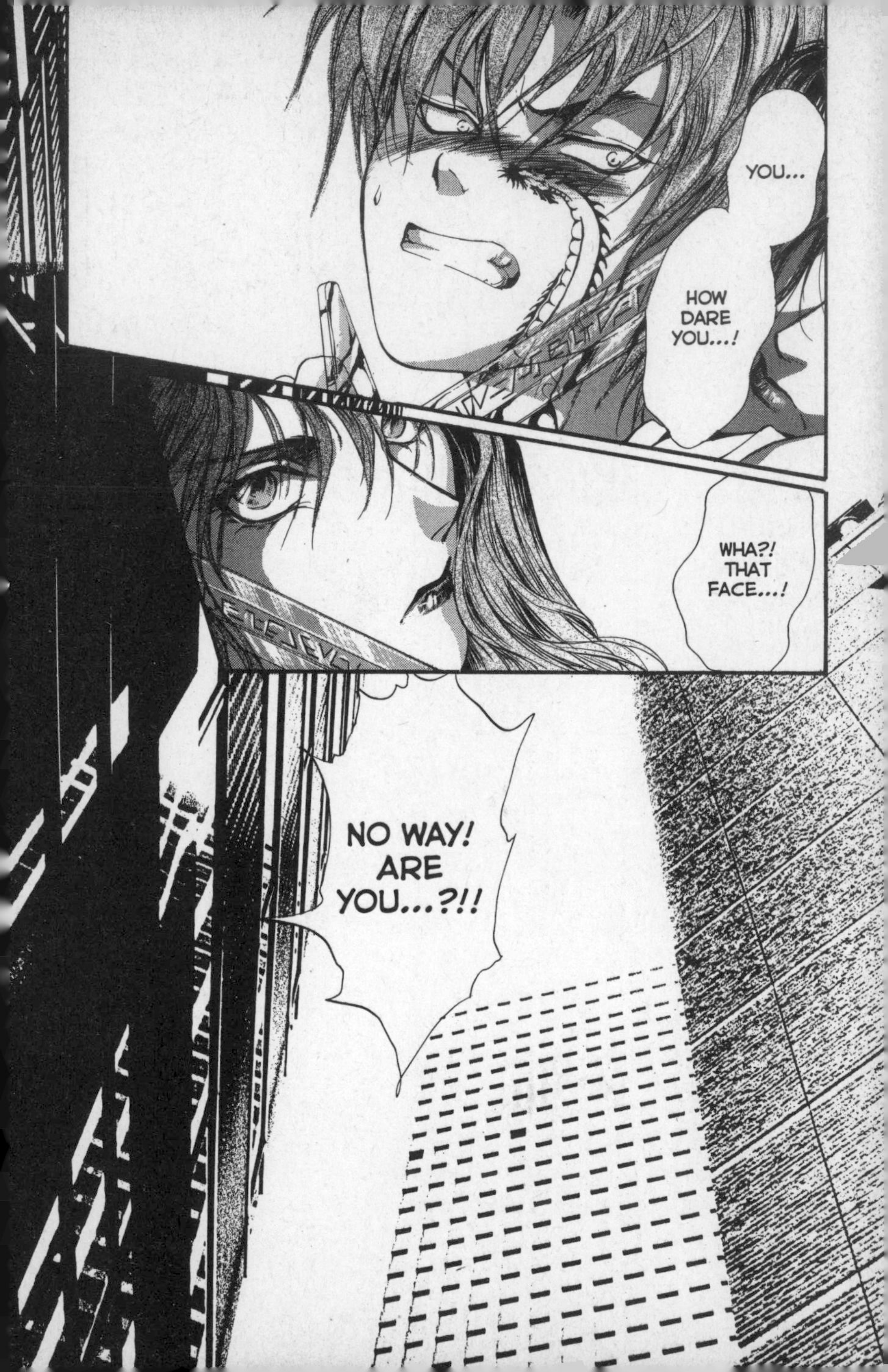
YOU...
HOW DARE YOU...!
WHA?! THAT FACE...!
NO WAY! ARE YOU...?!!

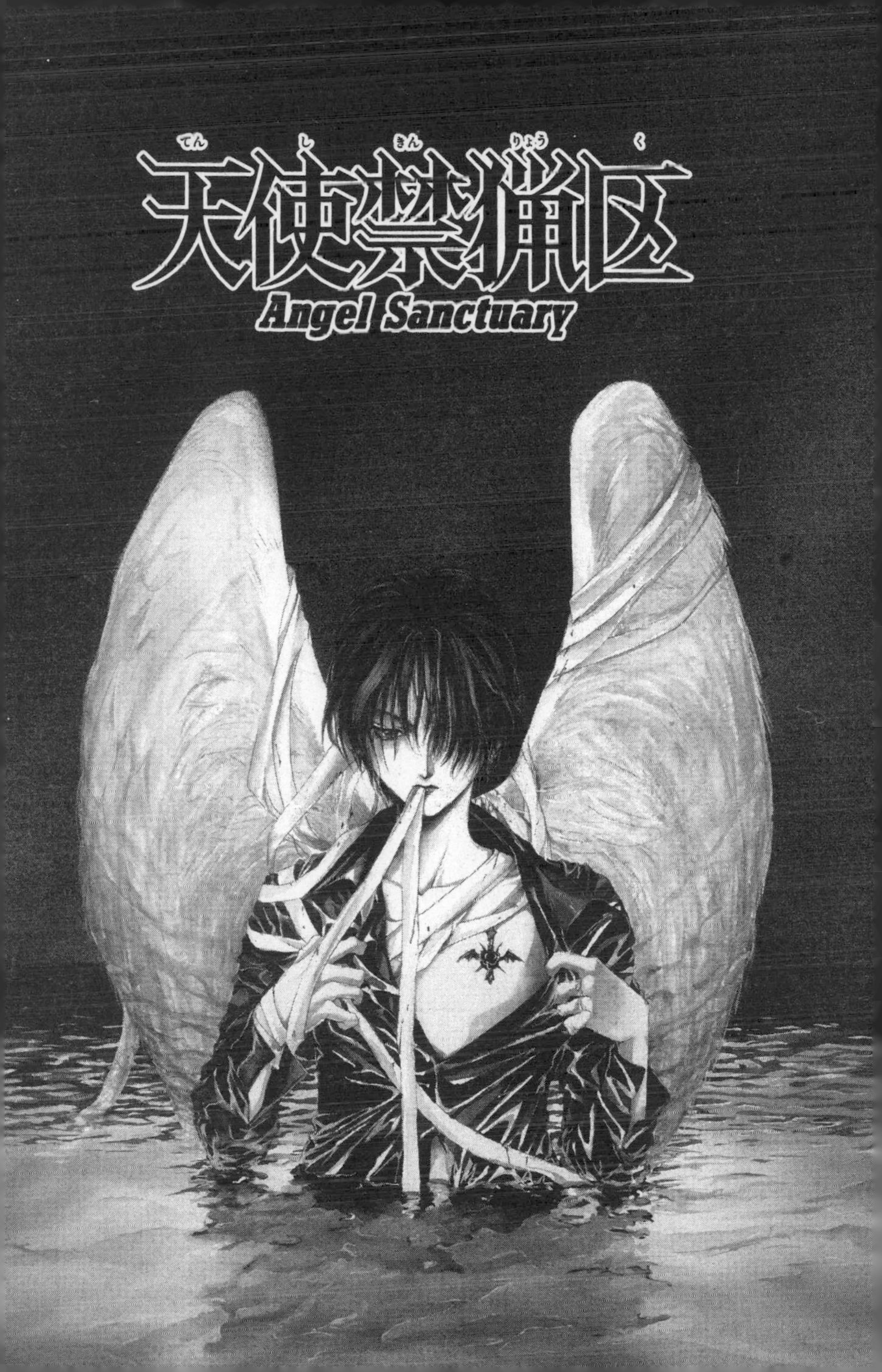
天使禁猟区
Angel Sanctuary

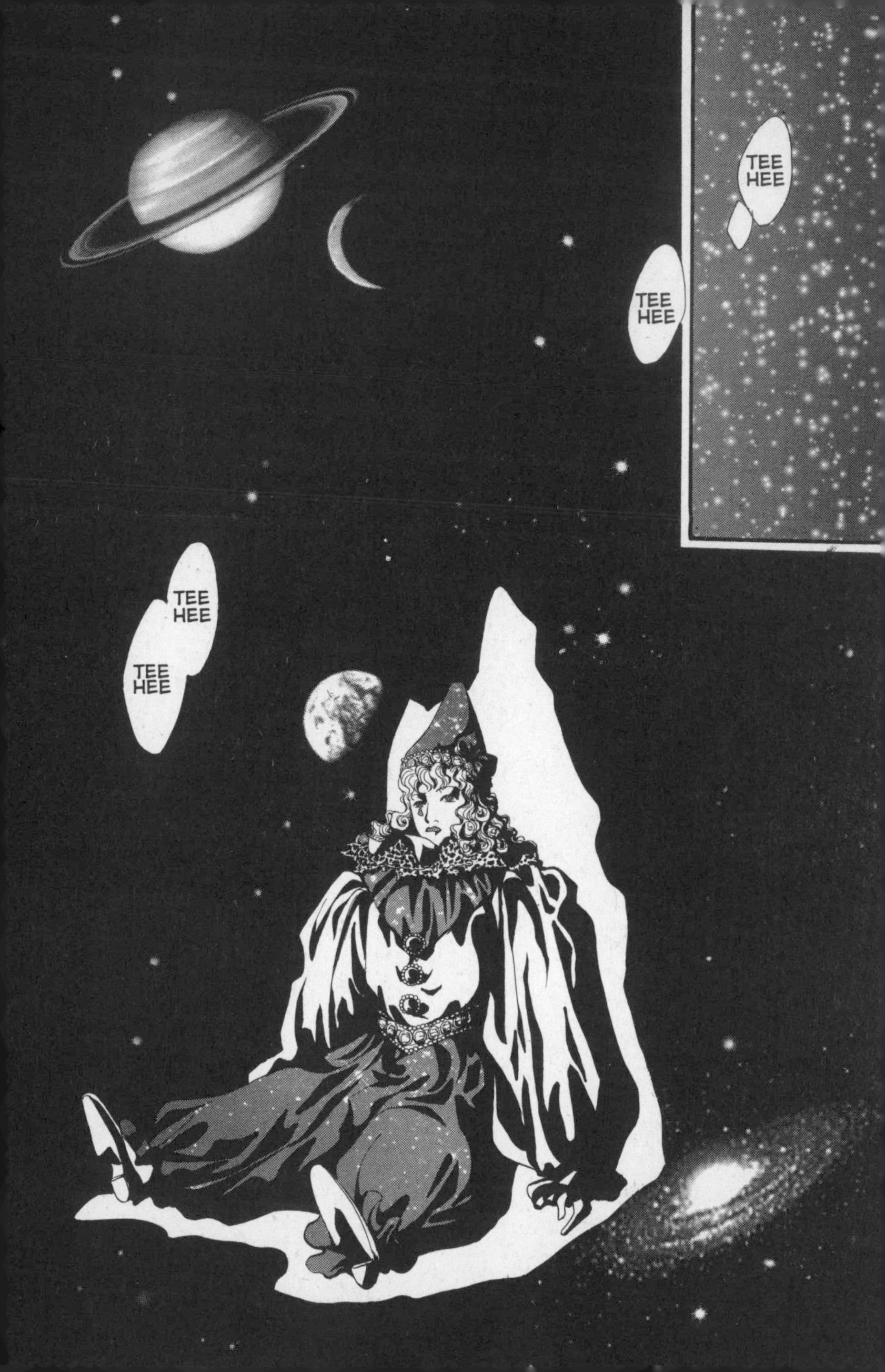
TEE HEE
TEE HEE
TEE HEE
TEE HEE

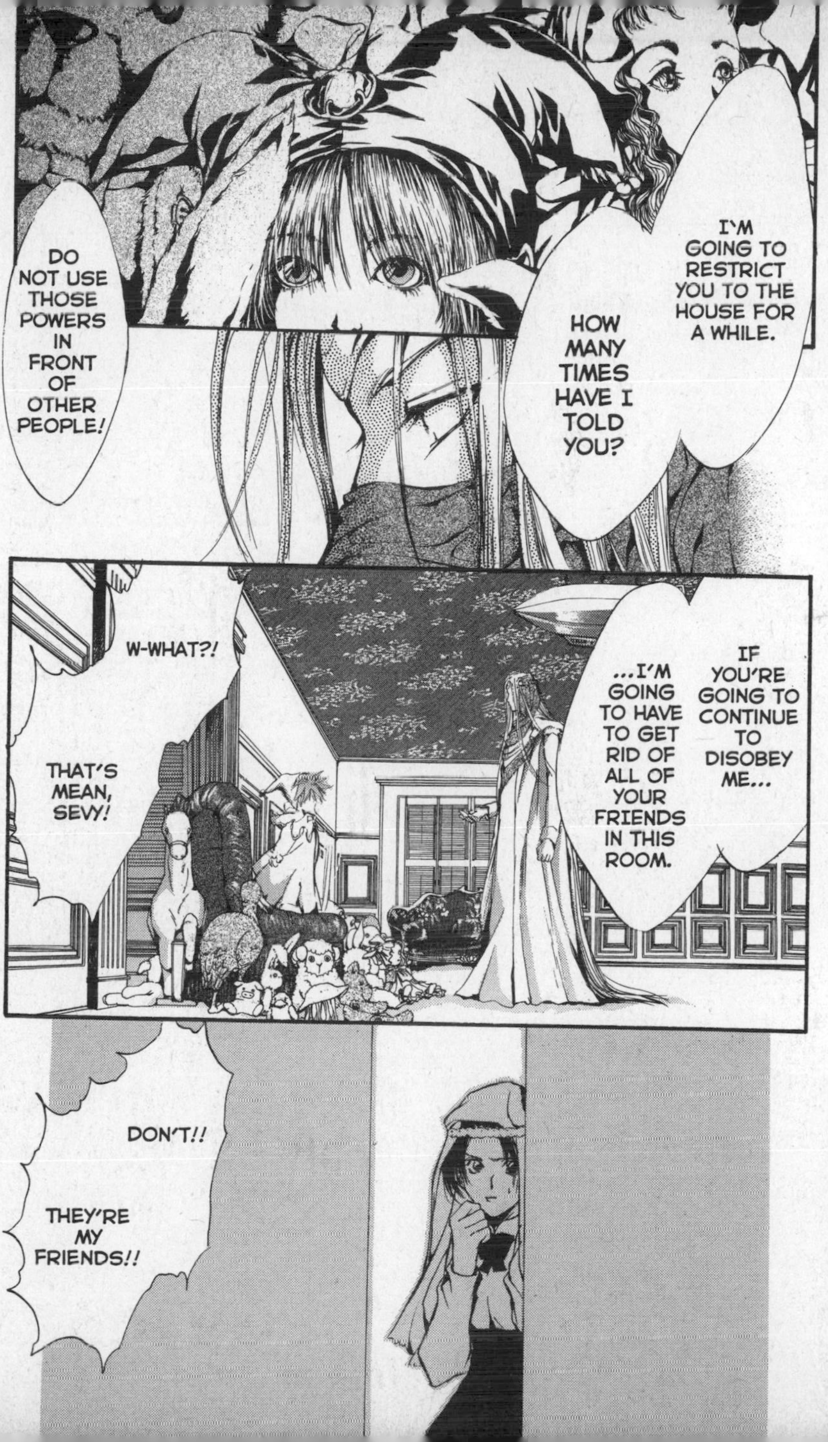
I'M GOING TO RESTRICT YOU TO THE HOUSE FOR A WHILE.
HOW MANY TIMES HAVE I TOLD YOU?
DO NOT USE THOSE POWERS IN FRONT OF OTHER PEOPLE!
IF YOU'RE GOING TO CONTINUE TO DISOBEY ME...
...I'M GOING TO HAVE TO GET RID OF ALL OF YOUR FRIENDS IN THIS ROOM.
W-WHAT?!
THAT'S MEAN, SEVY!
DON'T!!
THEY'RE MY FRIENDS!!

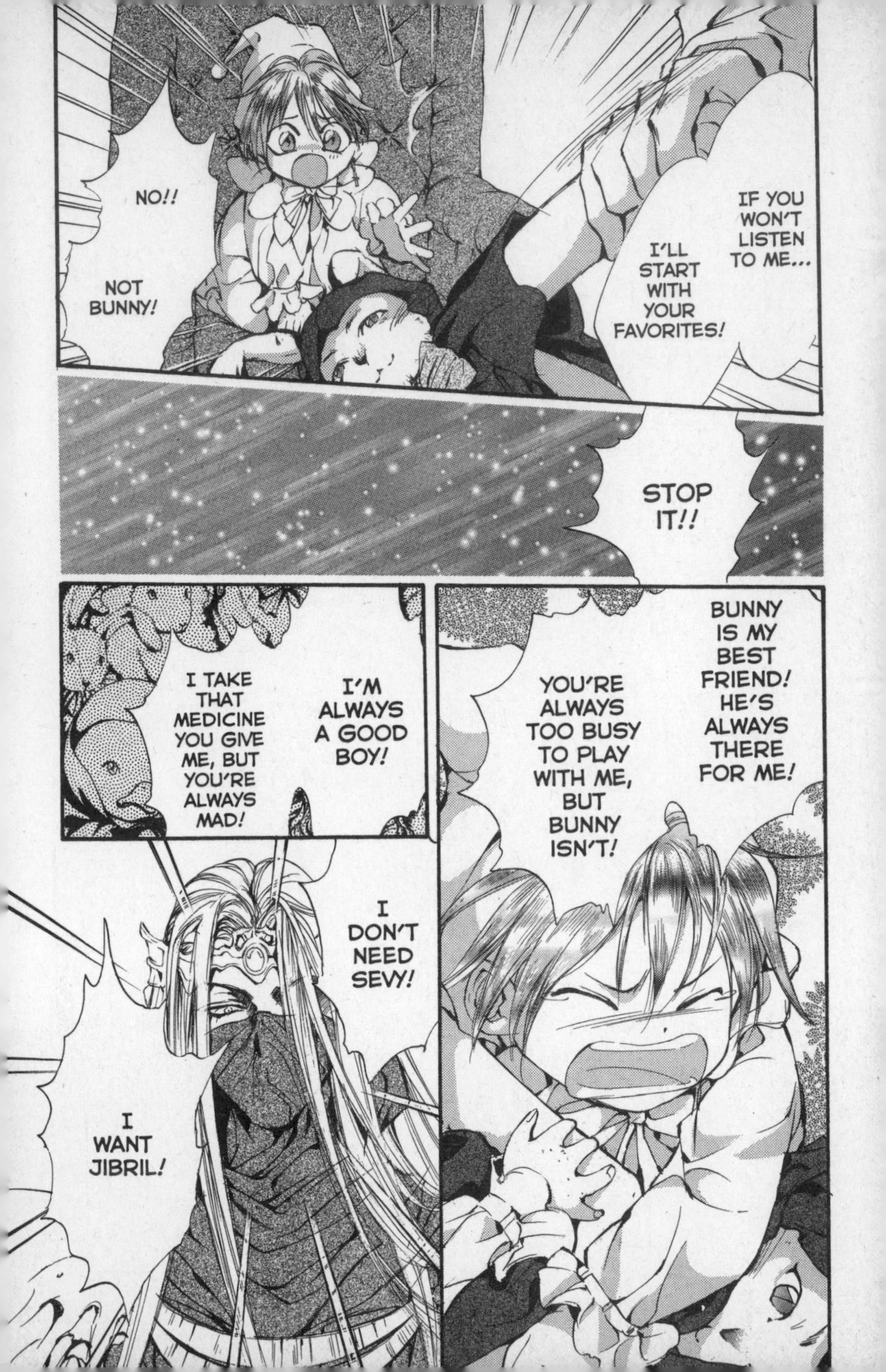
IF YOU WON'T LISTEN TO ME...
I'LL START WITH YOUR FAVORITES!
NO!!
NOT BUNNY!
STOP IT!!
BUNNY IS MY BEST FRIEND! HE'S ALWAYS THERE FOR ME!
YOU'RE ALWAYS TOO BUSY TO PLAY WITH ME, BUT BUNNY ISN'T!
I'M ALWAYS A GOOD BOY!
I TAKE THAT MEDICINE YOU GIVE ME, BUT YOU'RE ALWAYS MAD!
I DON'T NEED SEVY!
I WANT JIBRIL!

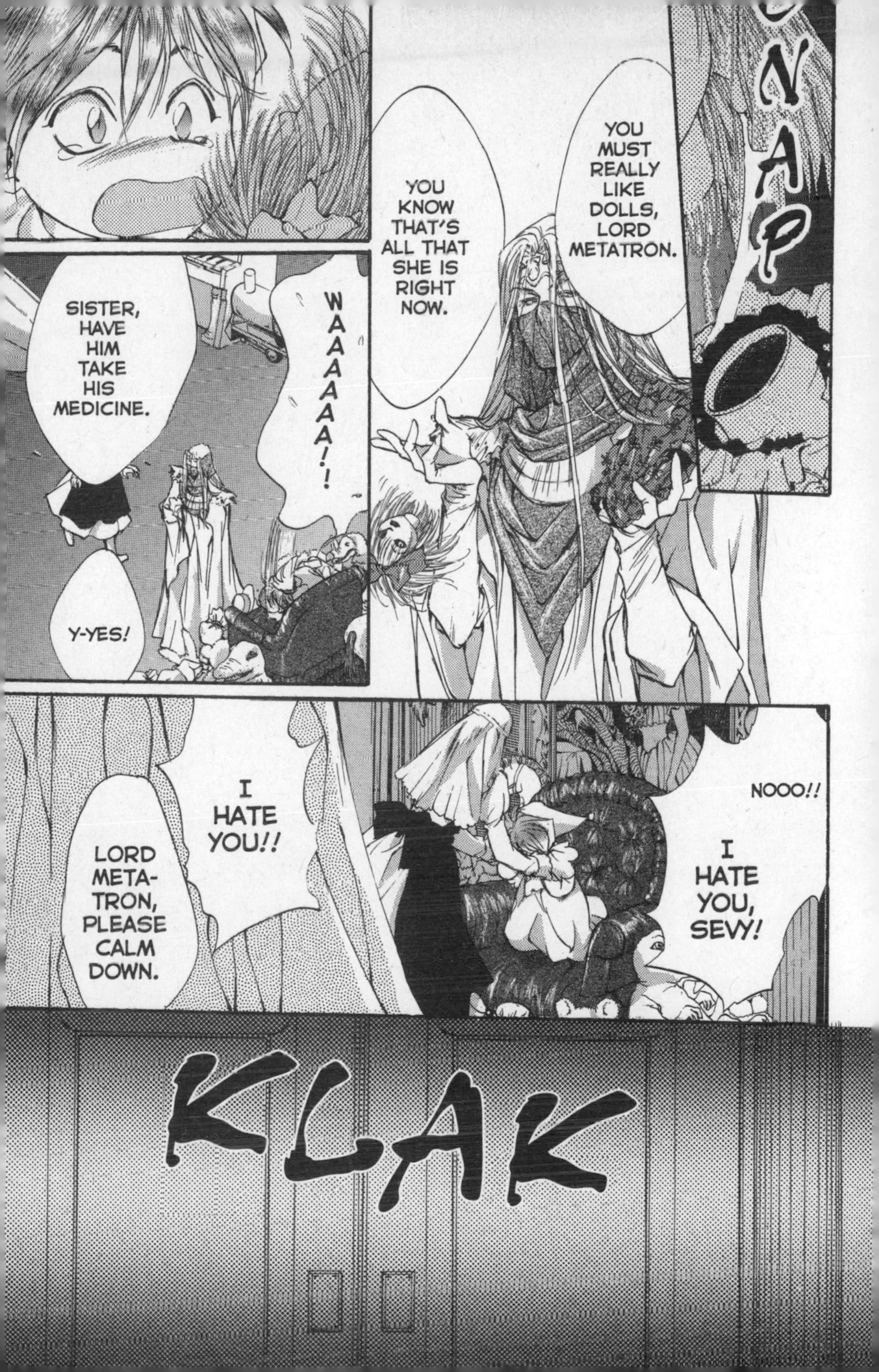
NAP
YOU MUST REALLY LIKE DOLLS, LORD METATRON.
YOU KNOW THAT'S ALL THAT SHE IS RIGHT NOW.
WAAAAAAA!!
SISTER, HAVE HIM TAKE HIS MEDICINE.
Y-YES!
NOOO!!
I HATE YOU, SEVY!
I HATE YOU!!
LORD META-TRON, PLEASE CALM DOWN.
KLAK

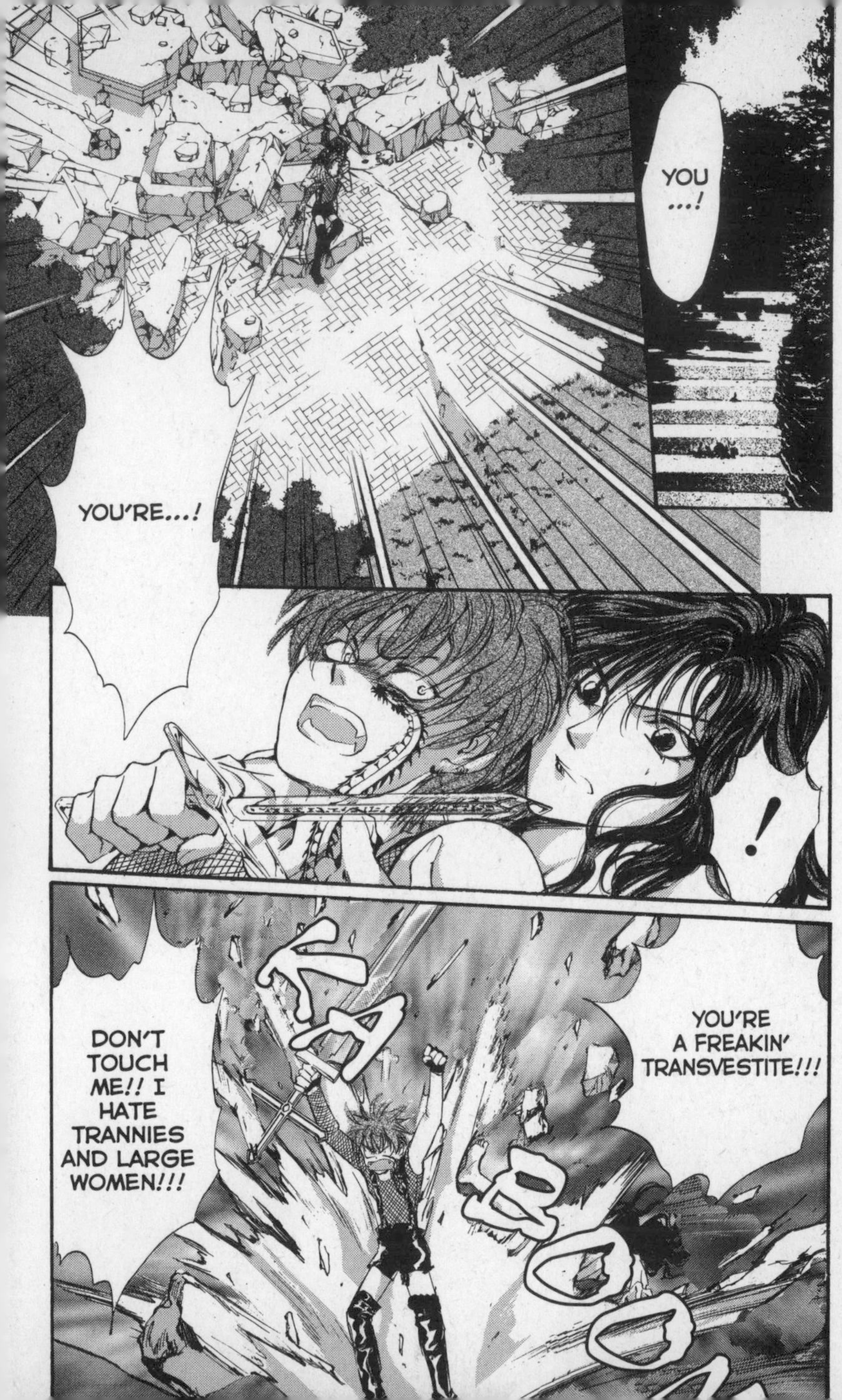
YOU ...!
YOU'RE...!
!
YOU'RE A FREAKIN' TRANSVESTITE!!!
DON'T TOUCH ME!! I HATE TRANNIES AND LARGE WOMEN!!!

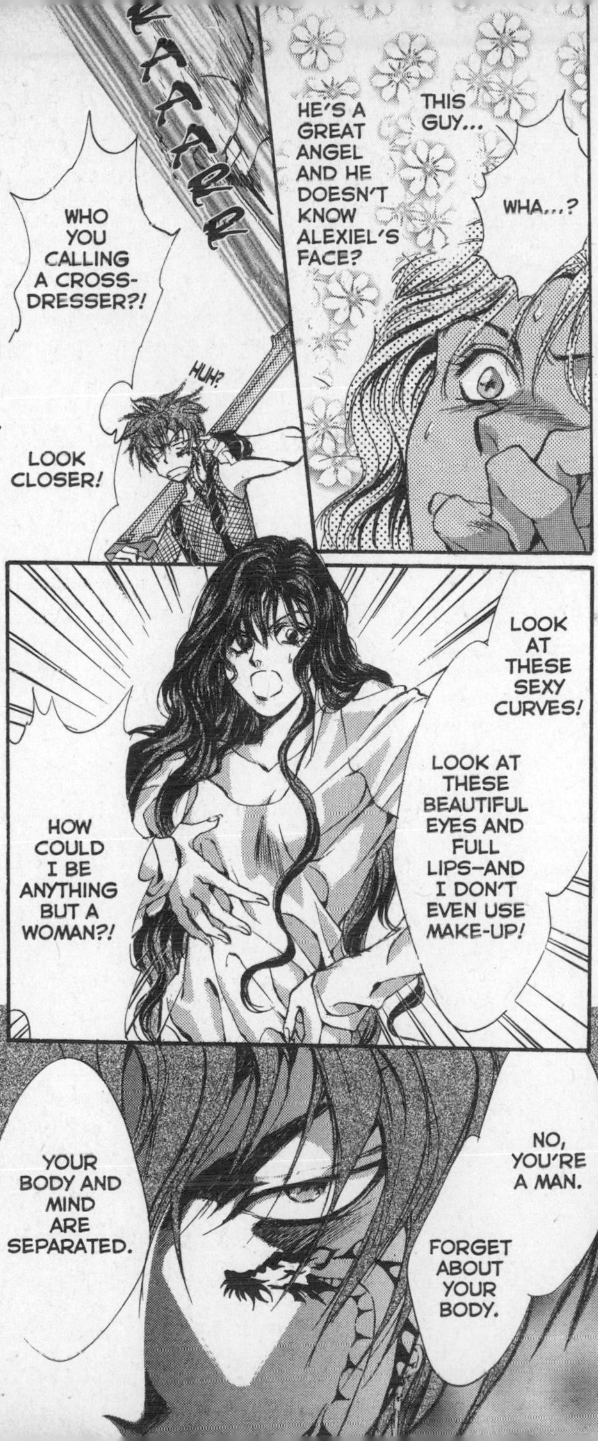
THIS GUY...
HE'S A GREAT ANGEL AND HE DOESN'T KNOW ALEXIEL'S FACE?
WHA...?
KAAAARR
WHO YOU CALLING A CROSS-DRESSER?!
HUH?
LOOK CLOSER!
LOOK AT THESE SEXY CURVES!
LOOK AT THESE BEAUTIFUL EYES AND FULL LIPS—AND I DON'T EVEN USE MAKE-UP!
HOW COULD I BE ANYTHING BUT A WOMAN?!
NO, YOU'RE A MAN.
FORGET ABOUT YOUR BODY.
YOUR BODY AND MIND ARE SEPARATED.

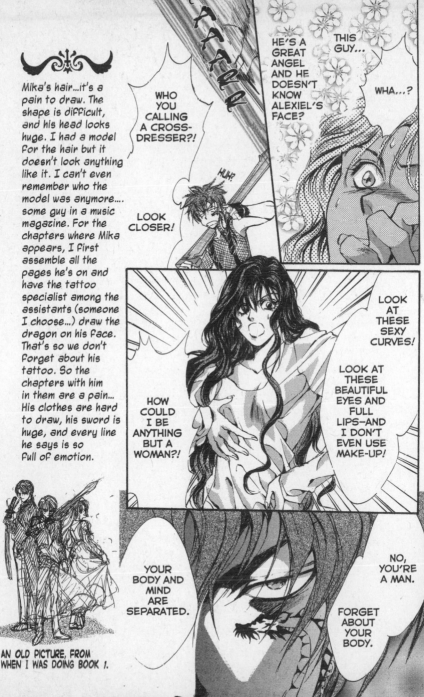

Mika's hair...it's a pain to draw. The shape is difficult, and his head looks huge. I had a model for the hair but it doesn't look anything like it. I can't even remember who the model was anymore.... some guy in a music magazine. For the chapters where Mika appears, I first assemble all the pages he's on and have the tattoo specialist among the assistants (someone I choose...) draw the dragon on his face. That's so we don't forget about his tattoo. So the chapters with him in them are a pain... His clothes are hard to draw, his sword is huge, and every line he says is so full of emotion.

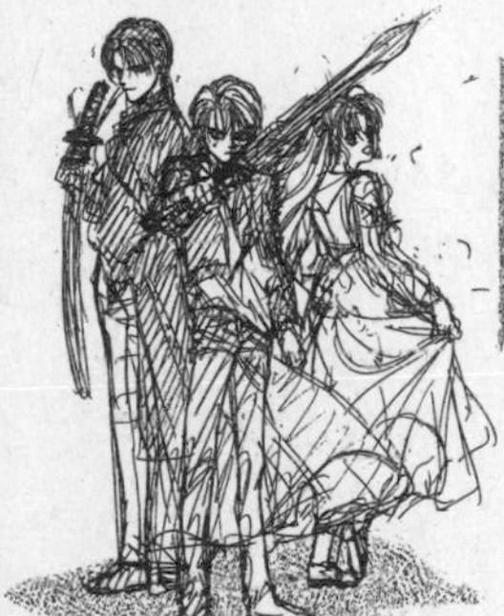

AN OLD PICTURE, FROM WHEN I WAS DOING BOOK 1.

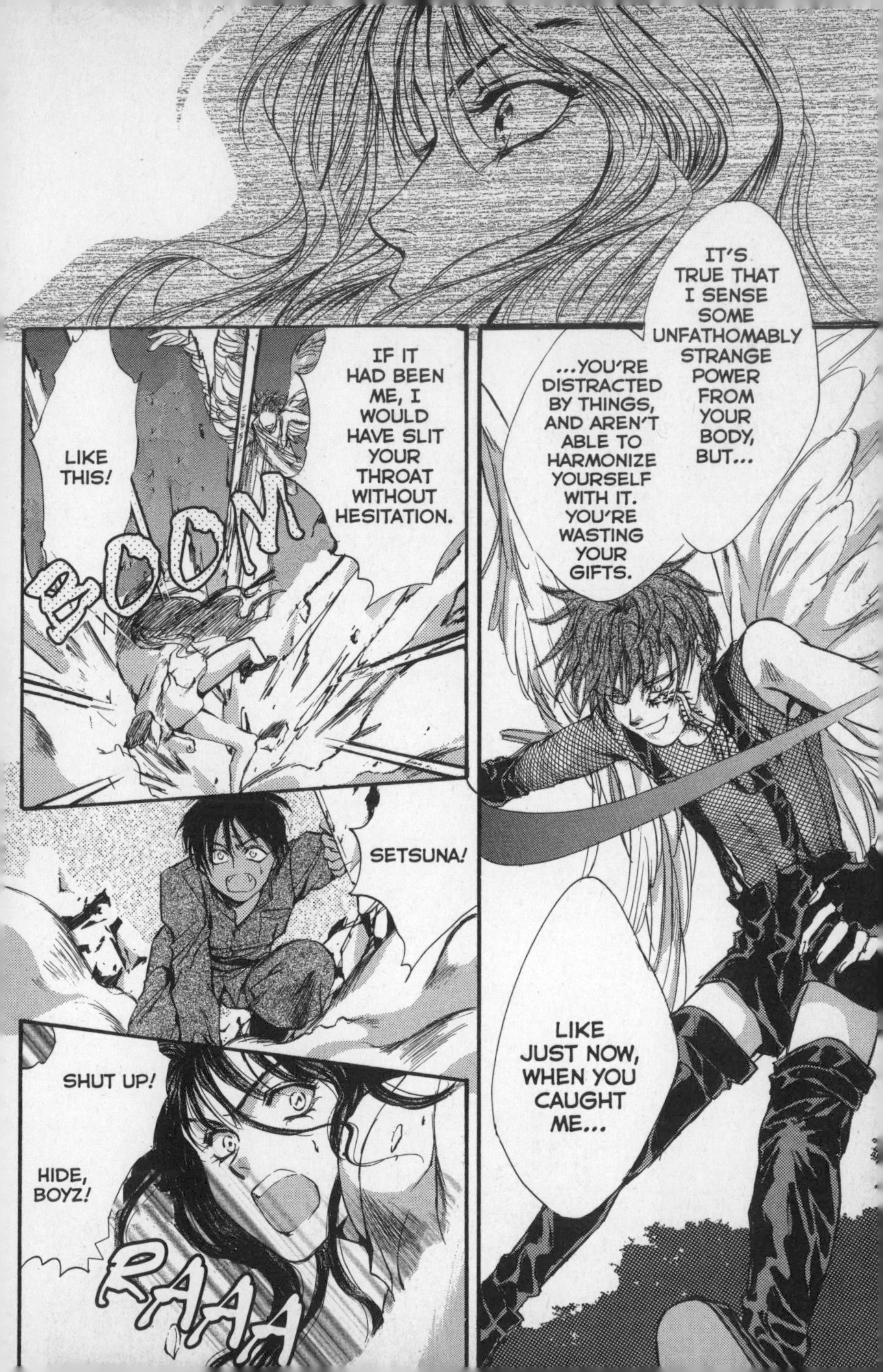

IT'S TRUE THAT I SENSE SOME UNFATHOMABLY STRANGE POWER FROM YOUR BODY, BUT...
...YOU'RE DISTRACTED BY THINGS, AND AREN'T ABLE TO HARMONIZE YOURSELF WITH IT. YOU'RE WASTING YOUR GIFTS.
LIKE JUST NOW, WHEN YOU CAUGHT ME...
IF IT HAD BEEN ME, I WOULD HAVE SLIT YOUR THROAT WITHOUT HESITATION.
LIKE THIS!
BOOM
SETSUNA!
SHUT UP!
HIDE, BOYZ!
RAAA

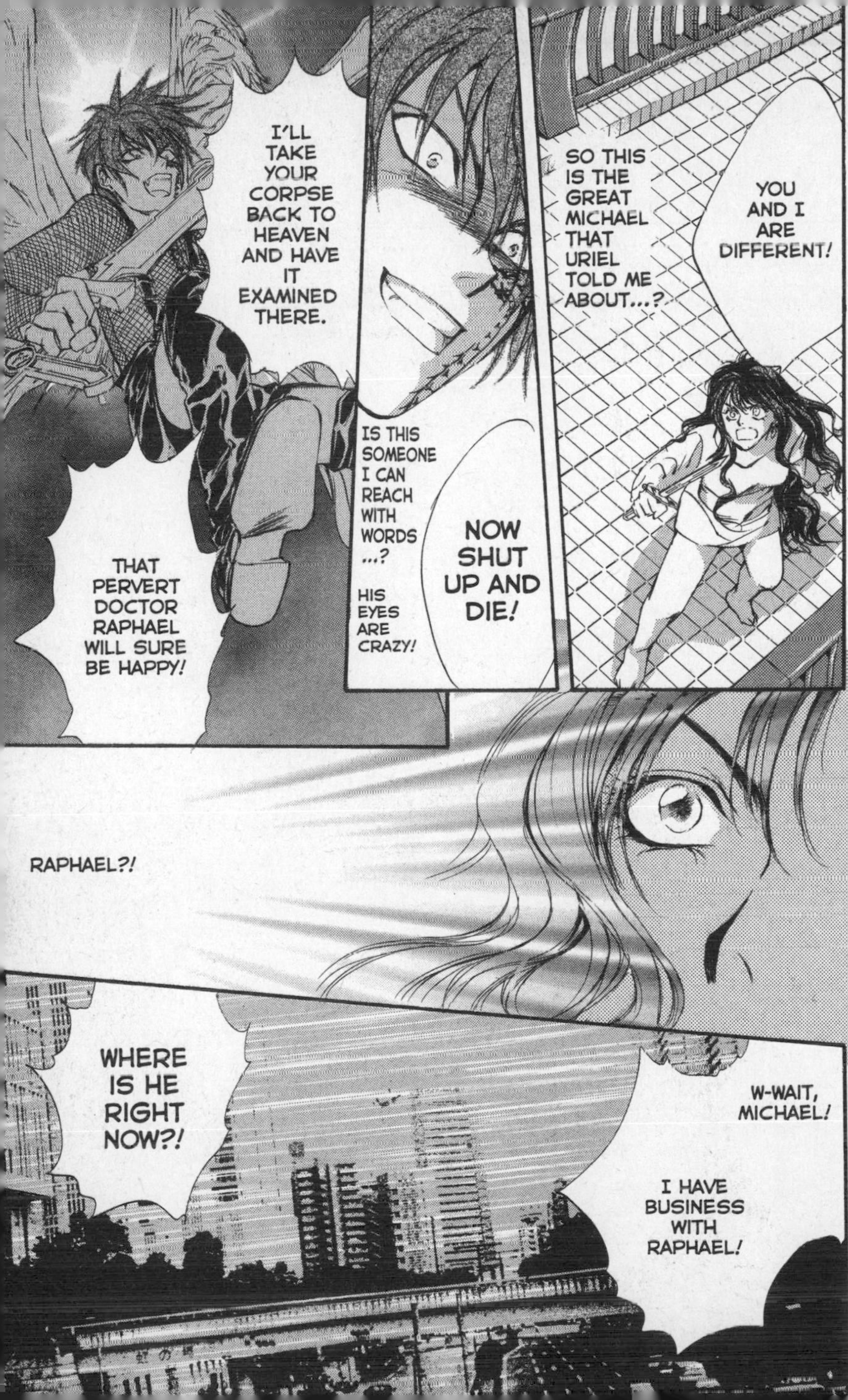
YOU AND I ARE DIFFERENT!
SO THIS IS THE GREAT MICHAEL THAT URIEL TOLD ME ABOUT...?
NOW SHUT UP AND DIE!
IS THIS SOMEONE I CAN REACH WITH WORDS ...?
HIS EYES ARE CRAZY!
I'LL TAKE YOUR CORPSE BACK TO HEAVEN AND HAVE IT EXAMINED THERE.
THAT PERVERT DOCTOR RAPHAEL WILL SURE BE HAPPY!
RAPHAEL?!
W-WAIT, MICHAEL!
I HAVE BUSINESS WITH RAPHAEL!
WHERE IS HE RIGHT NOW?!

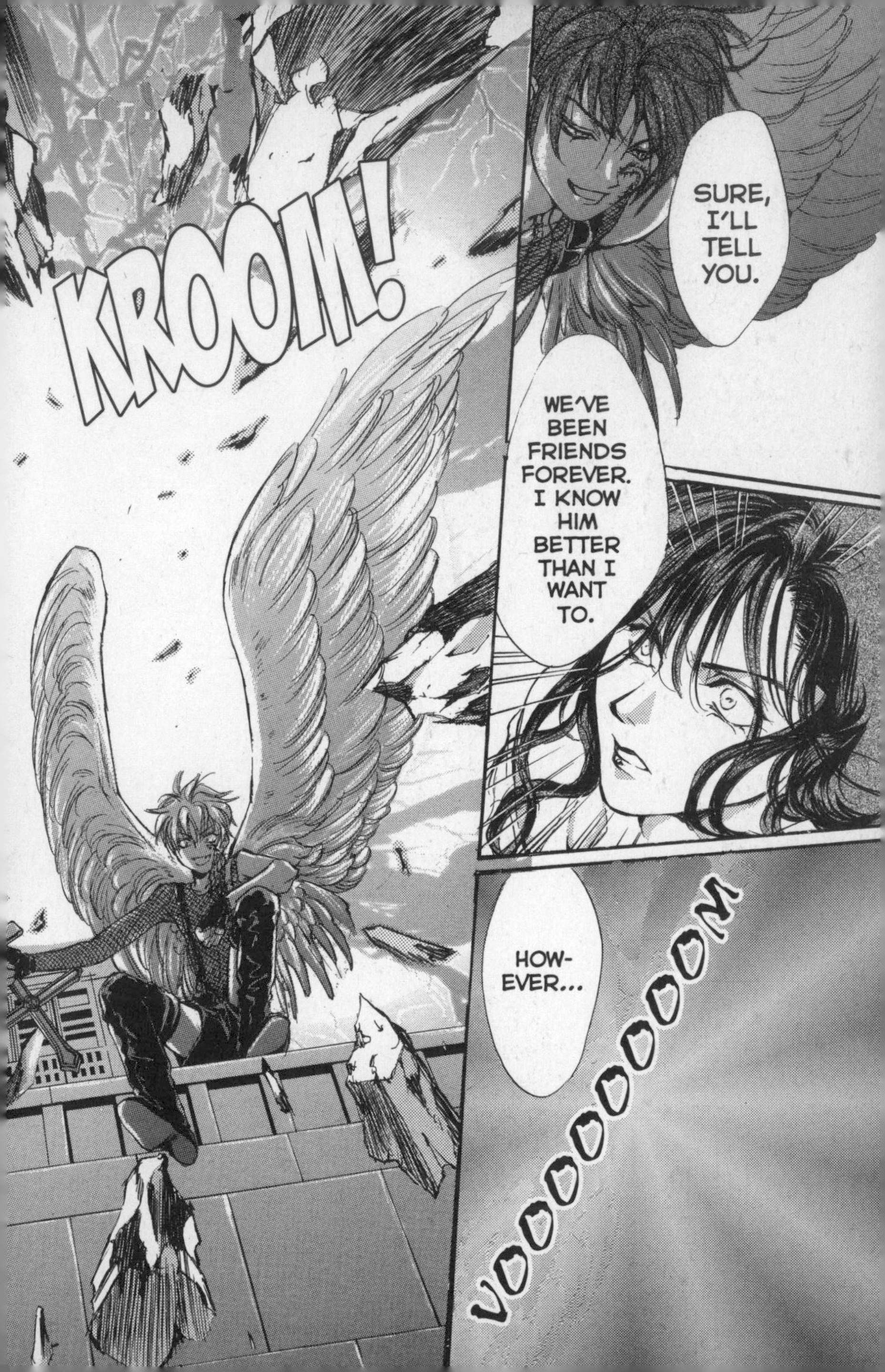
SURE, I'LL TELL YOU.
WE'VE BEEN FRIENDS FOREVER. I KNOW HIM BETTER THAN I WANT TO.
HOW-EVER...
VOOOOOOOOOOM
KROOM!

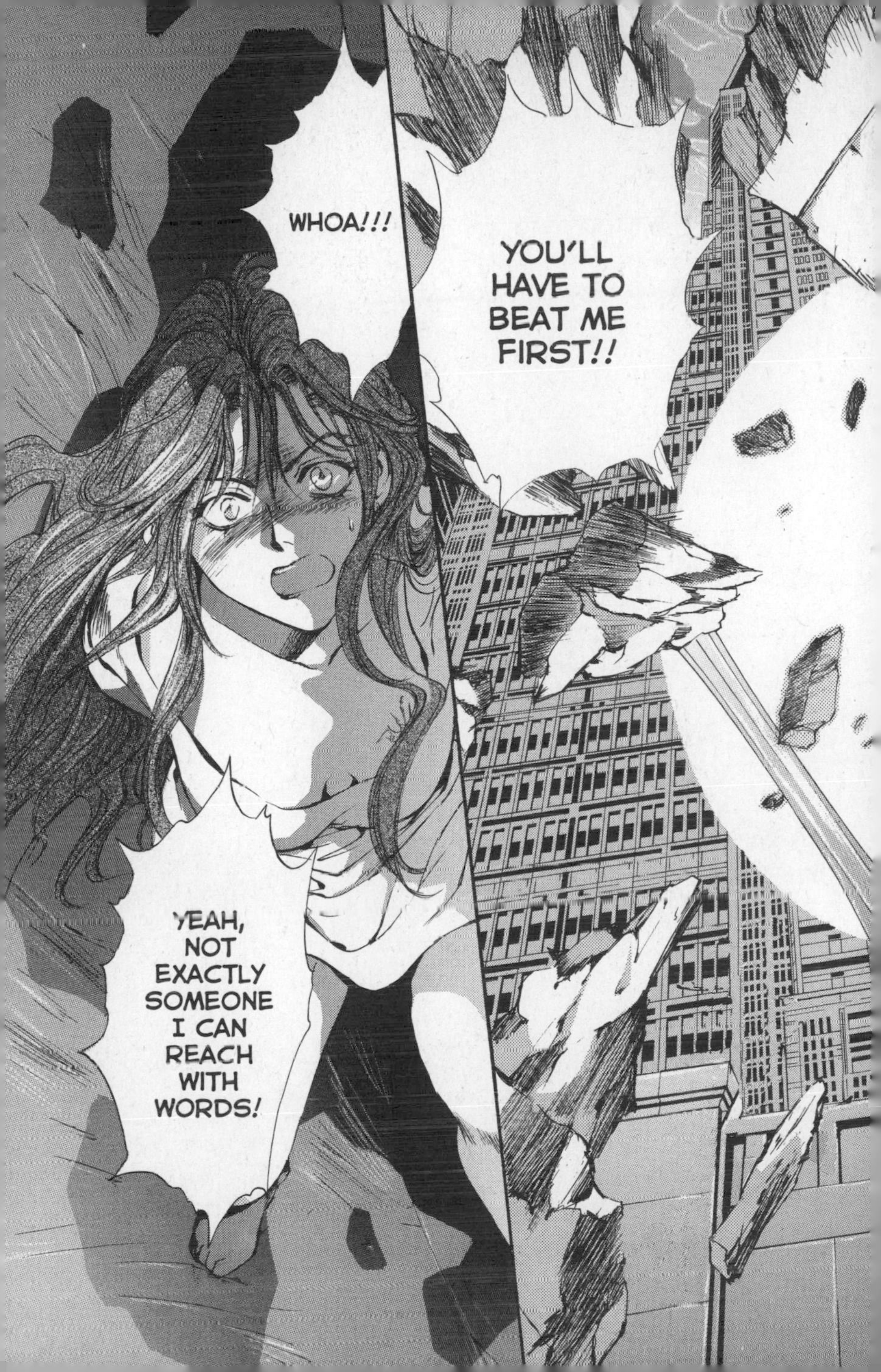
YOU'LL HAVE TO BEAT ME FIRST!!
WHOA!!!
YEAH, NOT EXACTLY SOMEONE I CAN REACH WITH WORDS!

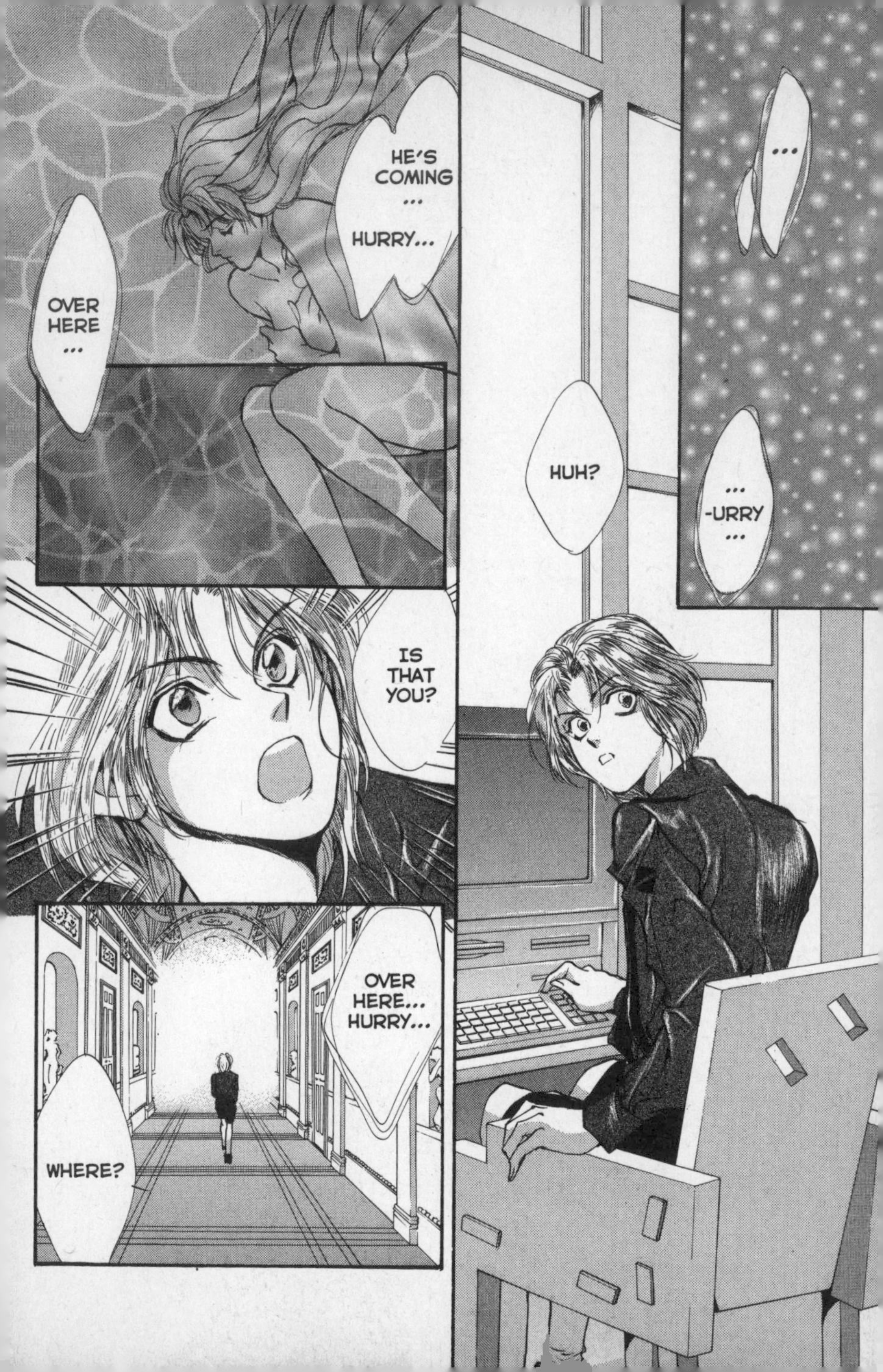
...
... -URRY ...
HUH?
HE'S COMING ... HURRY...
OVER HERE ...
IS THAT YOU?
OVER HERE... HURRY...
WHERE?

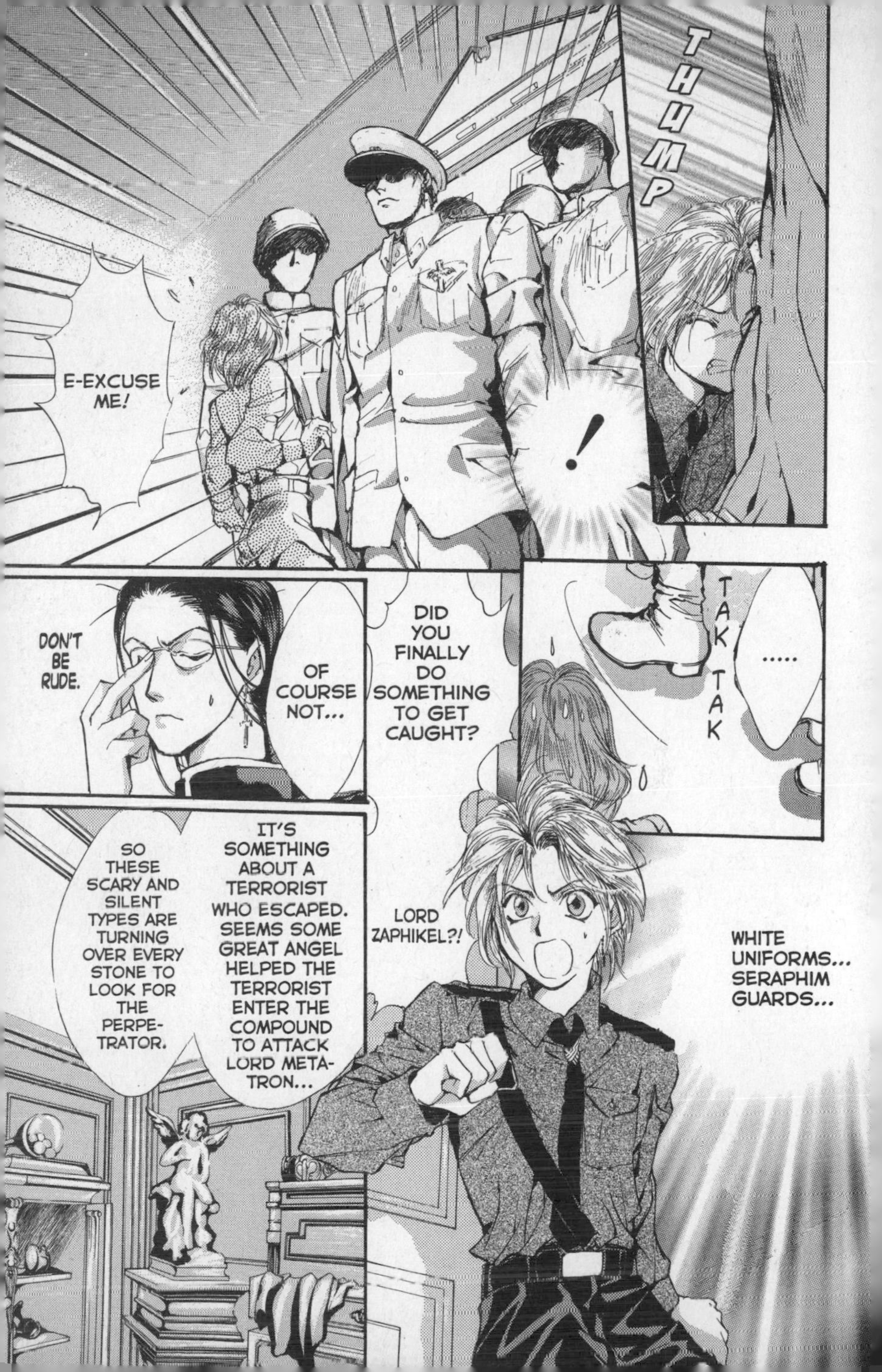
THUMP
E-EXCUSE ME!
!
TAK TAK
.....
DID YOU FINALLY DO SOMETHING TO GET CAUGHT?
OF COURSE NOT...
DON'T BE RUDE.
WHITE UNIFORMS... SERAPHIM GUARDS...
LORD ZAPHIKEL?!
IT'S SOMETHING ABOUT A TERRORIST WHO ESCAPED. SEEMS SOME GREAT ANGEL HELPED THE TERRORIST ENTER THE COMPOUND TO ATTACK LORD METATRON...
SO THESE SCARY AND SILENT TYPES ARE TURNING OVER EVERY STONE TO LOOK FOR THE PERPETRATOR.

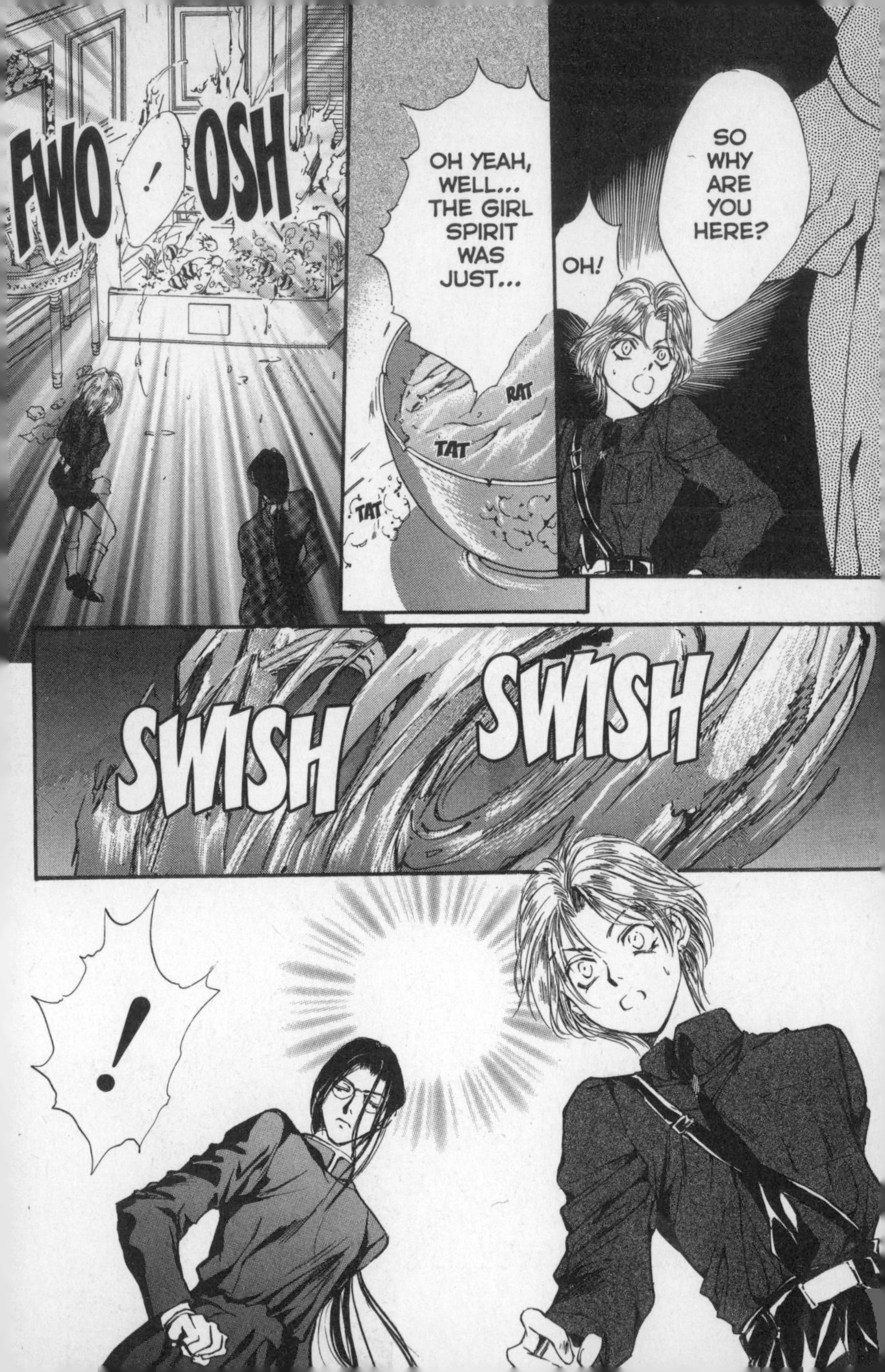
SO WHY ARE YOU HERE?
OH!
OH YEAH, WELL... THE GIRL SPIRIT WAS JUST...
RAT
TAT
TAT
FWO OSH
!
SWISH
SWISH
!

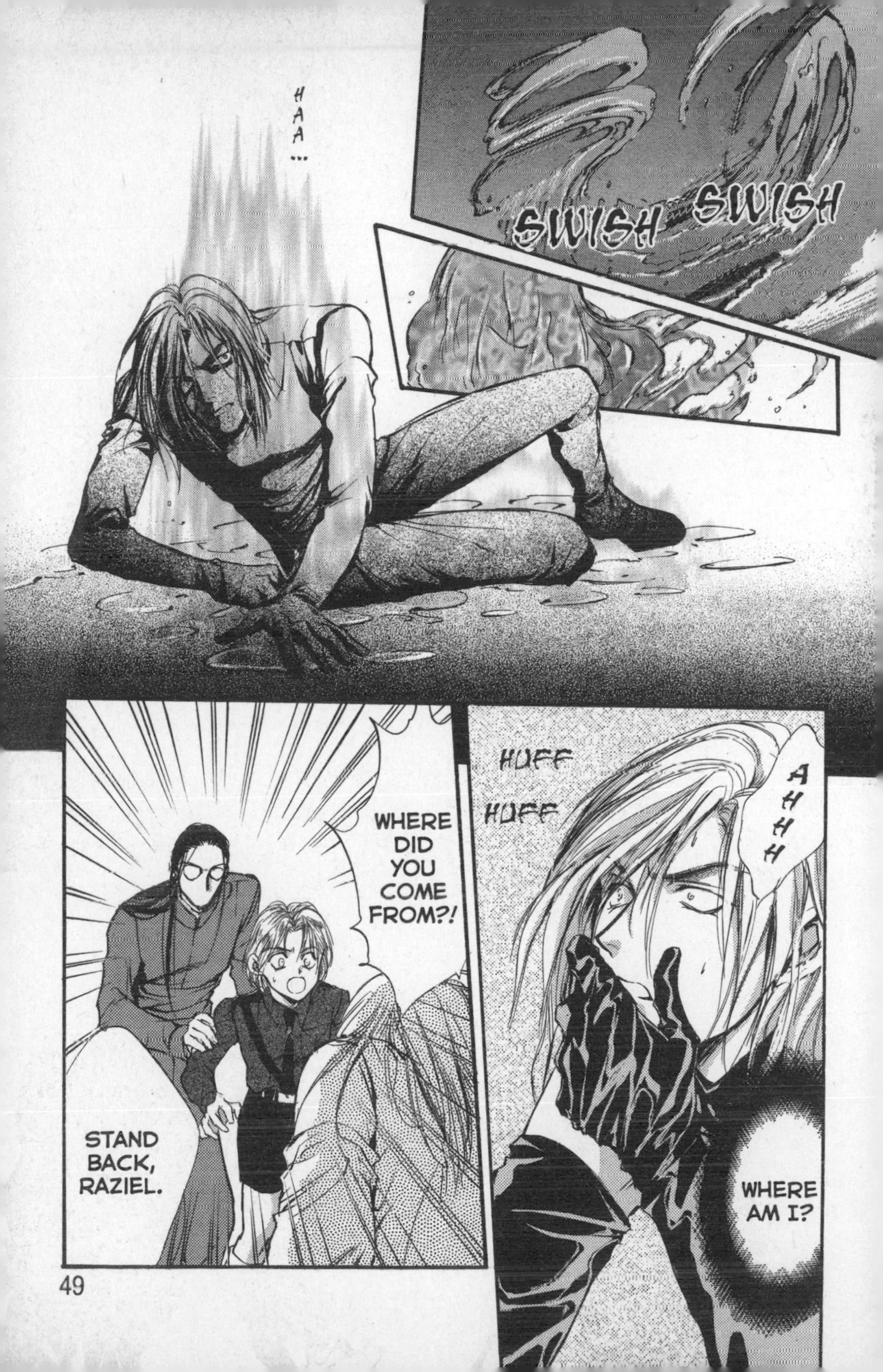
SWISH SWISH
HAA...
HUFF
HUFF
AHHH
WHERE AM I?
WHERE DID YOU COME FROM?!
STAND BACK, RAZIEL.

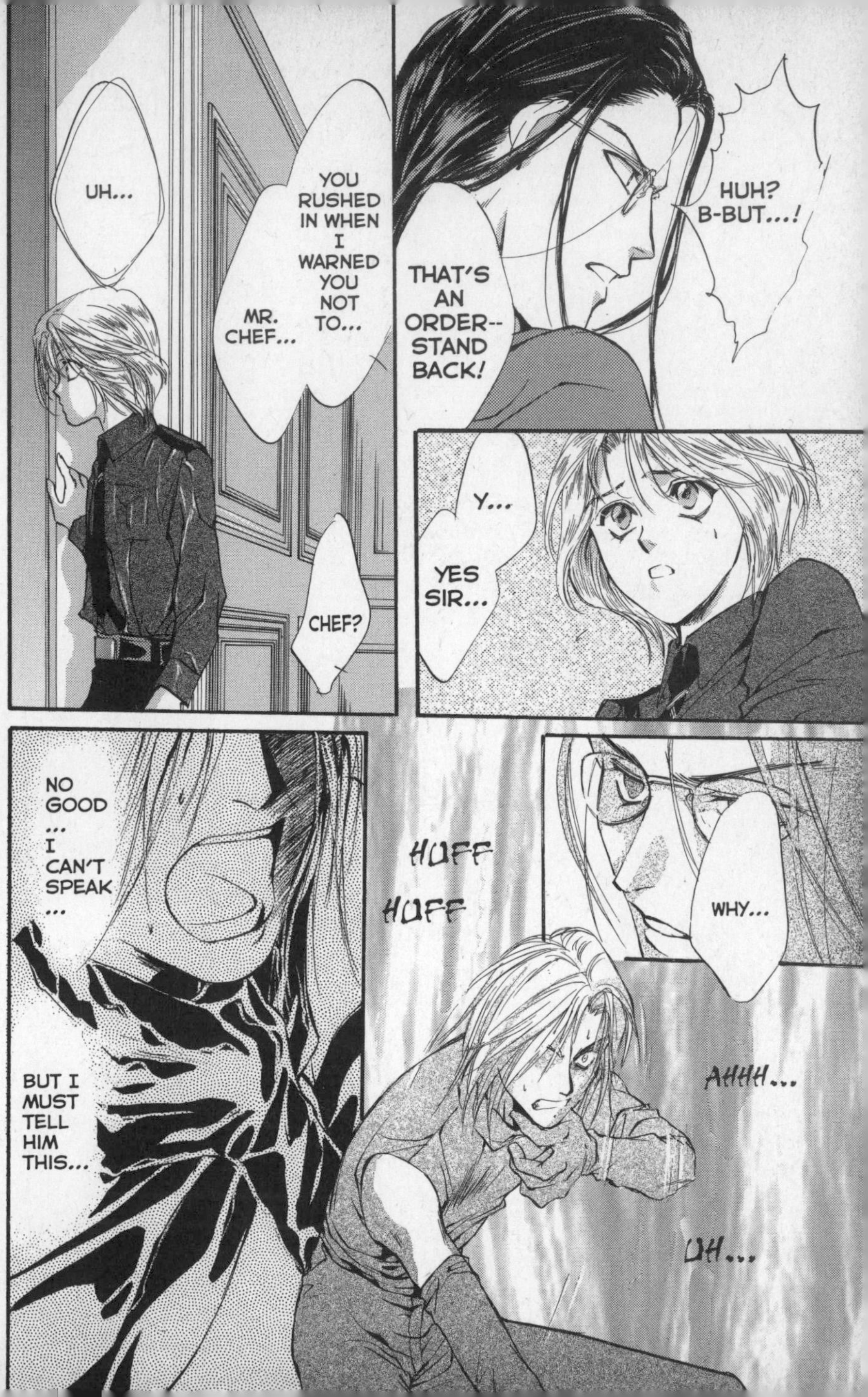
HUH? B-BUT...!
THAT'S AN ORDER-- STAND BACK!
Y...
YES SIR...
YOU RUSHED IN WHEN I WARNED YOU NOT TO...
MR. CHEF...
UH...
CHEF?
WHY...
AHHH...
HUFF
HUFF
UH...
NO GOOD ... I CAN'T SPEAK ...
BUT I MUST TELL HIM THIS...

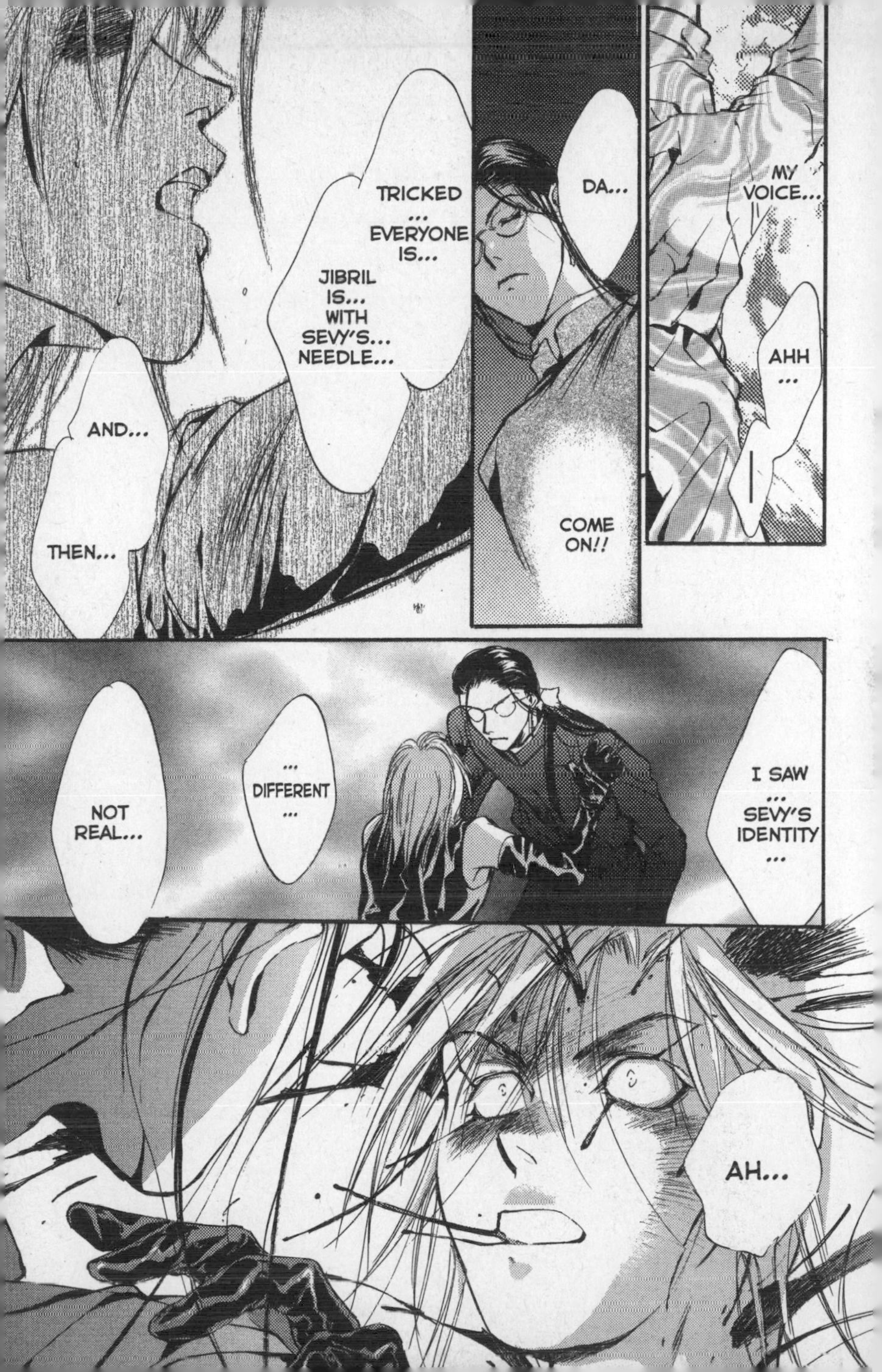
MY VOICE...
AHH ...
DA...
COME ON!!
TRICKED ... EVERYONE IS...
JIBRIL IS... WITH SEVY'S... NEEDLE...
AND... THEN...
I SAW ... SEVY'S IDENTITY ...
... DIFFERENT ...
NOT REAL...
AH...

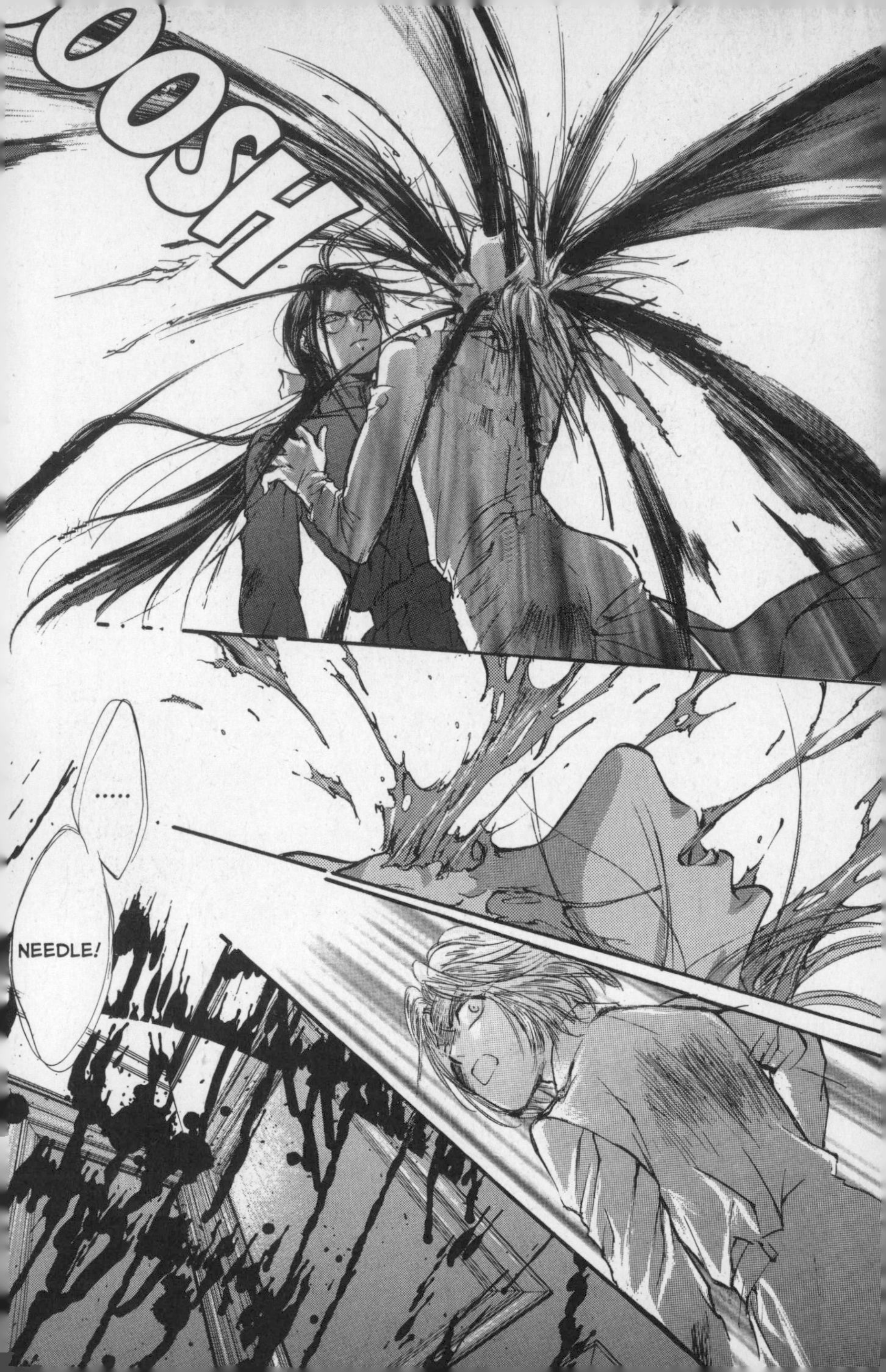
OOSH!
.....
NEEDLE!

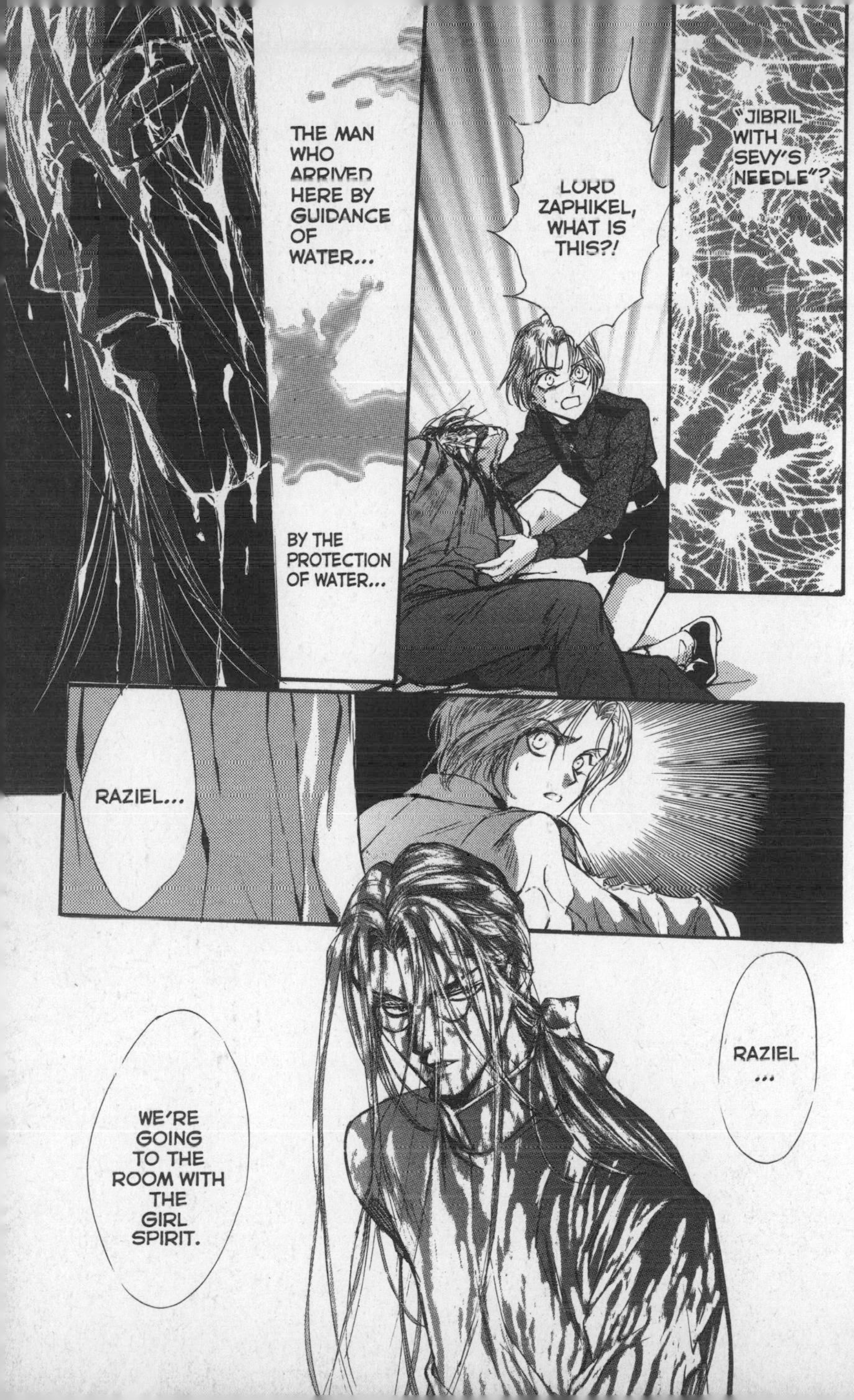
"JIBRIL WITH SEVY'S NEEDLE"?
LORD ZAPHIKEL, WHAT IS THIS?!
THE MAN WHO ARRIVED HERE BY GUIDANCE OF WATER...
BY THE PROTECTION OF WATER...
RAZIEL...
RAZIEL ...
WE'RE GOING TO THE ROOM WITH THE GIRL SPIRIT.

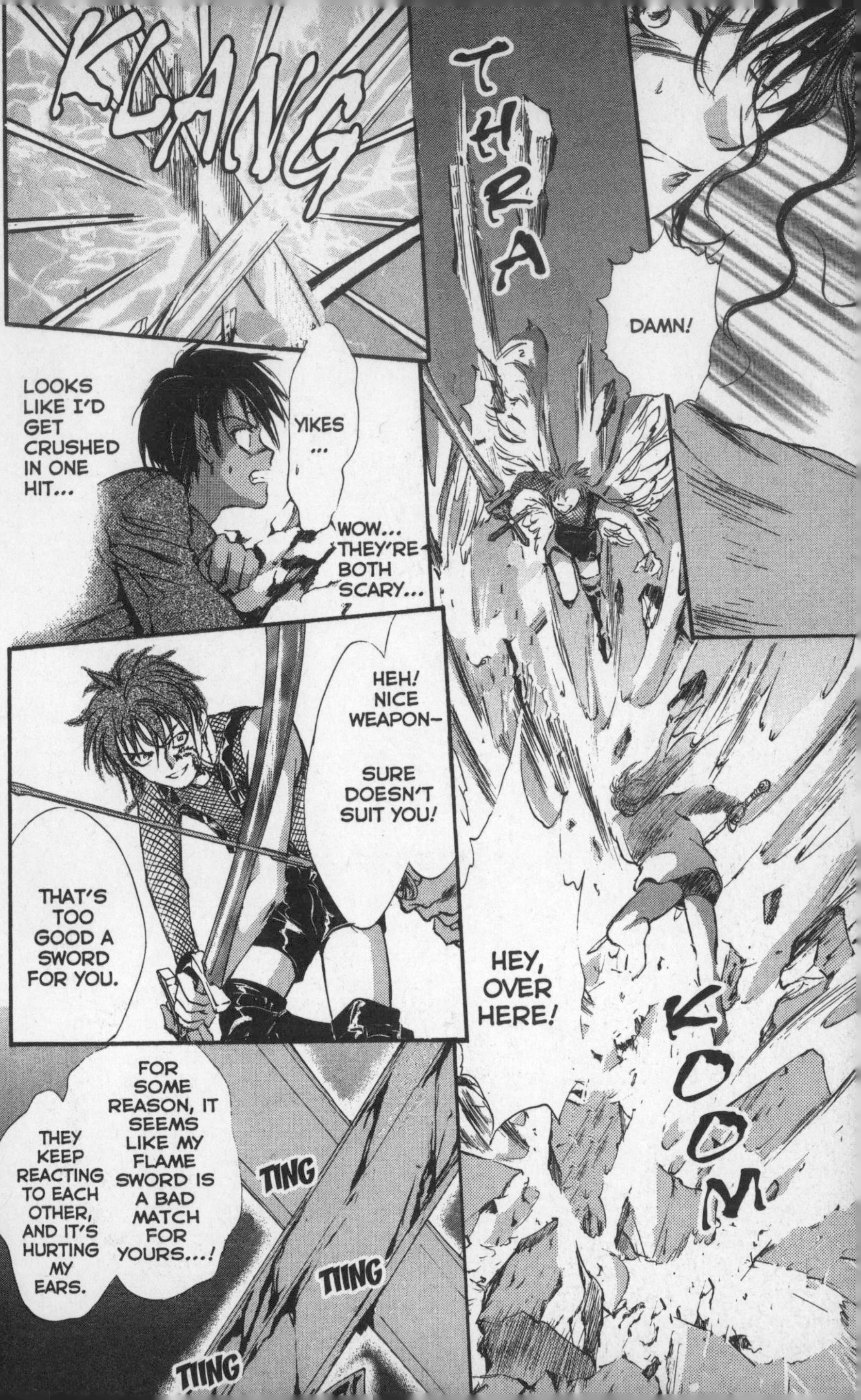
DAMN!
THRA
KLANG
YIKES...
LOOKS LIKE I'D GET CRUSHED IN ONE HIT...
WOW... THEY'RE BOTH SCARY...
HEY, OVER HERE!
KOOM
HEH! NICE WEAPON—
SURE DOESN'T SUIT YOU!
THAT'S TOO GOOD A SWORD FOR YOU.
FOR SOME REASON, IT SEEMS LIKE MY FLAME SWORD IS A BAD MATCH FOR YOURS...!
THEY KEEP REACTING TO EACH OTHER, AND IT'S HURTING MY EARS.
TIING
TIING
TIING

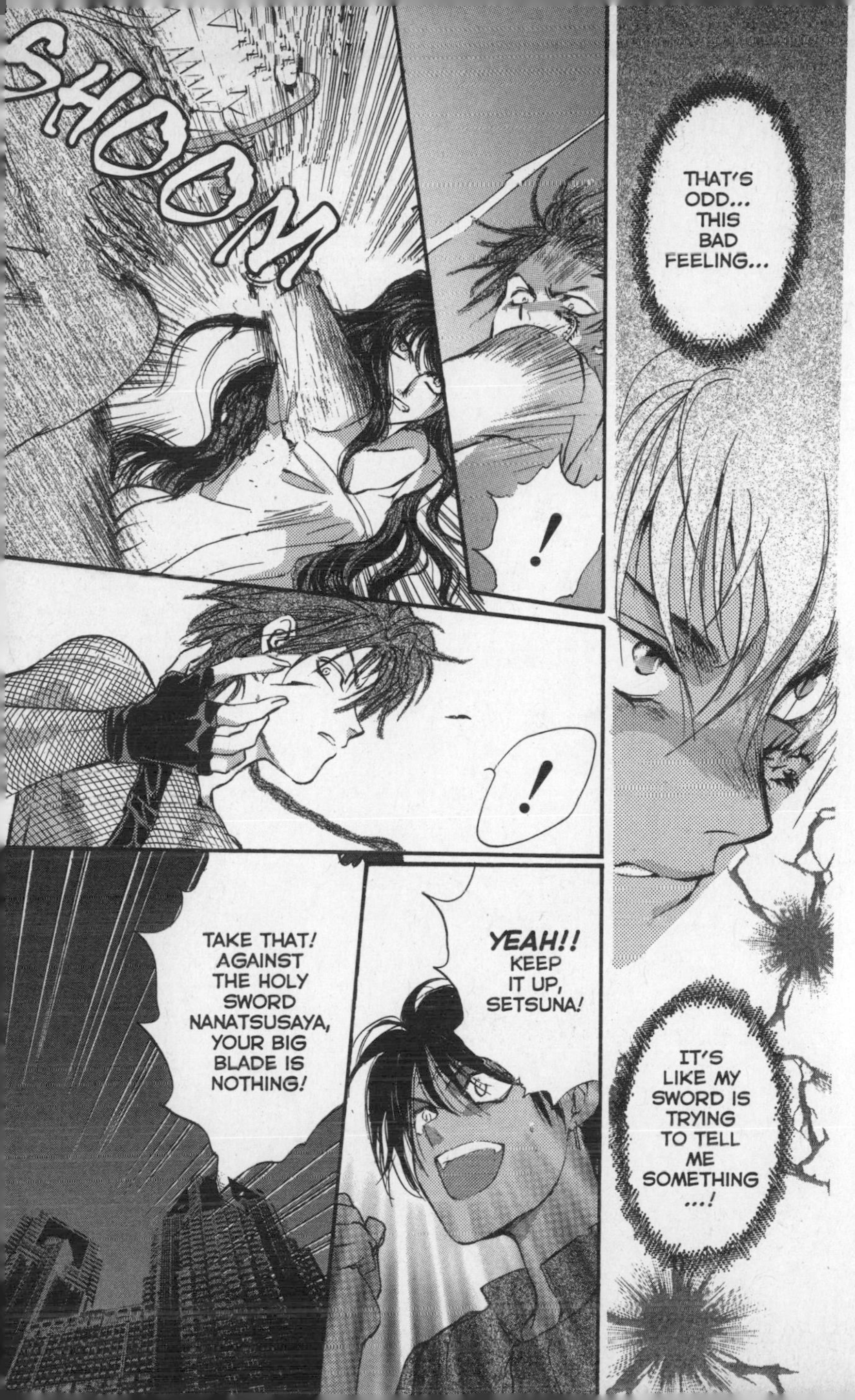
THAT'S ODD... THIS BAD FEELING...
IT'S LIKE MY SWORD IS TRYING TO TELL ME SOMETHING ...!
!
SHOOM
!
YEAH!! KEEP IT UP, SETSUNA!
TAKE THAT! AGAINST THE HOLY SWORD NANATSUSAYA, YOUR BIG BLADE IS NOTHING!

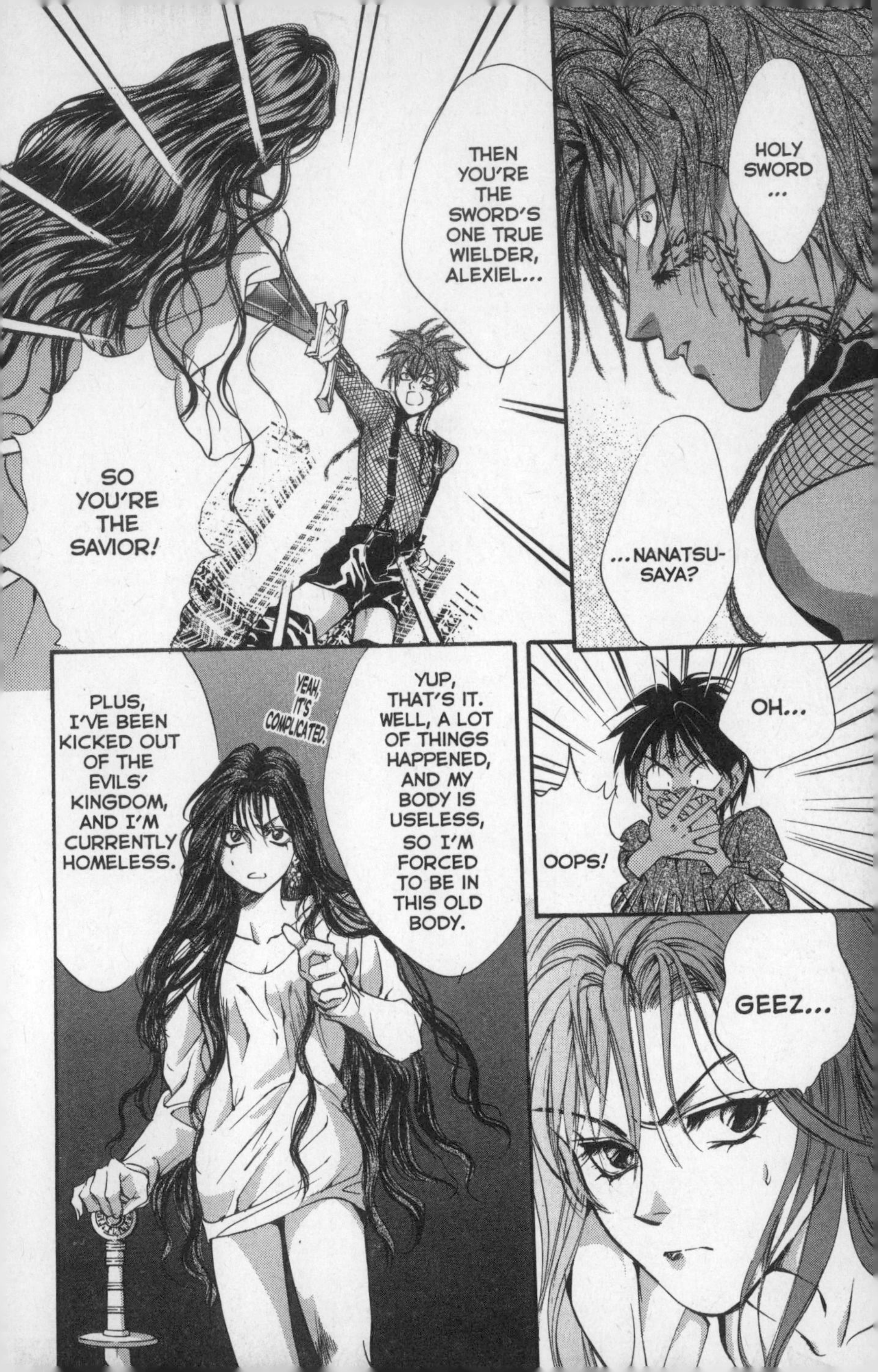
HOLY SWORD...
...NANATSU-SAYA?
THEN YOU'RE THE SWORD'S ONE TRUE WIELDER, ALEXIEL...
SO YOU'RE THE SAVIOR!
OH...
OOPS!
GEEZ...
YUP, THAT'S IT. WELL, A LOT OF THINGS HAPPENED, AND MY BODY IS USELESS, SO I'M FORCED TO BE IN THIS OLD BODY.
YEAH, IT'S COMPLICATED.
PLUS, I'VE BEEN KICKED OUT OF THE EVILS' KINGDOM, AND I'M CURRENTLY HOMELESS.

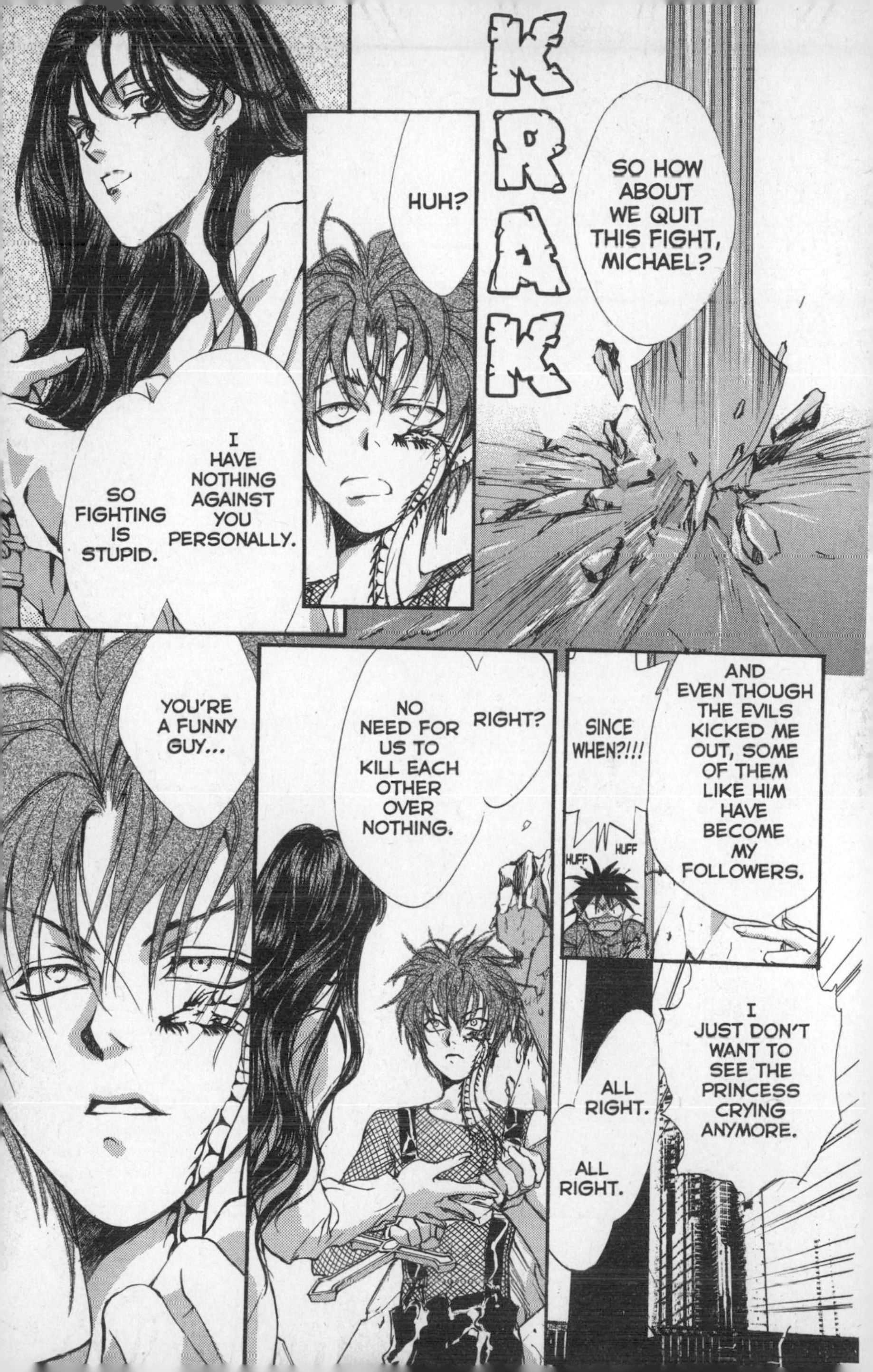
KRAK
SO HOW ABOUT WE QUIT THIS FIGHT, MICHAEL?
HUH?
I HAVE NOTHING AGAINST YOU PERSONALLY.
SO FIGHTING IS STUPID.
AND EVEN THOUGH THE EVILS KICKED ME OUT, SOME OF THEM LIKE HIM HAVE BECOME MY FOLLOWERS.
SINCE WHEN?!!!
HUFF
HUFF
I JUST DON'T WANT TO SEE THE PRINCESS CRYING ANYMORE.
RIGHT?
NO NEED FOR US TO KILL EACH OTHER OVER NOTHING.
ALL RIGHT.
ALL RIGHT.
YOU'RE A FUNNY GUY...

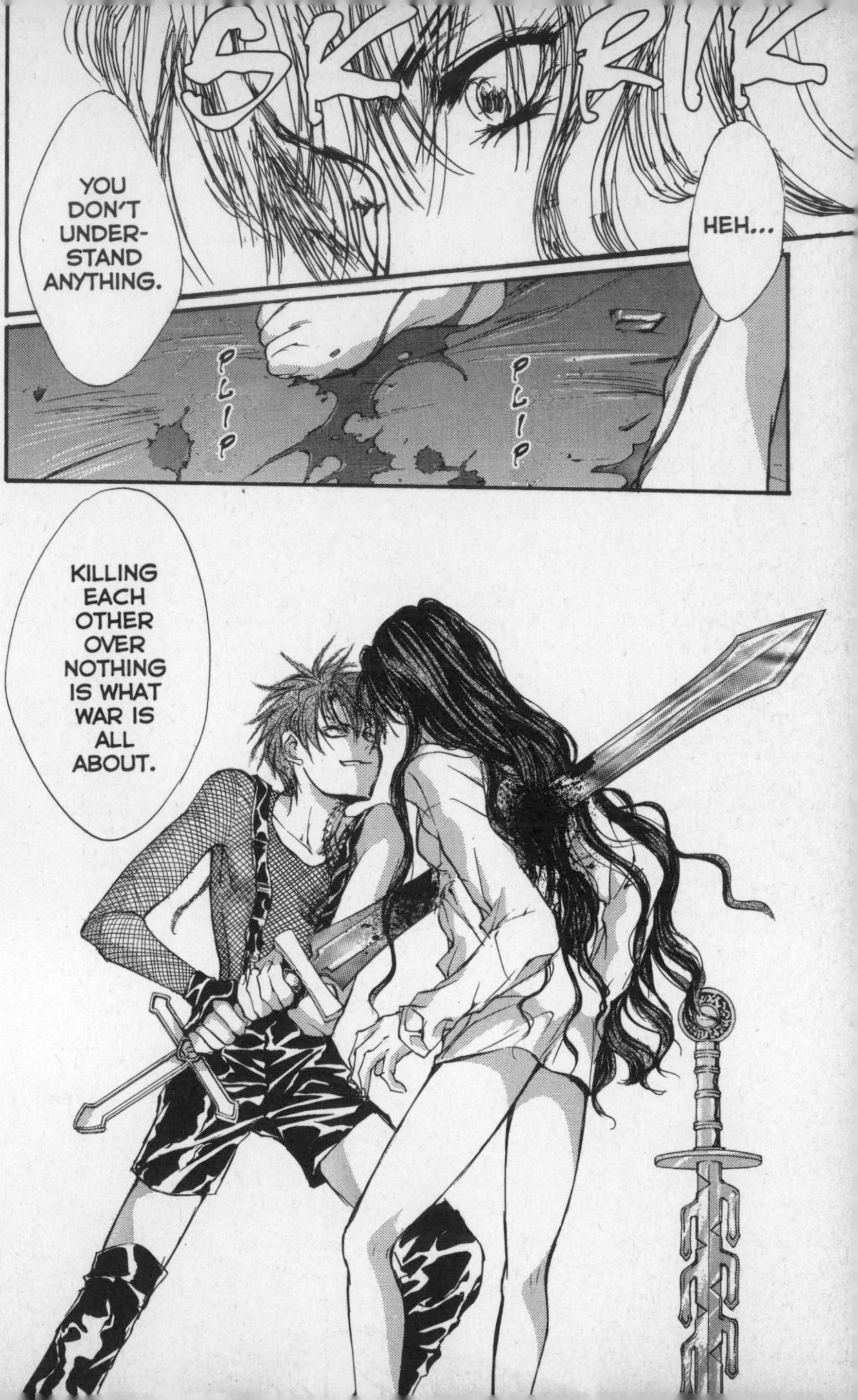
SKRIK
HEH...
YOU DON'T UNDER-STAND ANYTHING.
PLIP
PLIP
KILLING EACH OTHER OVER NOTHING IS WHAT WAR IS ALL ABOUT.

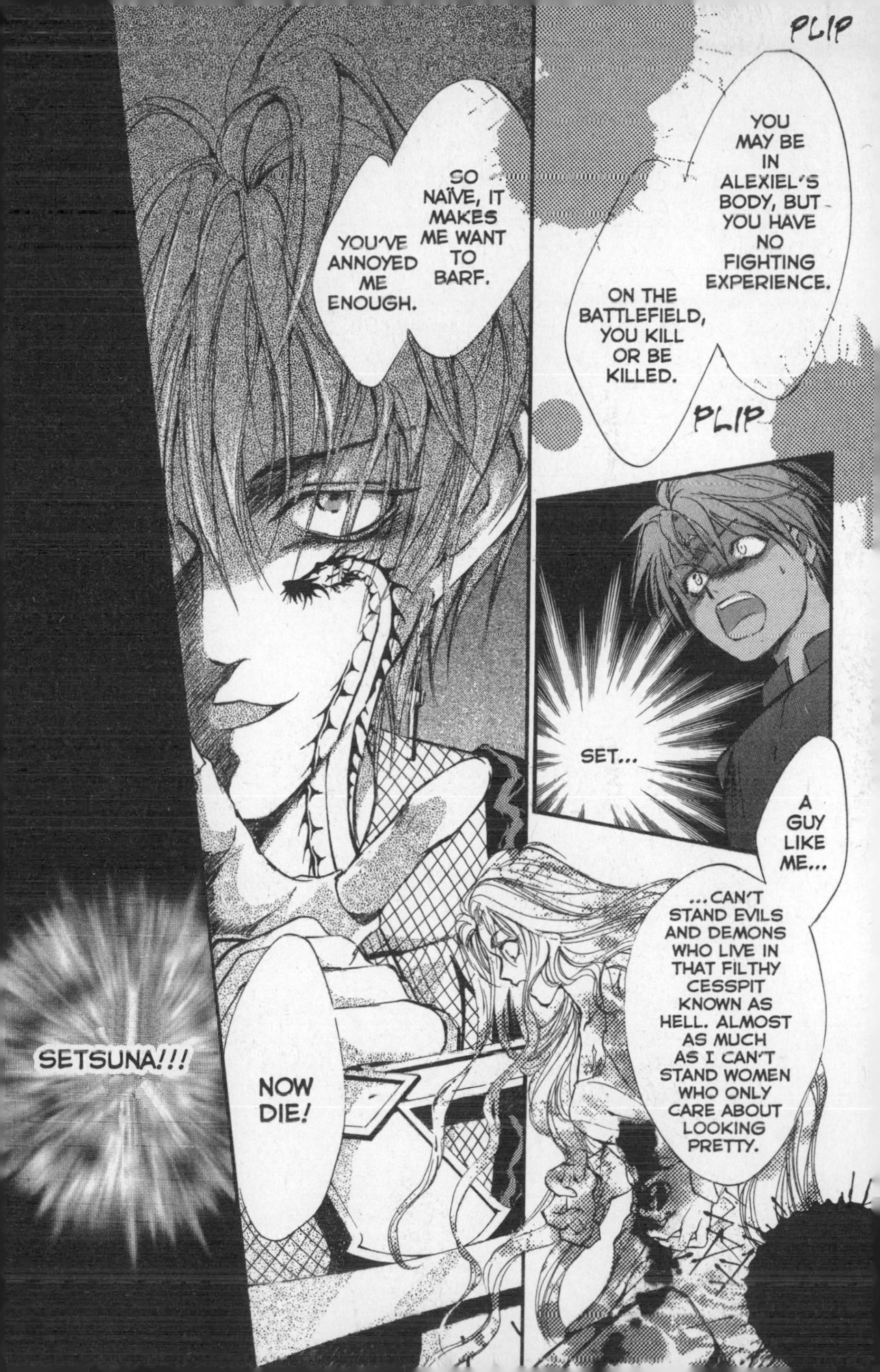
PLIP
YOU MAY BE IN ALEXIEL'S BODY, BUT YOU HAVE NO FIGHTING EXPERIENCE.
ON THE BATTLEFIELD, YOU KILL OR BE KILLED.
PLIP
SET...
A GUY LIKE ME...
...CAN'T STAND EVILS AND DEMONS WHO LIVE IN THAT FILTHY CESSPIT KNOWN AS HELL. ALMOST AS MUCH AS I CAN'T STAND WOMEN WHO ONLY CARE ABOUT LOOKING PRETTY.
SO NAÏVE, IT MAKES ME WANT TO BARF.
YOU'VE ANNOYED ME ENOUGH.
NOW DIE!
SETSUNA!!!

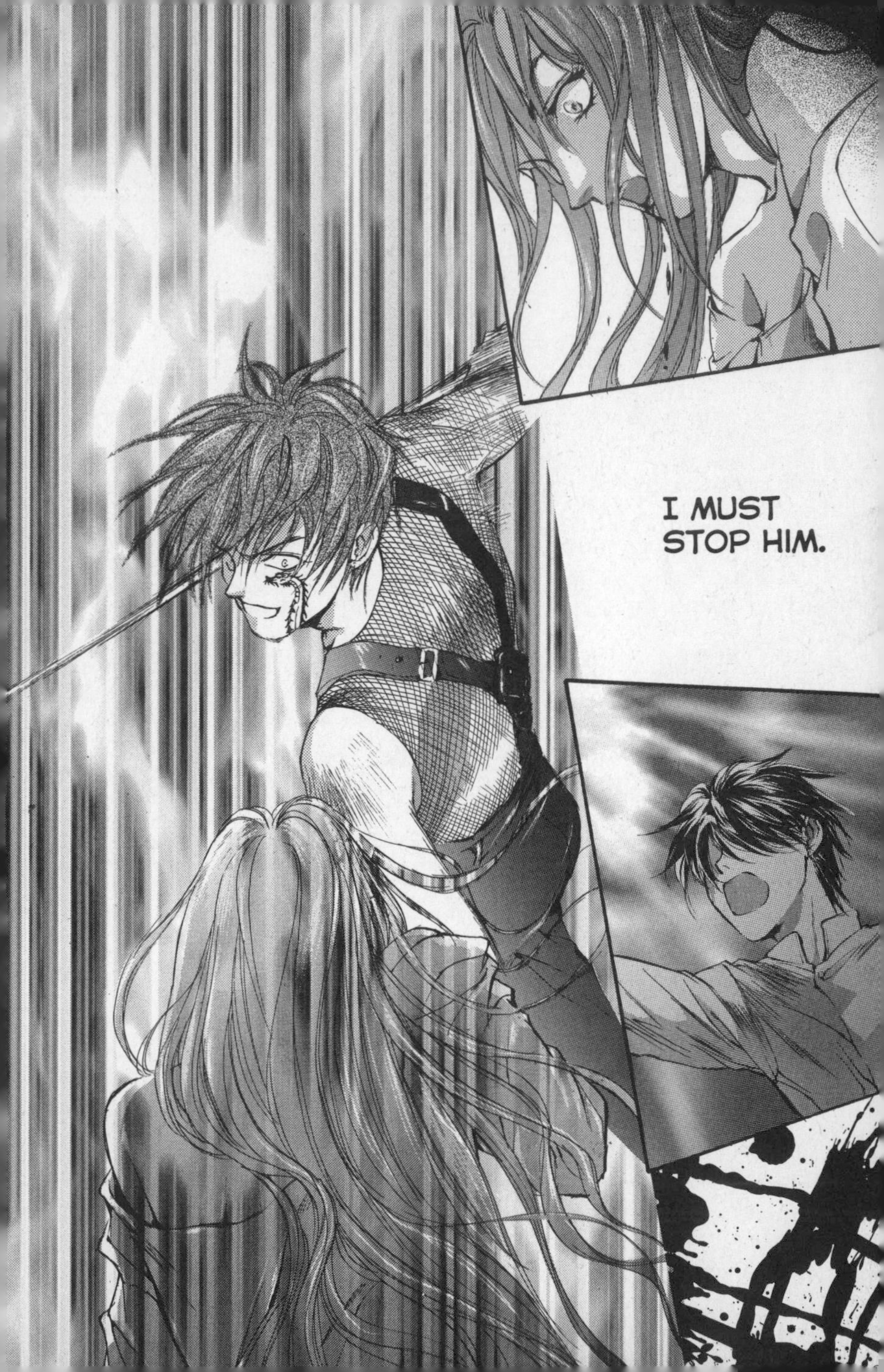
I MUST STOP HIM.

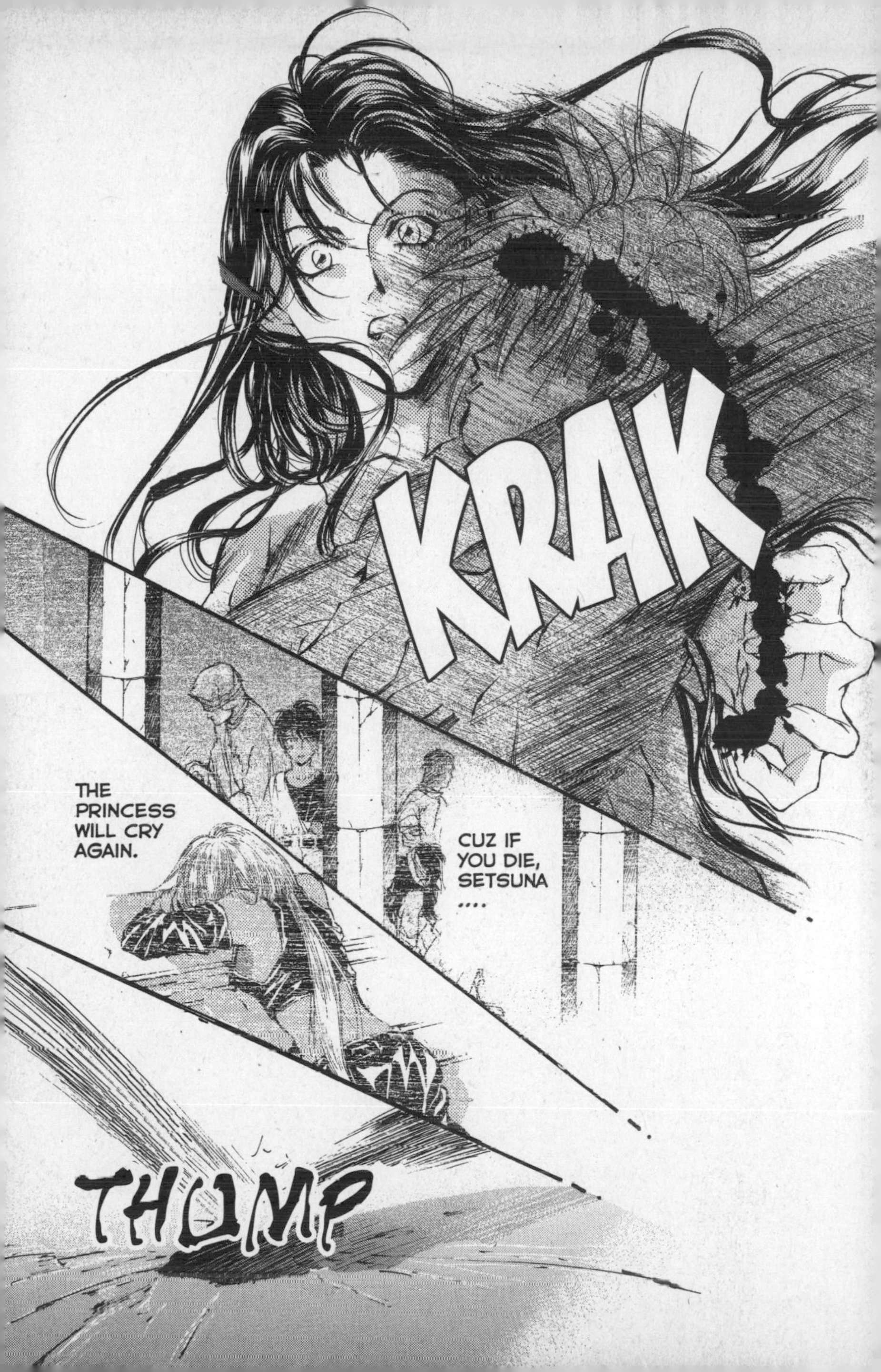
KRAK
CUZ IF YOU DIE, SETSUNA ....
THE PRINCESS WILL CRY AGAIN.
THUMP

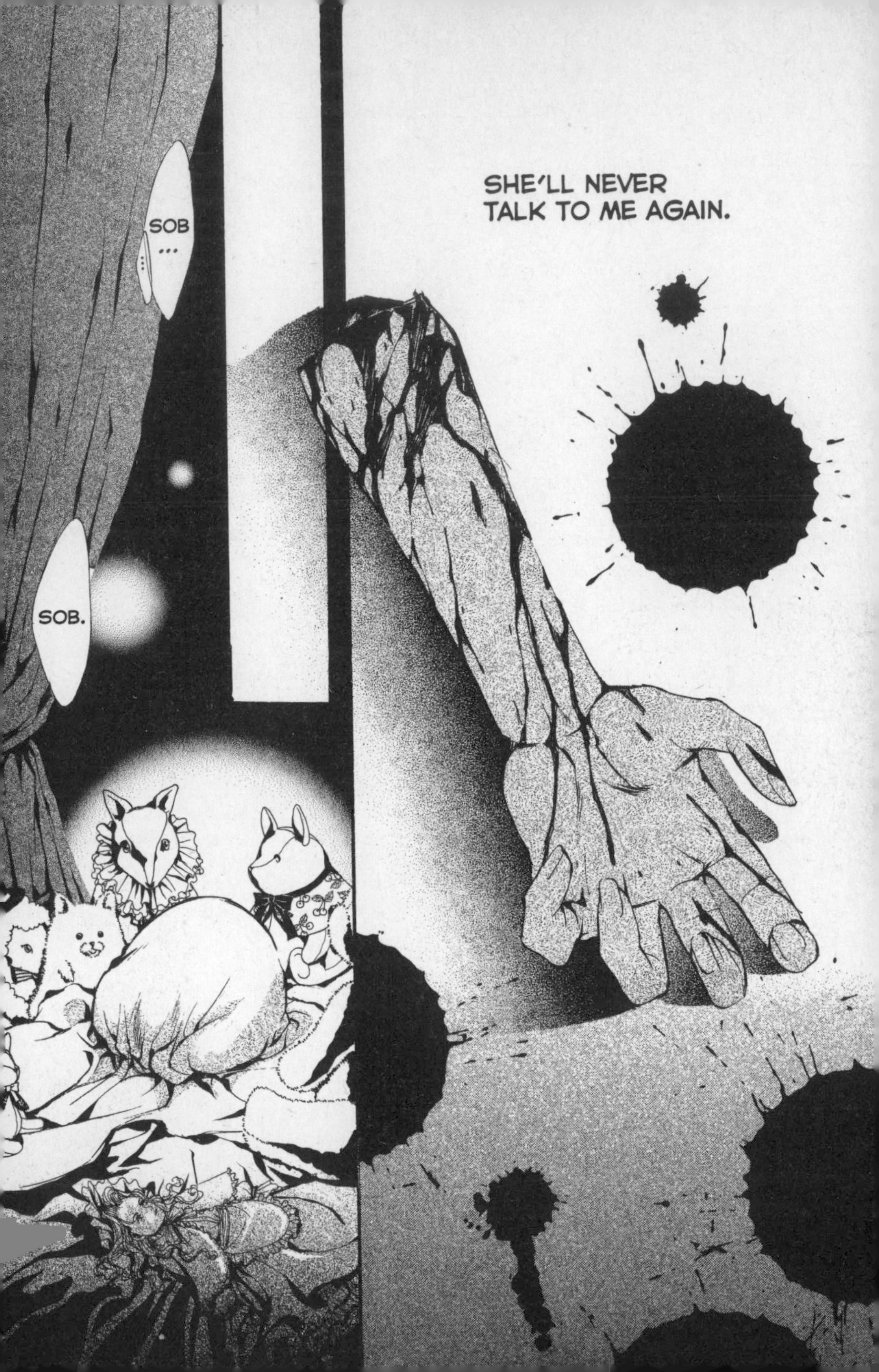
SHE'LL NEVER TALK TO ME AGAIN.
SOB ...
...
SOB.

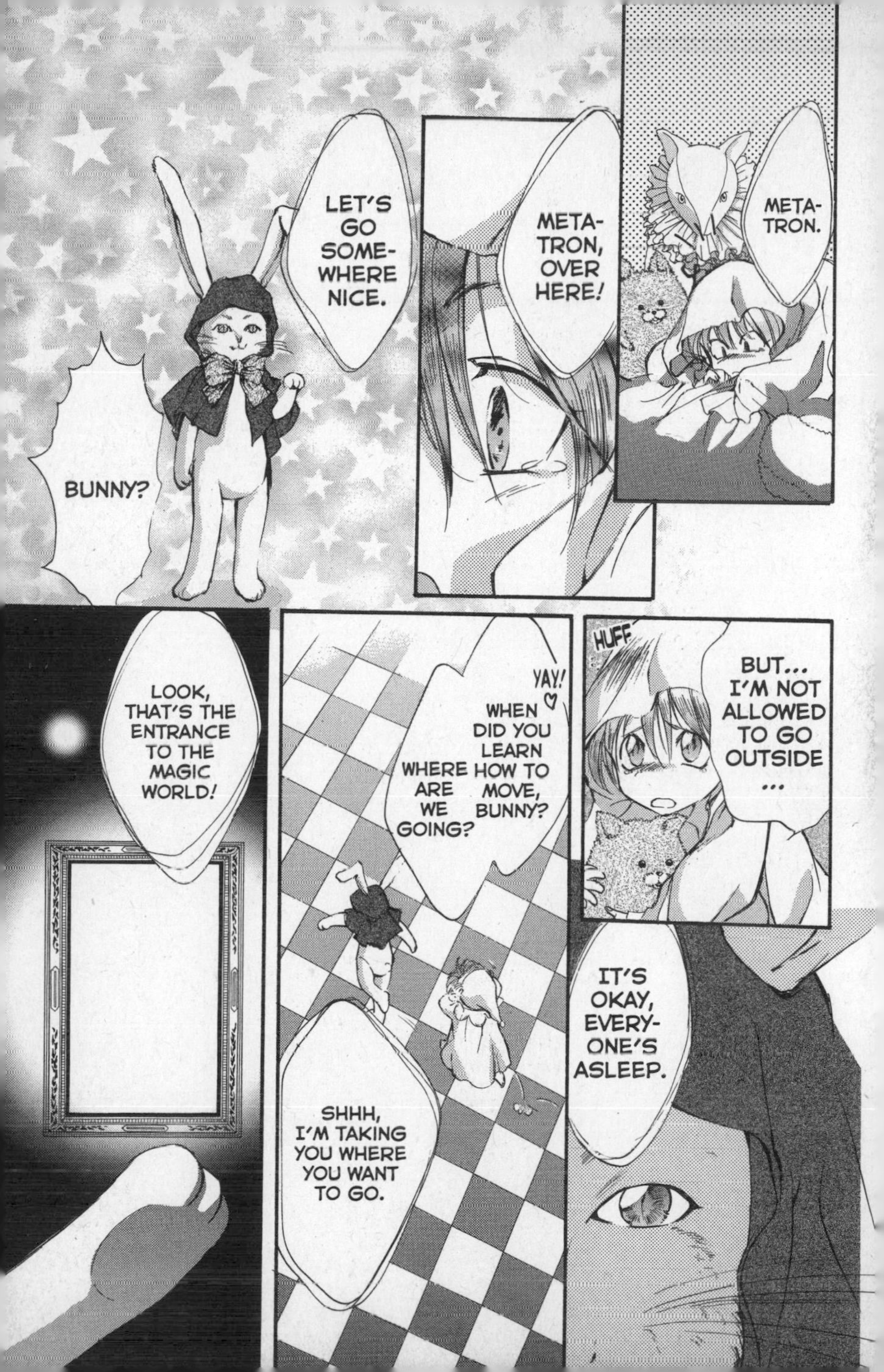
META-TRON.
META-TRON, OVER HERE!
LET'S GO SOME-WHERE NICE.
BUNNY?
HUFF
BUT... I'M NOT ALLOWED TO GO OUTSIDE ...
IT'S OKAY, EVERY-ONE'S ASLEEP.
YAY! ♡
WHEN DID YOU LEARN HOW TO MOVE, BUNNY?
WHERE ARE WE GOING?
SHHH, I'M TAKING YOU WHERE YOU WANT TO GO.
LOOK, THAT'S THE ENTRANCE TO THE MAGIC WORLD!

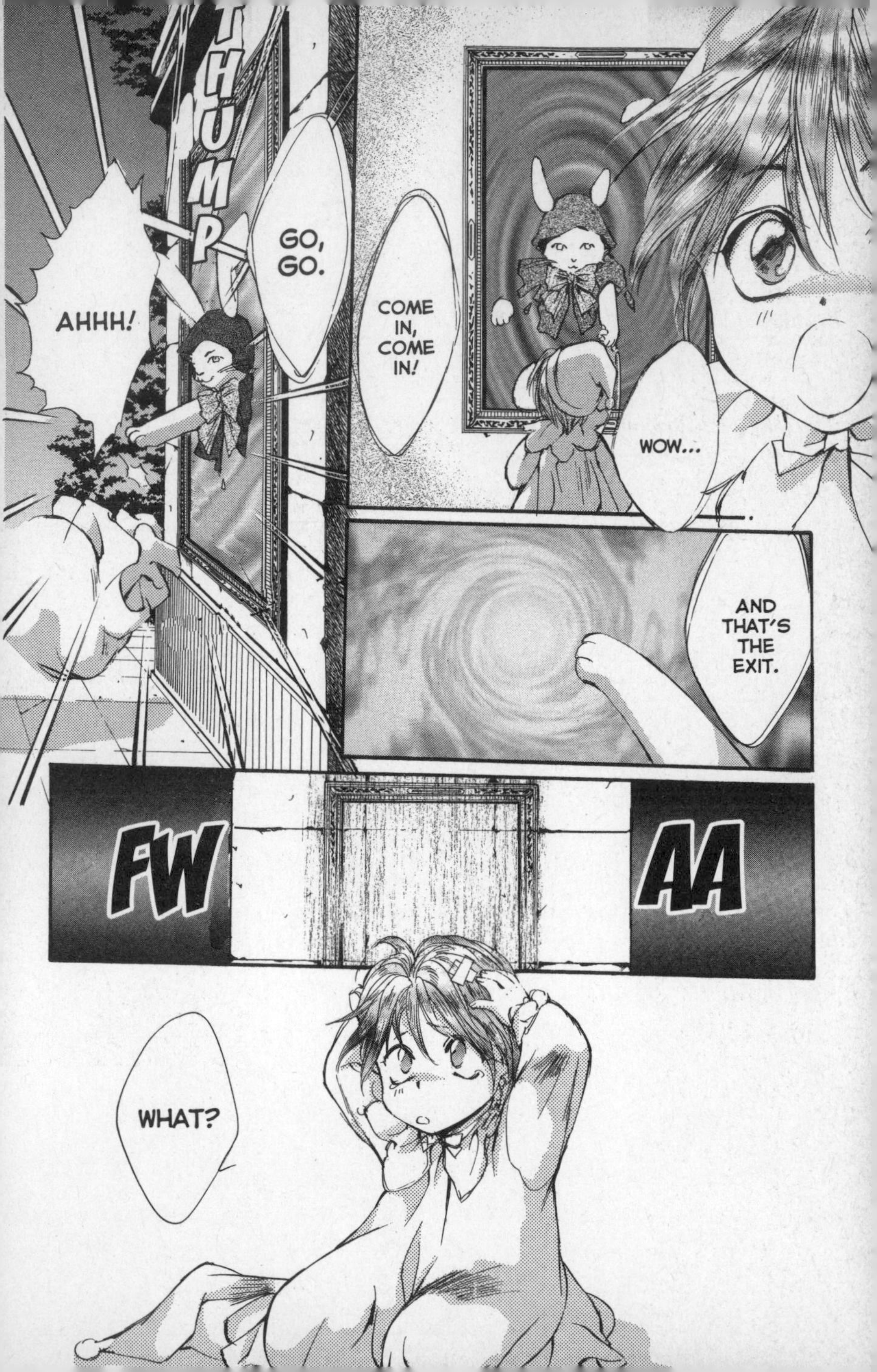
COME IN, COME IN!
WOW...
AND THAT'S THE EXIT.
GO, GO.
THUMP
AHHH!
FW AA
WHAT?

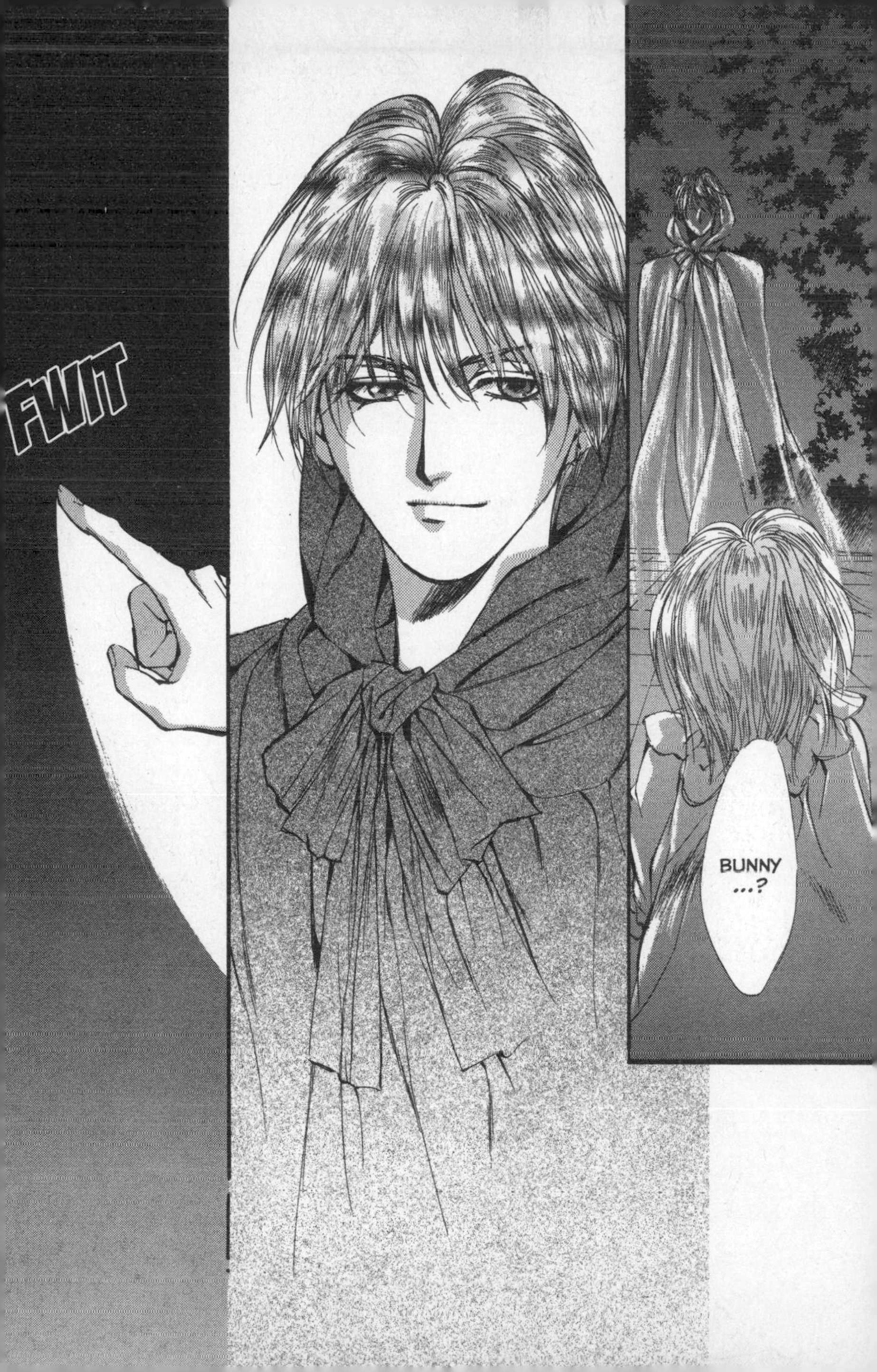
BUNNY ...?
FWIT

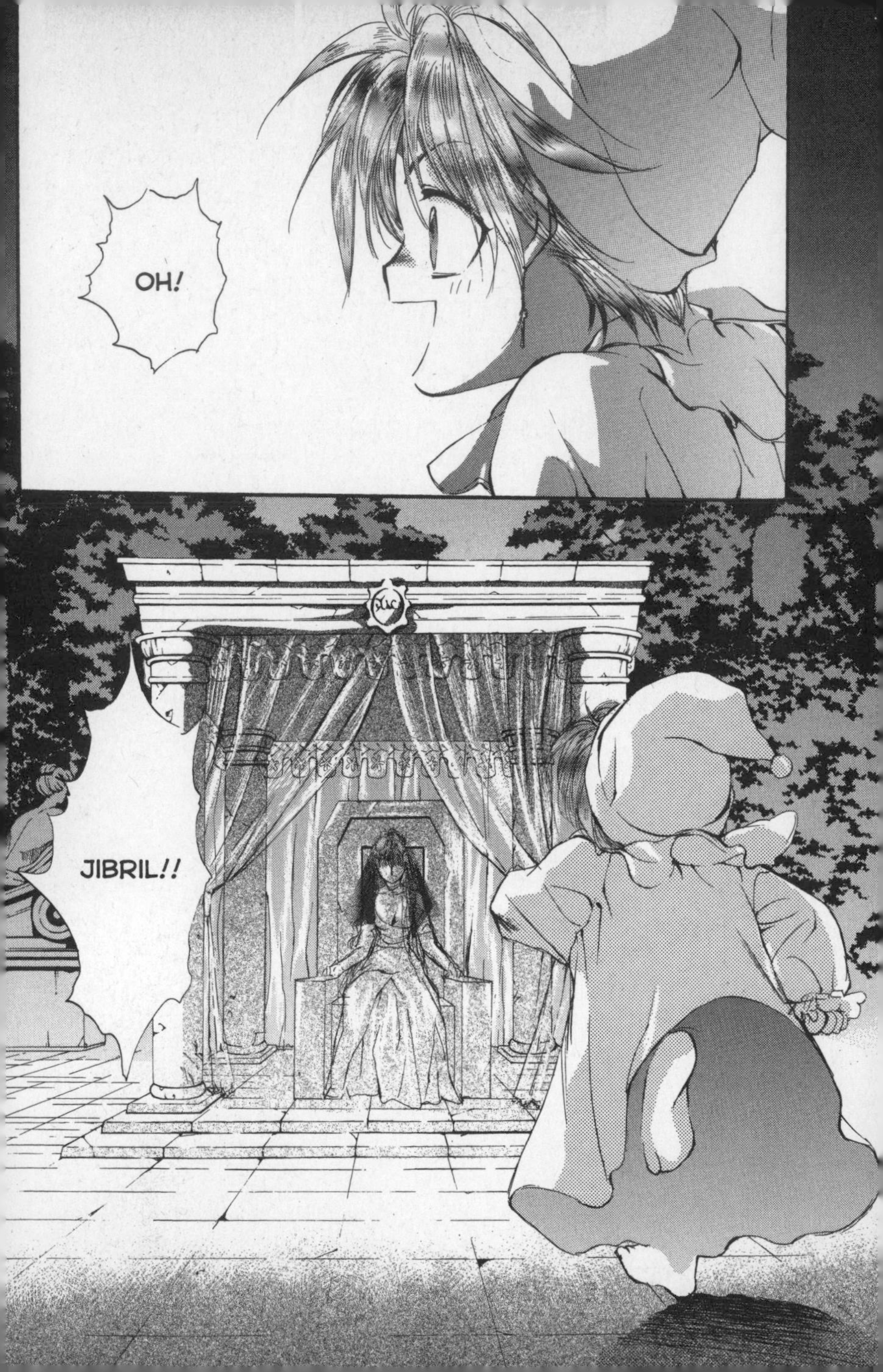
OH!
JIBRIL!!

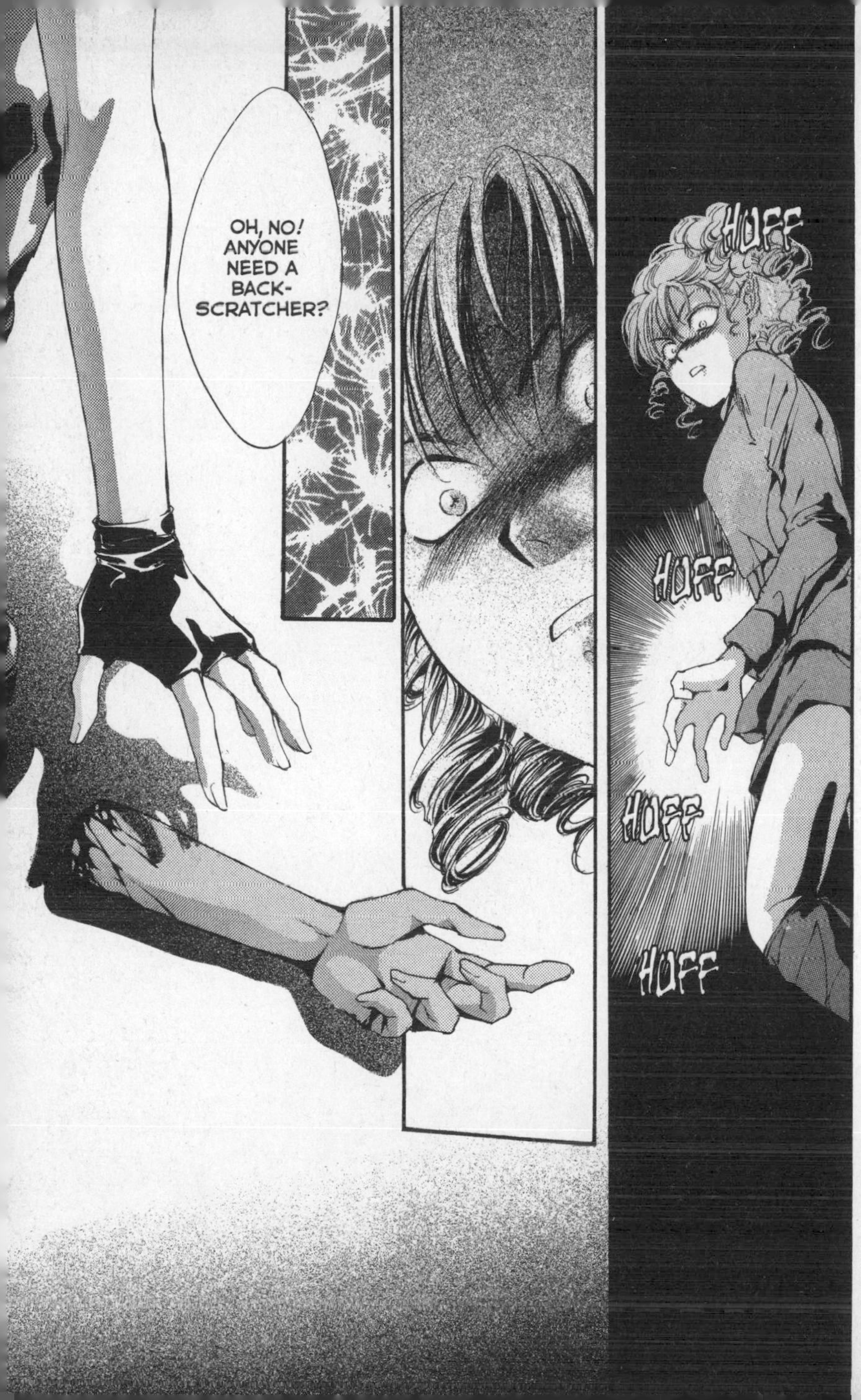
HUFF
HUFF
HUFF
HUFF
OH, NO! ANYONE NEED A BACK-SCRATCHER?

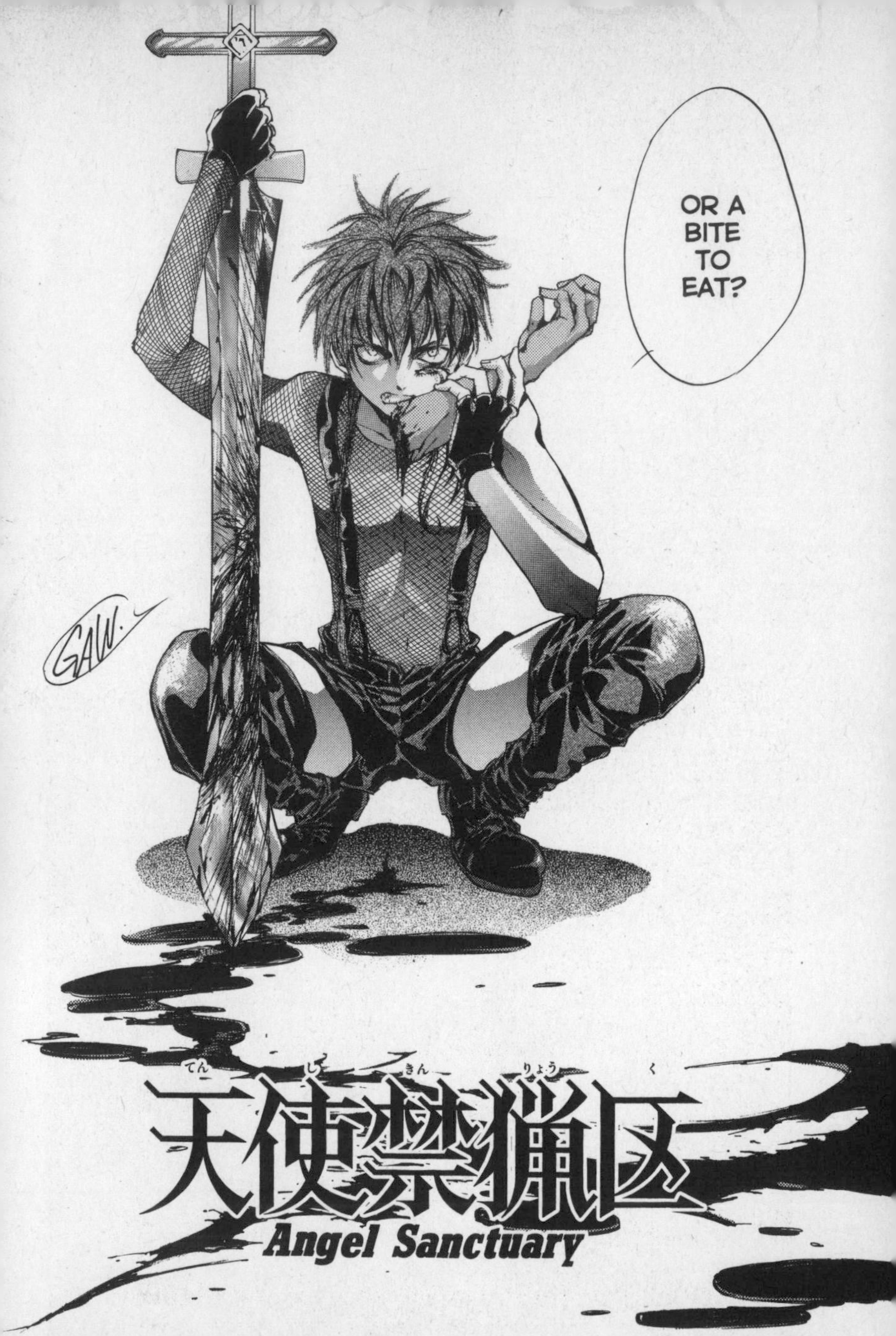
OR A BITE TO EAT?
GAW.
天使禁猟区
Angel Sanctuary

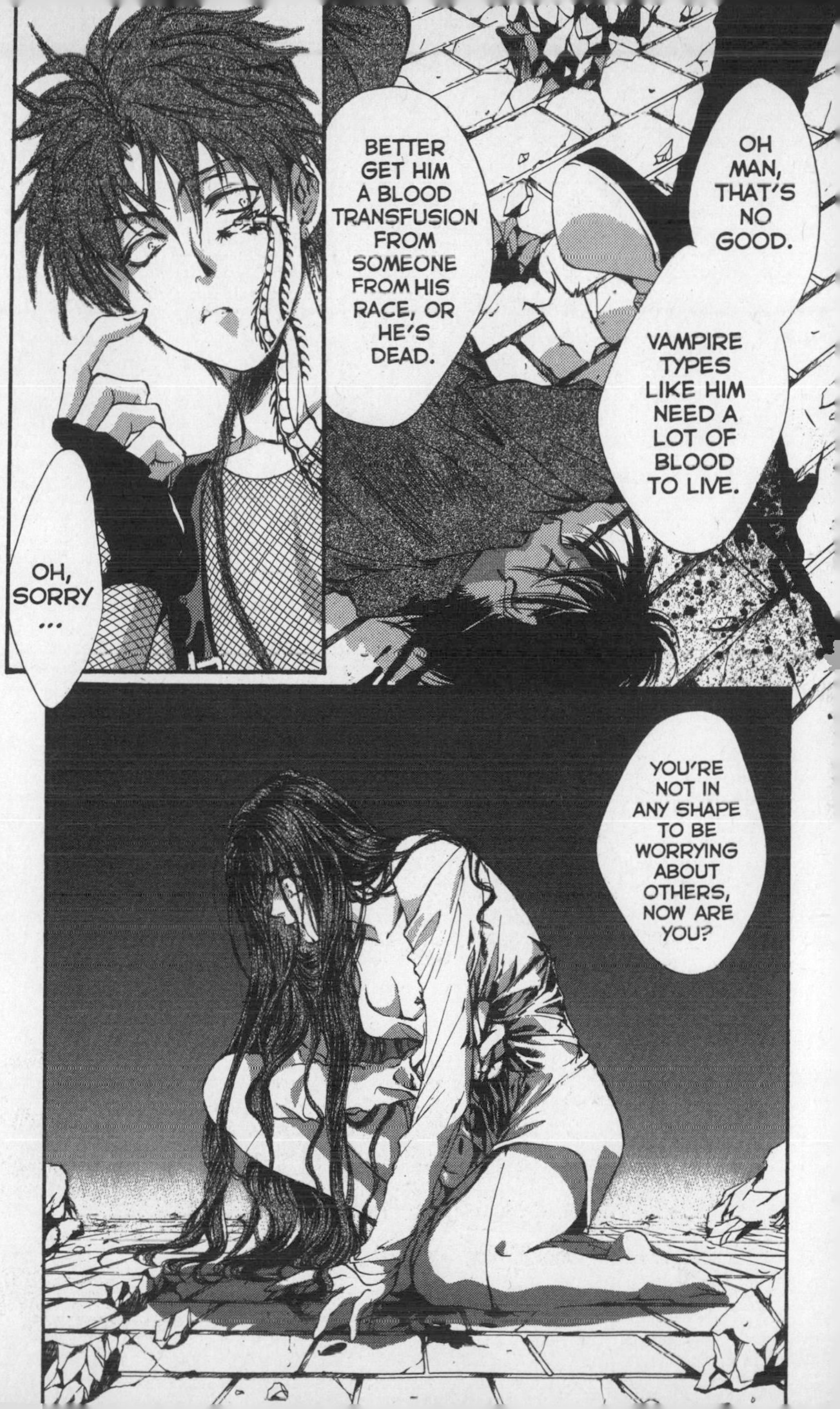
OH MAN, THAT'S NO GOOD.
VAMPIRE TYPES LIKE HIM NEED A LOT OF BLOOD TO LIVE.
BETTER GET HIM A BLOOD TRANSFUSION FROM SOMEONE FROM HIS RACE, OR HE'S DEAD.
OH, SORRY ...
YOU'RE NOT IN ANY SHAPE TO BE WORRYING ABOUT OTHERS, NOW ARE YOU?

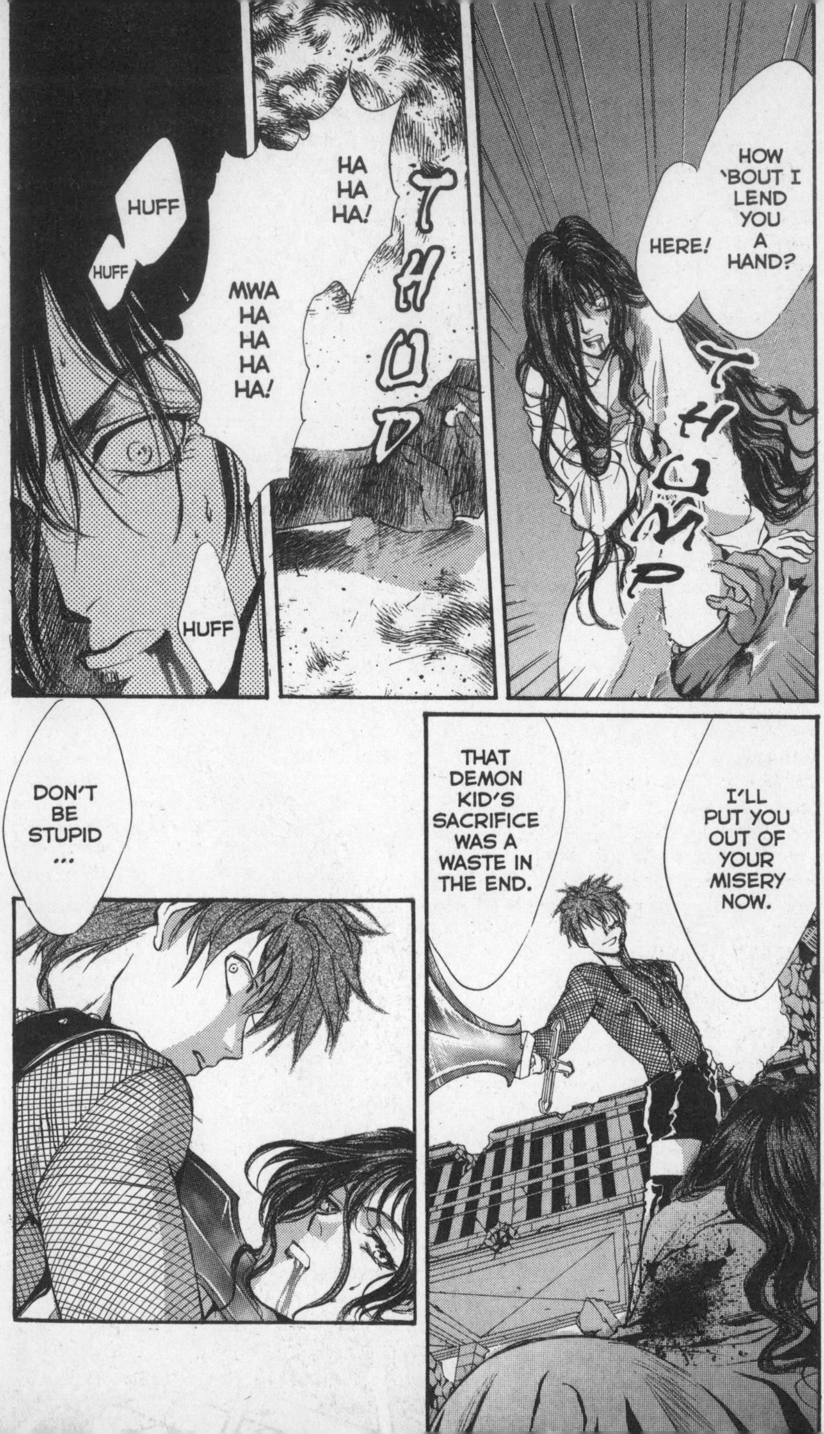
HOW 'BOUT I LEND YOU A HAND?
HERE!
THUMP
HA HA HA!
THUD
MWA HA HA HA HA!
HUFF
HUFF
HUFF
I'LL PUT YOU OUT OF YOUR MISERY NOW.
THAT DEMON KID'S SACRIFICE WAS A WASTE IN THE END.
DON'T BE STUPID ...

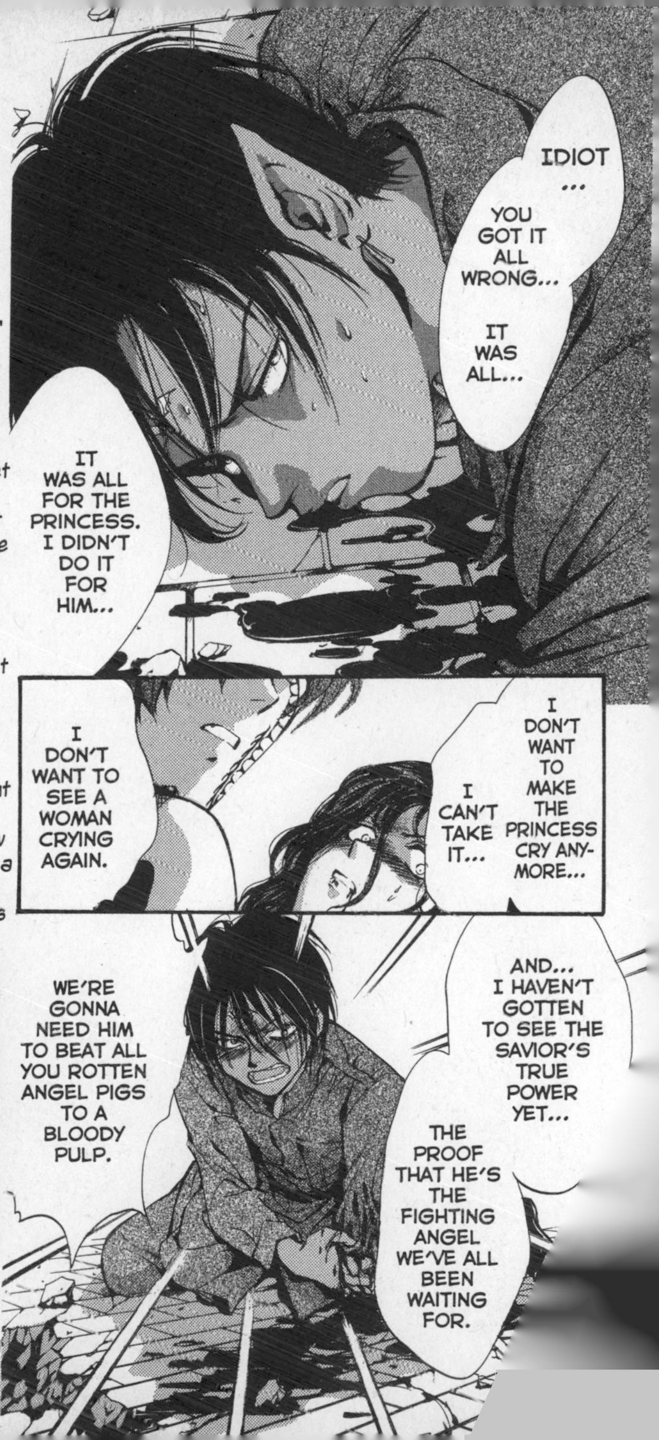
IDIOT ...
YOU GOT IT ALL WRONG...
IT WAS ALL...
IT WAS ALL FOR THE PRINCESS. I DIDN'T DO IT FOR HIM...
I DON'T WANT TO MAKE THE PRINCESS CRY ANY-MORE...
I CAN'T TAKE IT...
I DON'T WANT TO SEE A WOMAN CRYING AGAIN.
AND... I HAVEN'T GOTTEN TO SEE THE SAVIOR'S TRUE POWER YET...
THE PROOF THAT HE'S THE FIGHTING ANGEL WE'VE ALL BEEN WAITING FOR.
WE'RE GONNA NEED HIM TO BEAT ALL YOU ROTTEN ANGEL PIGS TO A BLOODY PULP.

"Who is the mysterious rabbit man?!" I got a lot of letters asking that question. Since he has the same hair as Meta, it seemed like some people did figure it out. But his part in the story is far, far away, so go ahead and forget about that. Hmm... I was surprised that not that many people started hating Mika after this chapter. I felt bad for Boyz, but I don't really care that much about him, so I can do whatever I want to him... Should I have just written that? He's not an important character and all. Oh, the picture below is the rough draft to a preview for chapter one. That sure brings back memories.

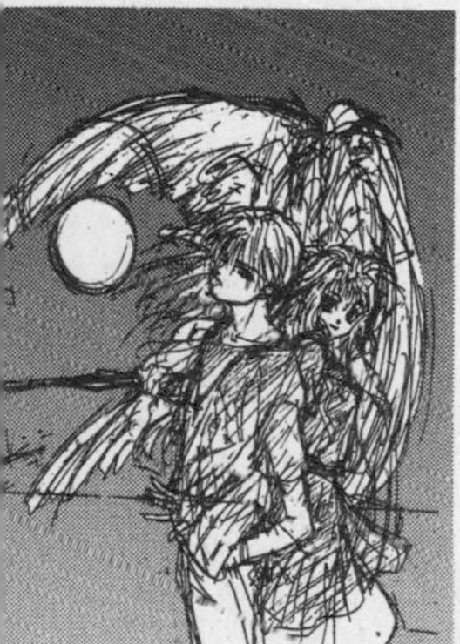

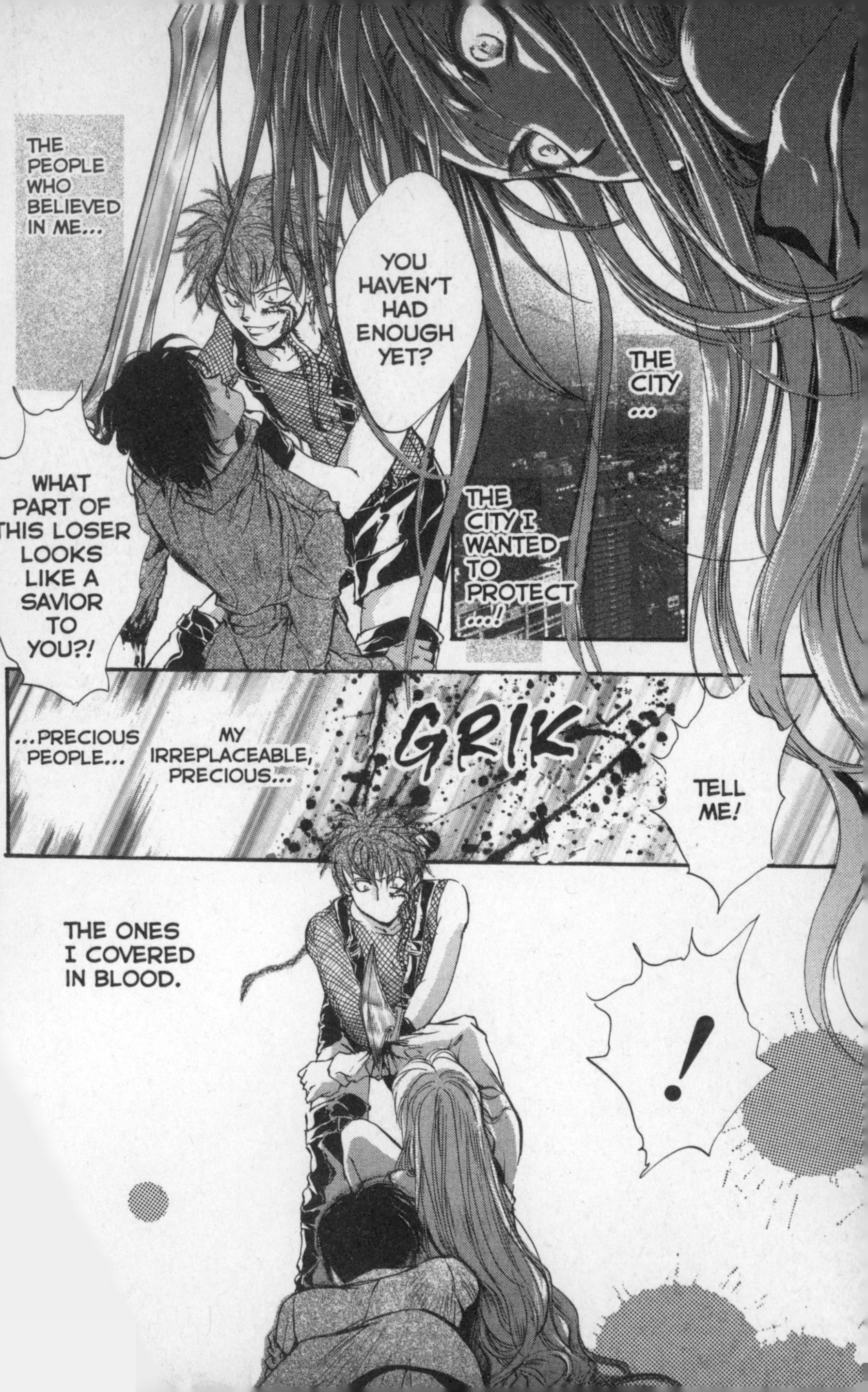
THE CITY ...
THE CITY I WANTED TO PROTECT ...!
YOU HAVEN'T HAD ENOUGH YET?
THE PEOPLE WHO BELIEVED IN ME...
WHAT PART OF THIS LOSER LOOKS LIKE A SAVIOR TO YOU?!
TELL ME!
GRIK
MY IRREPLACEABLE, PRECIOUS...
...PRECIOUS PEOPLE...
!
THE ONES I COVERED IN BLOOD.

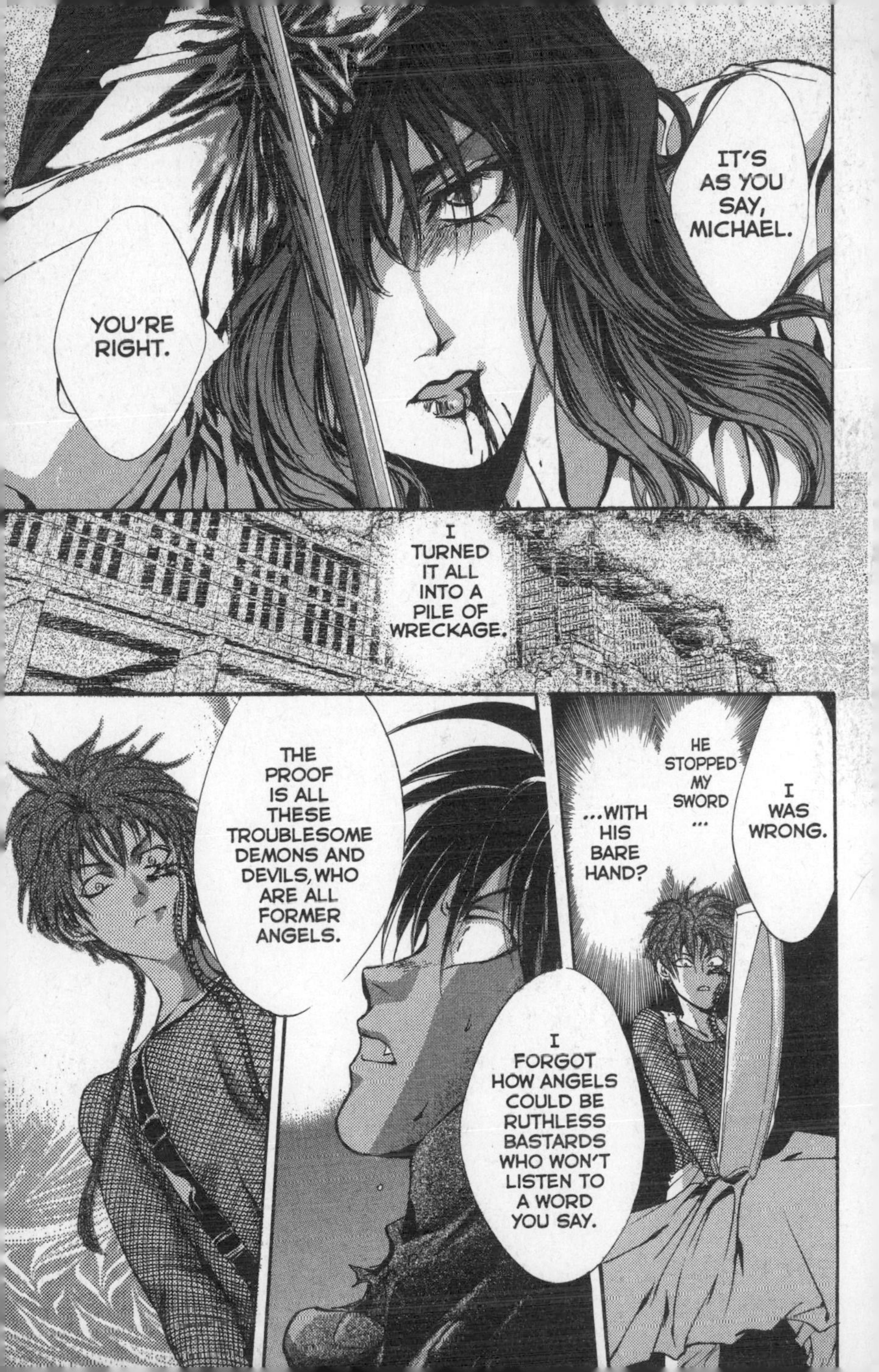
IT'S AS YOU SAY, MICHAEL.
YOU'RE RIGHT.
I TURNED IT ALL INTO A PILE OF WRECKAGE.
I WAS WRONG.
HE STOPPED MY SWORD ...
...WITH HIS BARE HAND?
I FORGOT HOW ANGELS COULD BE RUTHLESS BASTARDS WHO WON'T LISTEN TO A WORD YOU SAY.
THE PROOF IS ALL THESE TROUBLESOME DEMONS AND DEVILS, WHO ARE ALL FORMER ANGELS.

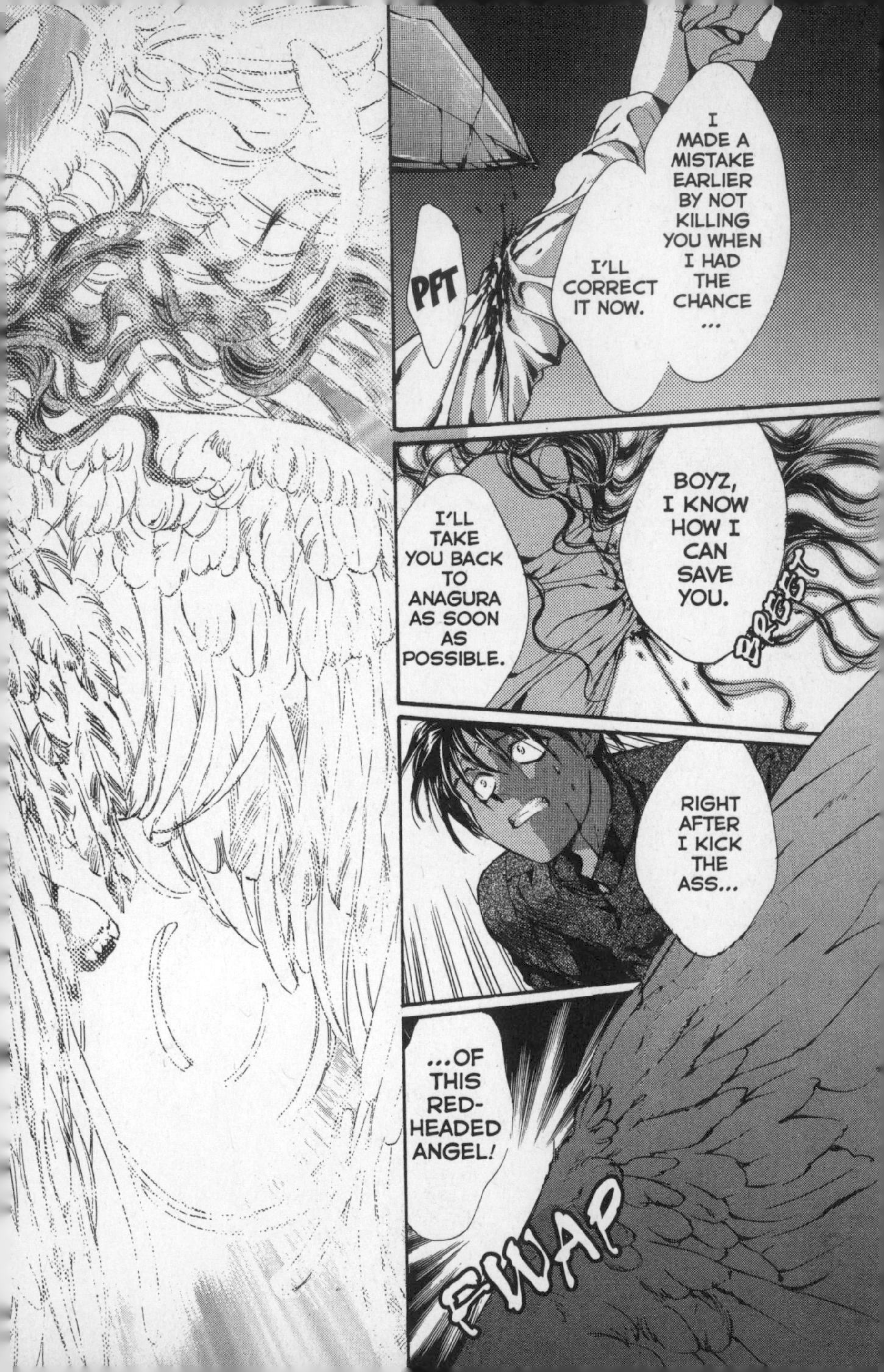
I MADE A MISTAKE EARLIER BY NOT KILLING YOU WHEN I HAD THE CHANCE...
I'LL CORRECT IT NOW.
PFT
BOYZ, I KNOW HOW I CAN SAVE YOU.
I'LL TAKE YOU BACK TO ANAGURA AS SOON AS POSSIBLE.
RIGHT AFTER I KICK THE ASS...
...OF THIS RED-HEADED ANGEL!
FWAP

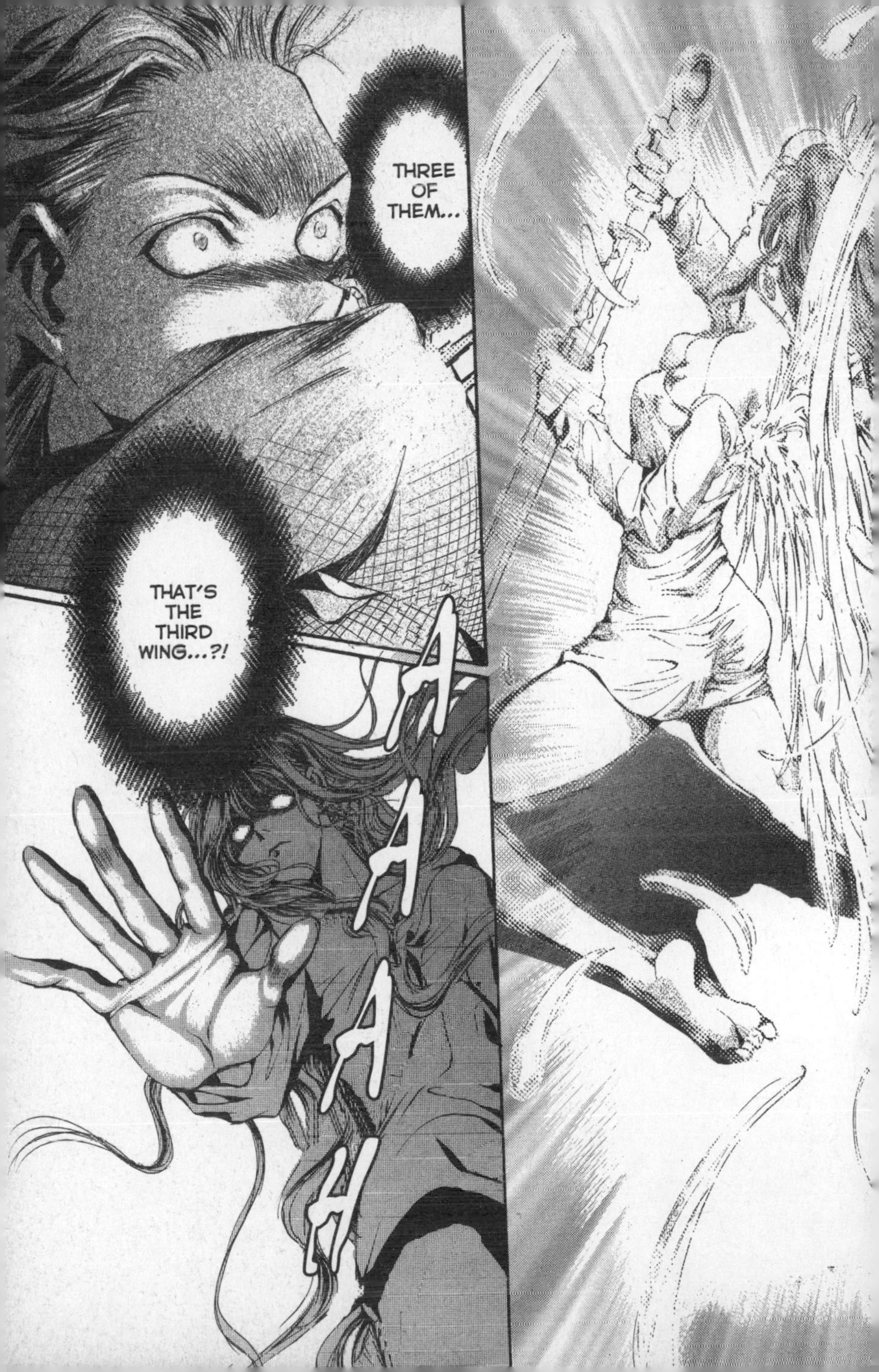
THREE OF THEM...
THAT'S THE THIRD WING...?!
AAAAAH

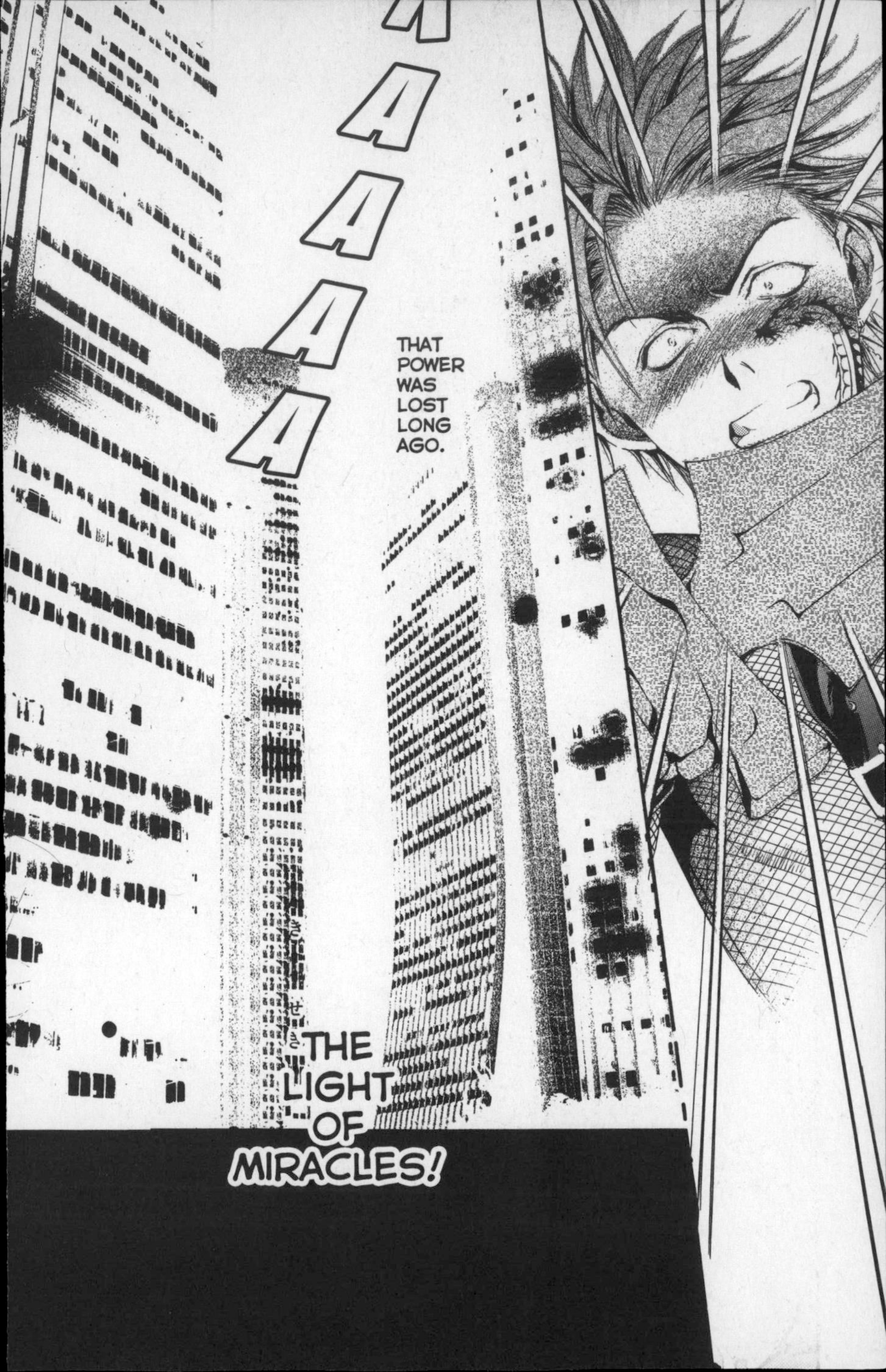
AAAAA
THAT POWER WAS LOST LONG AGO.
THE LIGHT OF MIRACLES!

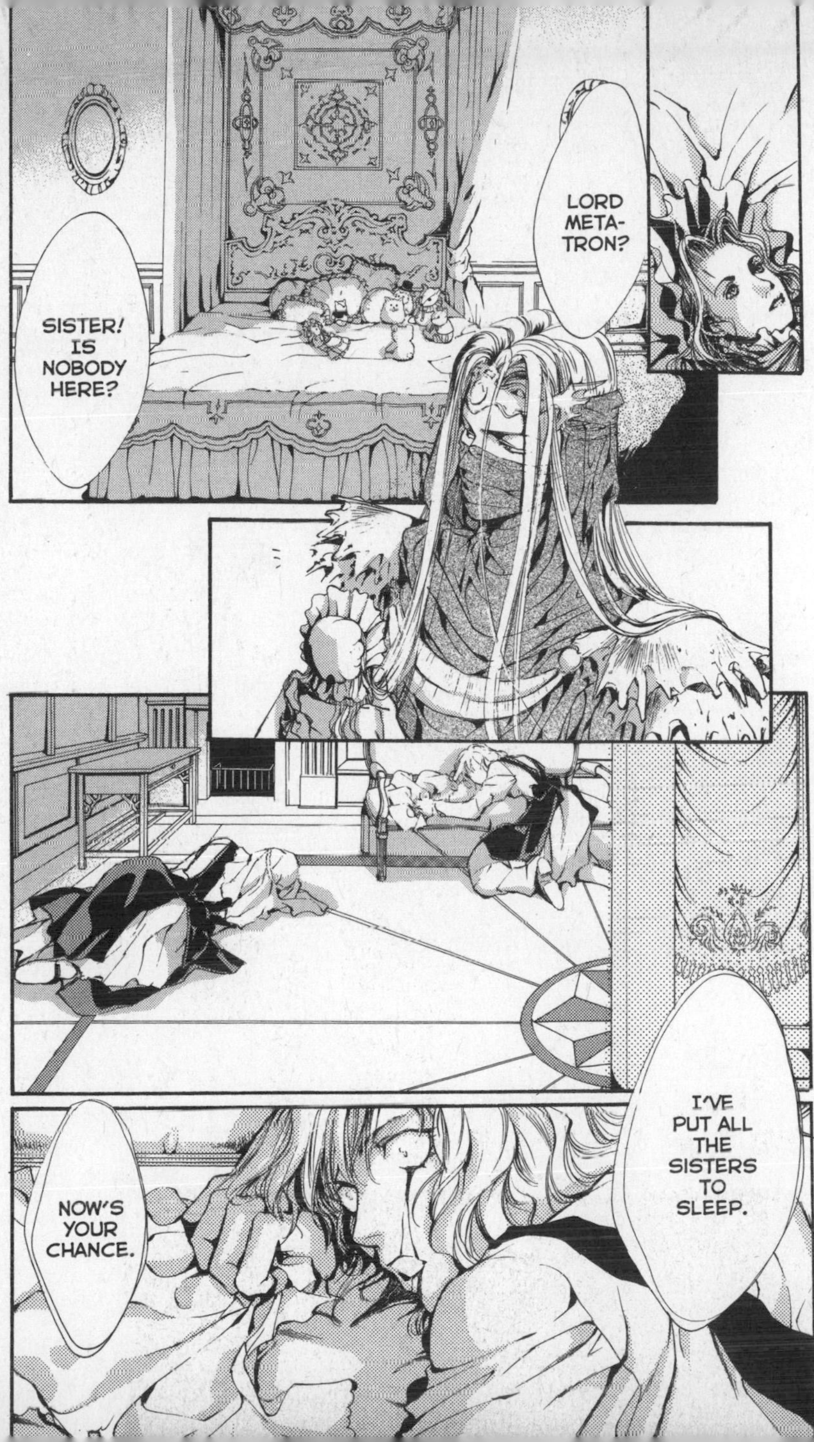
LORD METATRON?
SISTER! IS NOBODY HERE?
I'VE PUT ALL THE SISTERS TO SLEEP.
NOW'S YOUR CHANCE.

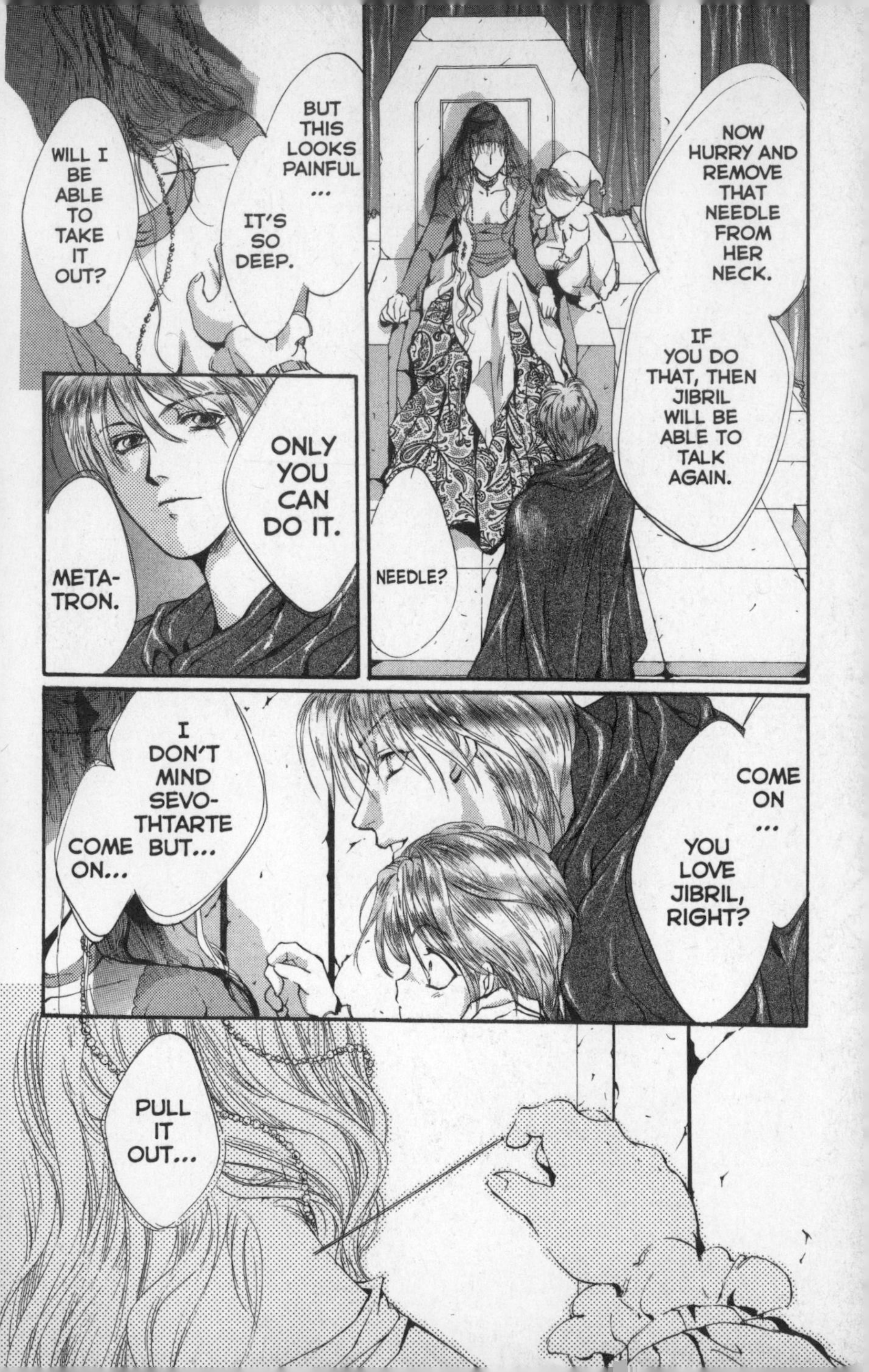
NOW HURRY AND REMOVE THAT NEEDLE FROM HER NECK.
IF YOU DO THAT, THEN JIBRIL WILL BE ABLE TO TALK AGAIN.
NEEDLE?
BUT THIS LOOKS PAINFUL ...
IT'S SO DEEP.
WILL I BE ABLE TO TAKE IT OUT?
ONLY YOU CAN DO IT.
METATRON.
COME ON ... YOU LOVE JIBRIL, RIGHT?
I DON'T MIND SEVOTHTARTE BUT...
COME ON...
PULL IT OUT...

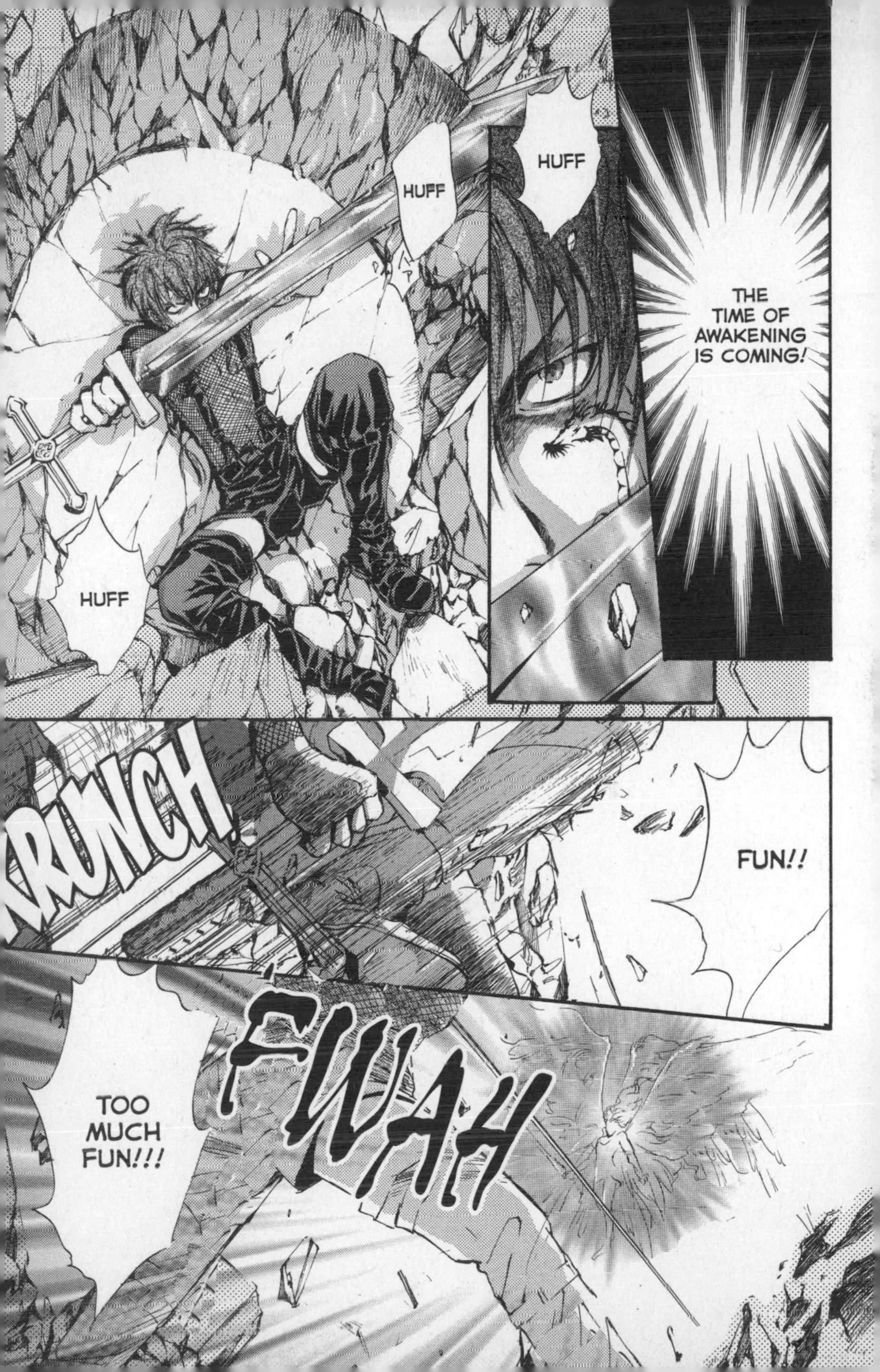
THE TIME OF AWAKENING IS COMING!
HUFF
HUFF
HUFF
FUN!!
RUNCH
FWAH
TOO MUCH FUN!!!

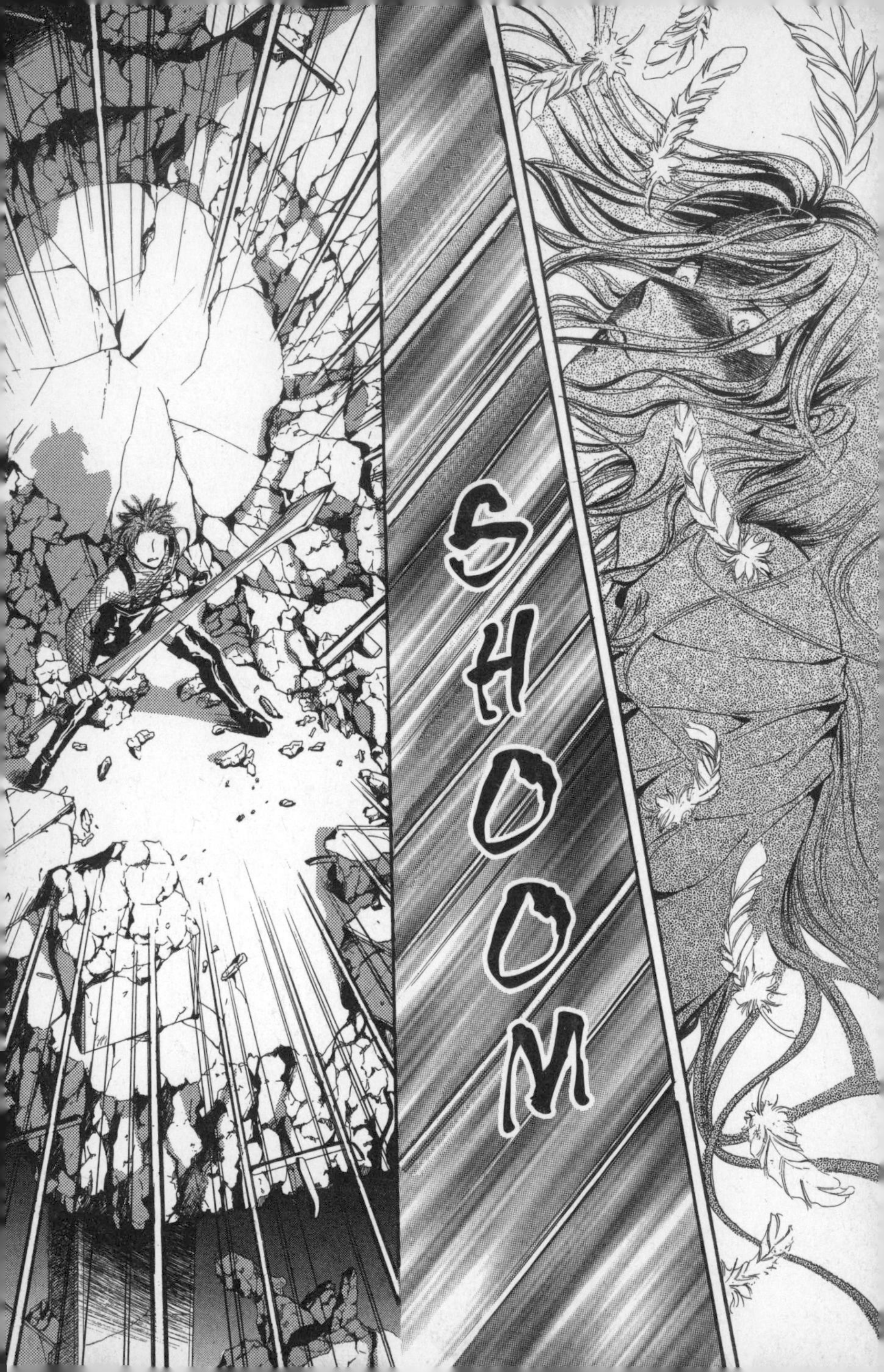
SHOOM

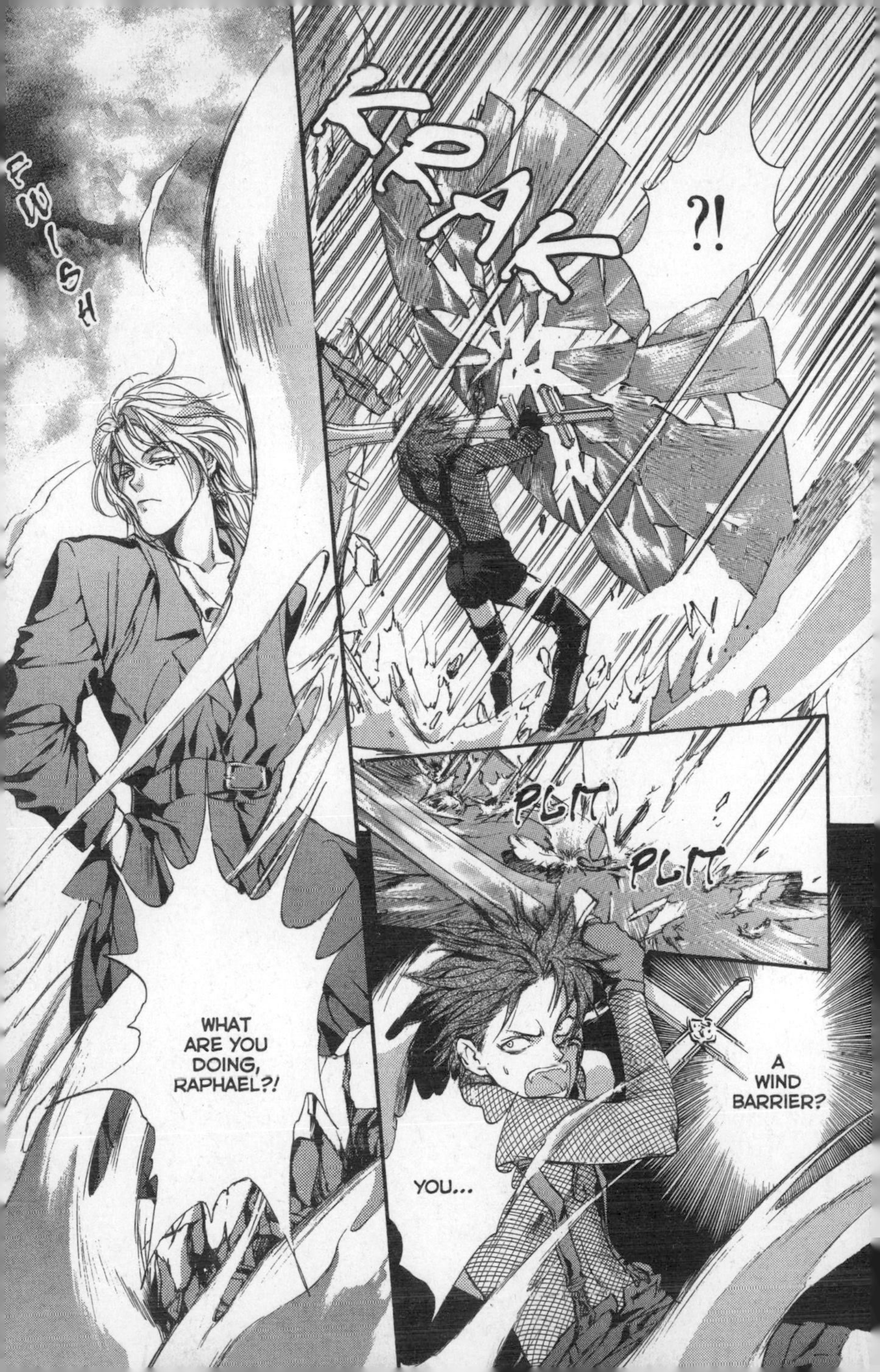
KRAK
?!
PLIT
PLIT
A WIND BARRIER?
YOU...
FWISH
WHAT ARE YOU DOING, RAPHAEL?!

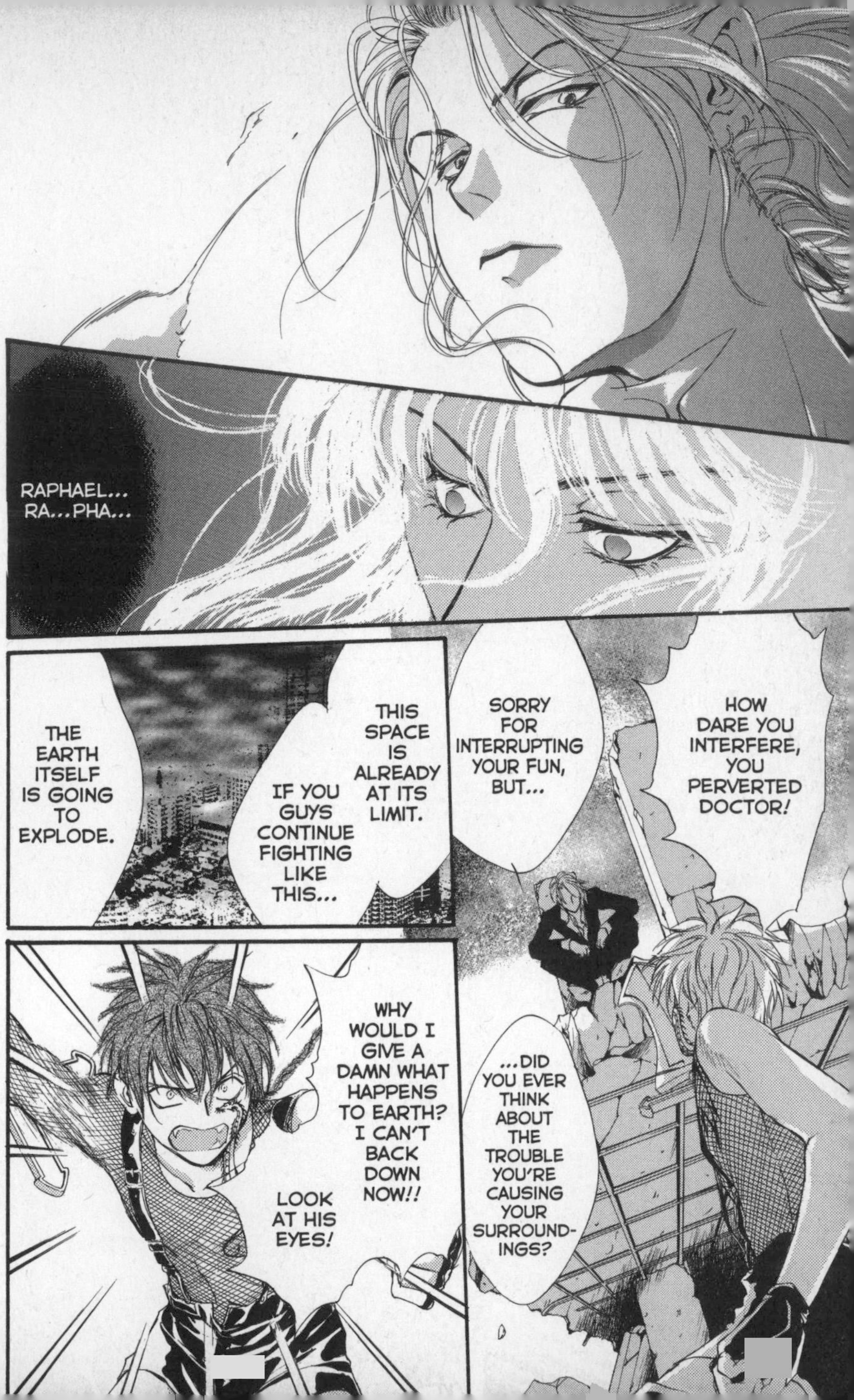
RAPHAEL... RA...PHA...
HOW DARE YOU INTERFERE, YOU PERVERTED DOCTOR!
SORRY FOR INTERRUPTING YOUR FUN, BUT...
...DID YOU EVER THINK ABOUT THE TROUBLE YOU'RE CAUSING YOUR SURROUNDINGS?
THIS SPACE IS ALREADY AT ITS LIMIT.
IF YOU GUYS CONTINUE FIGHTING LIKE THIS...
THE EARTH ITSELF IS GOING TO EXPLODE.
WHY WOULD I GIVE A DAMN WHAT HAPPENS TO EARTH? I CAN'T BACK DOWN NOW!!
LOOK AT HIS EYES!

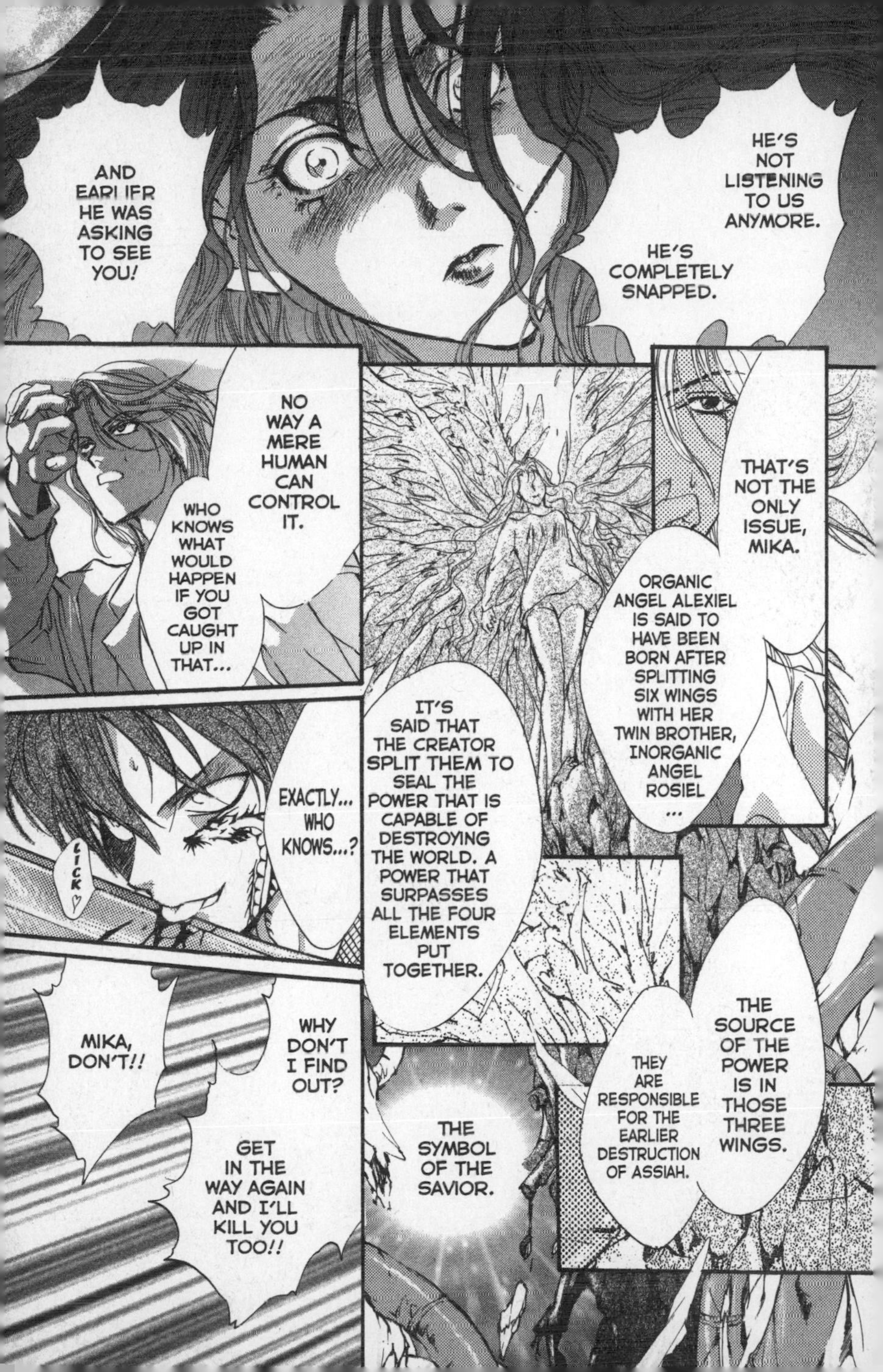
HE'S NOT LISTENING TO US ANYMORE.
HE'S COMPLETELY SNAPPED.
AND EARLIER HE WAS ASKING TO SEE YOU!
THAT'S NOT THE ONLY ISSUE, MIKA.
ORGANIC ANGEL ALEXIEL IS SAID TO HAVE BEEN BORN AFTER SPLITTING SIX WINGS WITH HER TWIN BROTHER, INORGANIC ANGEL ROSIEL...
IT'S SAID THAT THE CREATOR SPLIT THEM TO SEAL THE POWER THAT IS CAPABLE OF DESTROYING THE WORLD. A POWER THAT SURPASSES ALL THE FOUR ELEMENTS PUT TOGETHER.
NO WAY A MERE HUMAN CAN CONTROL IT.
WHO KNOWS WHAT WOULD HAPPEN IF YOU GOT CAUGHT UP IN THAT...
EXACTLY... WHO KNOWS...?
LICK
THE SOURCE OF THE POWER IS IN THOSE THREE WINGS.
THEY ARE RESPONSIBLE FOR THE EARLIER DESTRUCTION OF ASSIAH.
THE SYMBOL OF THE SAVIOR.
WHY DON'T I FIND OUT?
MIKA, DON'T!!
GET IN THE WAY AGAIN AND I'LL KILL YOU TOO!!

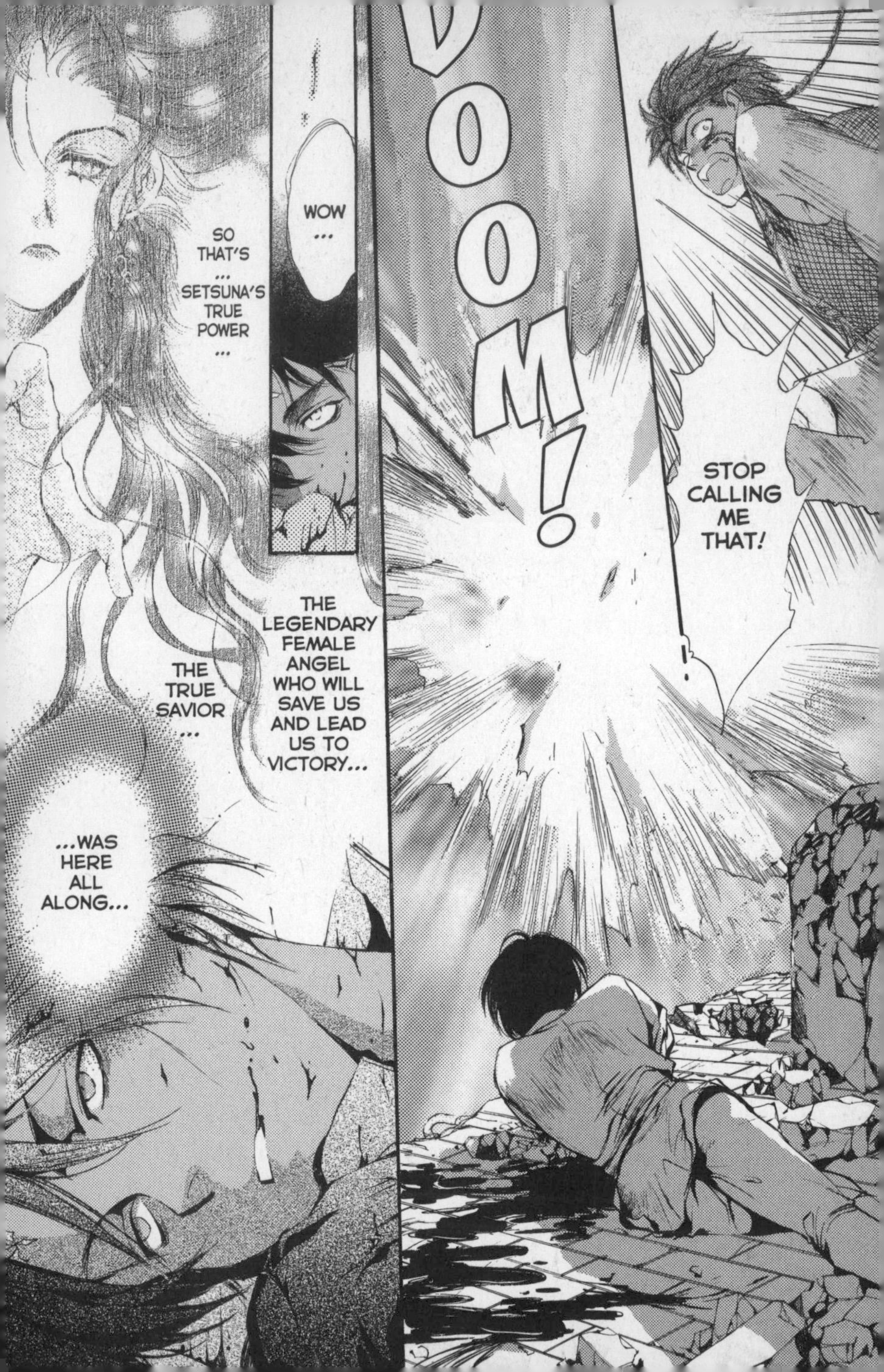
STOP CALLING ME THAT!
DOOM!
WOW ...
SO THAT'S ... SETSUNA'S TRUE POWER ...
THE LEGENDARY FEMALE ANGEL WHO WILL SAVE US AND LEAD US TO VICTORY...
THE TRUE SAVIOR ...
...WAS HERE ALL ALONG...

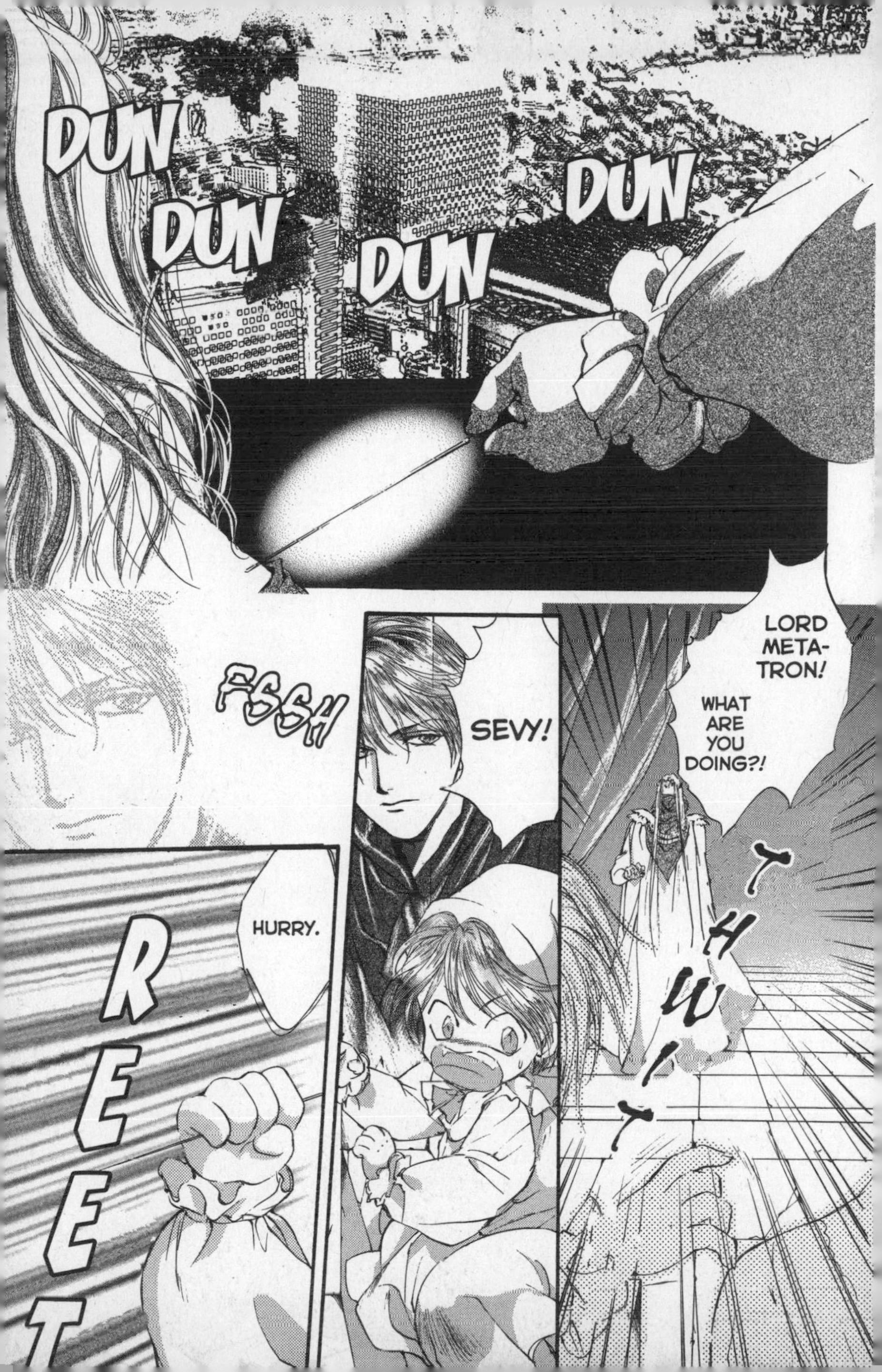
DUN
DUN
DUN
DUN
LORD META-TRON!
WHAT ARE YOU DOING?!
THWIT
SEVY!
FSSH
HURRY.
REEET

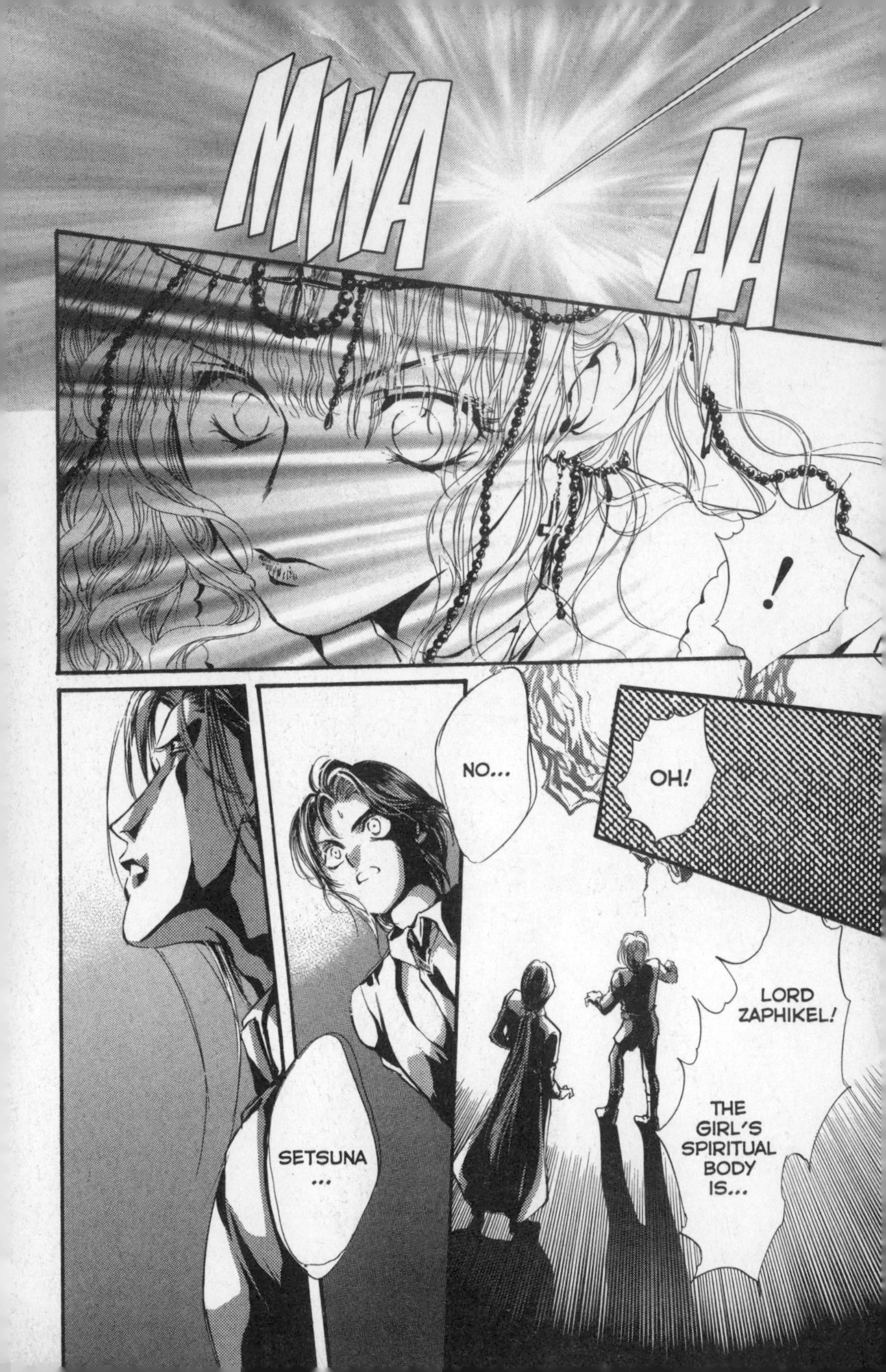
MWA
AA
!
OH!
LORD ZAPHIKEL!
THE GIRL'S SPIRITUAL BODY IS...
NO...
SETSUNA ...

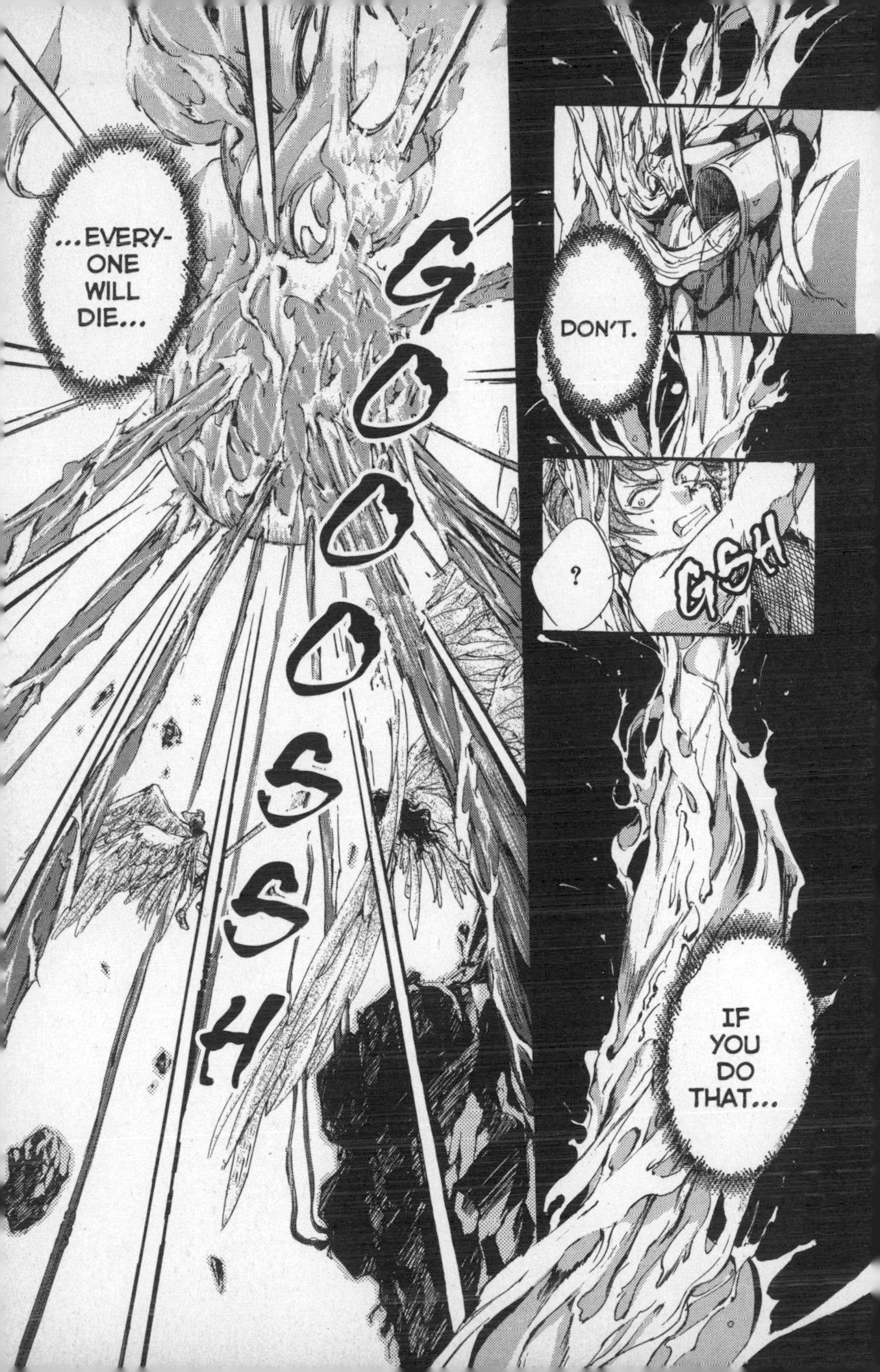
DON'T.
?
GSH
IF YOU DO THAT...
...EVERY-ONE WILL DIE...
GOOOSSH

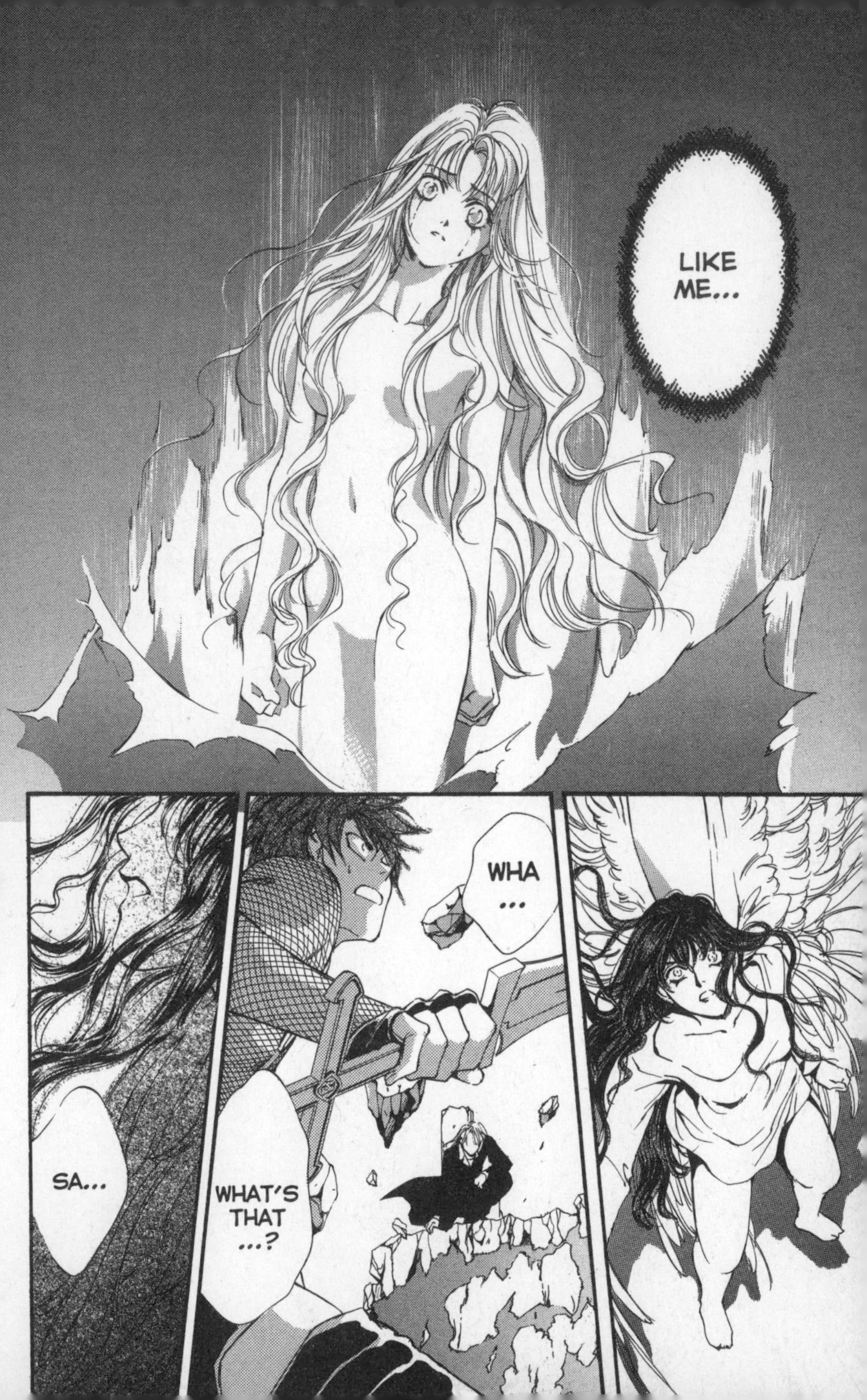
LIKE ME...
WHA ...
WHAT'S THAT ...?
SA...

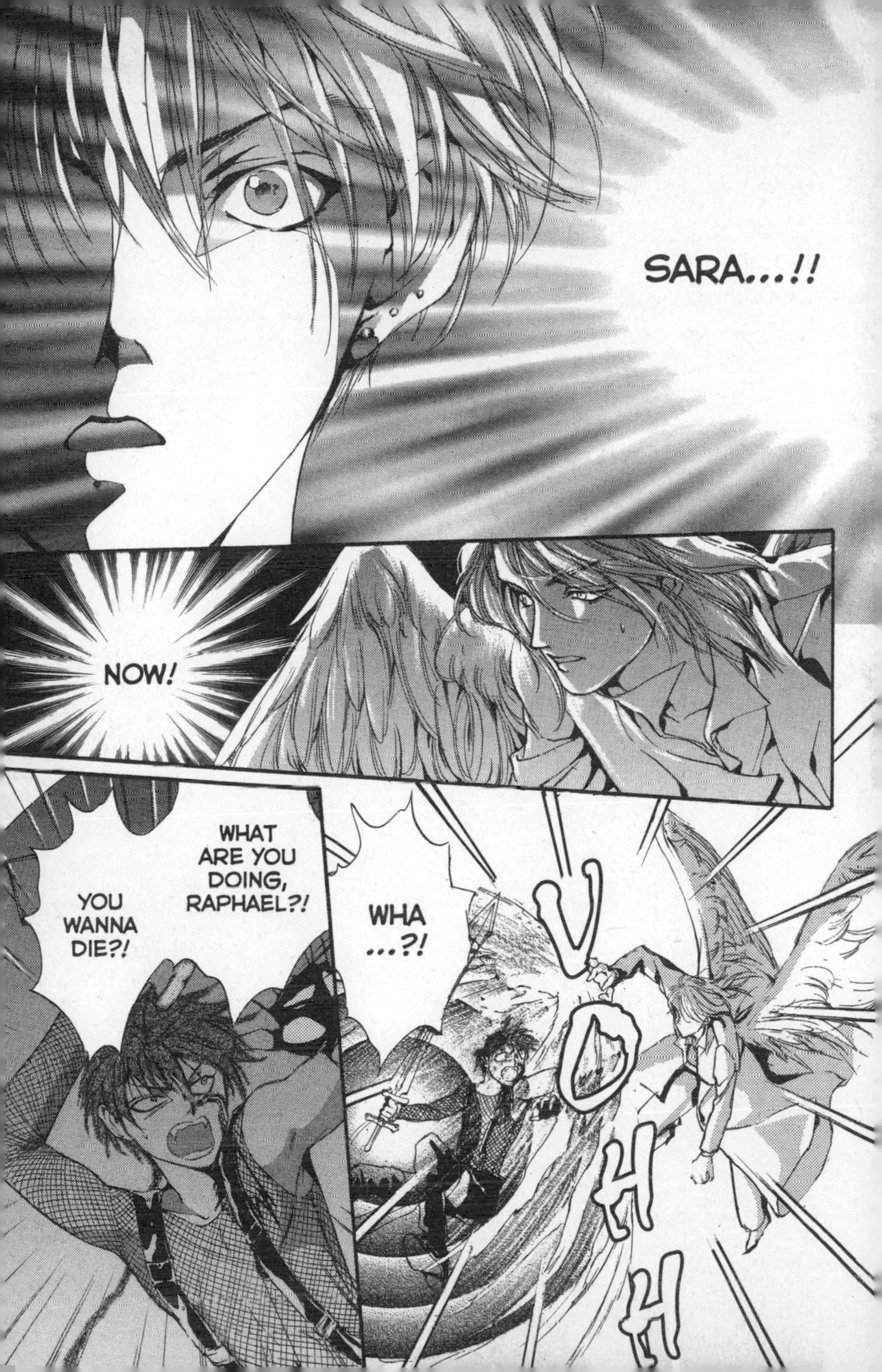
SARA...!!
NOW!
WHA ...?!
WHAT ARE YOU DOING, RAPHAEL?!
YOU WANNA DIE?!

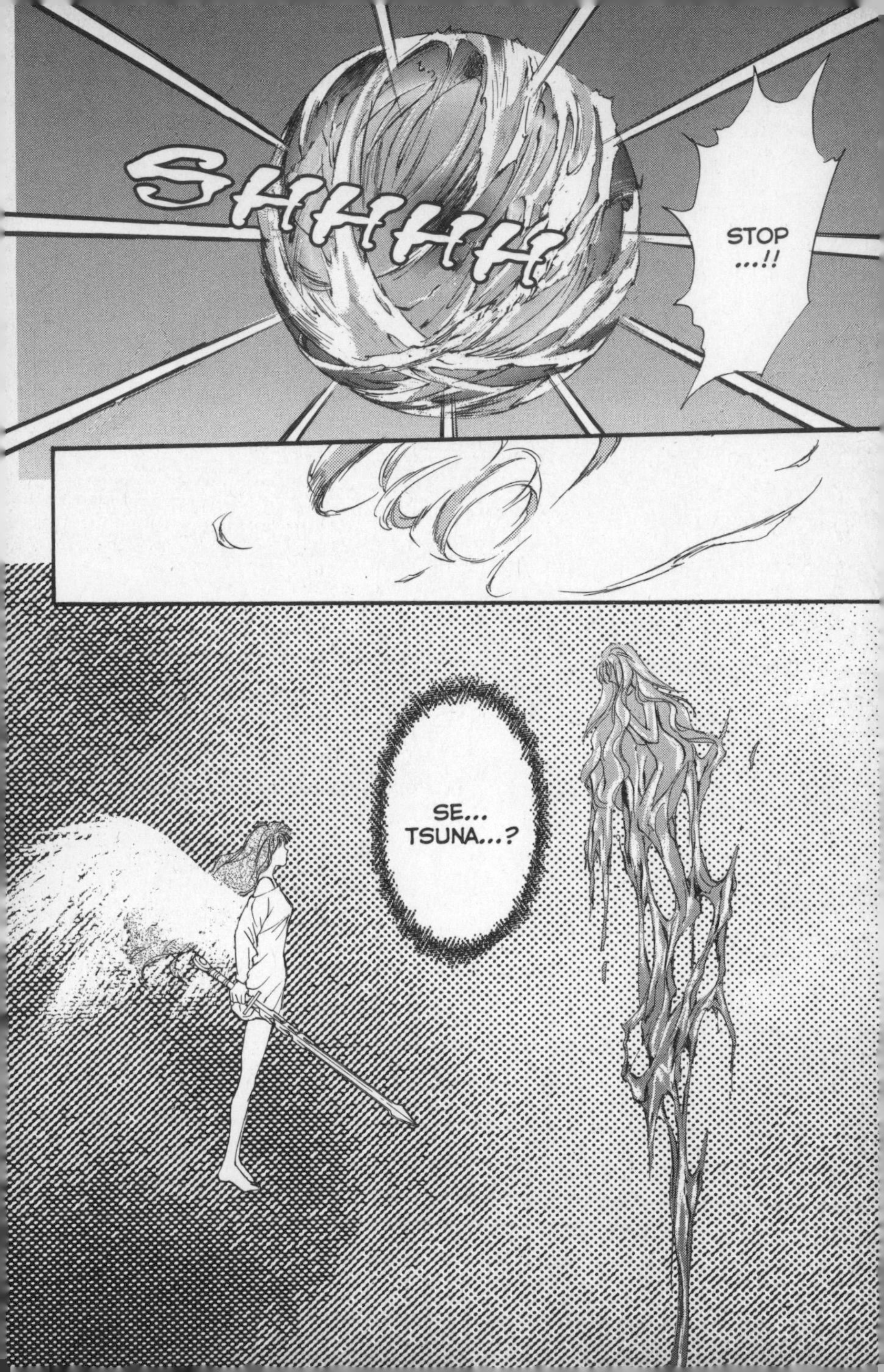
SHHHHH
STOP ...!!
SE... TSUNA...?

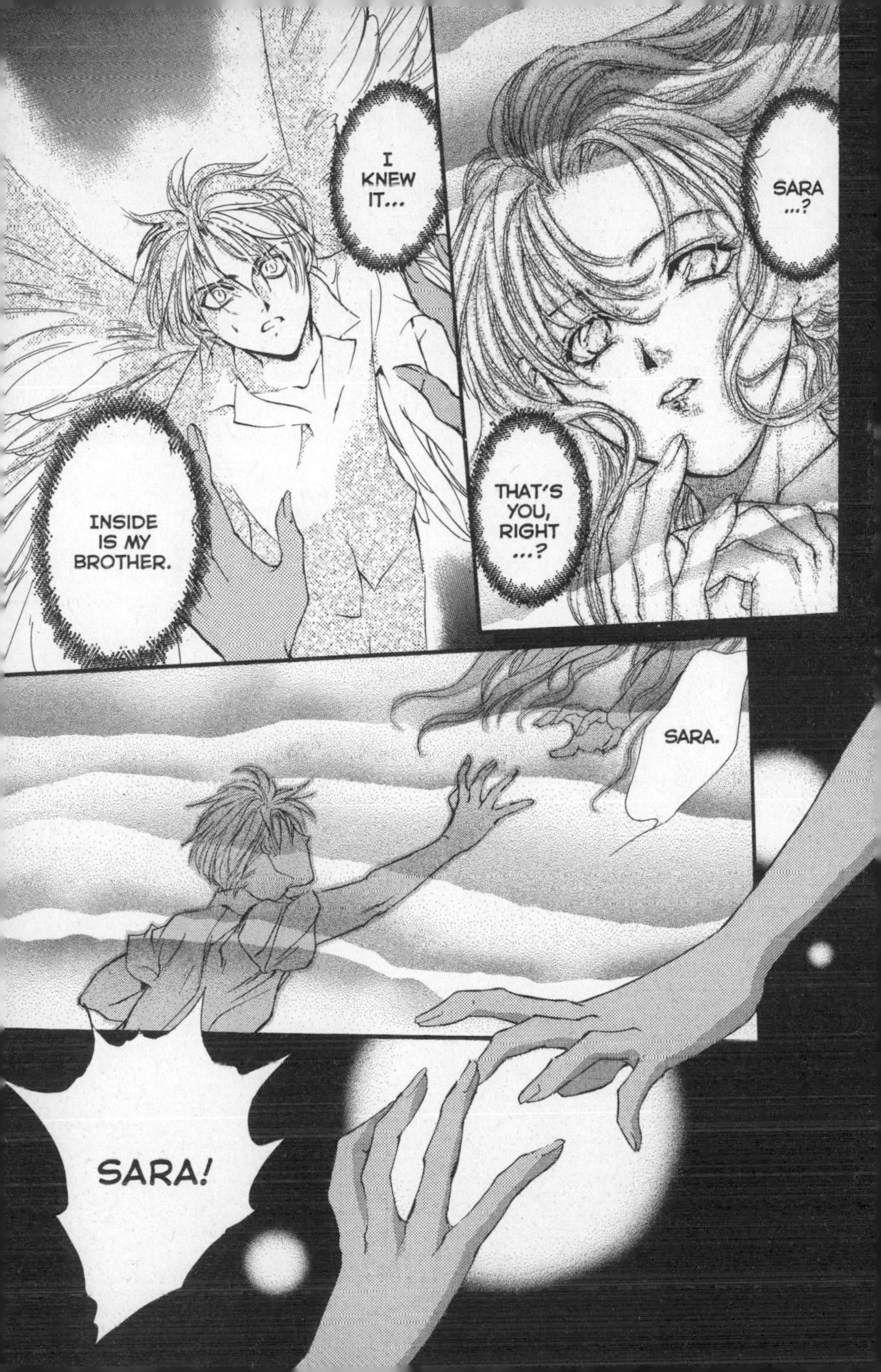
SARA ...?
THAT'S YOU, RIGHT ...?
I KNEW IT...
INSIDE IS MY BROTHER.
SARA.
SARA!

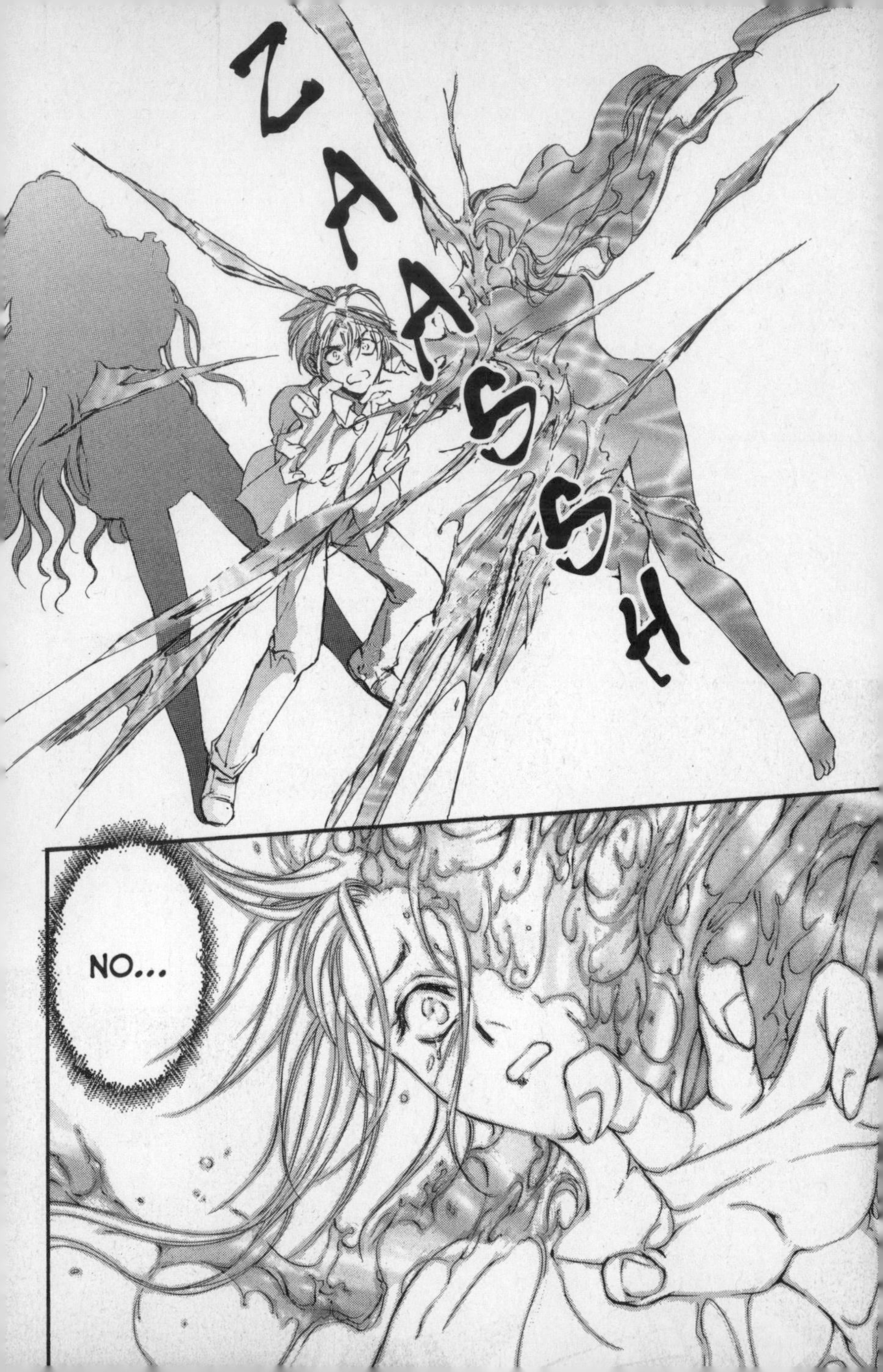
ZAAASSH
NO...

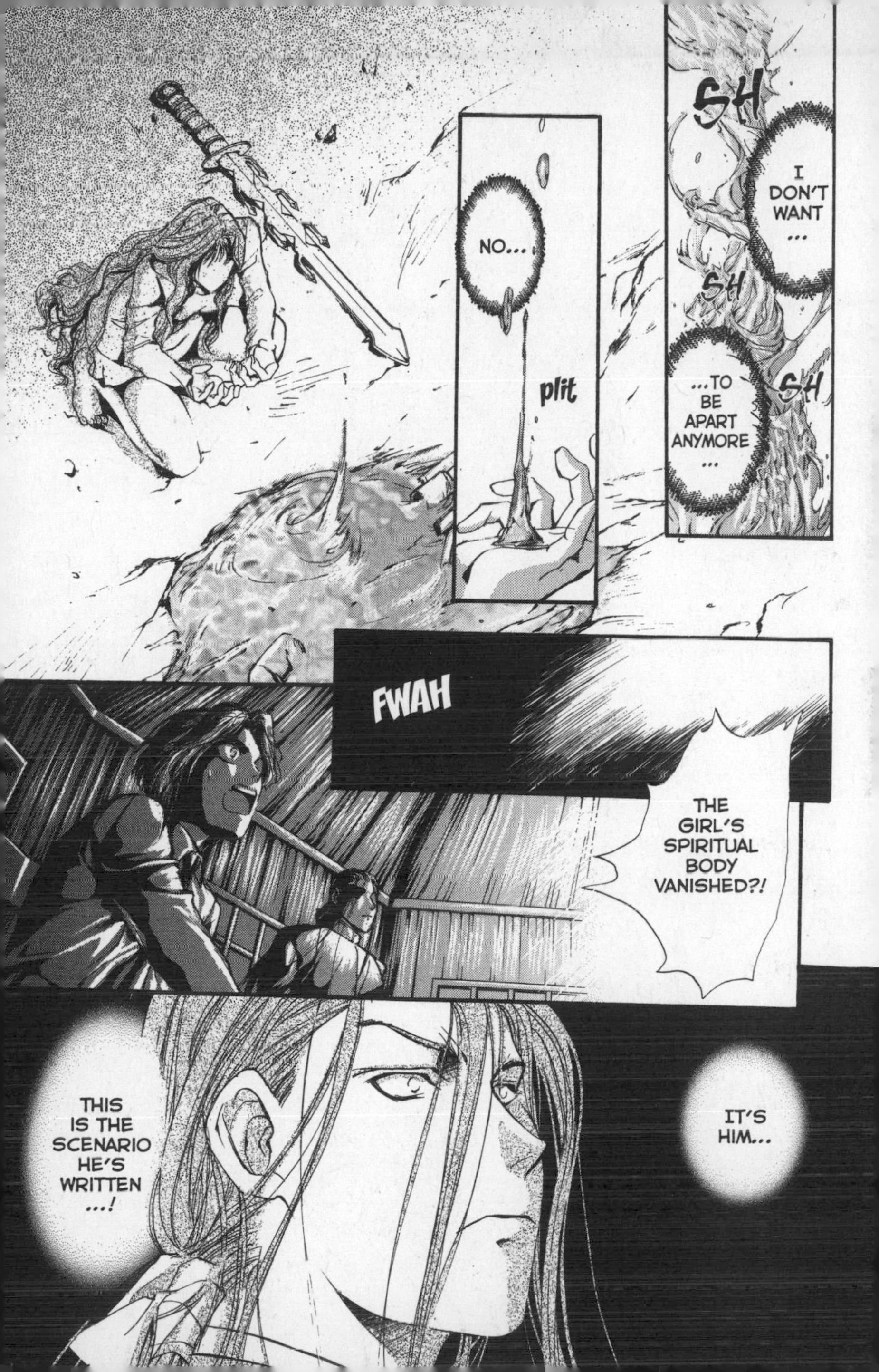
SH
I DON'T WANT ...
SH
...TO BE APART ANYMORE ...
SH
NO...
plit
FWAH
THE GIRL'S SPIRITUAL BODY VANISHED?!
IT'S HIM...
THIS IS THE SCENARIO HE'S WRITTEN ...!

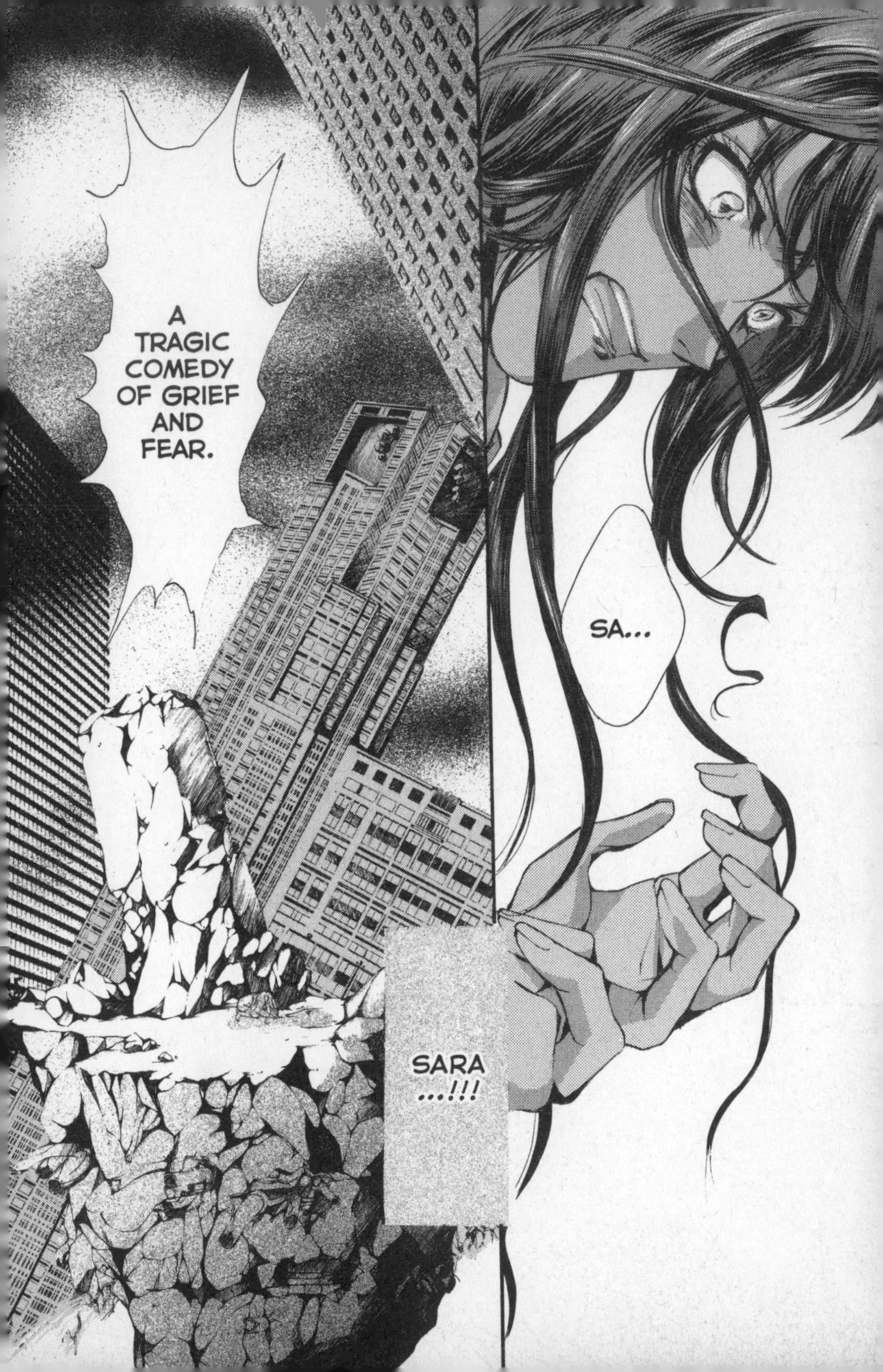
SA...
SARA ...!!!
A TRAGIC COMEDY OF GRIEF AND FEAR.

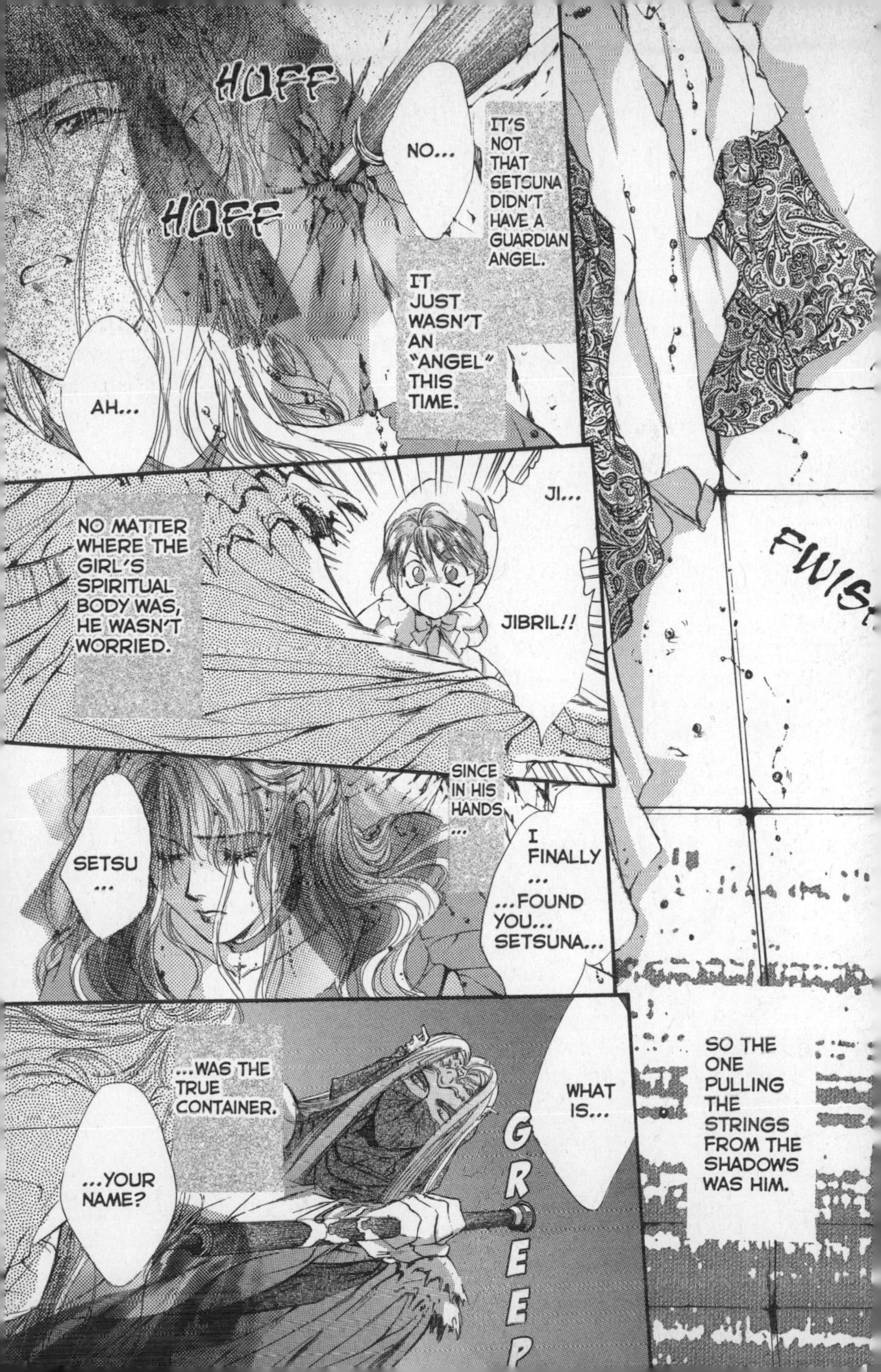
FWIS
HUFF
HUFF
NO...
IT'S NOT THAT SETSUNA DIDN'T HAVE A GUARDIAN ANGEL.
IT JUST WASN'T AN "ANGEL" THIS TIME.
AH...
JI...
JIBRIL!!
NO MATTER WHERE THE GIRL'S SPIRITUAL BODY WAS, HE WASN'T WORRIED.
SINCE IN HIS HANDS...
I FINALLY ... ...FOUND YOU... SETSUNA...
SETSU...
SO THE ONE PULLING THE STRINGS FROM THE SHADOWS WAS HIM.
WHAT IS...
GREEP
...WAS THE TRUE CONTAINER.
...YOUR NAME?

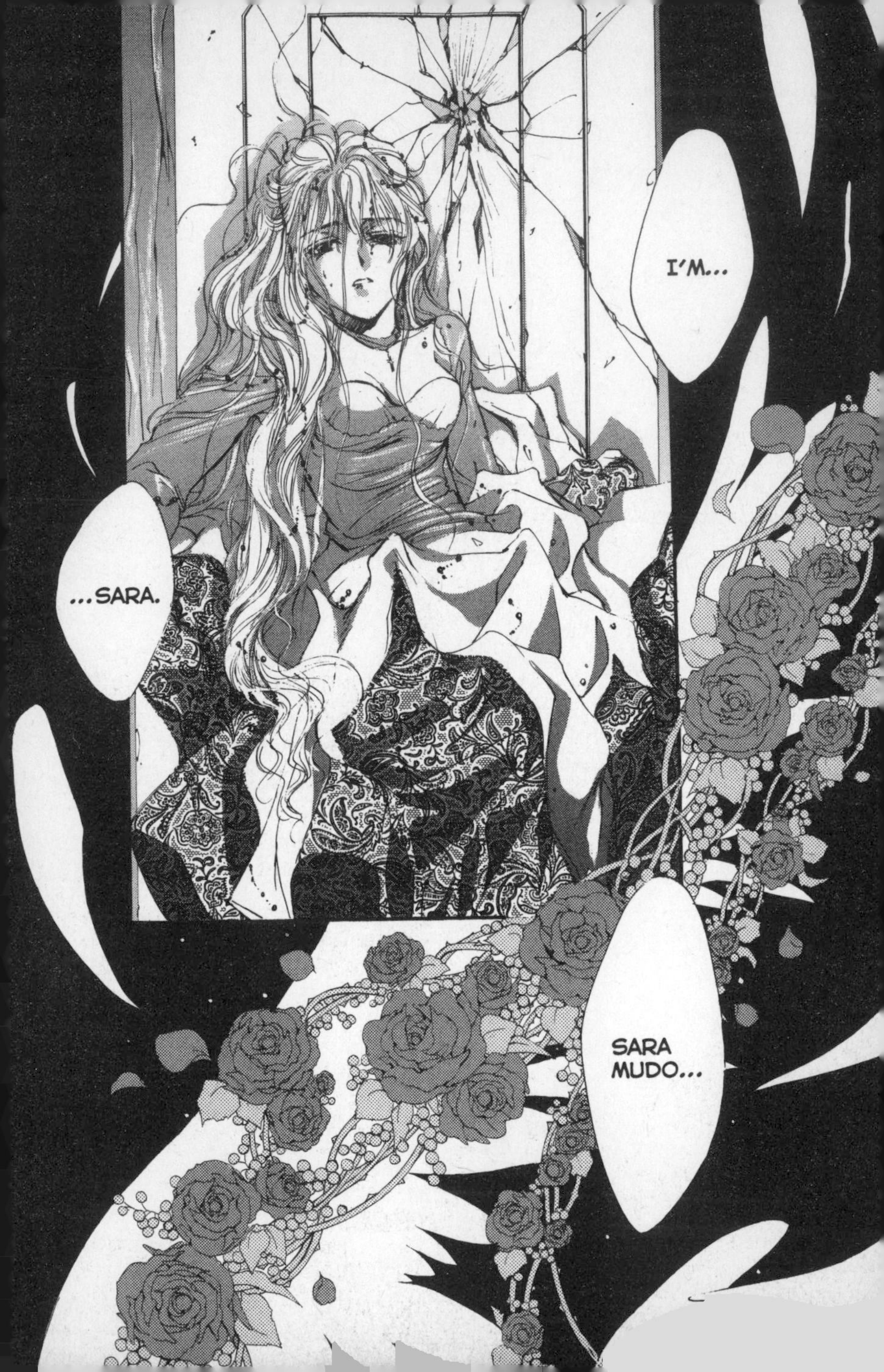
I'M...
...SARA.
SARA MUDO...

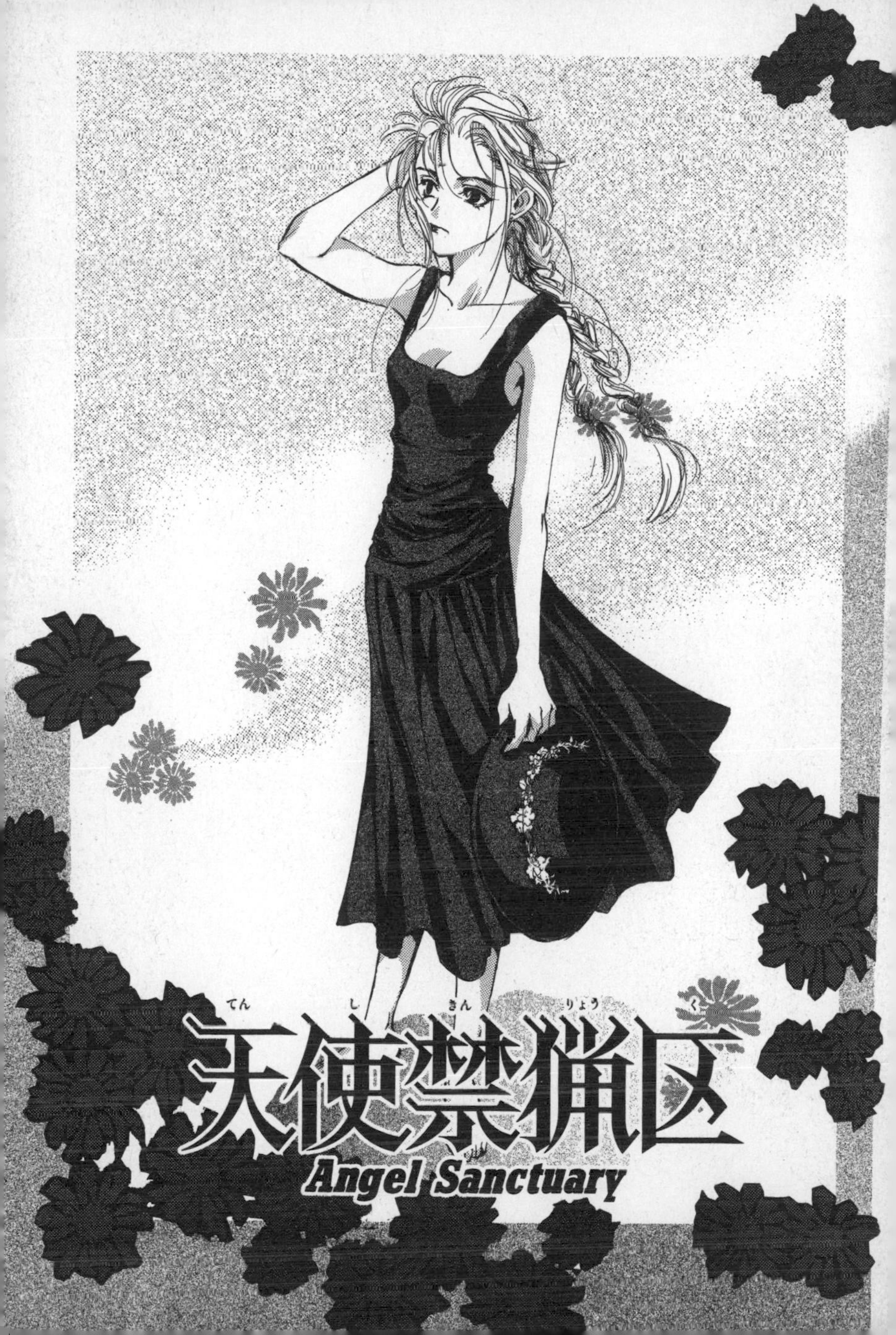
てんしきんりょうく
天使禁猟区
Angel Sanctuary

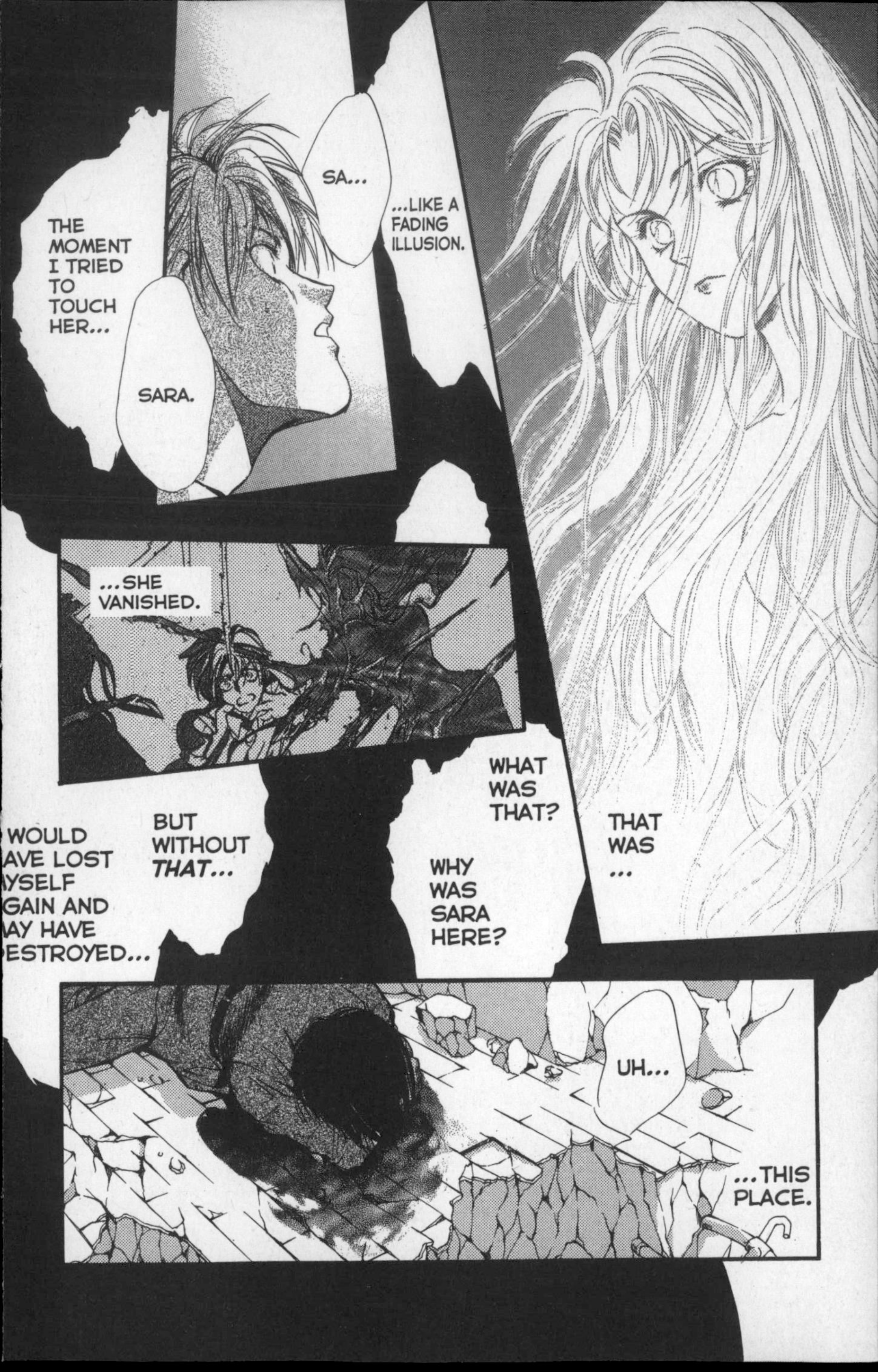

THAT WAS ...
SA...
...LIKE A FADING ILLUSION.
SARA.
THE MOMENT I TRIED TO TOUCH HER...
...SHE VANISHED.
WHAT WAS THAT?
WHY WAS SARA HERE?
BUT WITHOUT *THAT*...
WOULD AVE LOST YSELF GAIN AND AY HAVE ESTROYED...
UH...
...THIS PLACE.

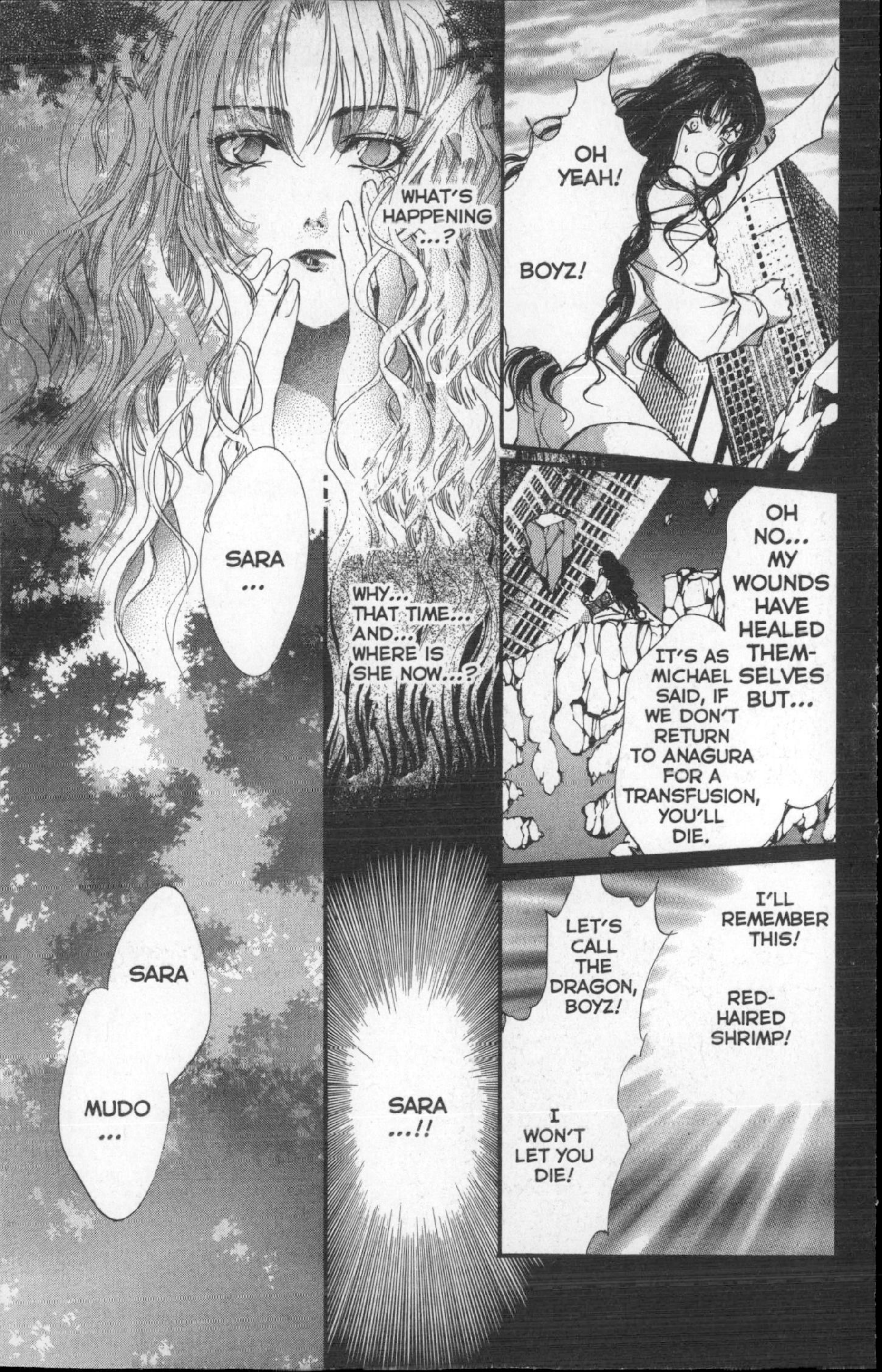
OH YEAH!
BOYZ!
OH NO... MY WOUNDS HAVE HEALED THEMSELVES BUT...
IT'S AS MICHAEL SAID, IF WE DON'T RETURN TO ANAGURA FOR A TRANSFUSION, YOU'LL DIE.
I'LL REMEMBER THIS!
RED-HAIRED SHRIMP!
LET'S CALL THE DRAGON, BOYZ!
I WON'T LET YOU DIE!
WHAT'S HAPPENING ...?
SARA ...
WHY... THAT TIME... AND... WHERE IS SHE NOW...?
SARA
MUDO ...
SARA ...!!

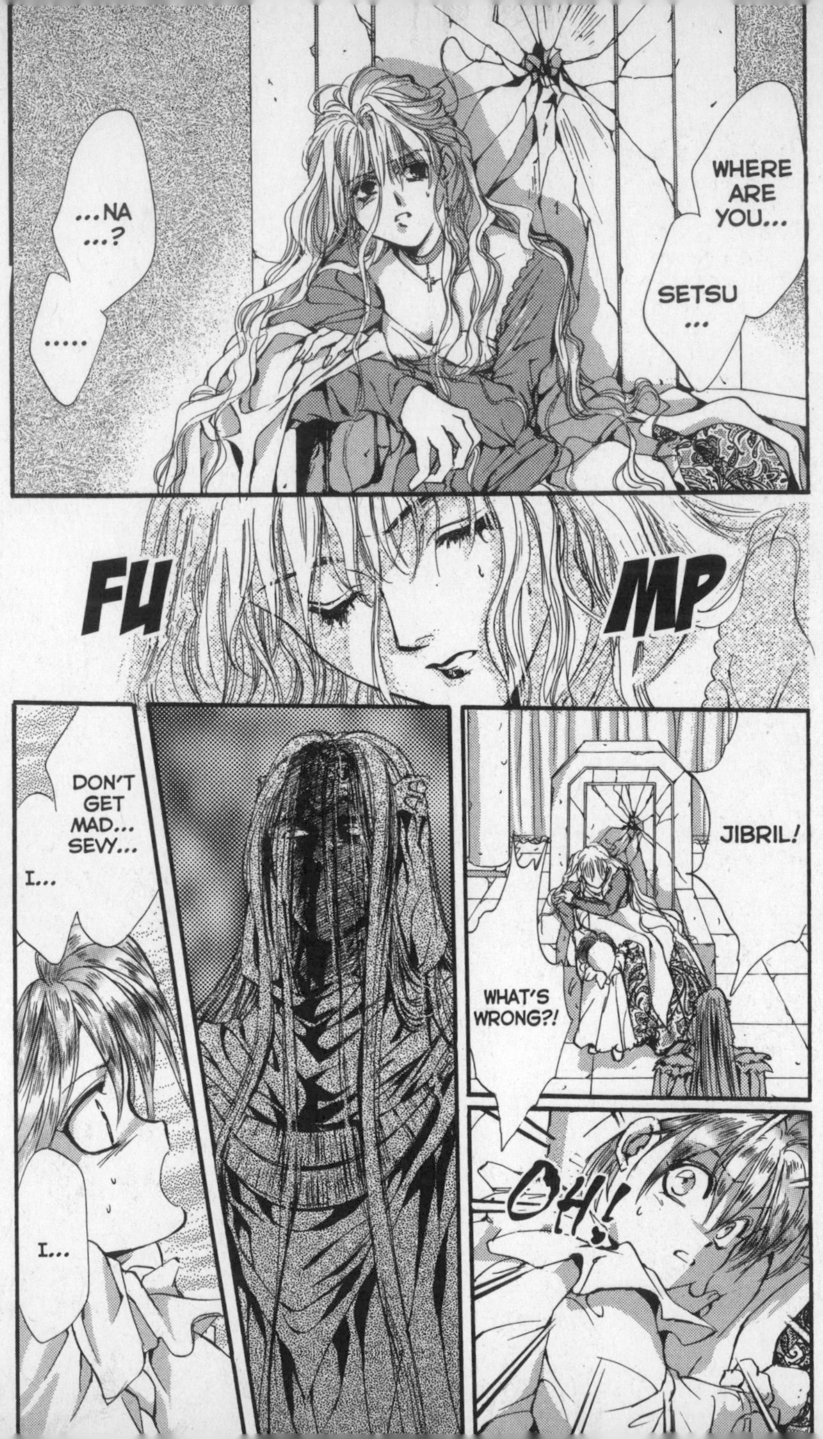
WHERE ARE YOU...
SETSU ...
...NA ...?
.....
FU MP
JIBRIL!
WHAT'S WRONG?!
OH!
DON'T GET MAD... SEVY...
I...
I...

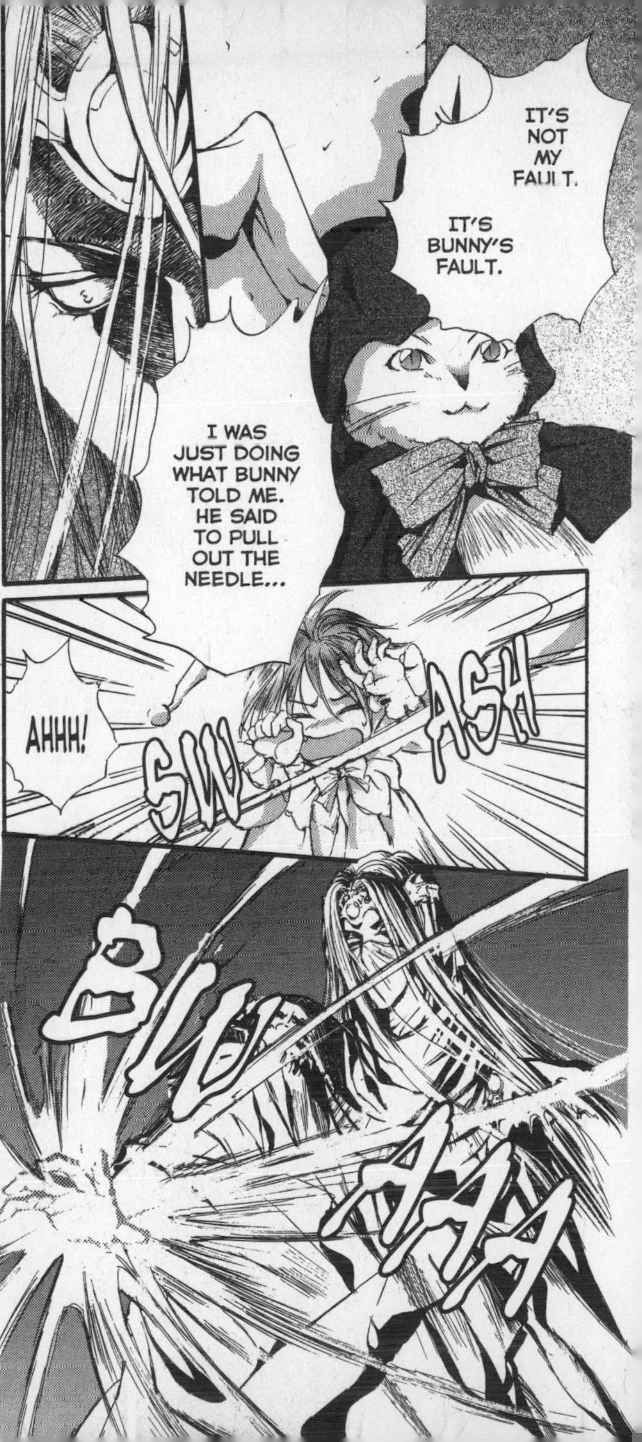
IT'S NOT MY FAULT.
IT'S BUNNY'S FAULT.
I WAS JUST DOING WHAT BUNNY TOLD ME. HE SAID TO PULL OUT THE NEEDLE...
SWASH
AHHH!

It's been so long since I drew Sara! I had forgotten how to separate her hair... And her face too, totally forgot. But that last chapter had a lot of plot development, so it got a big reaction. I guess that's because Setsuna and Sara's love is the main theme of the story (It is?). Oh, so what's up with Sevy's face? I got so many questions like that but you won't find that out for soooooo long. But maybe that's a good thing... ha ha ha. I got a feeling I'm going to get some letters saying "Stop being mean and just tell us!!" Come on, I can't reveal the whole plot now, right?!

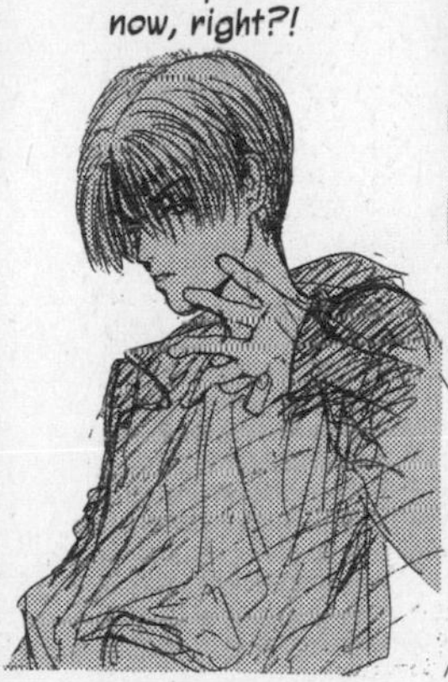

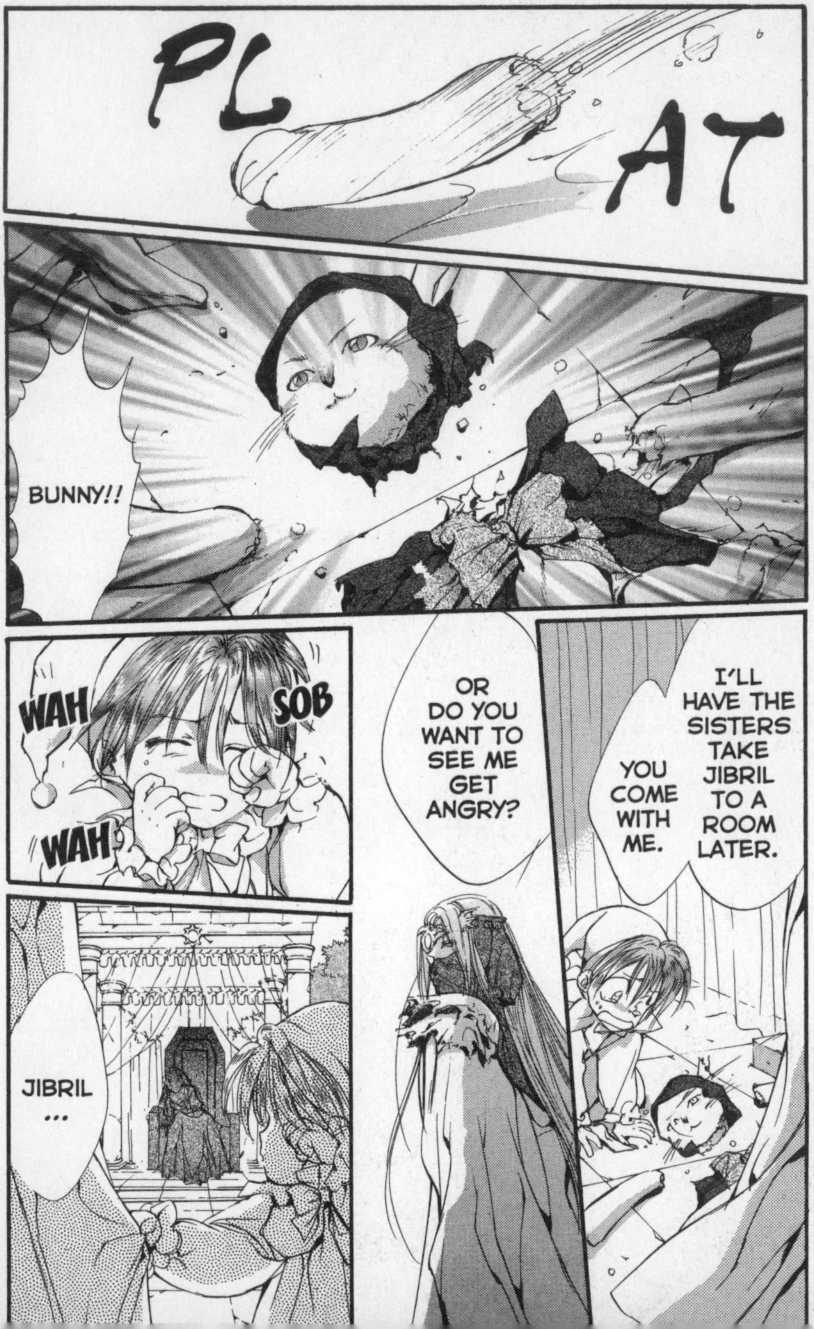
PL AT
BUNNY!!
I'LL HAVE THE SISTERS TAKE JIBRIL TO A ROOM LATER.
YOU COME WITH ME.
OR DO YOU WANT TO SEE ME GET ANGRY?
SOB
WAH
WAH
JIBRIL ...

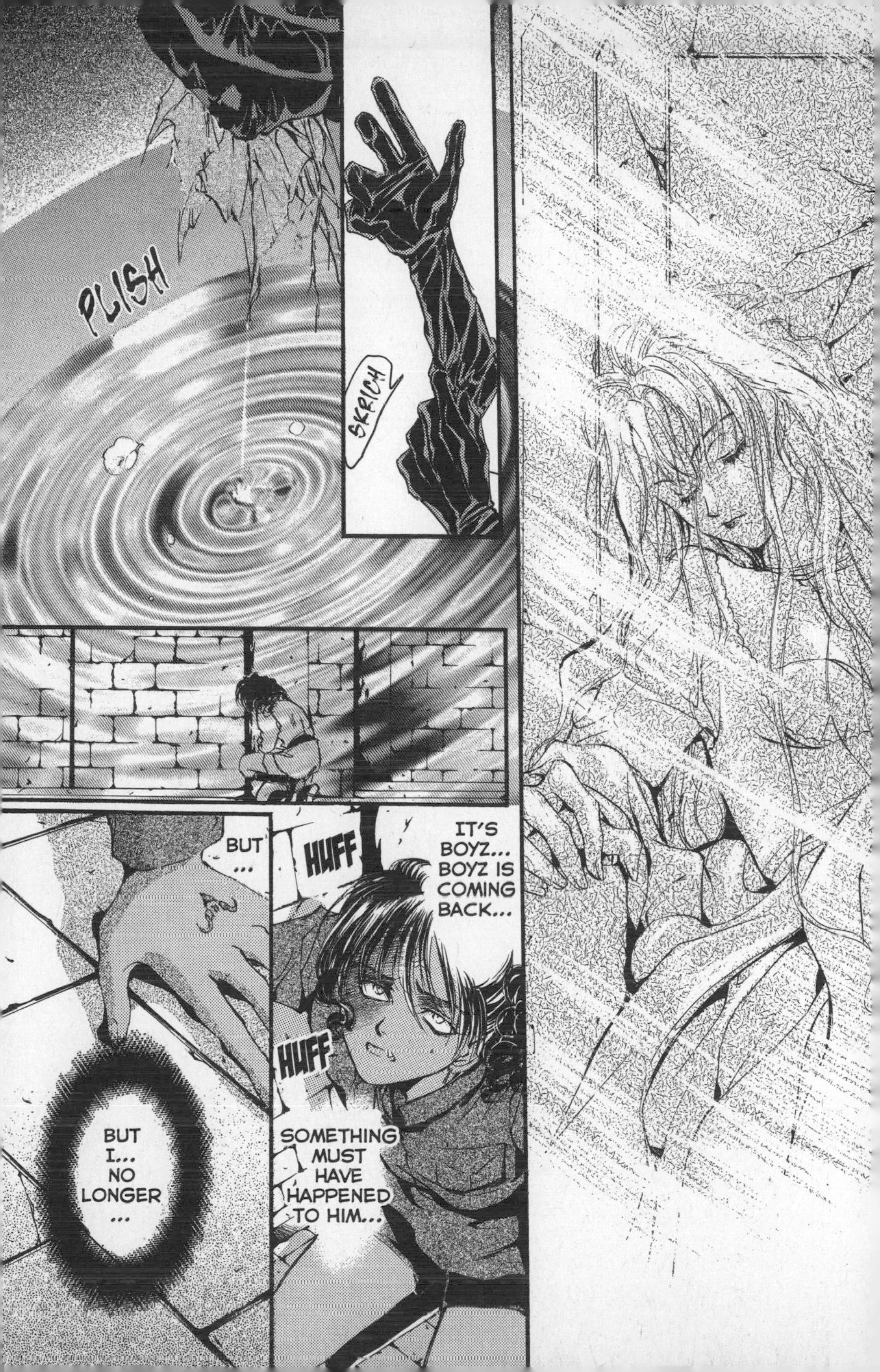
SKRICH
PLISH
IT'S BOYZ... BOYZ IS COMING BACK...
HUFF
HUFF
SOMETHING MUST HAVE HAPPENED TO HIM...
BUT ...
BUT I... NO LONGER ...

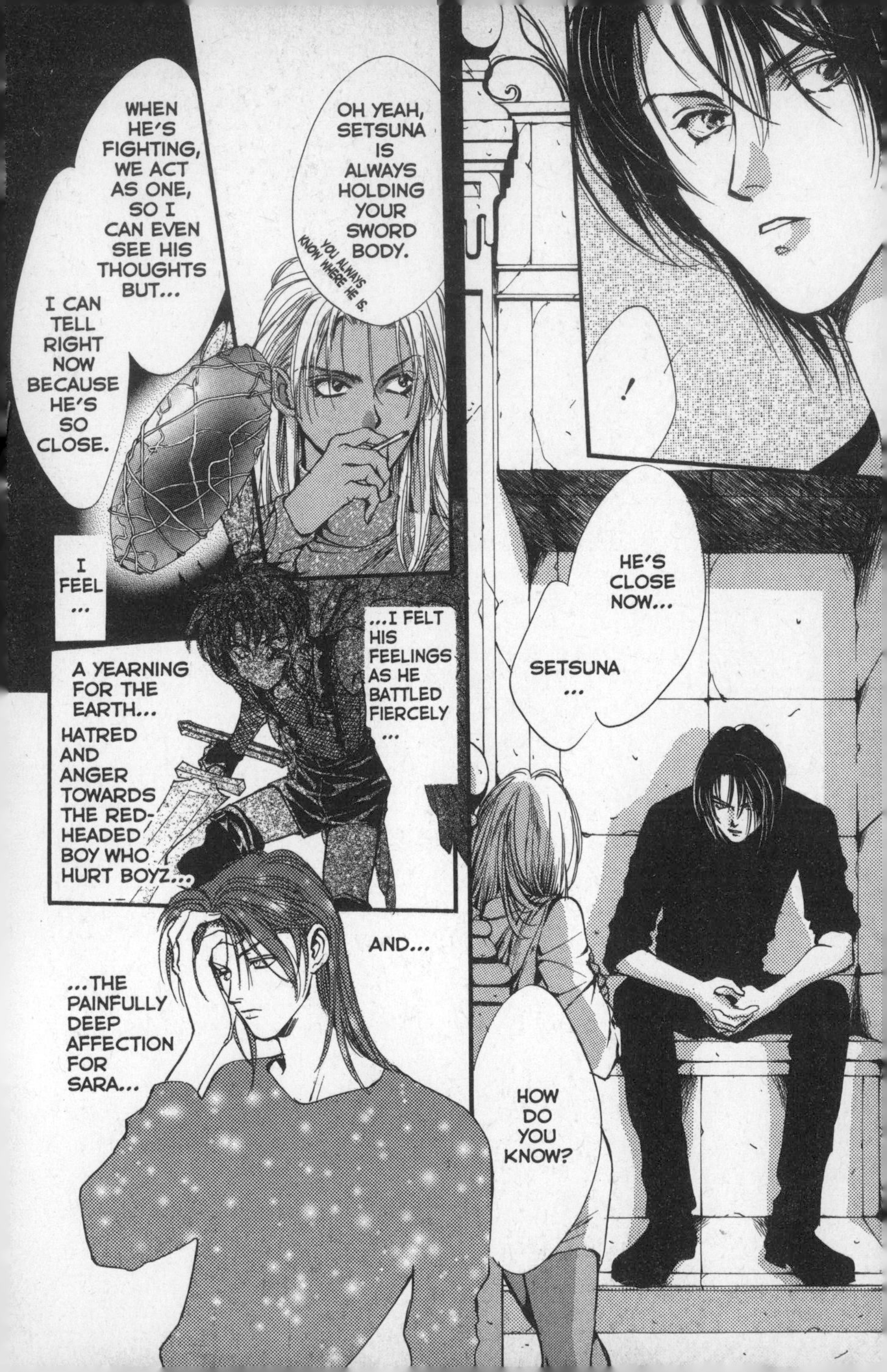
!
HE'S CLOSE NOW...
SETSUNA ...
HOW DO YOU KNOW?
WHEN HE'S FIGHTING, WE ACT AS ONE, SO I CAN EVEN SEE HIS THOUGHTS BUT...
I CAN TELL RIGHT NOW BECAUSE HE'S SO CLOSE.
OH YEAH, SETSUNA IS ALWAYS HOLDING YOUR SWORD BODY.
YOU ALWAYS KNOW WHERE HE IS.
I FEEL ...
...I FELT HIS FEELINGS AS HE BATTLED FIERCELY ...
A YEARNING FOR THE EARTH...
HATRED AND ANGER TOWARDS THE RED-HEADED BOY WHO HURT BOYZ...
AND...
...THE PAINFULLY DEEP AFFECTION FOR SARA...

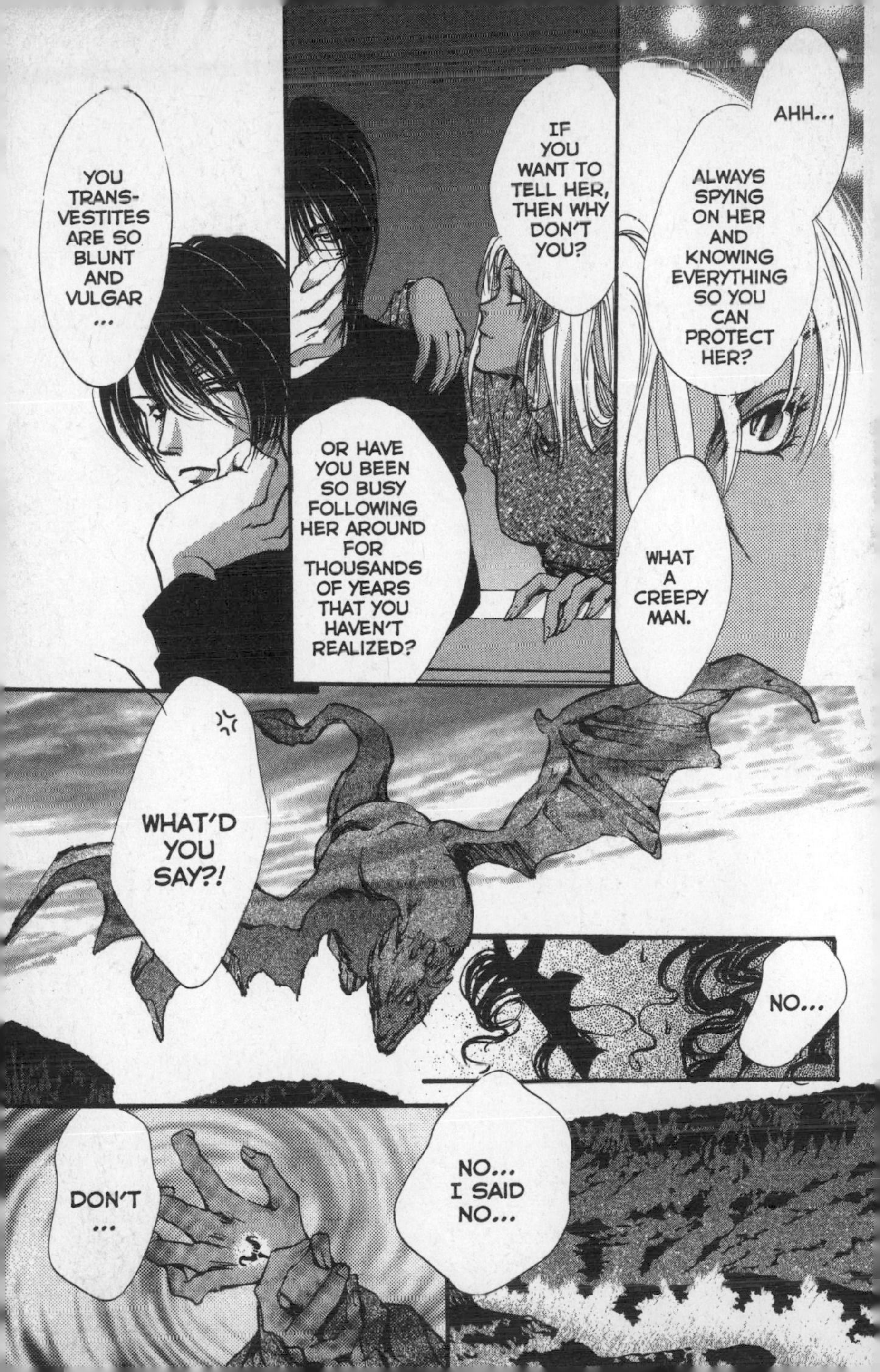
AHH...
ALWAYS SPYING ON HER AND KNOWING EVERYTHING SO YOU CAN PROTECT HER?
WHAT A CREEPY MAN.
IF YOU WANT TO TELL HER, THEN WHY DON'T YOU?
OR HAVE YOU BEEN SO BUSY FOLLOWING HER AROUND FOR THOUSANDS OF YEARS THAT YOU HAVEN'T REALIZED?
YOU TRANS-VESTITES ARE SO BLUNT AND VULGAR ...
WHAT'D YOU SAY?!
NO...
NO... I SAID NO...
DON'T ...

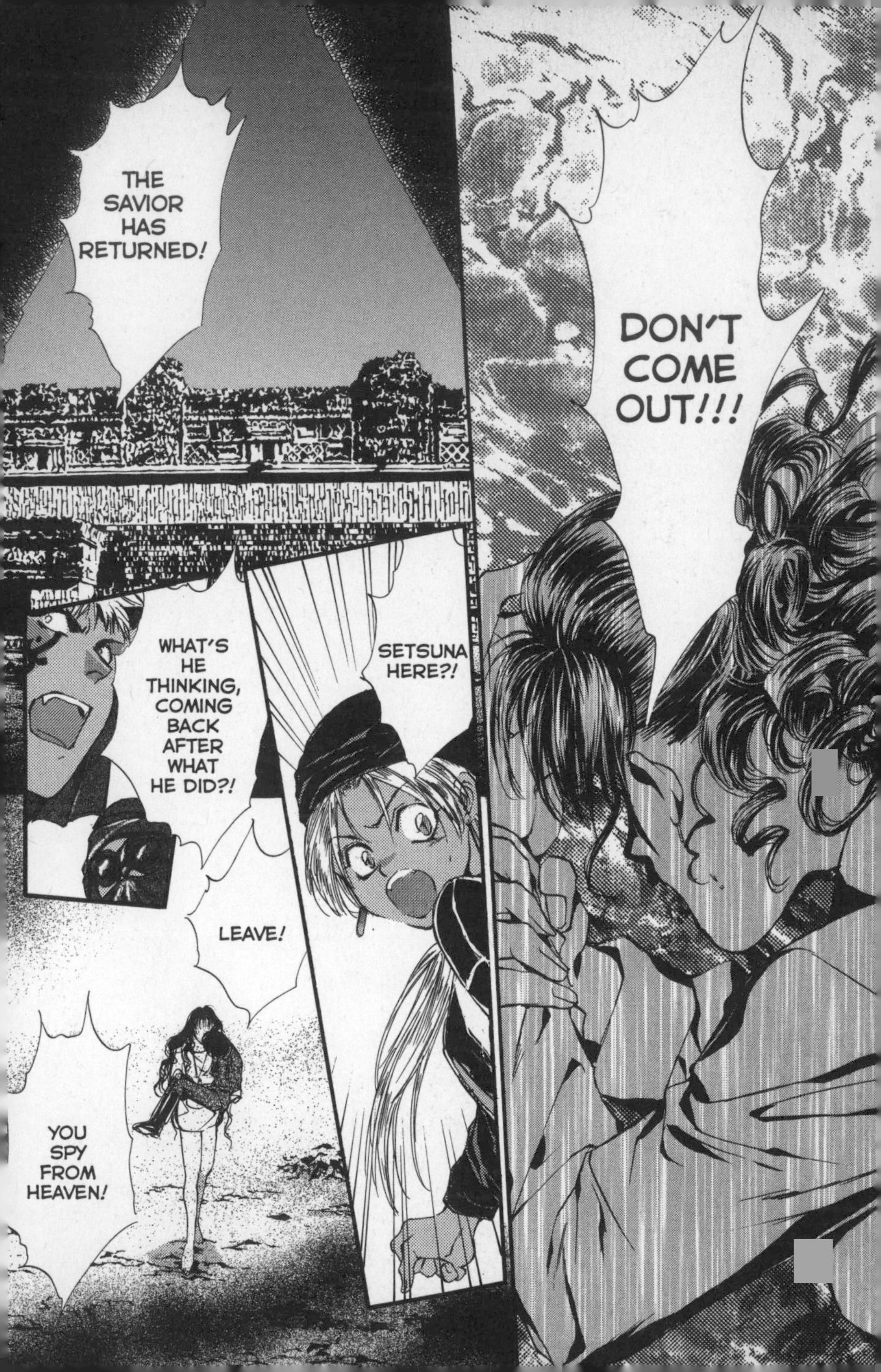
DON'T COME OUT!!!
THE SAVIOR HAS RETURNED!
SETSUNA HERE?!
WHAT'S HE THINKING, COMING BACK AFTER WHAT HE DID?!
LEAVE!
YOU SPY FROM HEAVEN!

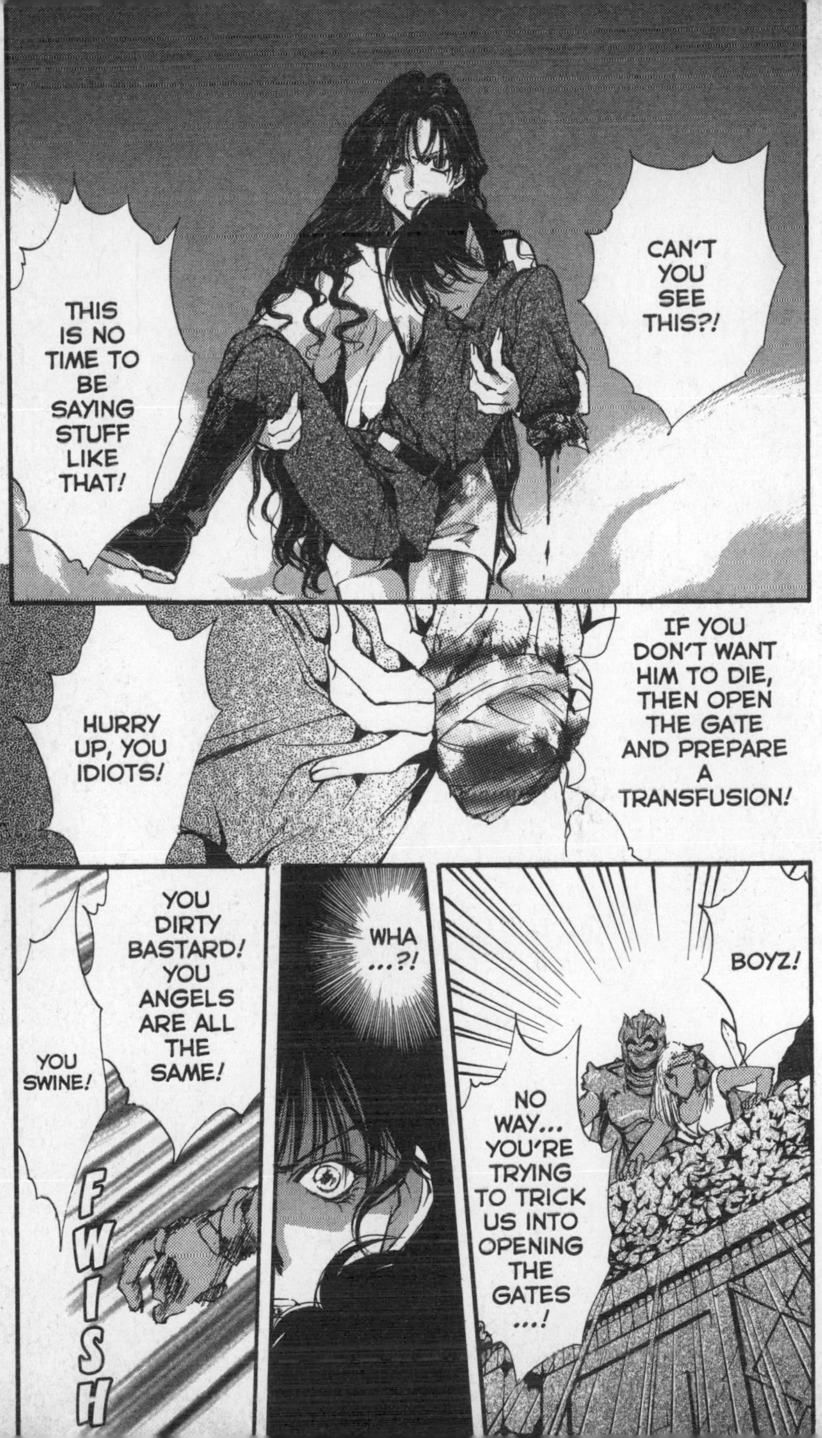
CAN'T YOU SEE THIS?!
THIS IS NO TIME TO BE SAYING STUFF LIKE THAT!
IF YOU DON'T WANT HIM TO DIE, THEN OPEN THE GATE AND PREPARE A TRANSFUSION!
HURRY UP, YOU IDIOTS!
BOYZ!
NO WAY... YOU'RE TRYING TO TRICK US INTO OPENING THE GATES...!
WHA ...?!
YOU DIRTY BASTARD! YOU ANGELS ARE ALL THE SAME!
YOU SWINE!
FWISH

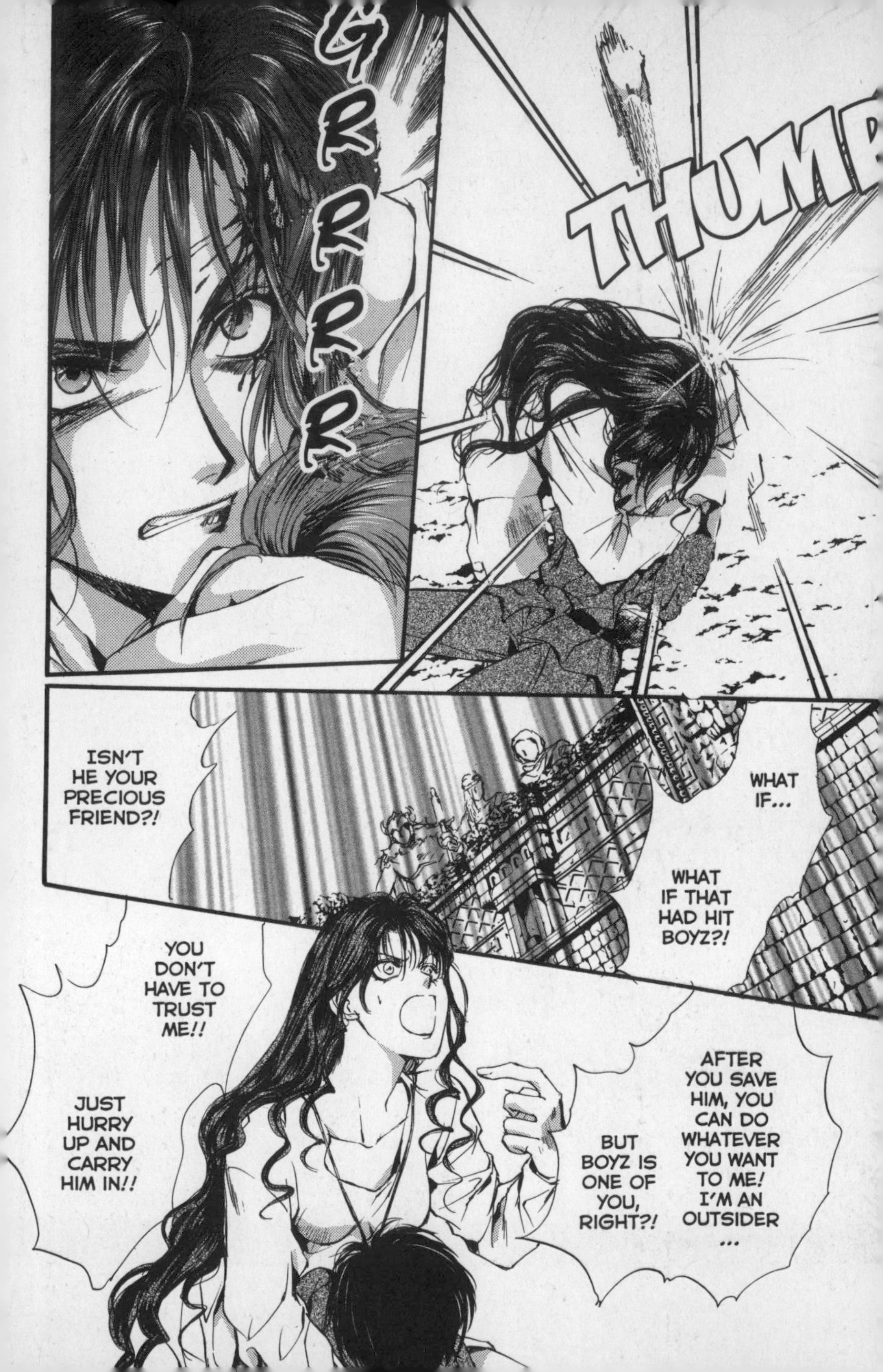
THUMP
GRRRR
WHAT IF...
WHAT IF THAT HAD HIT BOYZ?!
ISN'T HE YOUR PRECIOUS FRIEND?!
AFTER YOU SAVE HIM, YOU CAN DO WHATEVER YOU WANT TO ME! I'M AN OUTSIDER ...
BUT BOYZ IS ONE OF YOU, RIGHT?!
YOU DON'T HAVE TO TRUST ME!!
JUST HURRY UP AND CARRY HIM IN!!

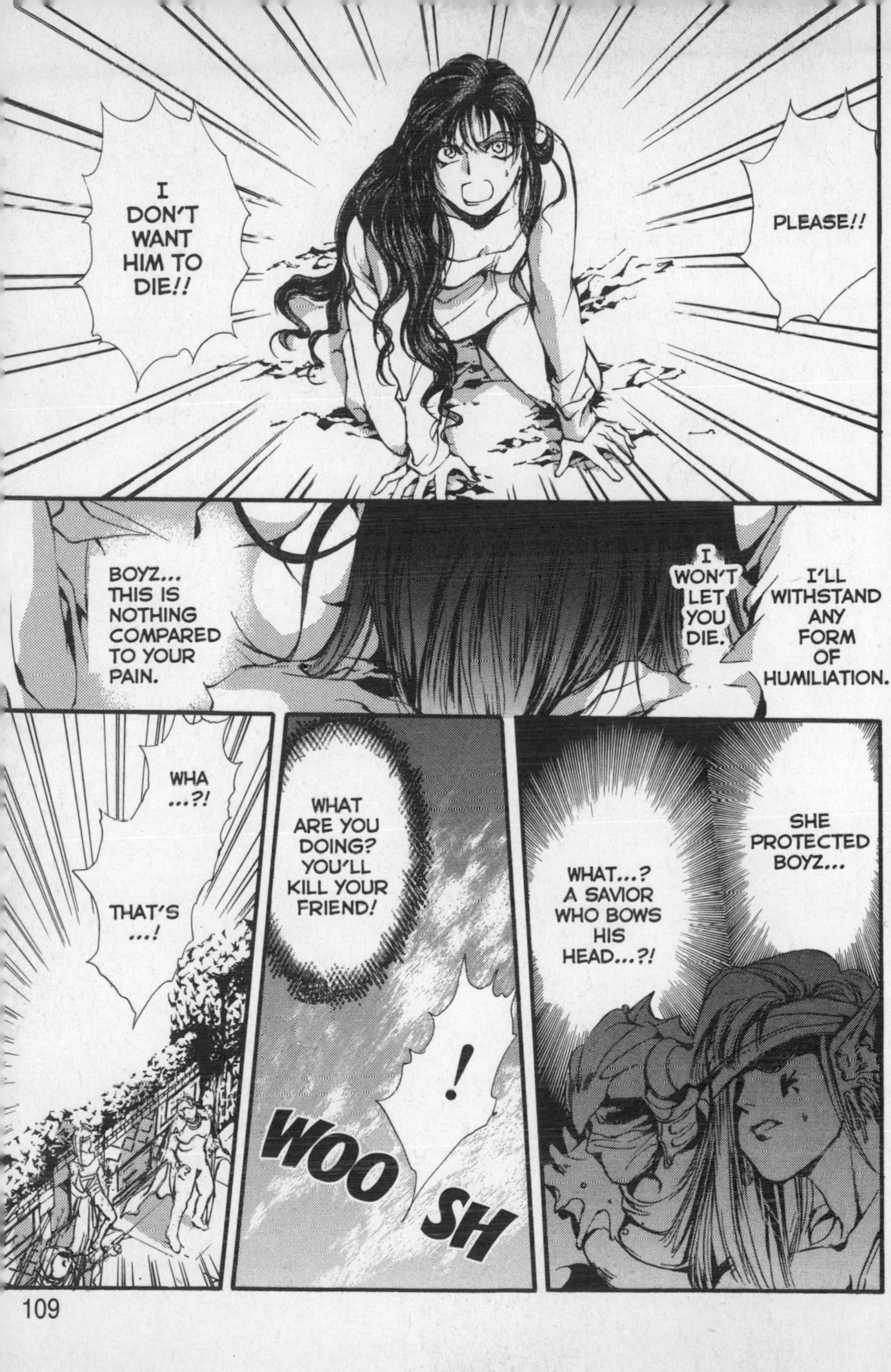
PLEASE!!
I DON'T WANT HIM TO DIE!!
I'LL WITHSTAND ANY FORM OF HUMILIATION.
I WON'T LET YOU DIE.
BOYZ... THIS IS NOTHING COMPARED TO YOUR PAIN.
SHE PROTECTED BOYZ...
WHAT...? A SAVIOR WHO BOWS HIS HEAD...?!
WHAT ARE YOU DOING? YOU'LL KILL YOUR FRIEND!
!
WOOSH
WHA...?!
THAT'S...!

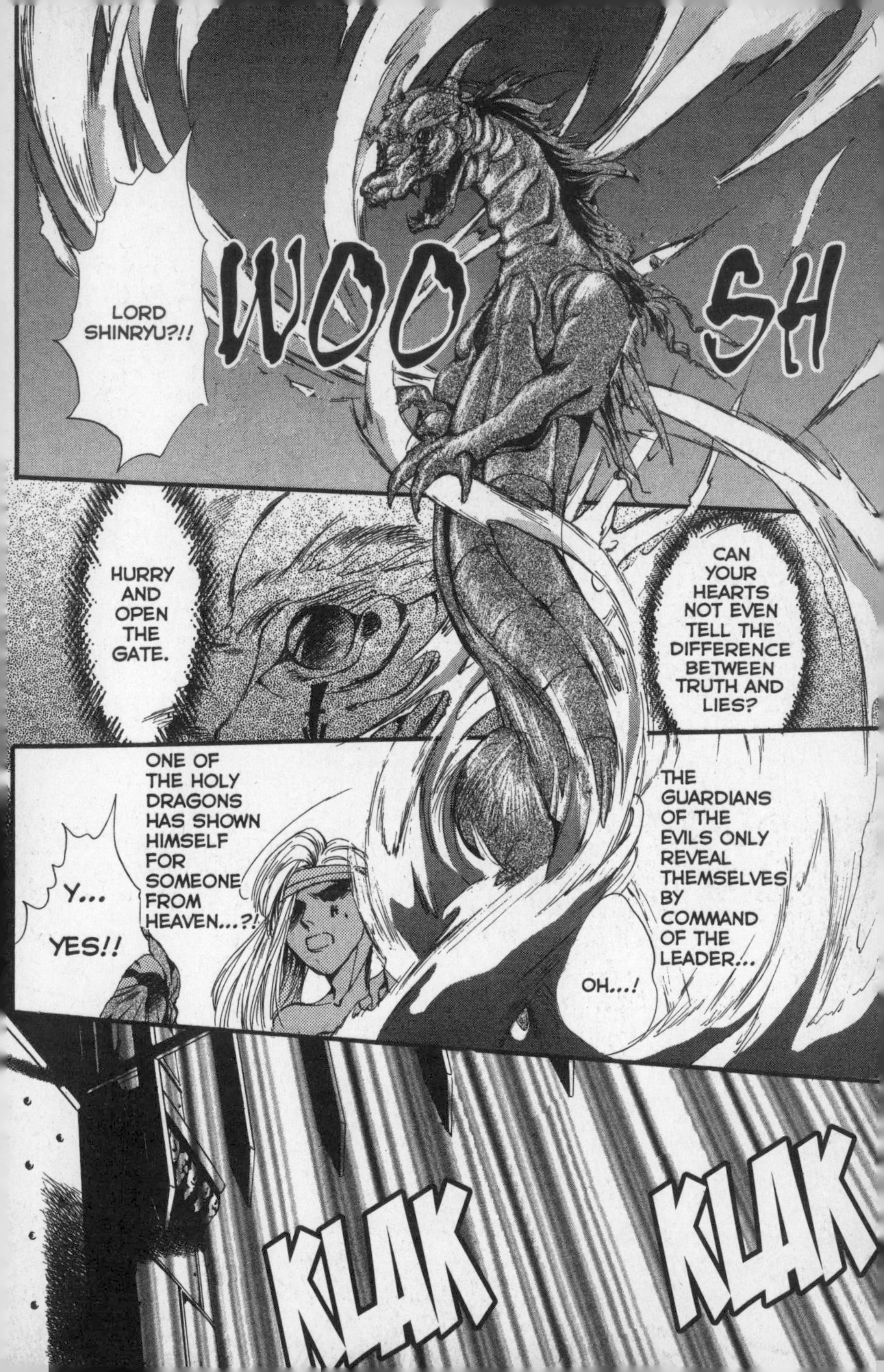
WOOSH
LORD SHINRYU?!!
CAN YOUR HEARTS NOT EVEN TELL THE DIFFERENCE BETWEEN TRUTH AND LIES?
HURRY AND OPEN THE GATE.
THE GUARDIANS OF THE EVILS ONLY REVEAL THEMSELVES BY COMMAND OF THE LEADER...
OH...!
ONE OF THE HOLY DRAGONS HAS SHOWN HIMSELF FOR SOMEONE FROM HEAVEN...?!
Y... YES!!
KLAK
KLAK

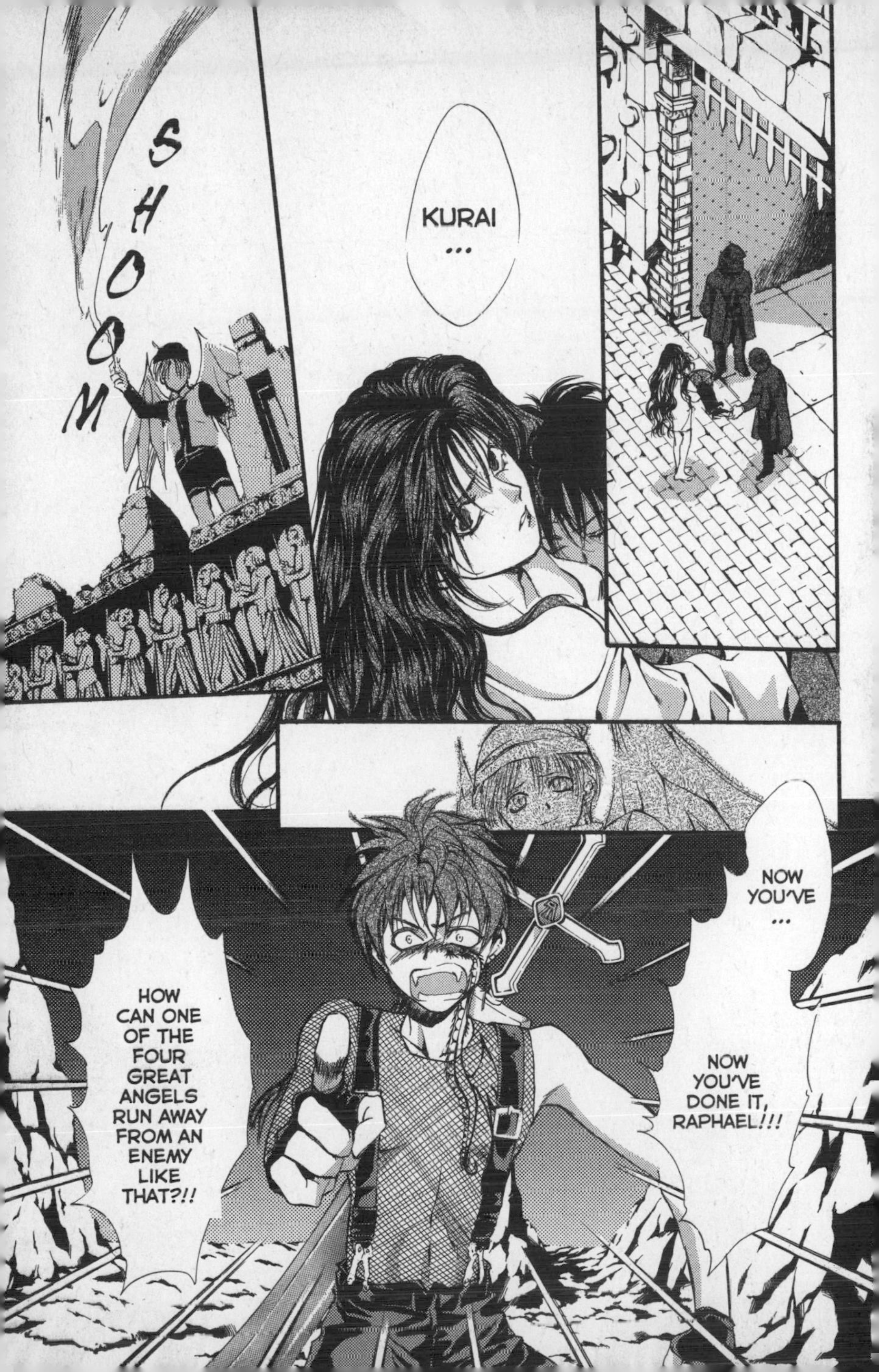
KURAI ...
SHOOOM
NOW YOU'VE ...
NOW YOU'VE DONE IT, RAPHAEL!!!
HOW CAN ONE OF THE FOUR GREAT ANGELS RUN AWAY FROM AN ENEMY LIKE THAT?!!

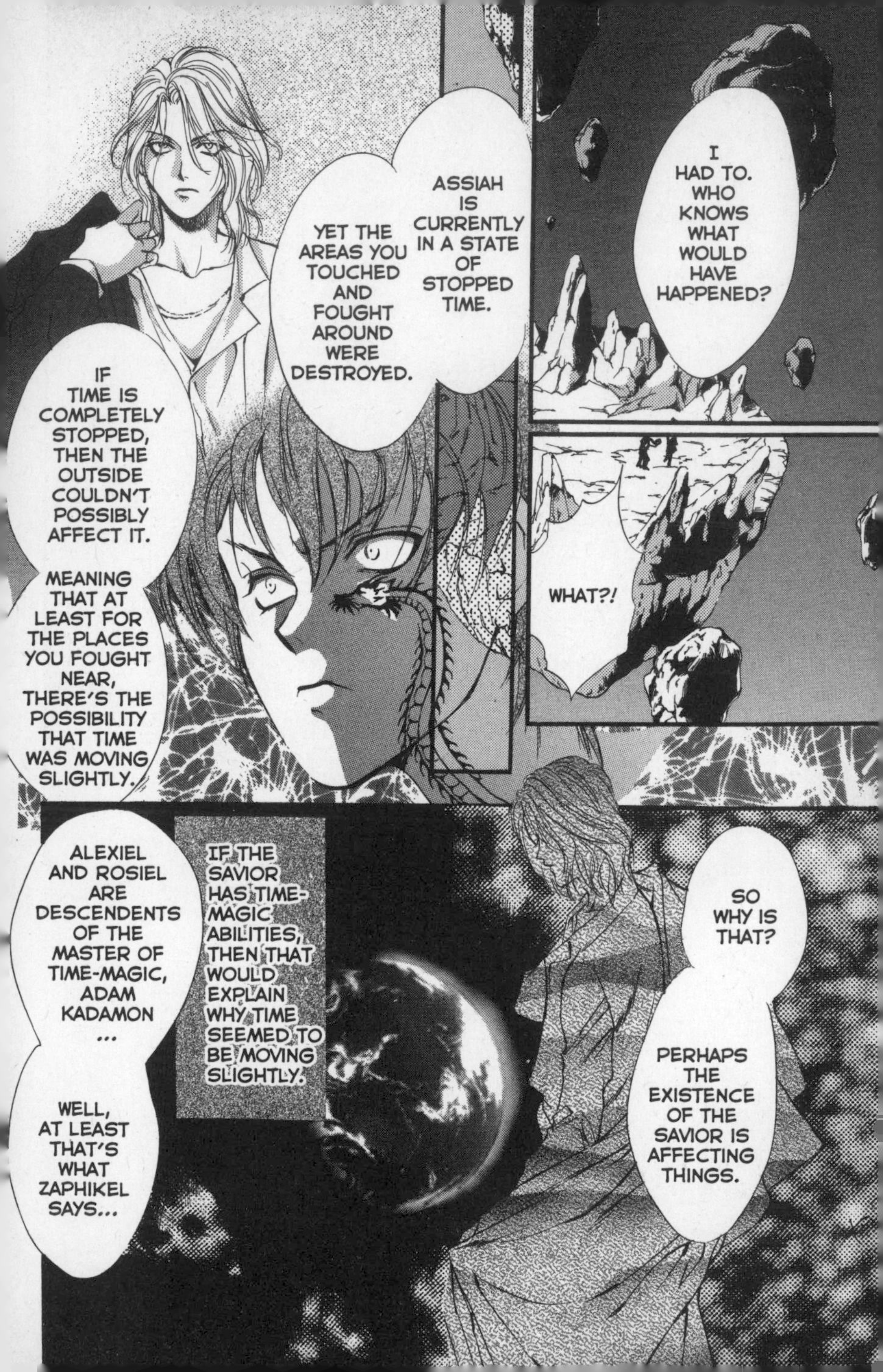
I HAD TO. WHO KNOWS WHAT WOULD HAVE HAPPENED?
WHAT?!
ASSIAH IS CURRENTLY IN A STATE OF STOPPED TIME.
YET THE AREAS YOU TOUCHED AND FOUGHT AROUND WERE DESTROYED.
IF TIME IS COMPLETELY STOPPED, THEN THE OUTSIDE COULDN'T POSSIBLY AFFECT IT.
MEANING THAT AT LEAST FOR THE PLACES YOU FOUGHT NEAR, THERE'S THE POSSIBILITY THAT TIME WAS MOVING SLIGHTLY.
SO WHY IS THAT?
PERHAPS THE EXISTENCE OF THE SAVIOR IS AFFECTING THINGS.
IF THE SAVIOR HAS TIME-MAGIC ABILITIES, THEN THAT WOULD EXPLAIN WHY TIME SEEMED TO BE MOVING SLIGHTLY.
ALEXIEL AND ROSIEL ARE DESCENDENTS OF THE MASTER OF TIME-MAGIC, ADAM KADAMON ...
WELL, AT LEAST THAT'S WHAT ZAPHIKEL SAYS...

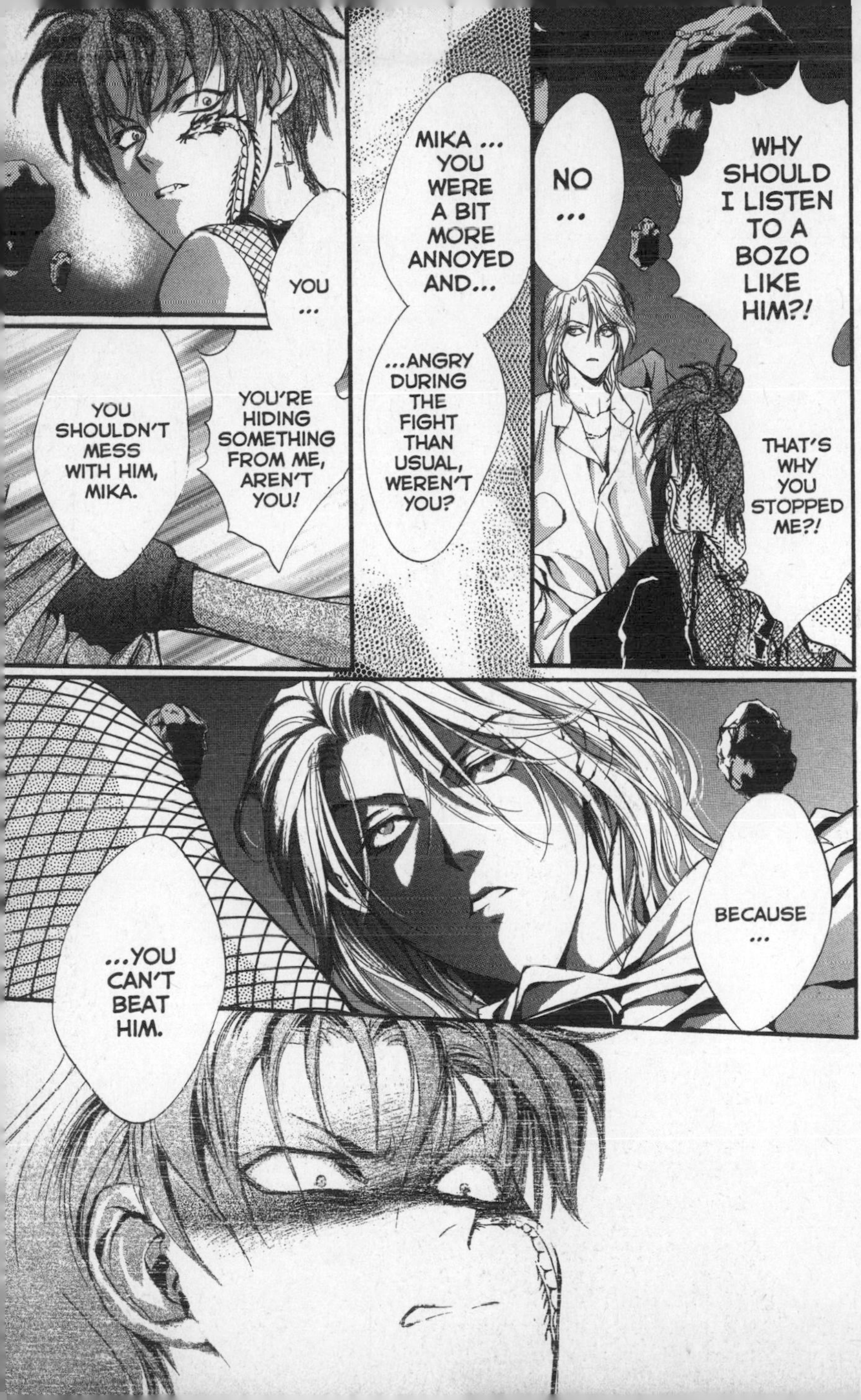
WHY SHOULD I LISTEN TO A BOZO LIKE HIM?!
NO ...
THAT'S WHY YOU STOPPED ME?!
MIKA ... YOU WERE A BIT MORE ANNOYED AND...
...ANGRY DURING THE FIGHT THAN USUAL, WEREN'T YOU?
YOU ...
YOU'RE HIDING SOMETHING FROM ME, AREN'T YOU!
YOU SHOULDN'T MESS WITH HIM, MIKA.
BECAUSE ...
...YOU CAN'T BEAT HIM.

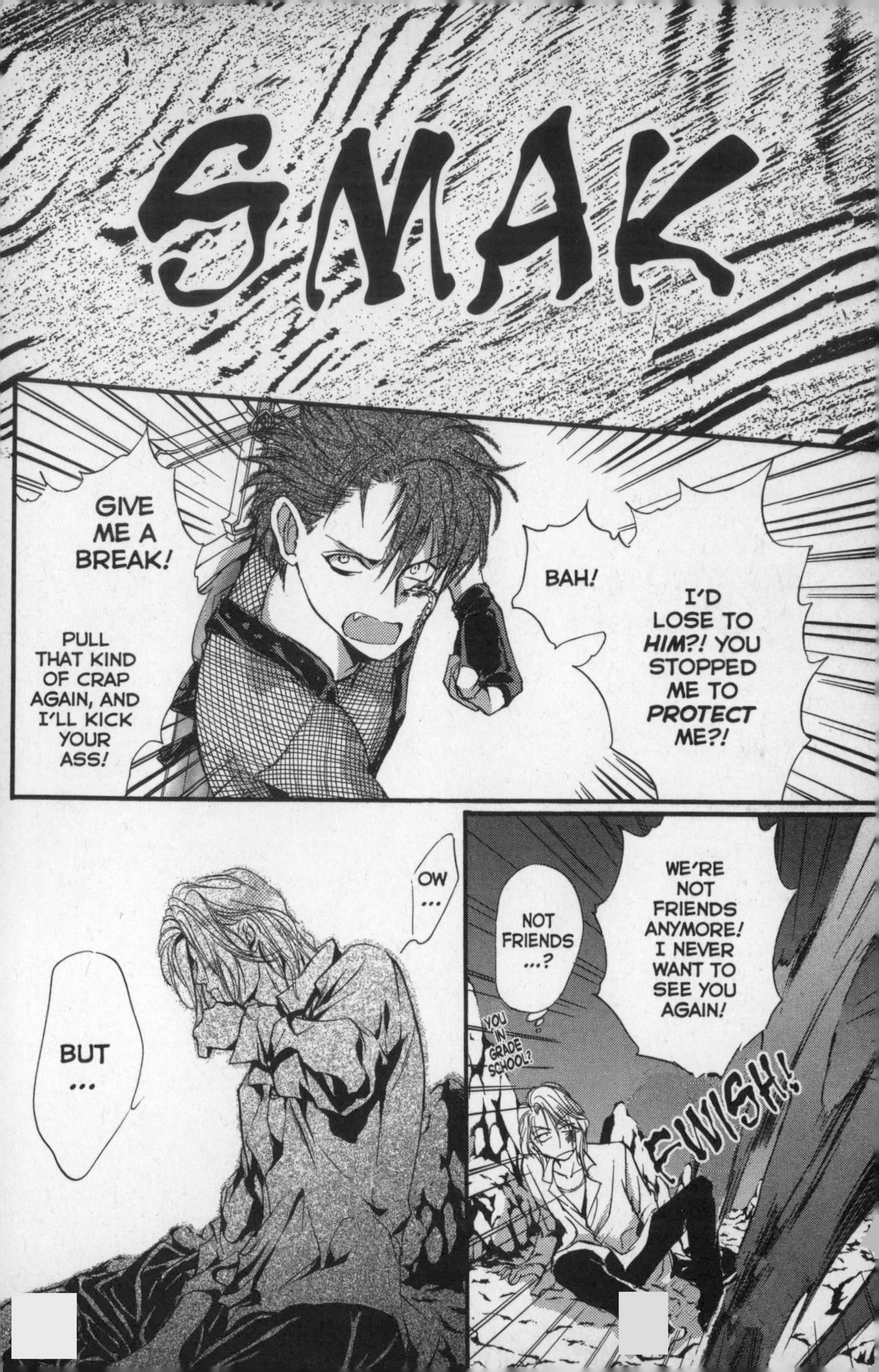
SMAK
I'D LOSE TO HIM?! YOU STOPPED ME TO PROTECT ME?!
BAH!
GIVE ME A BREAK!
PULL THAT KIND OF CRAP AGAIN, AND I'LL KICK YOUR ASS!
WE'RE NOT FRIENDS ANYMORE! I NEVER WANT TO SEE YOU AGAIN!
FWISH!
NOT FRIENDS ...?
YOU IN GRADE SCHOOL?
OW ...
BUT ...

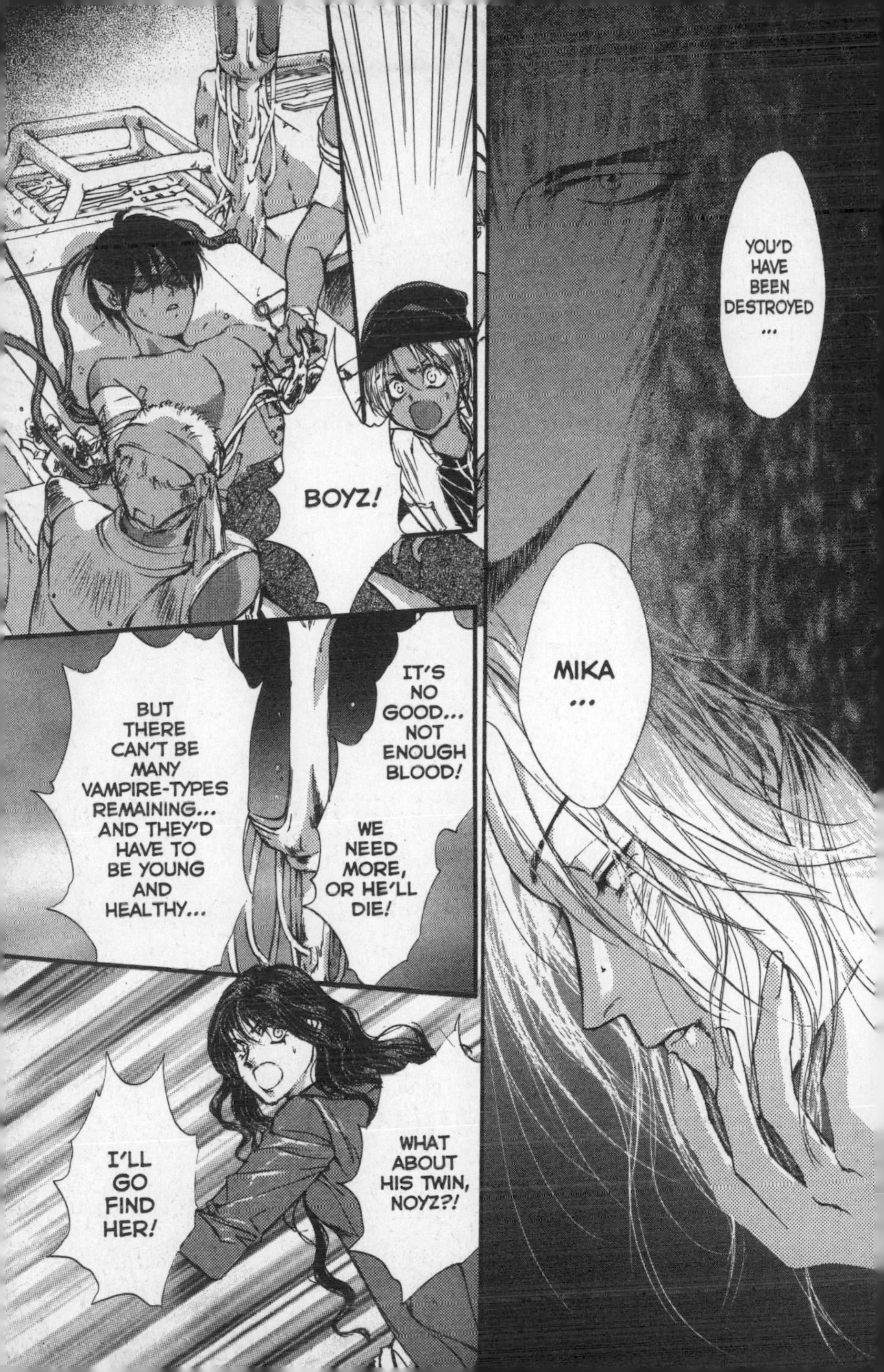
YOU'D HAVE BEEN DESTROYED ...
MIKA ...
BOYZ!
IT'S NO GOOD... NOT ENOUGH BLOOD!
WE NEED MORE, OR HE'LL DIE!
BUT THERE CAN'T BE MANY VAMPIRE-TYPES REMAINING... AND THEY'D HAVE TO BE YOUNG AND HEALTHY...
WHAT ABOUT HIS TWIN, NOYZ?!
I'LL GO FIND HER!

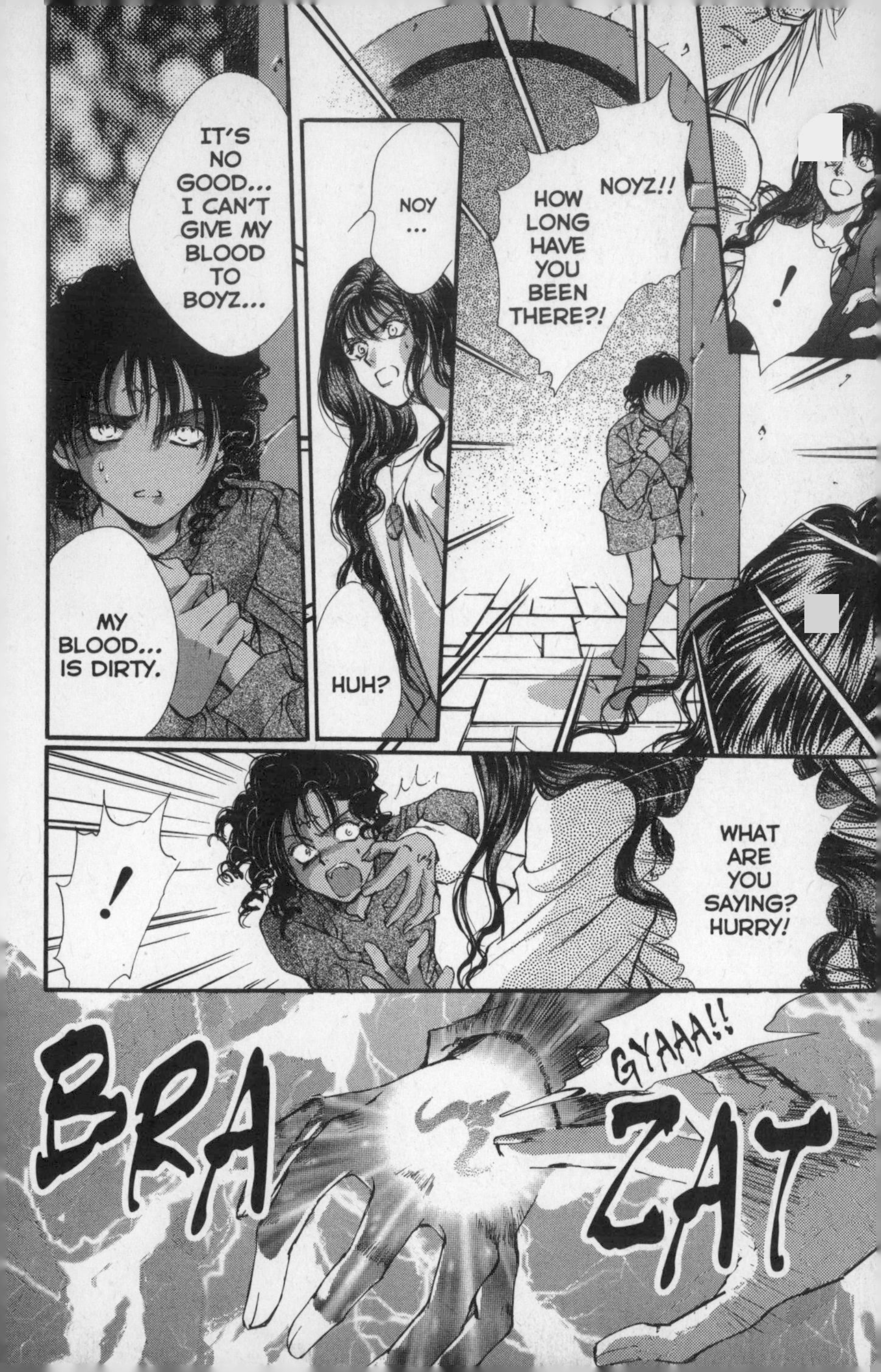
!
NOYZ!!
HOW LONG HAVE YOU BEEN THERE?!
NOY ...
HUH?
IT'S NO GOOD... I CAN'T GIVE MY BLOOD TO BOYZ...
MY BLOOD... IS DIRTY.
WHAT ARE YOU SAYING? HURRY!
!
GYAAA!!
BRA
ZAT

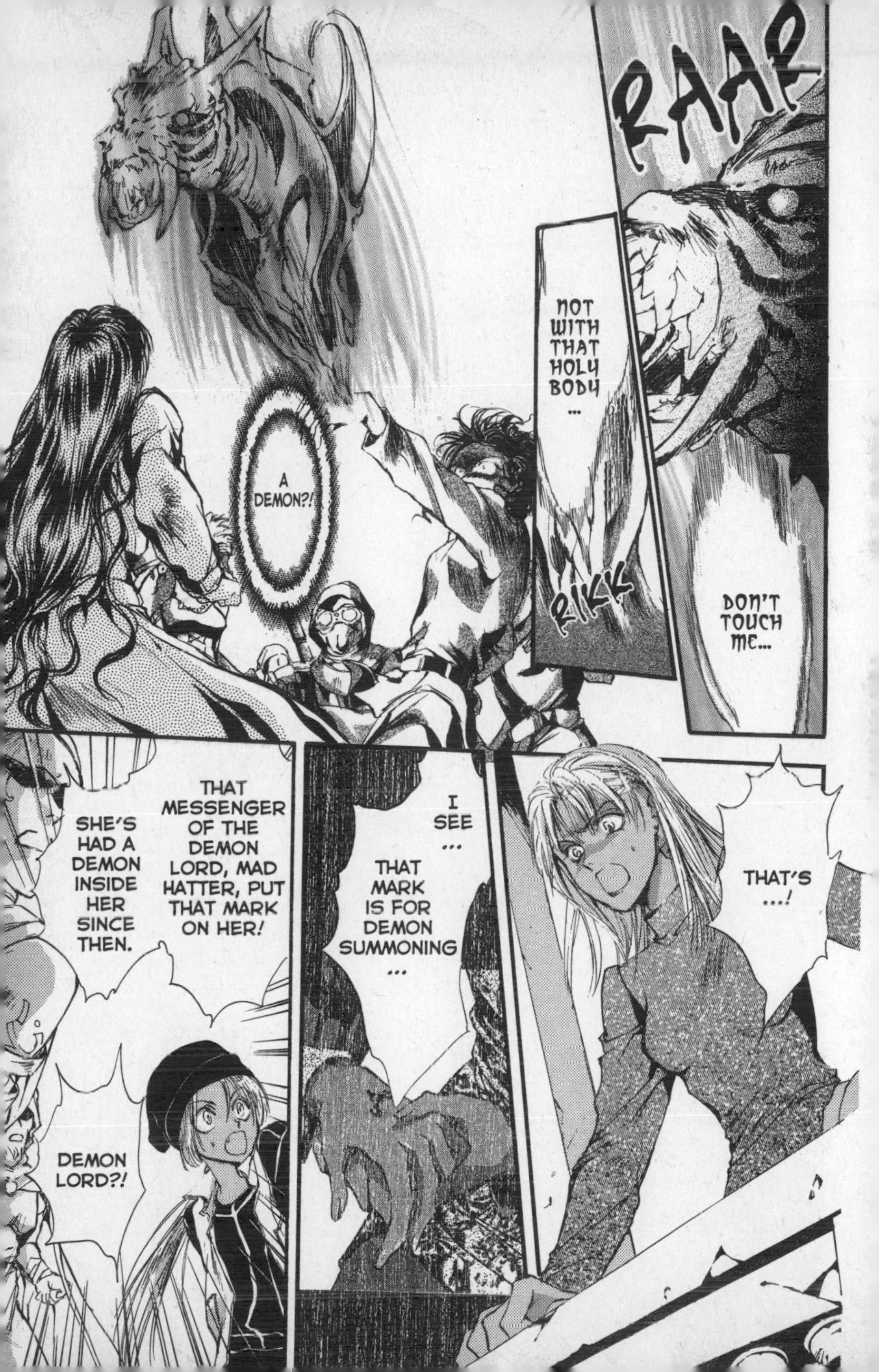
RAAR
NOT WITH THAT HOLY BODY...
RIKK
DON'T TOUCH ME...
A DEMON?!
THAT'S ...!
I SEE ...
THAT MARK IS FOR DEMON SUMMONING ...
THAT MESSENGER OF THE DEMON LORD, MAD HATTER, PUT THAT MARK ON HER!
SHE'S HAD A DEMON INSIDE HER SINCE THEN.
DEMON LORD?!

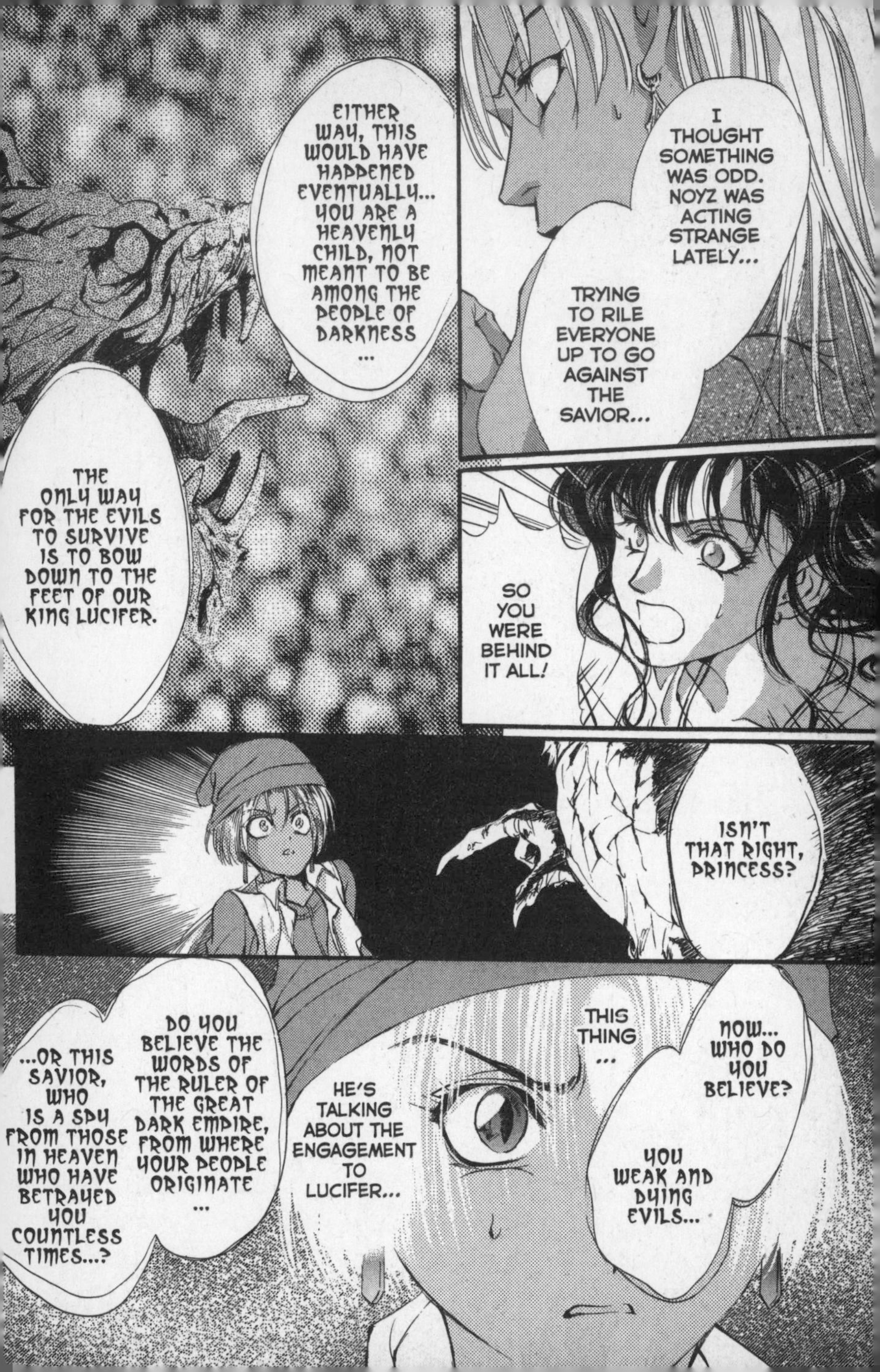
I THOUGHT SOMETHING WAS ODD. NOYZ WAS ACTING STRANGE LATELY...
TRYING TO RILE EVERYONE UP TO GO AGAINST THE SAVIOR...
SO YOU WERE BEHIND IT ALL!
EITHER WAY, THIS WOULD HAVE HAPPENED EVENTUALLY... YOU ARE A HEAVENLY CHILD, NOT MEANT TO BE AMONG THE PEOPLE OF DARKNESS...
THE ONLY WAY FOR THE EVILS TO SURVIVE IS TO BOW DOWN TO THE FEET OF OUR KING LUCIFER.
ISN'T THAT RIGHT, PRINCESS?
NOW... WHO DO YOU BELIEVE?
YOU WEAK AND DYING EVILS...
DO YOU BELIEVE THE WORDS OF THE RULER OF THE GREAT DARK EMPIRE, FROM WHERE YOUR PEOPLE ORIGINATE...
...OR THIS SAVIOR, WHO IS A SPY FROM THOSE IN HEAVEN WHO HAVE BETRAYED YOU COUNTLESS TIMES...?
THIS THING...
HE'S TALKING ABOUT THE ENGAGEMENT TO LUCIFER...

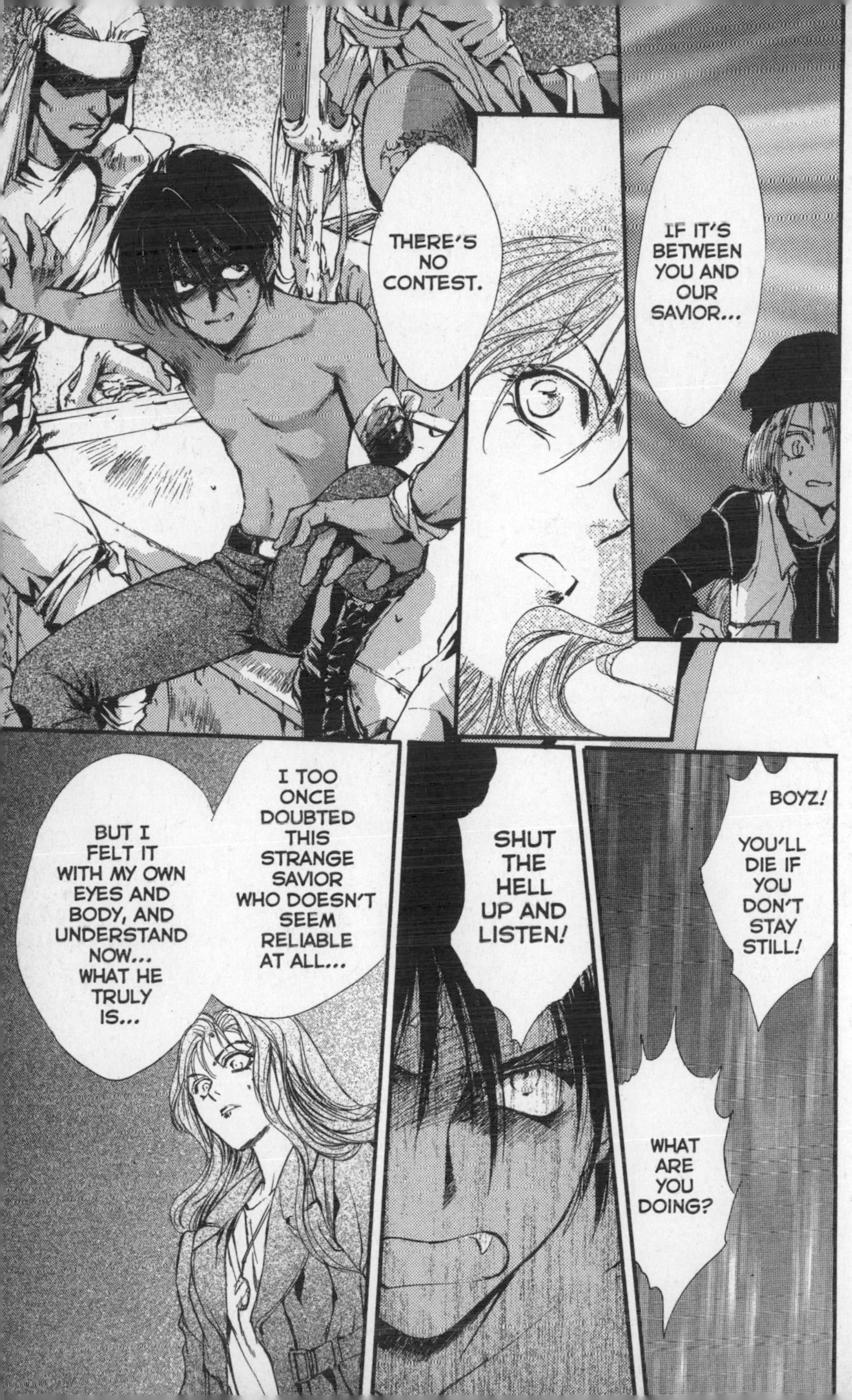
IF IT'S BETWEEN YOU AND OUR SAVIOR...
THERE'S NO CONTEST.
BOYZ!
YOU'LL DIE IF YOU DON'T STAY STILL!
WHAT ARE YOU DOING?
SHUT THE HELL UP AND LISTEN!
I TOO ONCE DOUBTED THIS STRANGE SAVIOR WHO DOESN'T SEEM RELIABLE AT ALL...
BUT I FELT IT WITH MY OWN EYES AND BODY, AND UNDERSTAND NOW... WHAT HE TRULY IS...

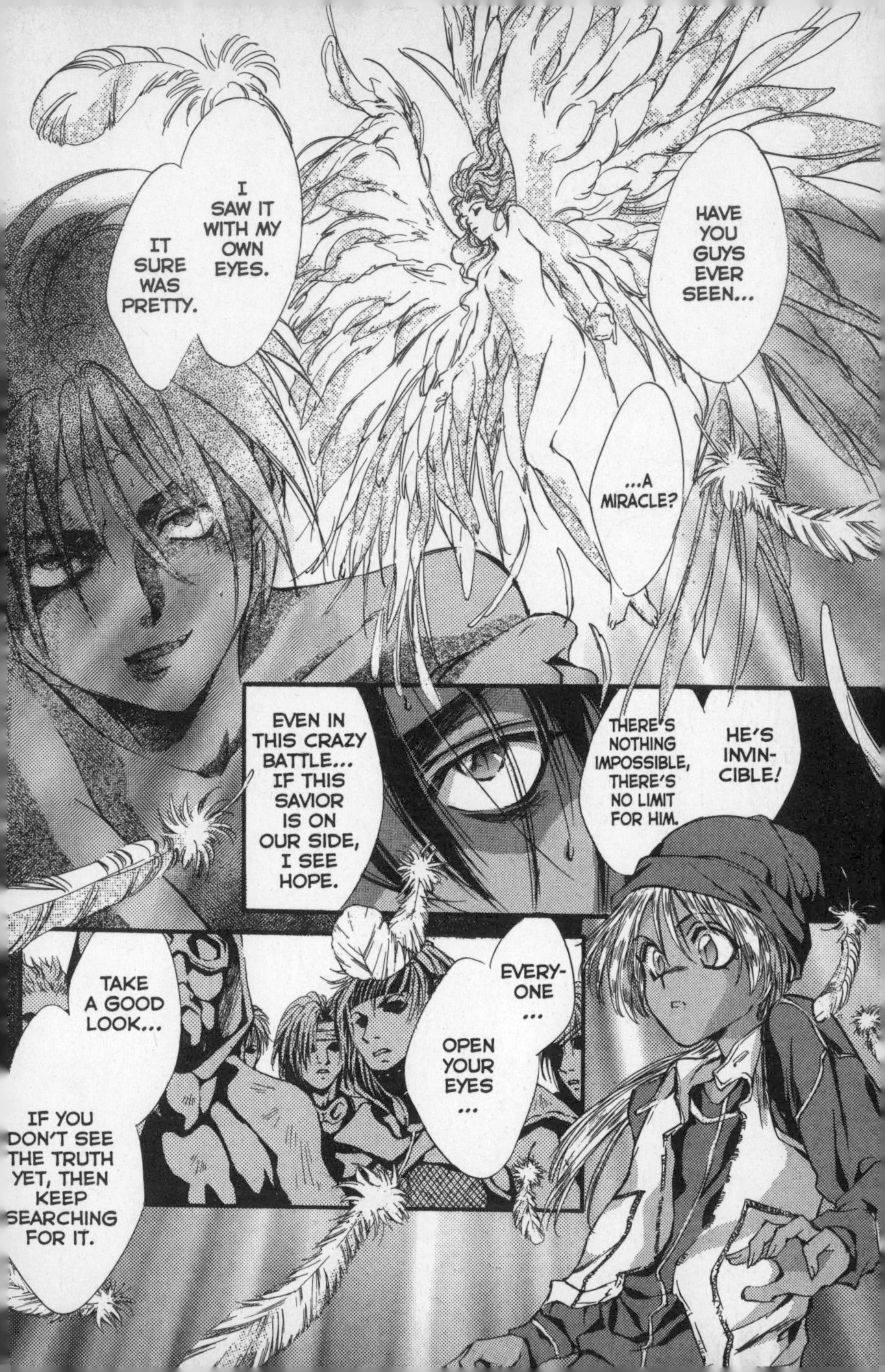
HAVE YOU GUYS EVER SEEN...
...A MIRACLE?
I SAW IT WITH MY OWN EYES.
IT SURE WAS PRETTY.
HE'S INVINCIBLE!
THERE'S NOTHING IMPOSSIBLE, THERE'S NO LIMIT FOR HIM.
EVEN IN THIS CRAZY BATTLE... IF THIS SAVIOR IS ON OUR SIDE, I SEE HOPE.
EVERYONE ...
OPEN YOUR EYES ...
TAKE A GOOD LOOK...
IF YOU DON'T SEE THE TRUTH YET, THEN KEEP SEARCHING FOR IT.

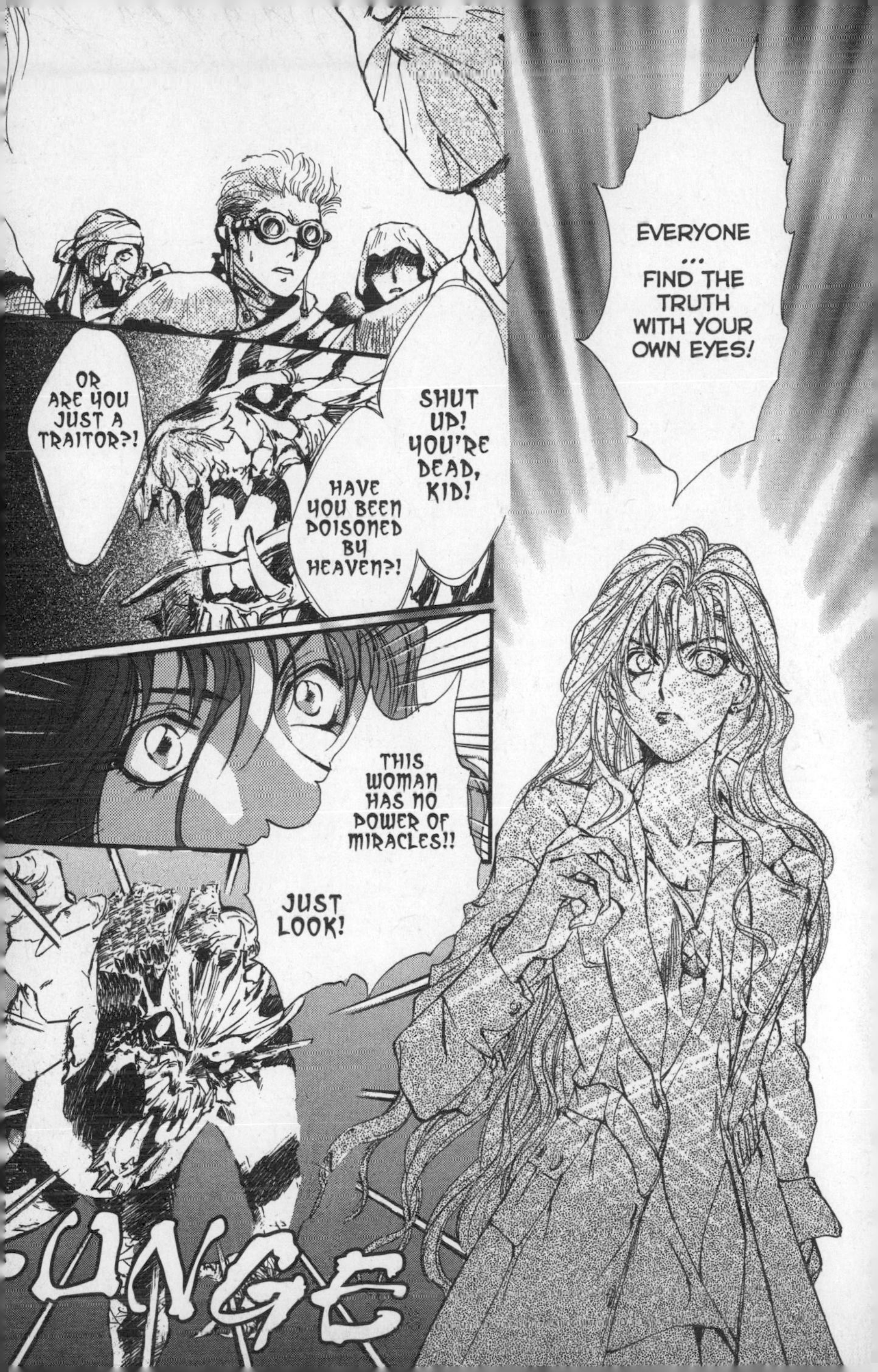
EVERYONE ... FIND THE TRUTH WITH YOUR OWN EYES!
SHUT UP! YOU'RE DEAD, KID!
HAVE YOU BEEN POISONED BY HEAVEN?!
OR ARE YOU JUST A TRAITOR?!
THIS WOMAN HAS NO POWER OF MIRACLES!!
JUST LOOK!
UNGE

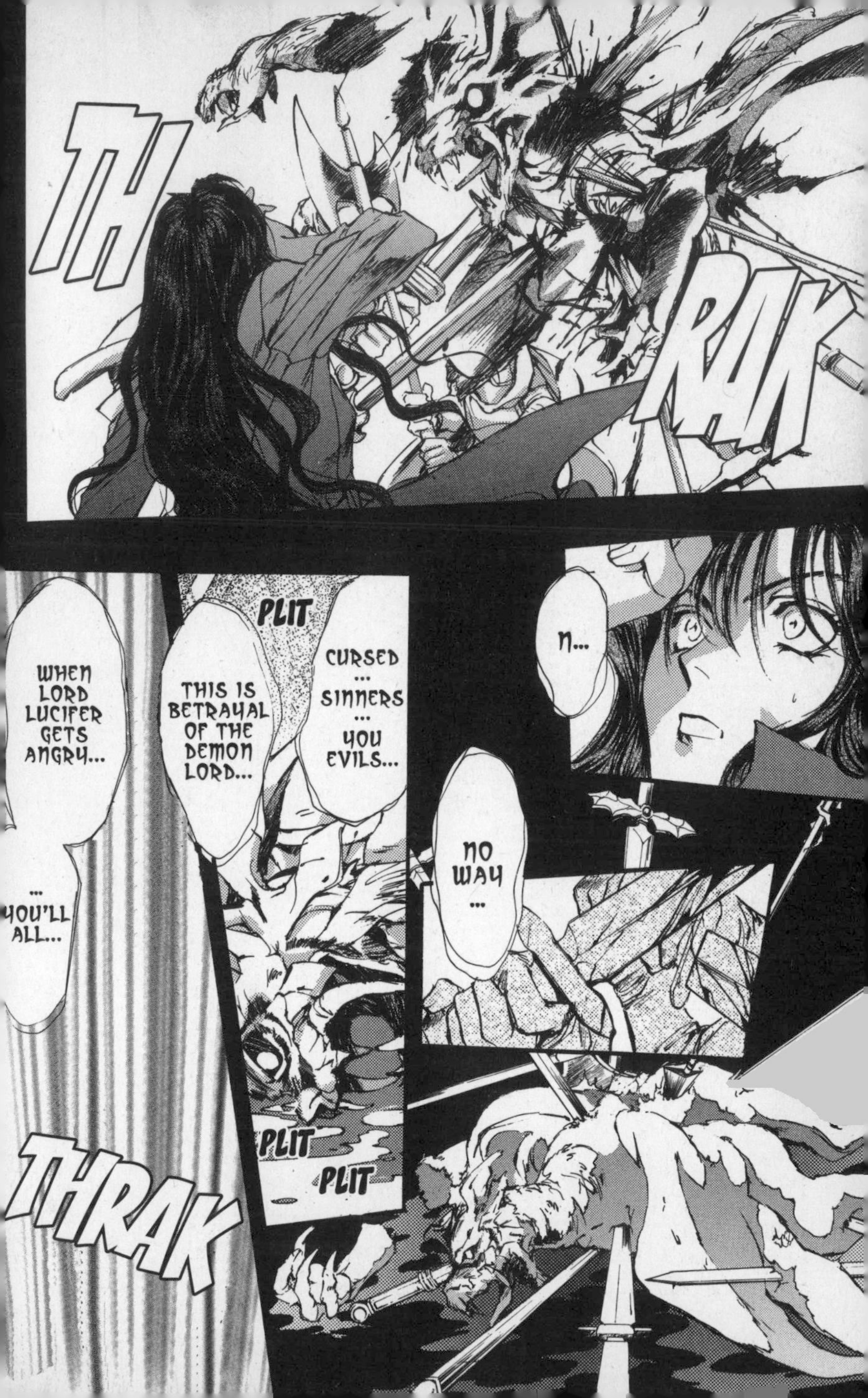
TH
RAK
n...
NO WAY ...
PLIT
CURSED ... SINNERS ... YOU EVILS...
THIS IS BETRAYAL OF THE DEMON LORD...
PLIT
PLIT
WHEN LORD LUCIFER GETS ANGRY...
... YOU'LL ALL...
THRAK

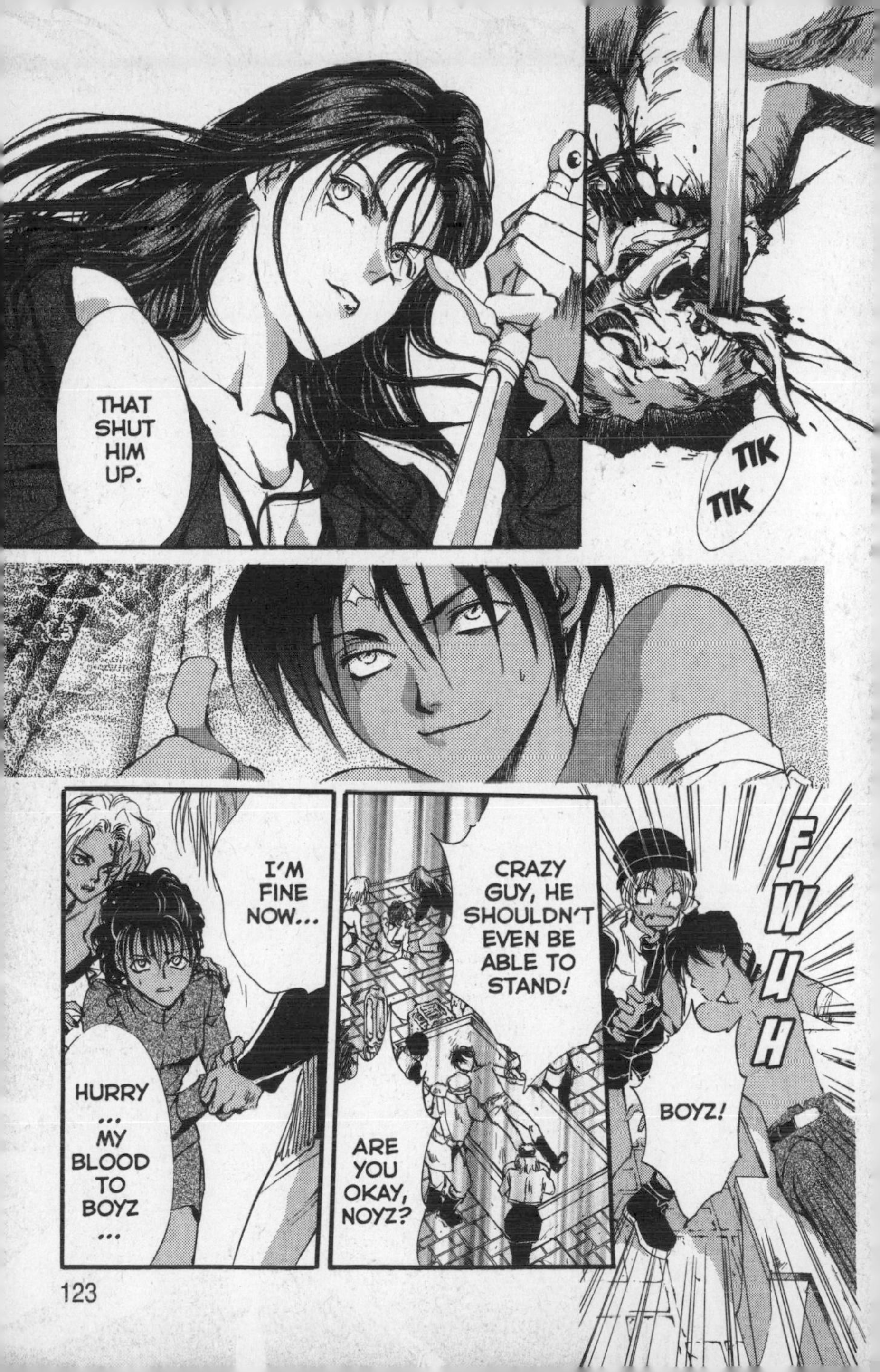
TIK TIK
THAT SHUT HIM UP.
FWUHH
BOYZ!
CRAZY GUY, HE SHOULDN'T EVEN BE ABLE TO STAND!
ARE YOU OKAY, NOYZ?
I'M FINE NOW...
HURRY ... MY BLOOD TO BOYZ ...

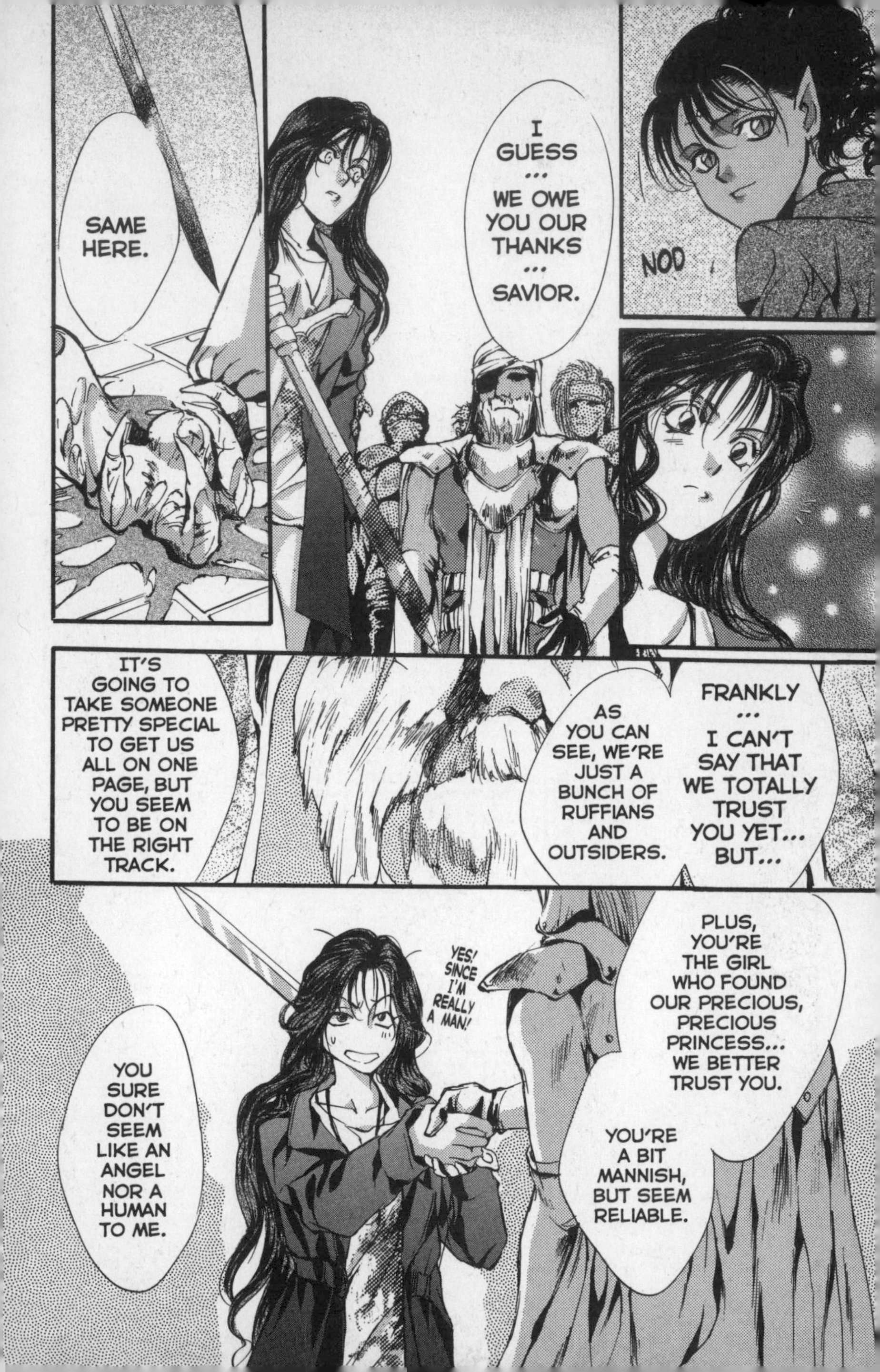
NOD
I GUESS ... WE OWE YOU OUR THANKS ... SAVIOR.
SAME HERE.
FRANKLY ... I CAN'T SAY THAT WE TOTALLY TRUST YOU YET... BUT...
AS YOU CAN SEE, WE'RE JUST A BUNCH OF RUFFIANS AND OUTSIDERS.
IT'S GOING TO TAKE SOMEONE PRETTY SPECIAL TO GET US ALL ON ONE PAGE, BUT YOU SEEM TO BE ON THE RIGHT TRACK.
PLUS, YOU'RE THE GIRL WHO FOUND OUR PRECIOUS, PRECIOUS PRINCESS... WE BETTER TRUST YOU.
YOU'RE A BIT MANNISH, BUT SEEM RELIABLE.
YES! SINCE I'M REALLY A MAN!
YOU SURE DON'T SEEM LIKE AN ANGEL NOR A HUMAN TO ME.

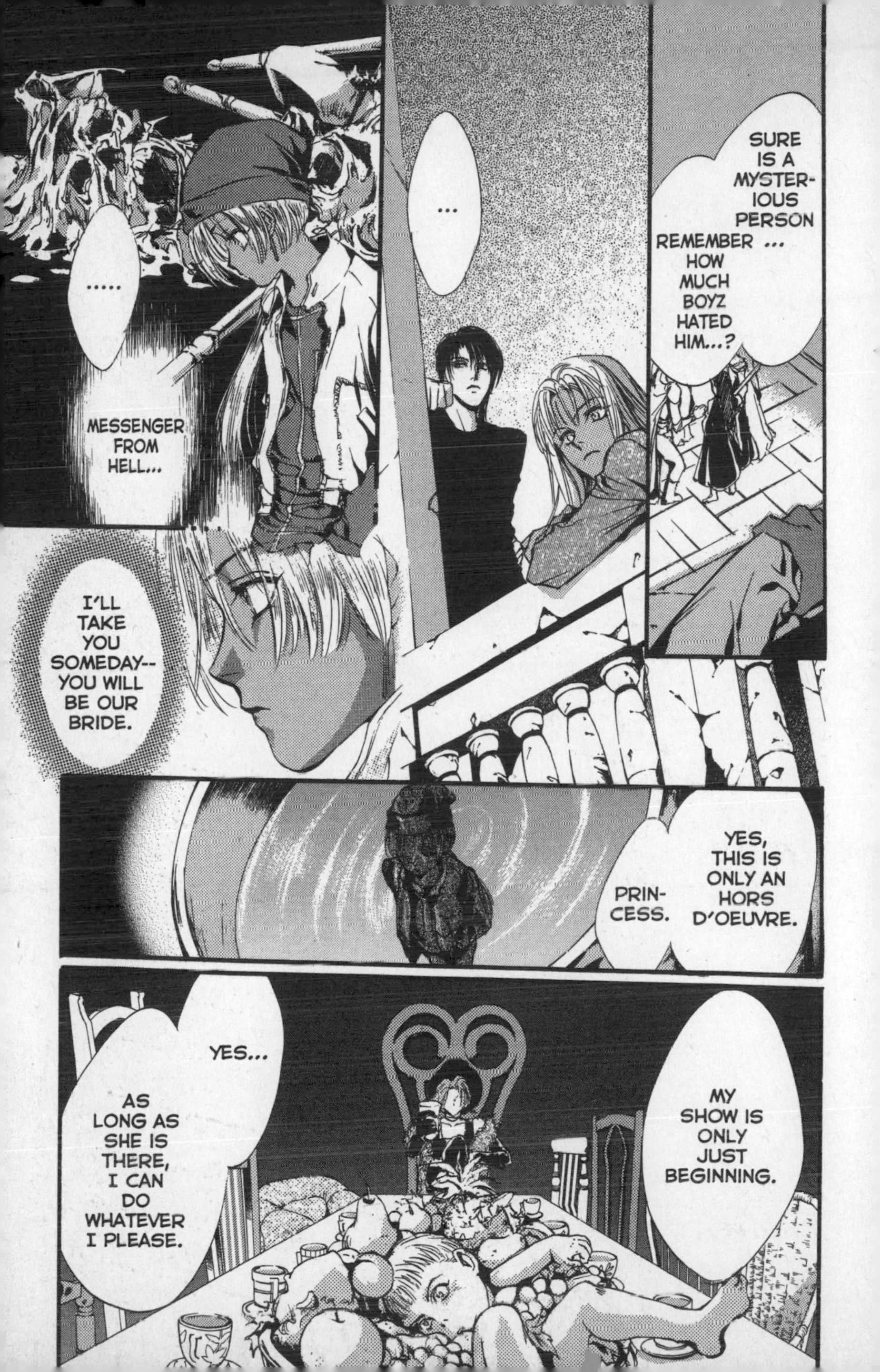
SURE IS A MYSTERIOUS PERSON
REMEMBER ... HOW MUCH BOYZ HATED HIM...?
...
.....
MESSENGER FROM HELL...
I'LL TAKE YOU SOMEDAY-- YOU WILL BE OUR BRIDE.
YES, THIS IS ONLY AN HORS D'OEUVRE.
PRIN-CESS.
MY SHOW IS ONLY JUST BEGINNING.
YES...
AS LONG AS SHE IS THERE, I CAN DO WHATEVER I PLEASE.

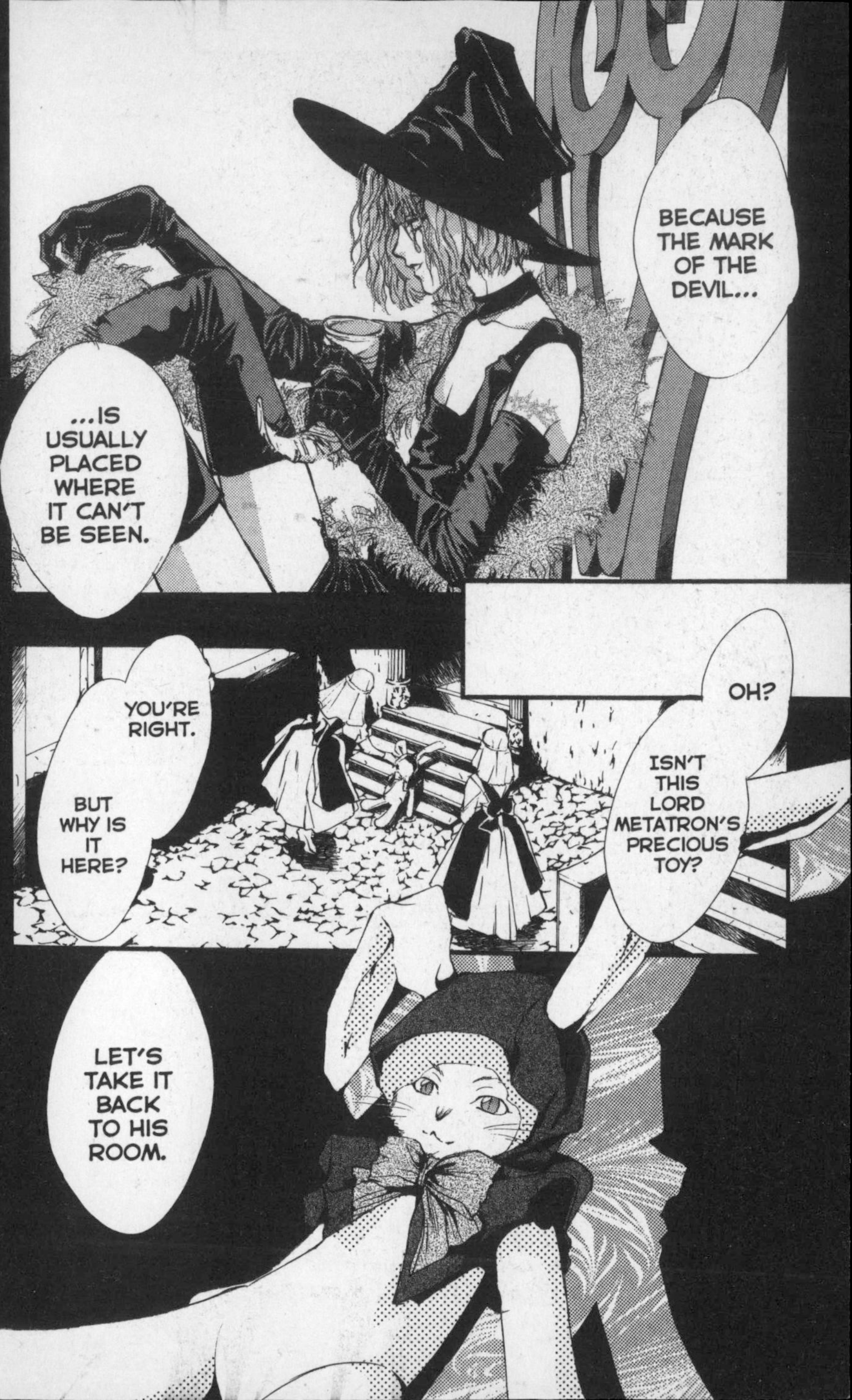
BECAUSE THE MARK OF THE DEVIL...
...IS USUALLY PLACED WHERE IT CAN'T BE SEEN.
OH?
ISN'T THIS LORD METATRON'S PRECIOUS TOY?
YOU'RE RIGHT.
BUT WHY IS IT HERE?
LET'S TAKE IT BACK TO HIS ROOM.

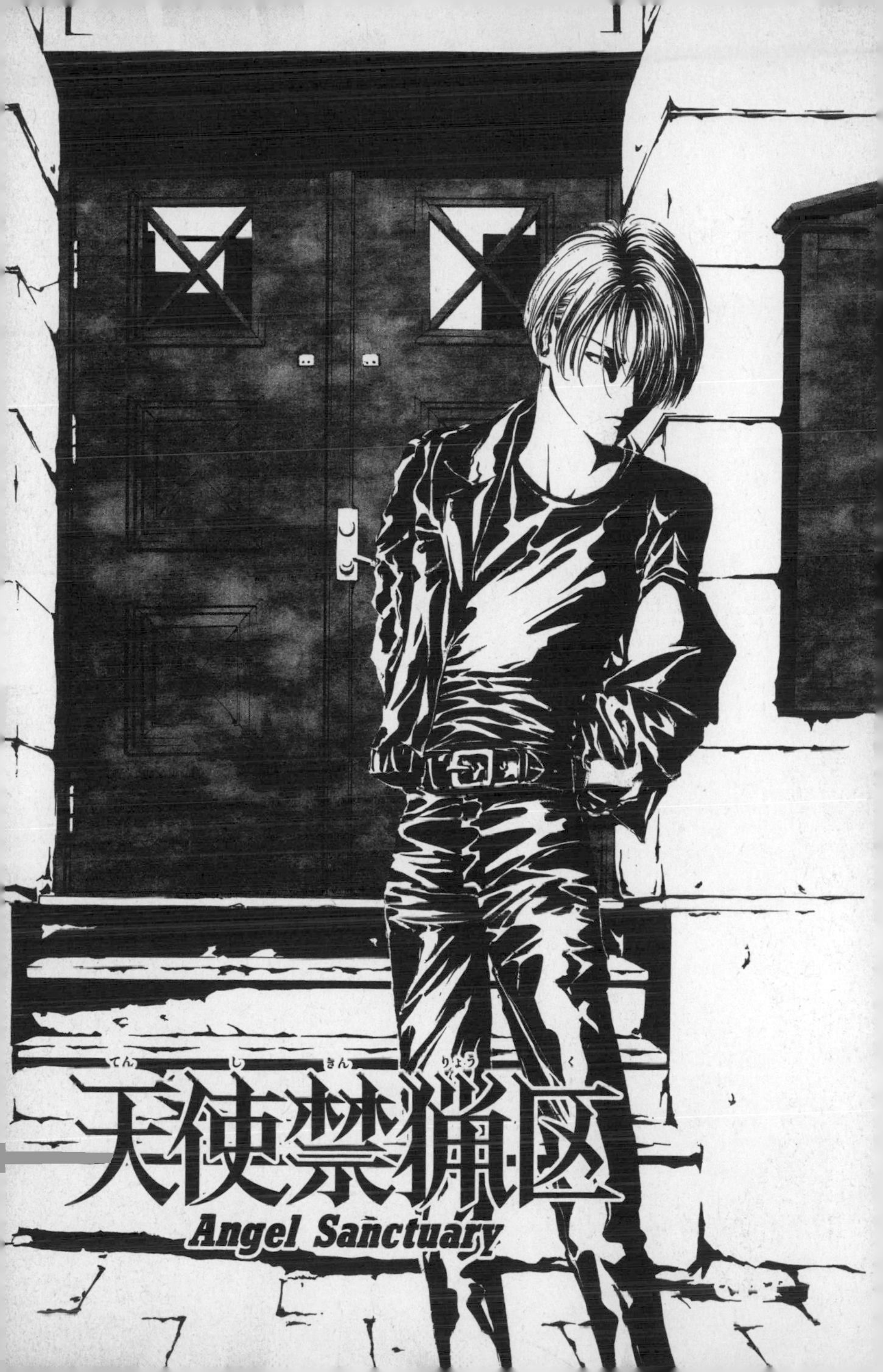
天使禁猟区
Angel Sanctuary

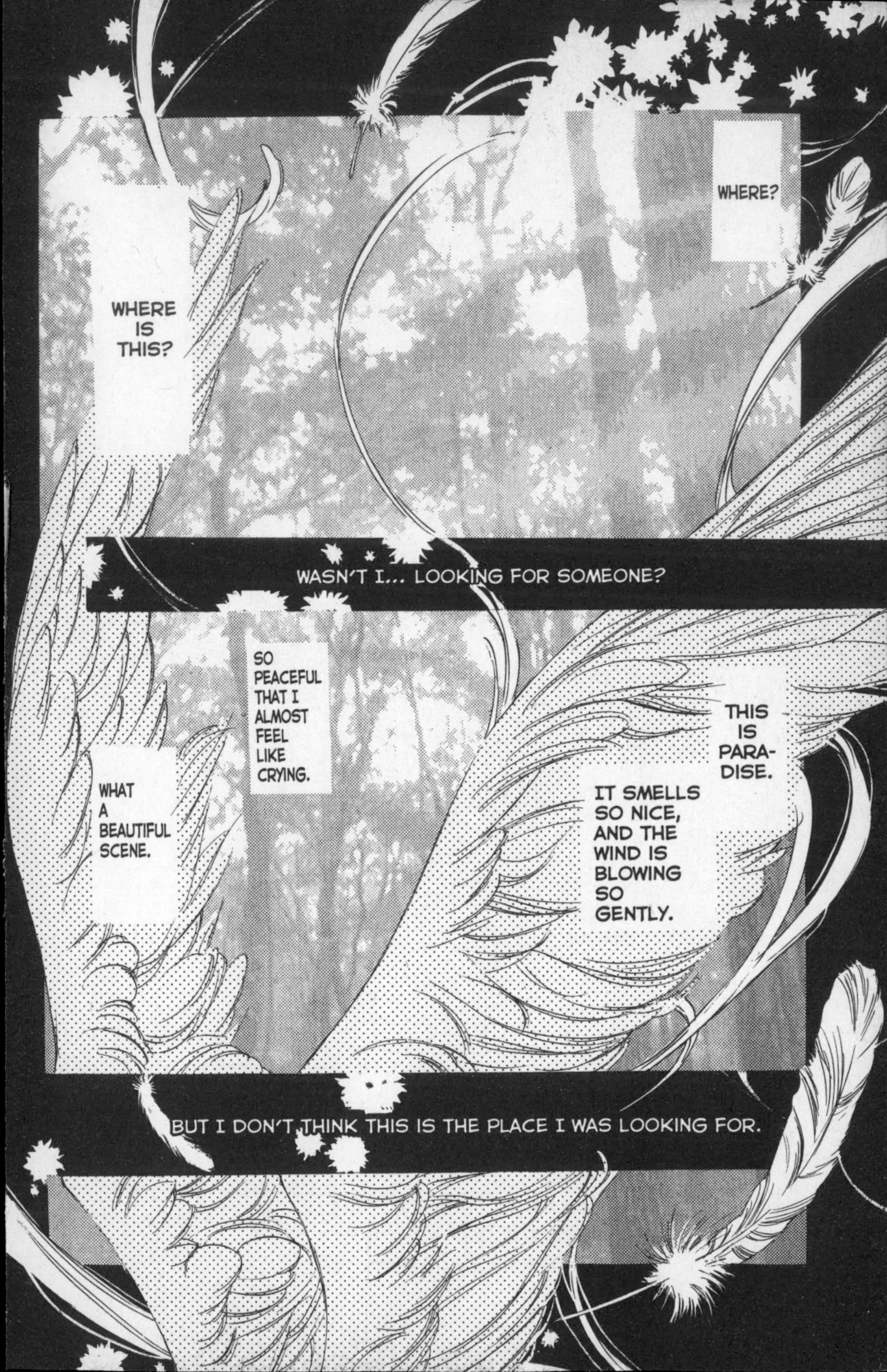
WHERE?
WHERE IS THIS?
WASN'T I... LOOKING FOR SOMEONE?
THIS IS PARA-DISE.
IT SMELLS SO NICE, AND THE WIND IS BLOWING SO GENTLY.
SO PEACEFUL THAT I ALMOST FEEL LIKE CRYING.
WHAT A BEAUTIFUL SCENE.
BUT I DON'T THINK THIS IS THE PLACE I WAS LOOKING FOR.

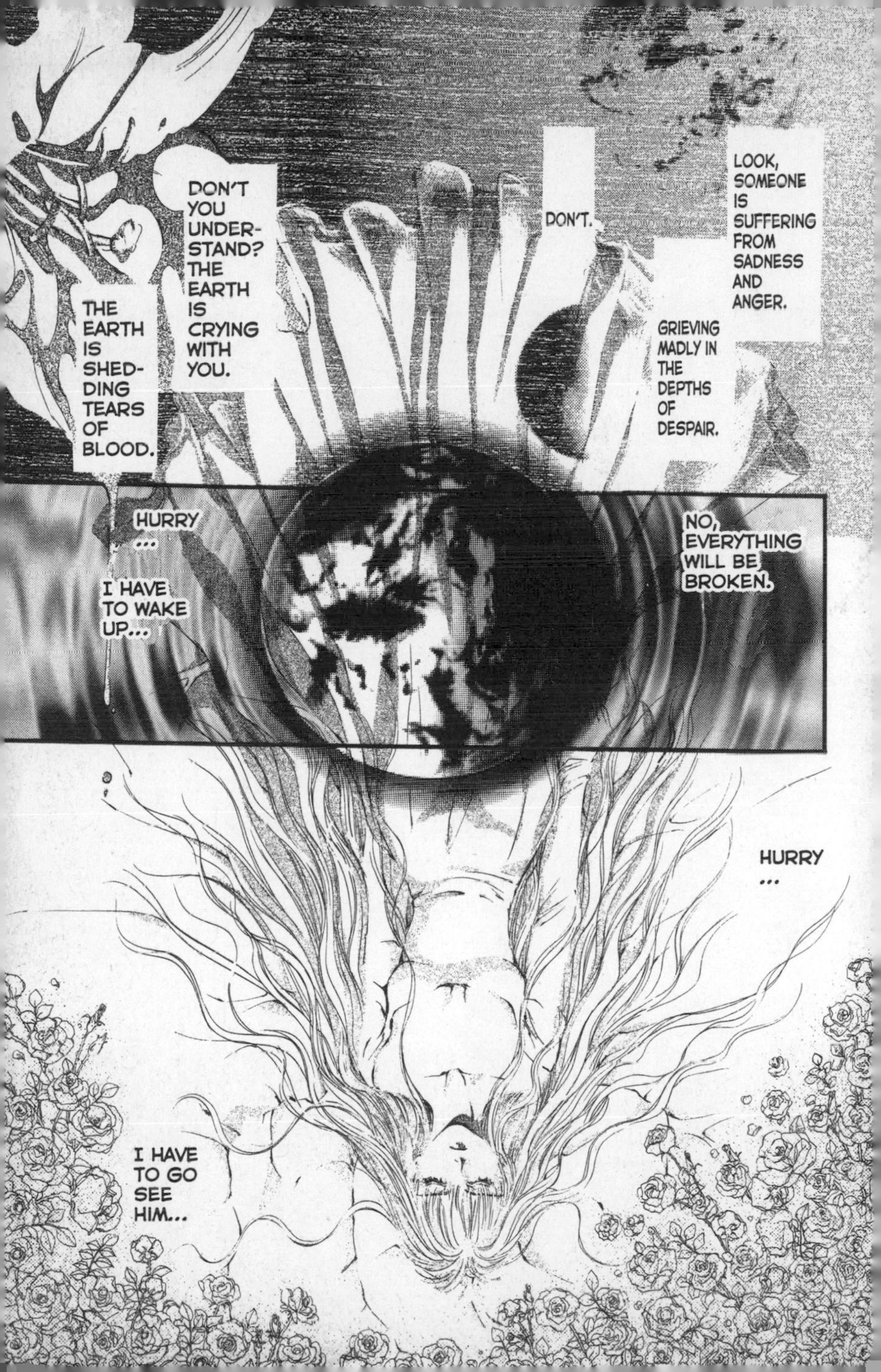
LOOK, SOMEONE IS SUFFERING FROM SADNESS AND ANGER.
GRIEVING MADLY IN THE DEPTHS OF DESPAIR.
DON'T.
DON'T YOU UNDER-STAND? THE EARTH IS CRYING WITH YOU.
THE EARTH IS SHED-DING TEARS OF BLOOD.
NO, EVERYTHING WILL BE BROKEN.
HURRY...
I HAVE TO WAKE UP...
HURRY...
I HAVE TO GO SEE HIM...

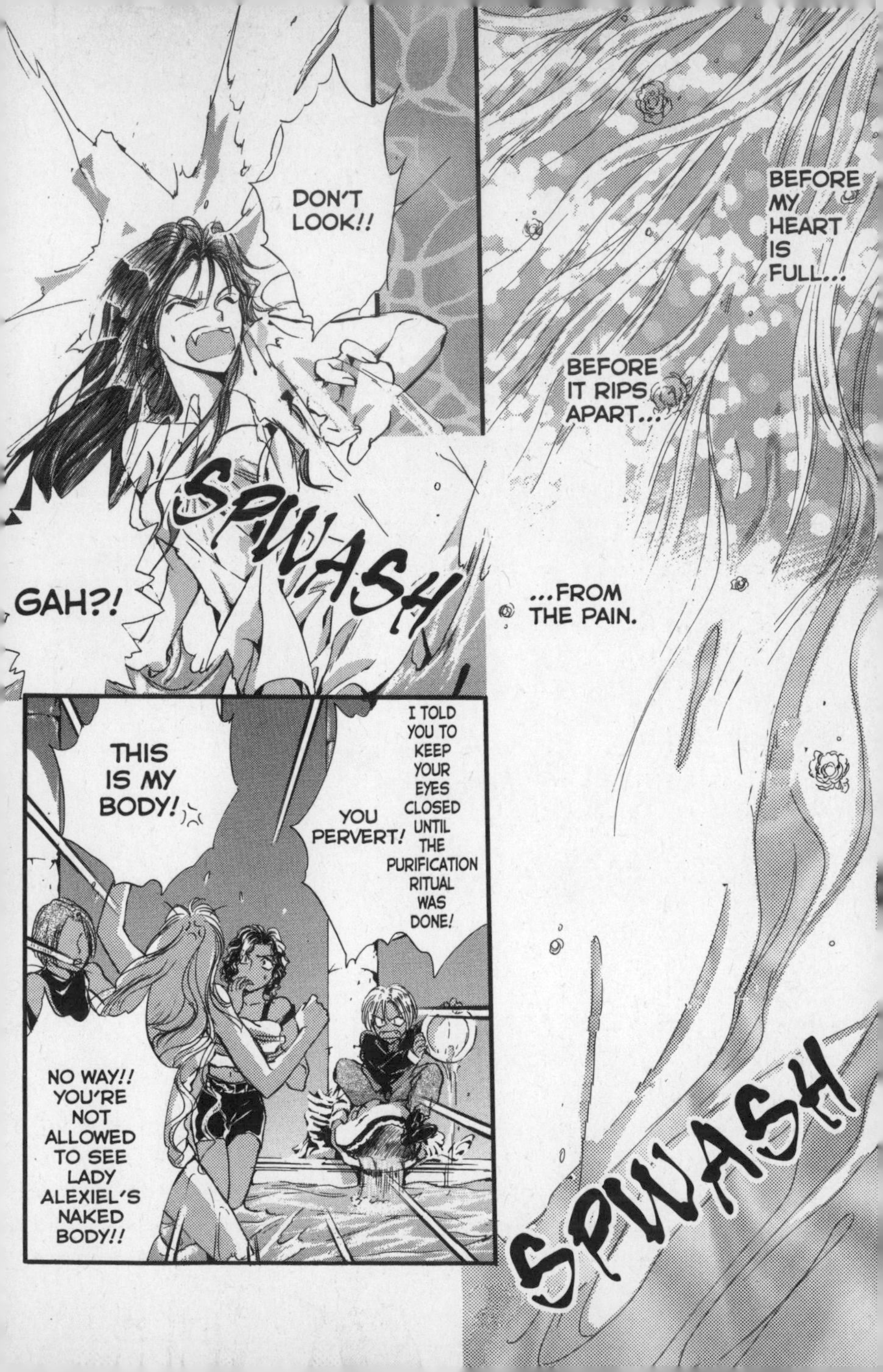
BEFORE MY HEART IS FULL...
BEFORE IT RIPS APART...
...FROM THE PAIN.
SPWASH
DON'T LOOK!!
SPWASH
GAH?!
I TOLD YOU TO KEEP YOUR EYES CLOSED UNTIL THE PURIFICATION RITUAL WAS DONE!
YOU PERVERT!
THIS IS MY BODY!
NO WAY!! YOU'RE NOT ALLOWED TO SEE LADY ALEXIEL'S NAKED BODY!!

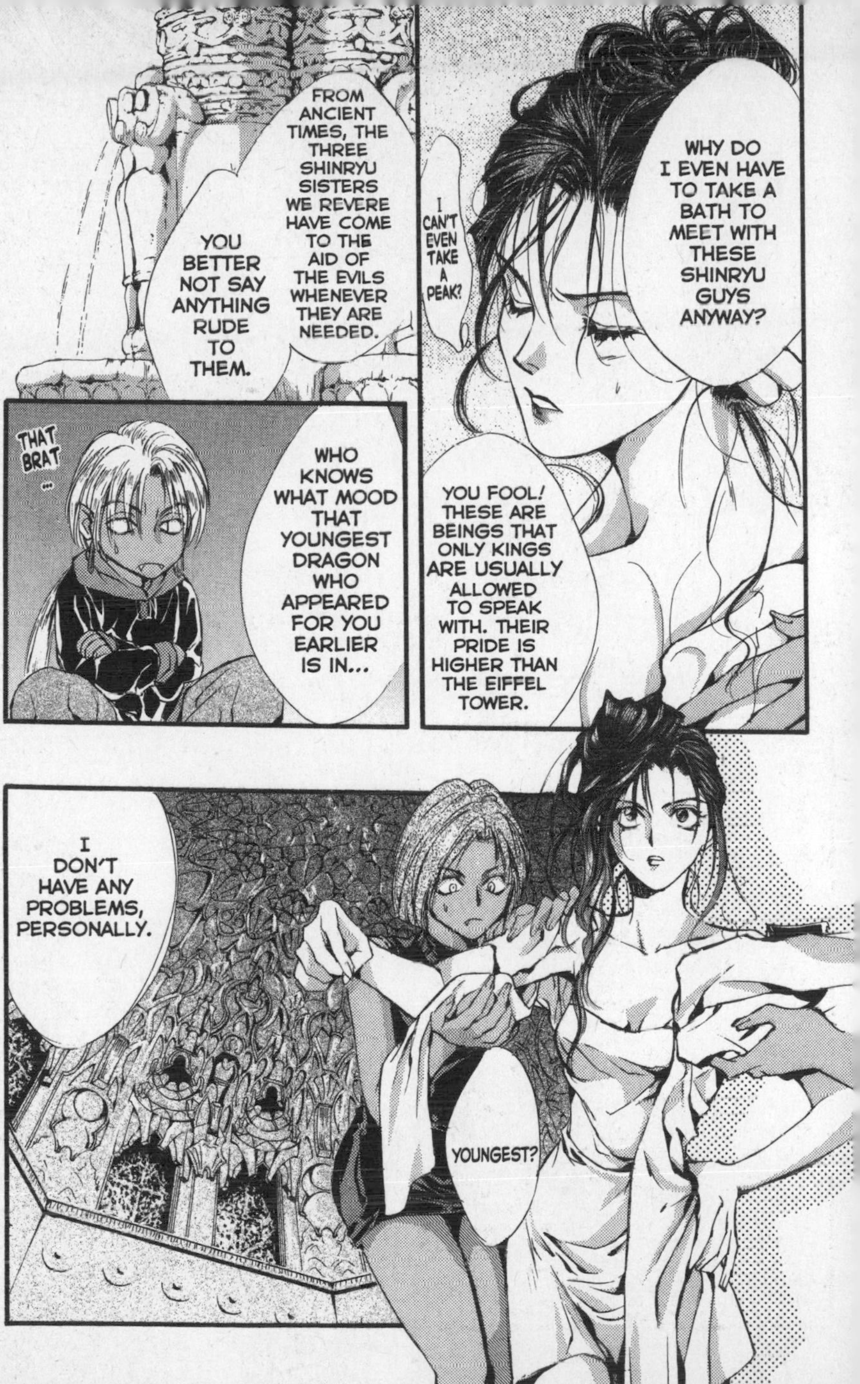
WHY DO I EVEN HAVE TO TAKE A BATH TO MEET WITH THESE SHINRYU GUYS ANYWAY?
I CAN'T EVEN TAKE A PEAK?
YOU FOOL! THESE ARE BEINGS THAT ONLY KINGS ARE USUALLY ALLOWED TO SPEAK WITH. THEIR PRIDE IS HIGHER THAN THE EIFFEL TOWER.
FROM ANCIENT TIMES, THE THREE SHINRYU SISTERS WE REVERE HAVE COME TO THE AID OF THE EVILS WHENEVER THEY ARE NEEDED.
YOU BETTER NOT SAY ANYTHING RUDE TO THEM.
WHO KNOWS WHAT MOOD THAT YOUNGEST DRAGON WHO APPEARED FOR YOU EARLIER IS IN...
THAT BRAT ...
YOUNGEST?
I DON'T HAVE ANY PROBLEMS, PERSONALLY.

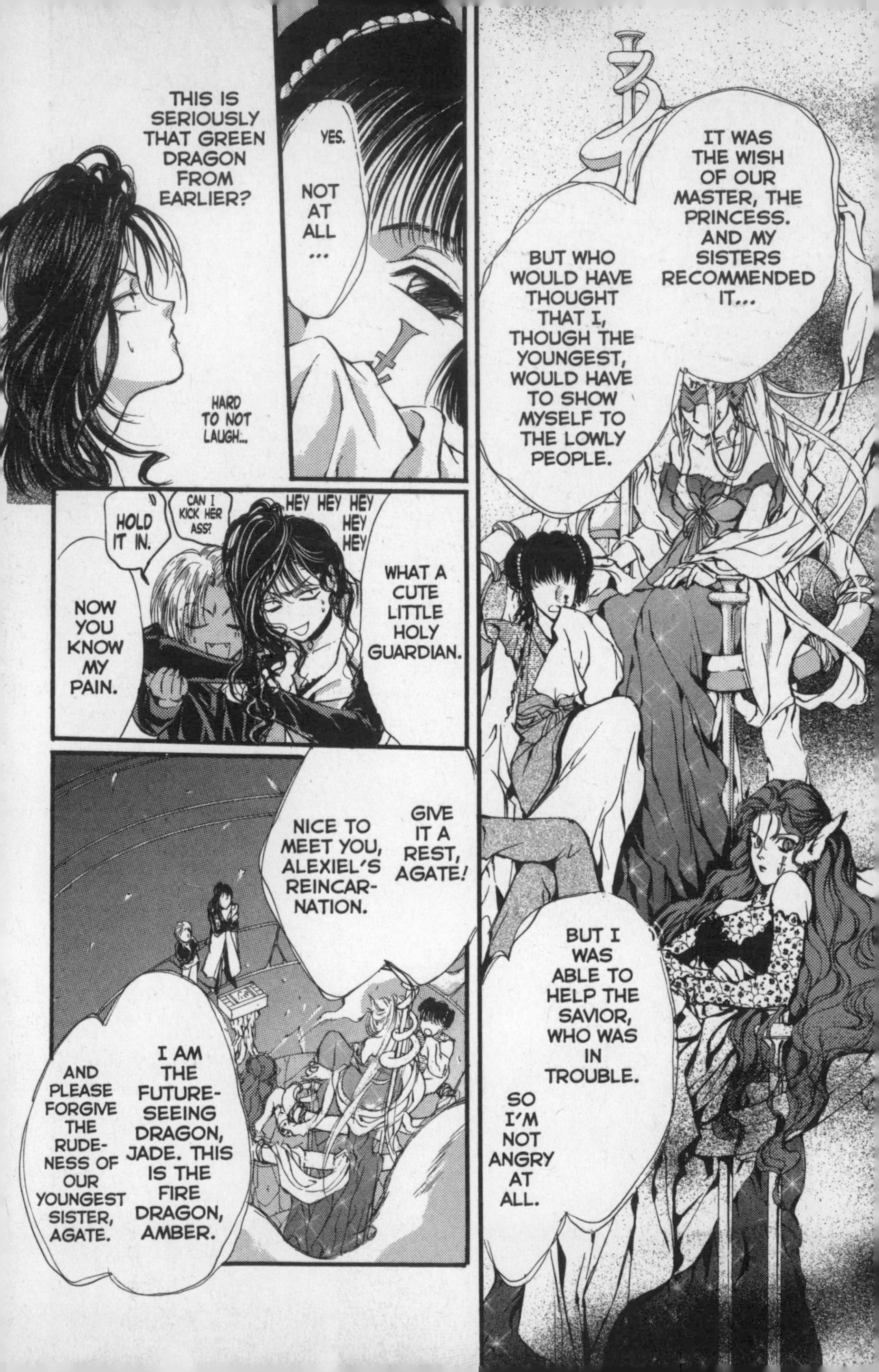
IT WAS THE WISH OF OUR MASTER, THE PRINCESS. AND MY SISTERS RECOMMENDED IT...
BUT WHO WOULD HAVE THOUGHT THAT I, THOUGH THE YOUNGEST, WOULD HAVE TO SHOW MYSELF TO THE LOWLY PEOPLE.
BUT I WAS ABLE TO HELP THE SAVIOR, WHO WAS IN TROUBLE.
SO I'M NOT ANGRY AT ALL.
YES.
NOT AT ALL ...
THIS IS SERIOUSLY THAT GREEN DRAGON FROM EARLIER?
HARD TO NOT LAUGH...
HEY HEY HEY HEY HEY
WHAT A CUTE LITTLE HOLY GUARDIAN.
CAN I KICK HER ASS?
HOLD IT IN.
NOW YOU KNOW MY PAIN.
GIVE IT A REST, AGATE!
NICE TO MEET YOU, ALEXIEL'S REINCARNATION.
I AM THE FUTURE-SEEING DRAGON, JADE. THIS IS THE FIRE DRAGON, AMBER.
AND PLEASE FORGIVE THE RUDENESS OF OUR YOUNGEST SISTER, AGATE.

Yay... Hatter showed up a lot in this chapter, so I enjoyed drawing it (just those parts). Well, he's just really easy to draw. Plus, he's kind of sexy. So the one acting as Alexiel's stylist is probably Arachne. If Setsuna was in charge, it would probably be no bra and a t-shirt. Kurai's probably really strict and makes sure Alexiel's hair is taken care of. I bet Setsuna is really annoyed with all those servant girls. You think he peeked at his new naked body at least once? I'm not sure I want to think about that... yeah...

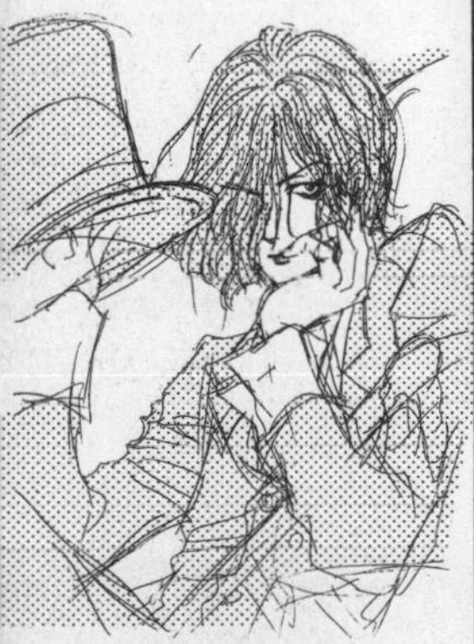

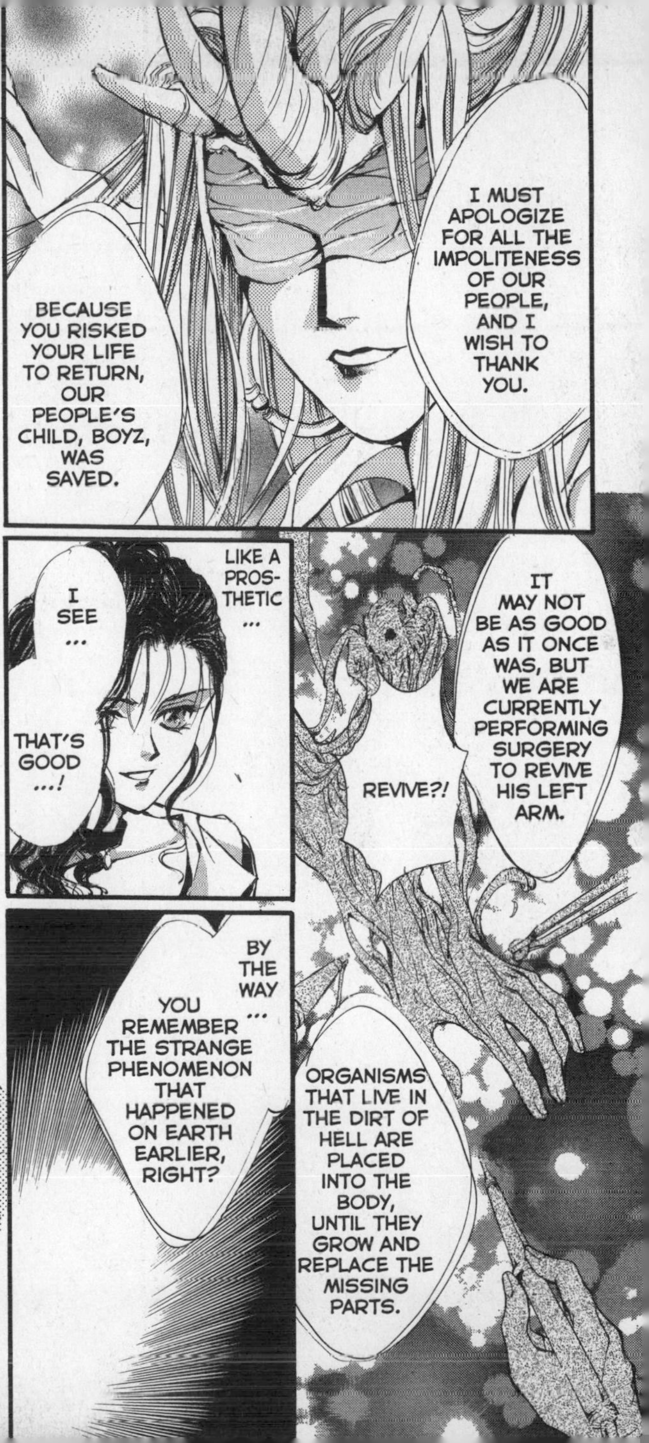
I MUST APOLOGIZE FOR ALL THE IMPOLITENESS OF OUR PEOPLE, AND I WISH TO THANK YOU.
BECAUSE YOU RISKED YOUR LIFE TO RETURN, OUR PEOPLE'S CHILD, BOYZ, WAS SAVED.
IT MAY NOT BE AS GOOD AS IT ONCE WAS, BUT WE ARE CURRENTLY PERFORMING SURGERY TO REVIVE HIS LEFT ARM.
REVIVE?!
LIKE A PROS-THETIC ...
I SEE ...
THAT'S GOOD ...!
ORGANISMS THAT LIVE IN THE DIRT OF HELL ARE PLACED INTO THE BODY, UNTIL THEY GROW AND REPLACE THE MISSING PARTS.
BY THE WAY ...
YOU REMEMBER THE STRANGE PHENOMENON THAT HAPPENED ON EARTH EARLIER, RIGHT?

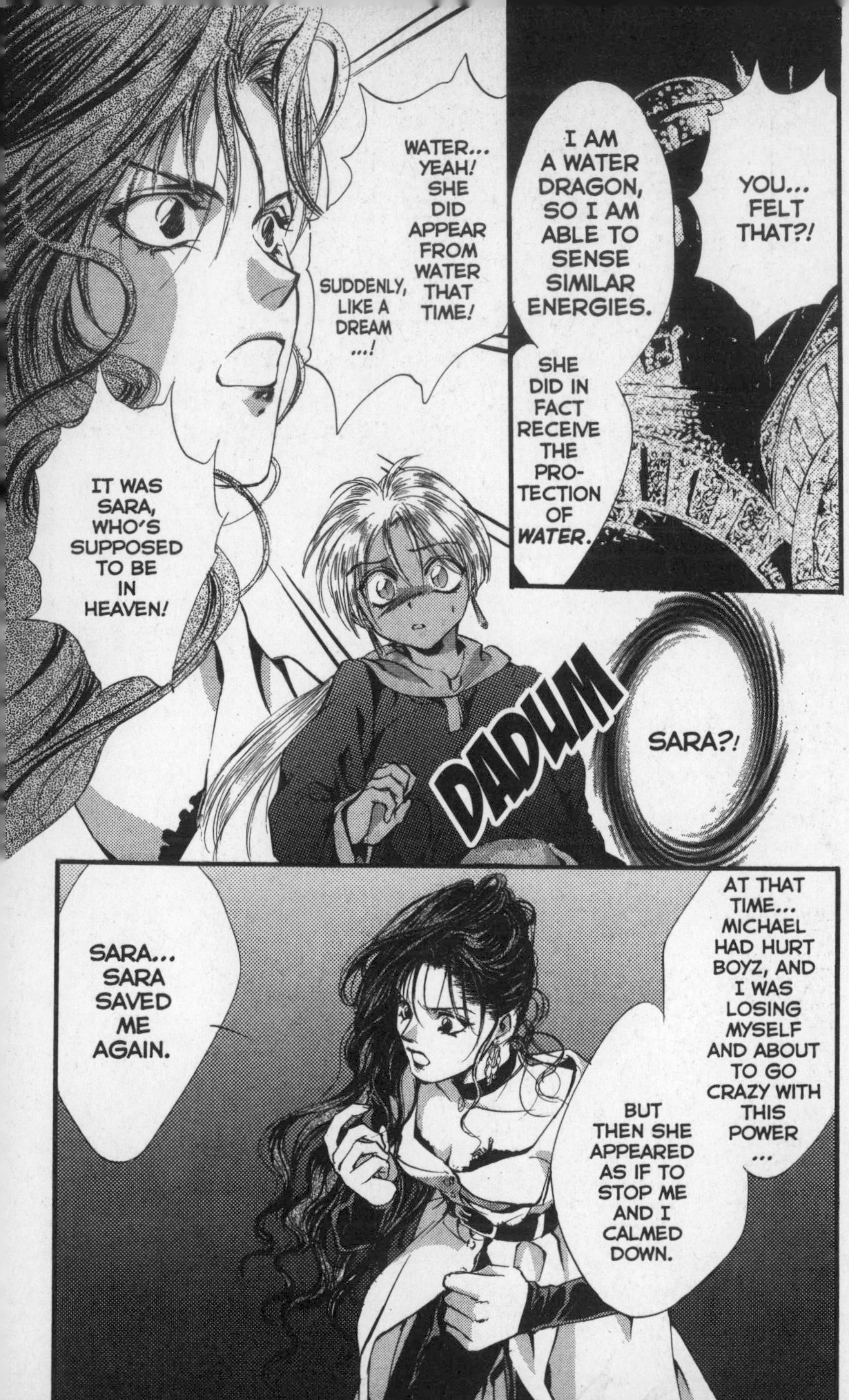
YOU... FELT THAT?!
I AM A WATER DRAGON, SO I AM ABLE TO SENSE SIMILAR ENERGIES.
SHE DID IN FACT RECEIVE THE PROTECTION OF WATER.
WATER... YEAH! SHE DID APPEAR FROM WATER THAT TIME!
SUDDENLY, LIKE A DREAM ...!
IT WAS SARA, WHO'S SUPPOSED TO BE IN HEAVEN!
DADUM
SARA?!
AT THAT TIME... MICHAEL HAD HURT BOYZ, AND I WAS LOSING MYSELF AND ABOUT TO GO CRAZY WITH THIS POWER ...
BUT THEN SHE APPEARED AS IF TO STOP ME AND I CALMED DOWN.
SARA... SARA SAVED ME AGAIN.

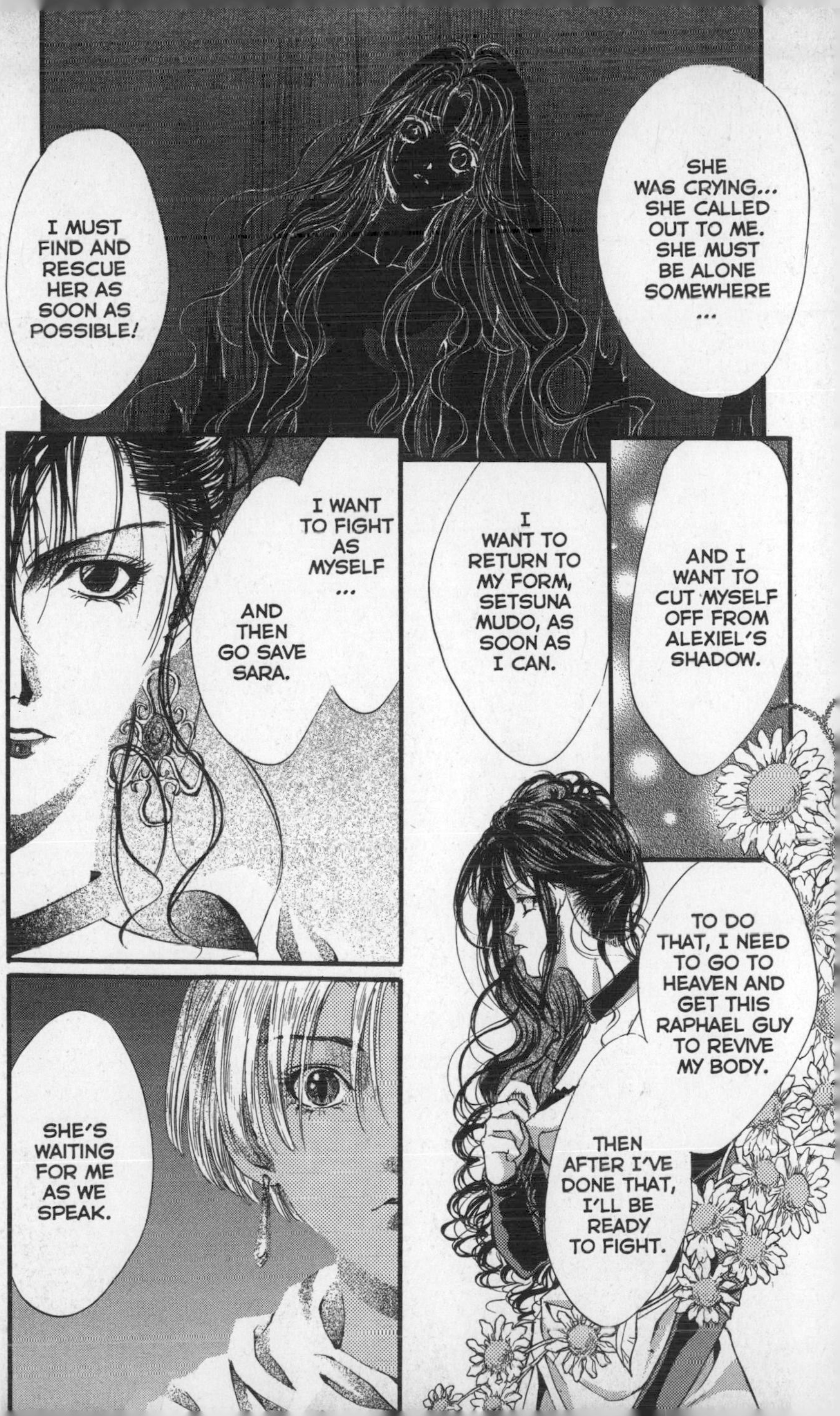
SHE WAS CRYING... SHE CALLED OUT TO ME. SHE MUST BE ALONE SOMEWHERE ...
I MUST FIND AND RESCUE HER AS SOON AS POSSIBLE!
AND I WANT TO CUT MYSELF OFF FROM ALEXIEL'S SHADOW.
I WANT TO RETURN TO MY FORM, SETSUNA MUDO, AS SOON AS I CAN.
I WANT TO FIGHT AS MYSELF ...
AND THEN GO SAVE SARA.
TO DO THAT, I NEED TO GO TO HEAVEN AND GET THIS RAPHAEL GUY TO REVIVE MY BODY.
THEN AFTER I'VE DONE THAT, I'LL BE READY TO FIGHT.
SHE'S WAITING FOR ME AS WE SPEAK.

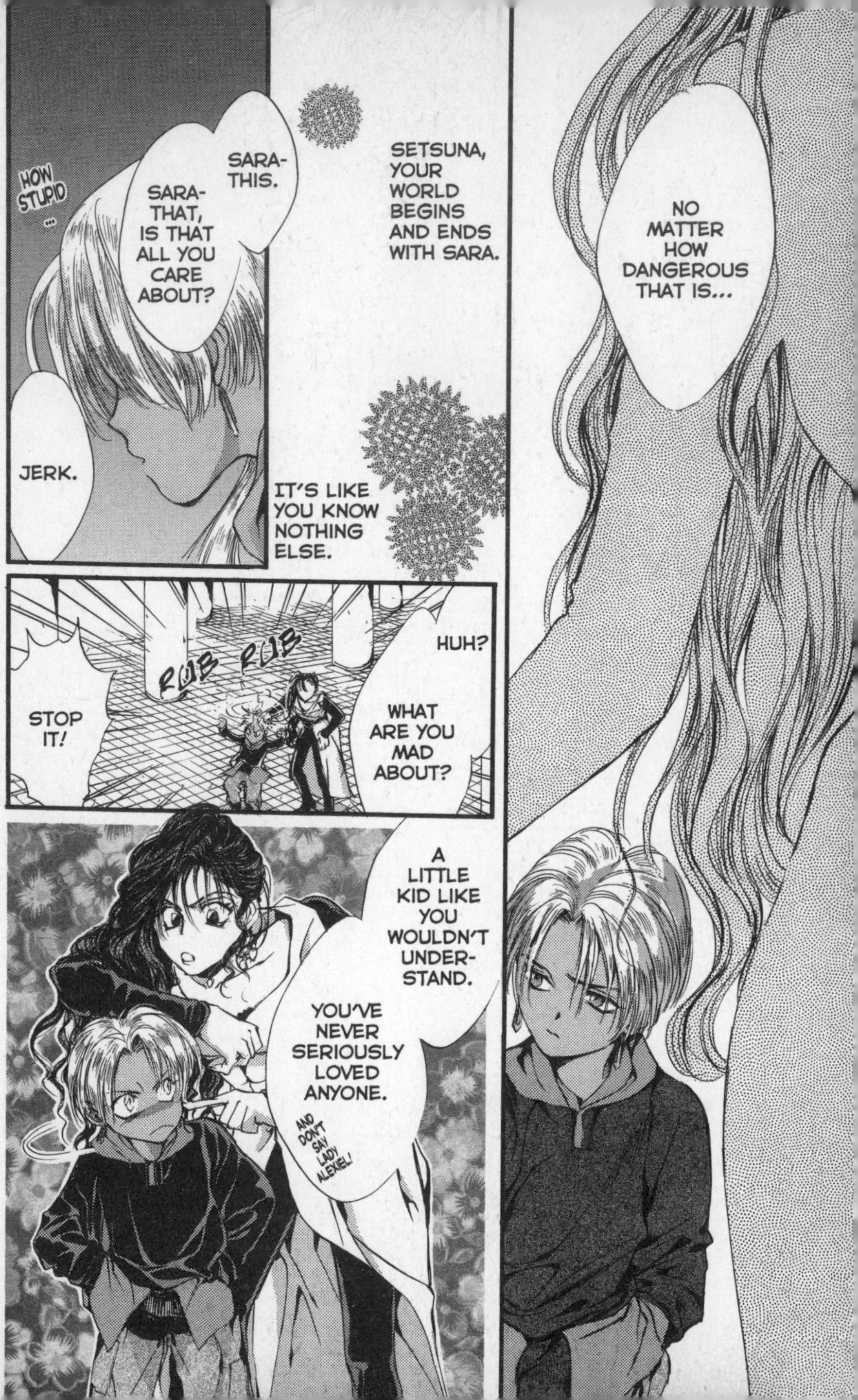
NO MATTER HOW DANGEROUS THAT IS...
SETSUNA, YOUR WORLD BEGINS AND ENDS WITH SARA.
SARA-THIS.
SARA-THAT, IS THAT ALL YOU CARE ABOUT?
HOW STUPID ...
JERK.
IT'S LIKE YOU KNOW NOTHING ELSE.
HUH?
RUB RUB
STOP IT!
WHAT ARE YOU MAD ABOUT?
A LITTLE KID LIKE YOU WOULDN'T UNDER-STAND.
YOU'VE NEVER SERIOUSLY LOVED ANYONE.
AND DON'T SAY LADY ALEXIEL!

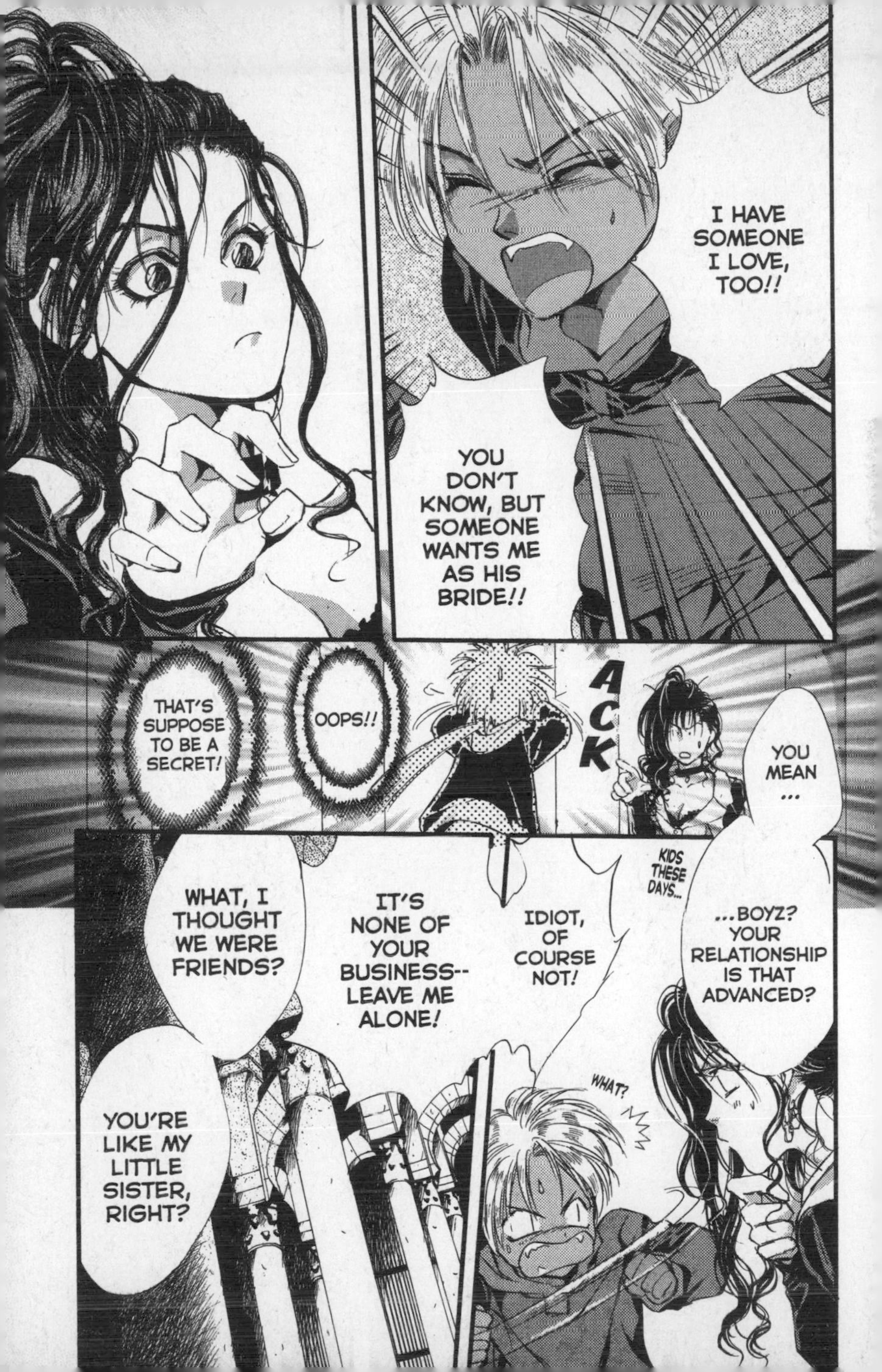
I HAVE SOMEONE I LOVE, TOO!!
YOU DON'T KNOW, BUT SOMEONE WANTS ME AS HIS BRIDE!!
YOU MEAN ...
ACK
OOPS!!
THAT'S SUPPOSE TO BE A SECRET!
...BOYZ? YOUR RELATIONSHIP IS THAT ADVANCED?
KIDS THESE DAYS...
IDIOT, OF COURSE NOT!
WHAT?
IT'S NONE OF YOUR BUSINESS-- LEAVE ME ALONE!
WHAT, I THOUGHT WE WERE FRIENDS?
YOU'RE LIKE MY LITTLE SISTER, RIGHT?

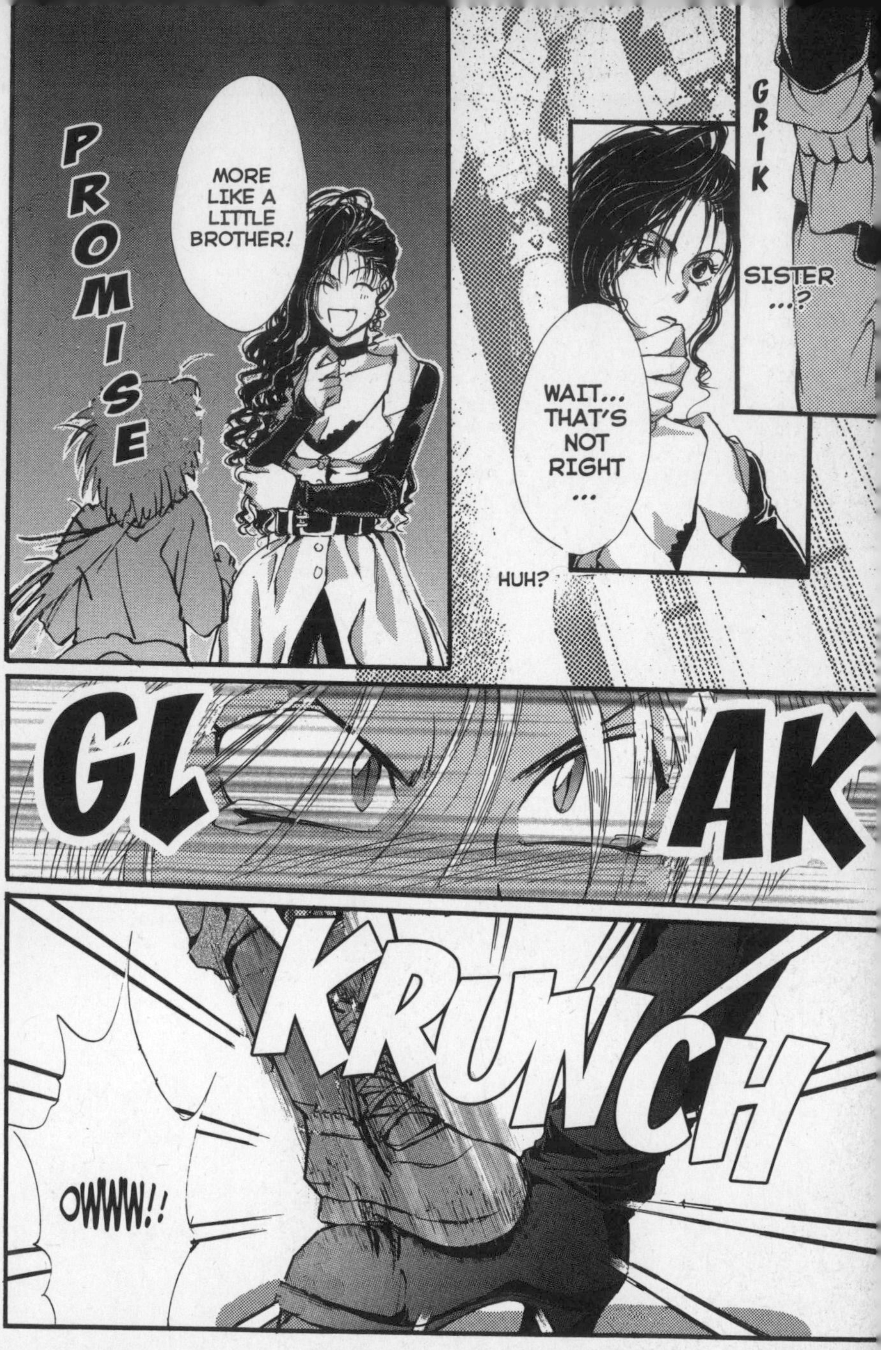
GRIK
SISTER ...?
WAIT... THAT'S NOT RIGHT ...
HUH?
MORE LIKE A LITTLE BROTHER!
PROMISE
GL AK
KRUNCH
OWWW!!

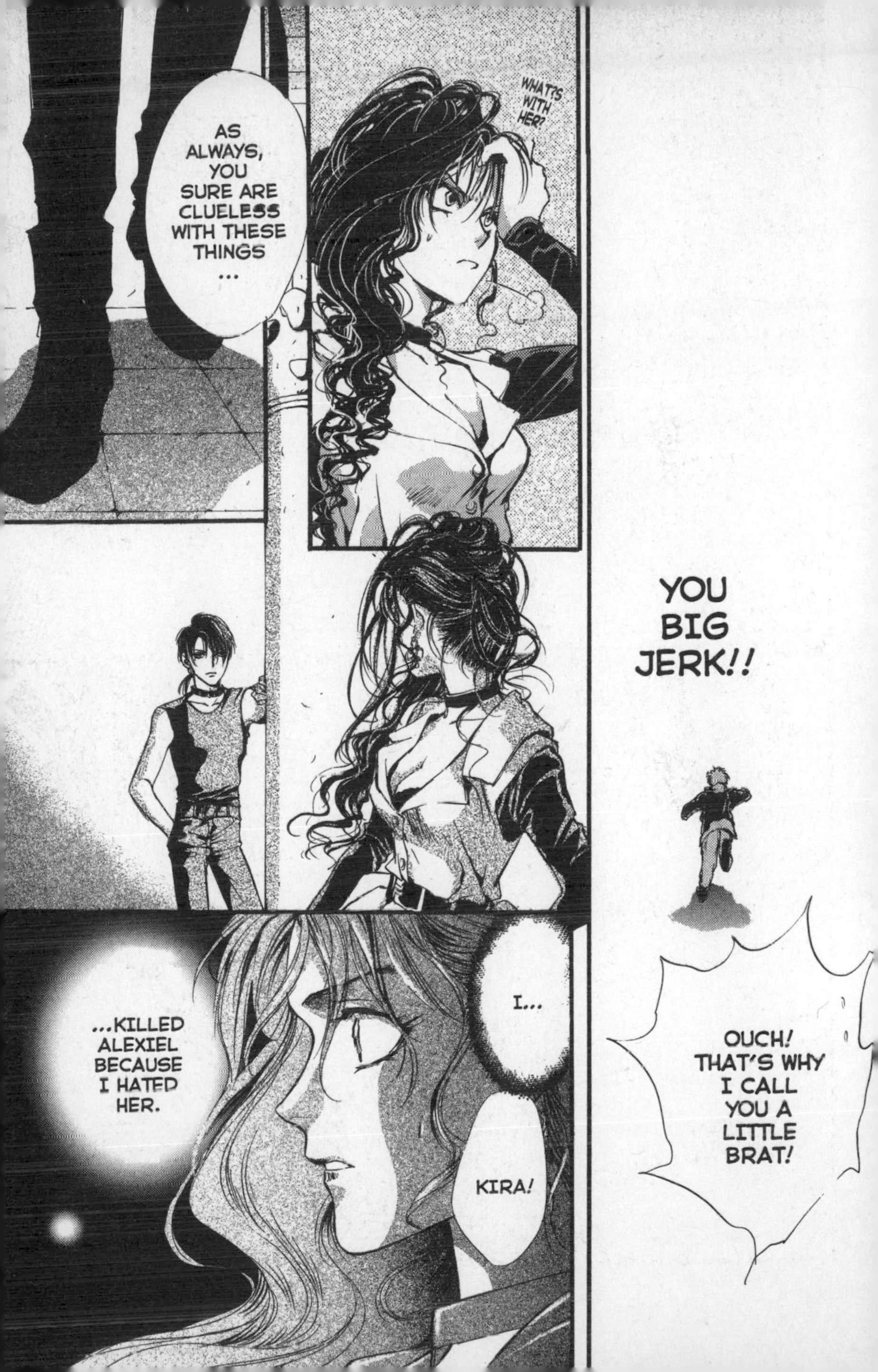
YOU BIG JERK!!
OUCH! THAT'S WHY I CALL YOU A LITTLE BRAT!
WHAT?S WITH HER?
AS ALWAYS, YOU SURE ARE CLUELESS WITH THESE THINGS ...
I...
KIRA!
...KILLED ALEXIEL BECAUSE I HATED HER.

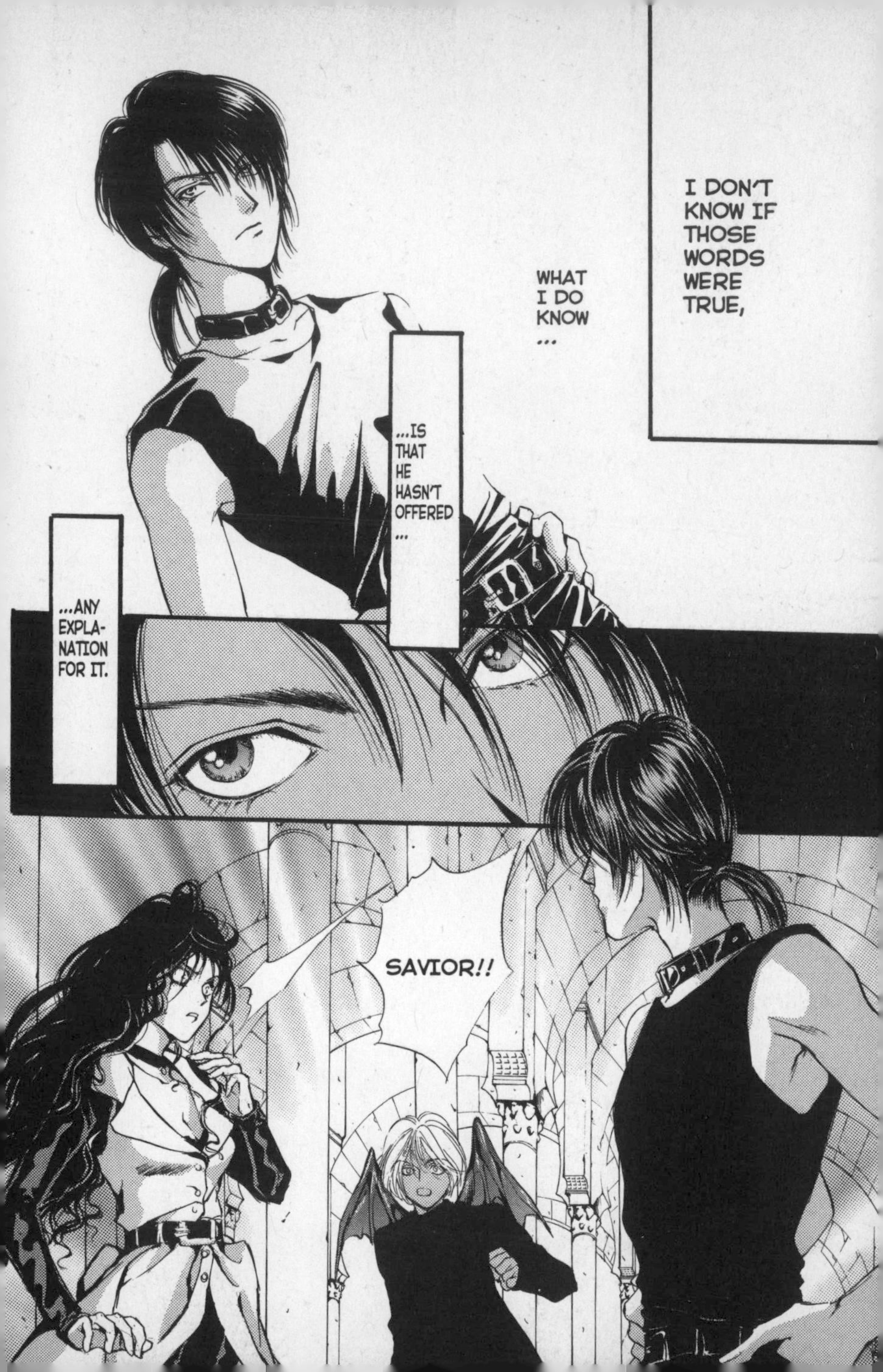
I DON'T KNOW IF THOSE WORDS WERE TRUE,
WHAT I DO KNOW ...
...IS THAT HE HASN'T OFFERED ...
...ANY EXPLA-NATION FOR IT.
SAVIOR!!

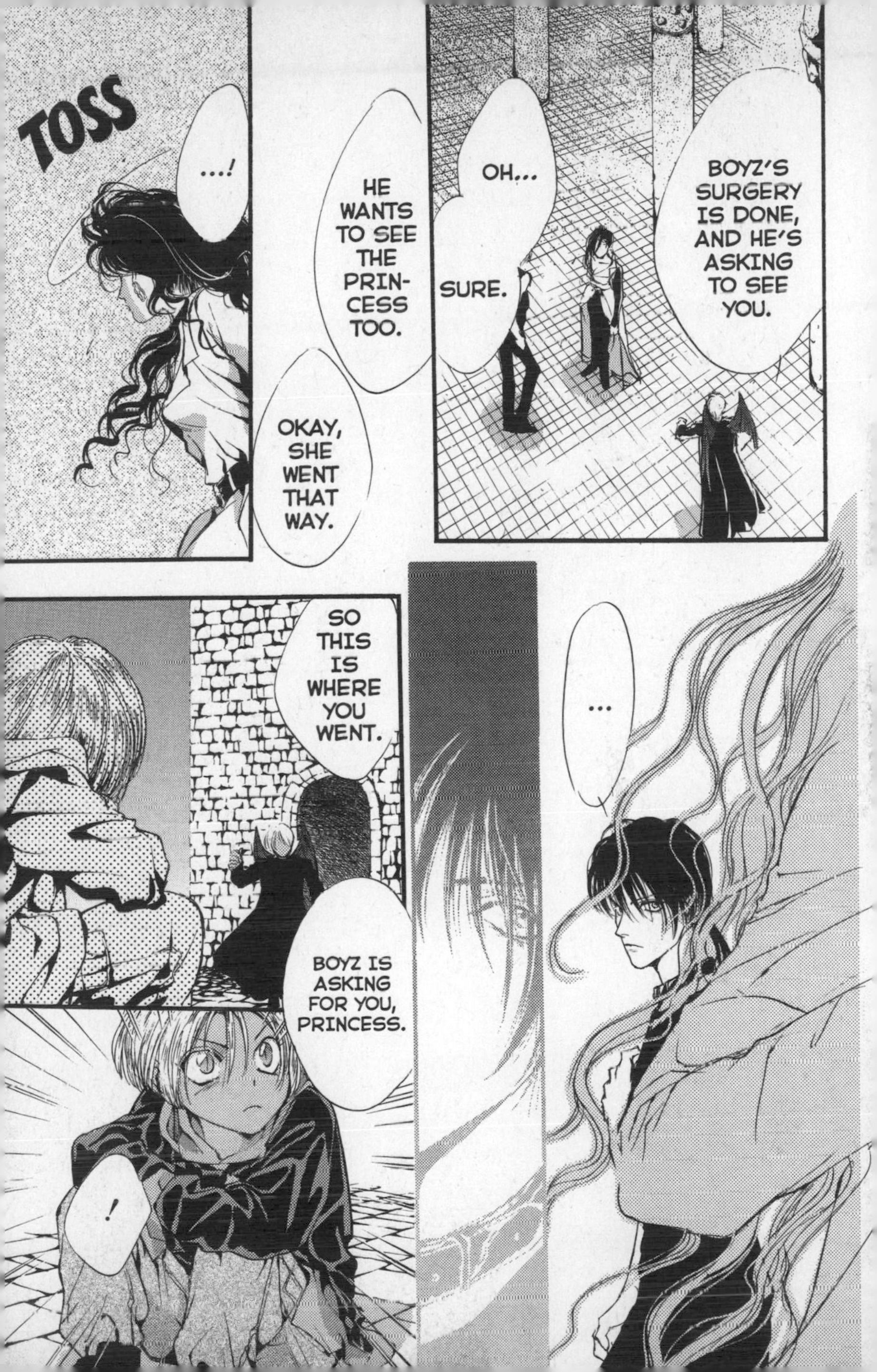
BOYZ'S SURGERY IS DONE, AND HE'S ASKING TO SEE YOU.
OH...
SURE.
HE WANTS TO SEE THE PRIN-CESS TOO.
OKAY, SHE WENT THAT WAY.
TOSS
...!
...
SO THIS IS WHERE YOU WENT.
BOYZ IS ASKING FOR YOU, PRINCESS.
!

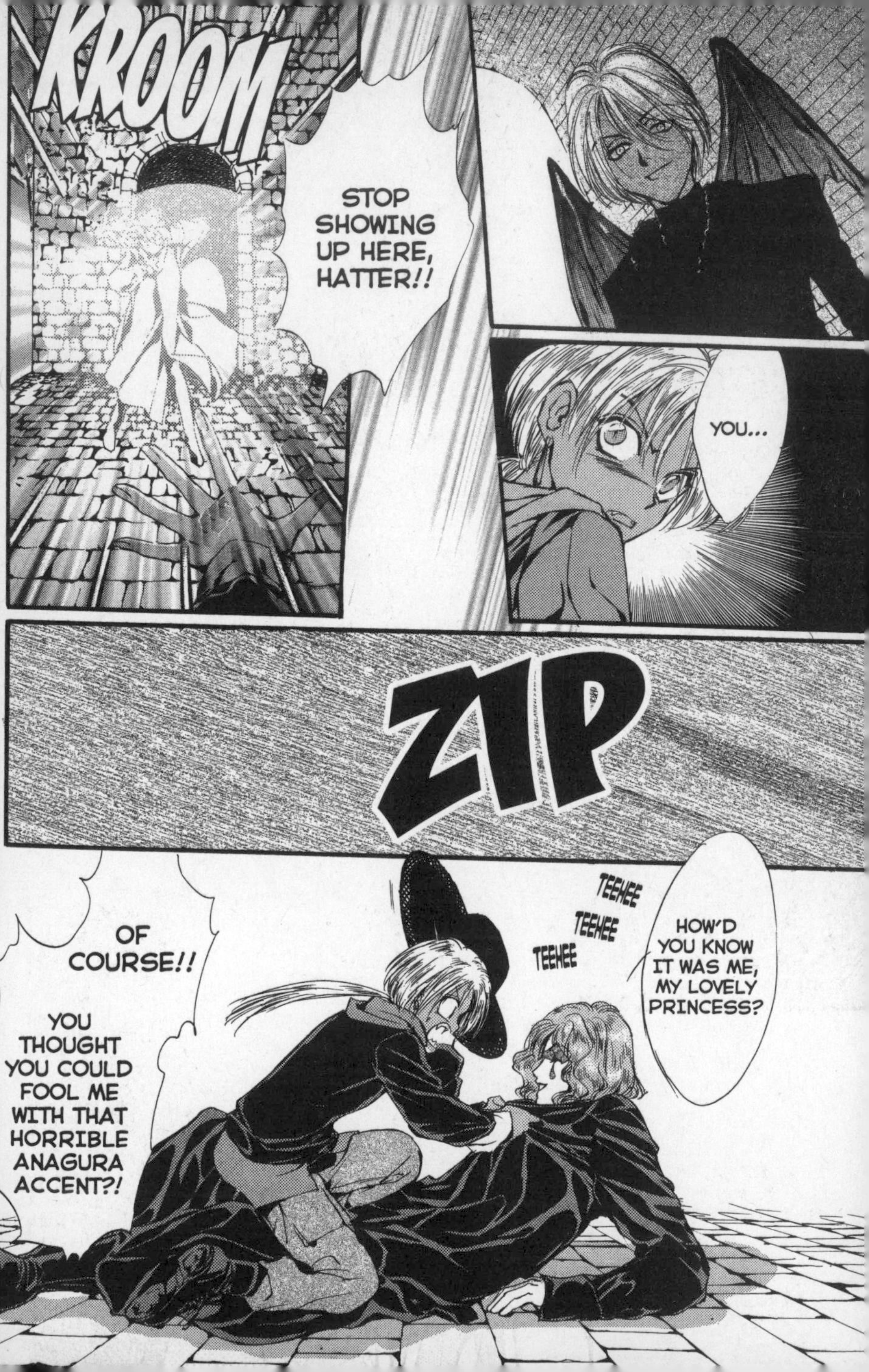

YOU...
KROOM
STOP SHOWING UP HERE, HATTER!!
ZIP
TEEHEE
TEEHEE
TEEHEE
HOW'D YOU KNOW IT WAS ME, MY LOVELY PRINCESS?
OF COURSE!!
YOU THOUGHT YOU COULD FOOL ME WITH THAT HORRIBLE ANAGURA ACCENT?!

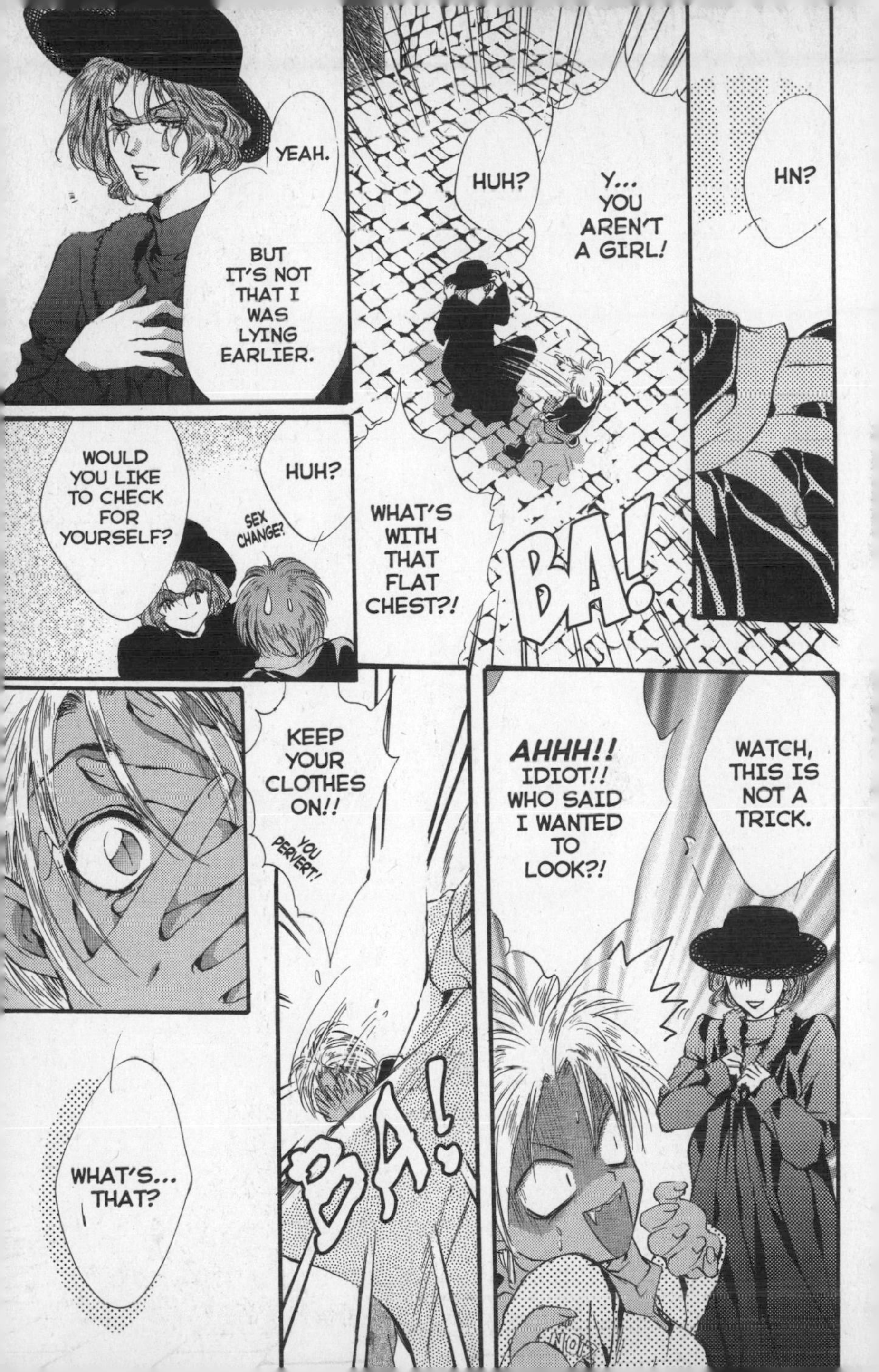
HN?
Y... YOU AREN'T A GIRL!
HUH?
BA!
WHAT'S WITH THAT FLAT CHEST?!
YEAH.
BUT IT'S NOT THAT I WAS LYING EARLIER.
HUH?
SEX CHANGE?
WOULD YOU LIKE TO CHECK FOR YOURSELF?
WATCH, THIS IS NOT A TRICK.
AHHH!! IDIOT!! WHO SAID I WANTED TO LOOK?!
KEEP YOUR CLOTHES ON!!
YOU PERVERT!
BA!
WHAT'S... THAT?

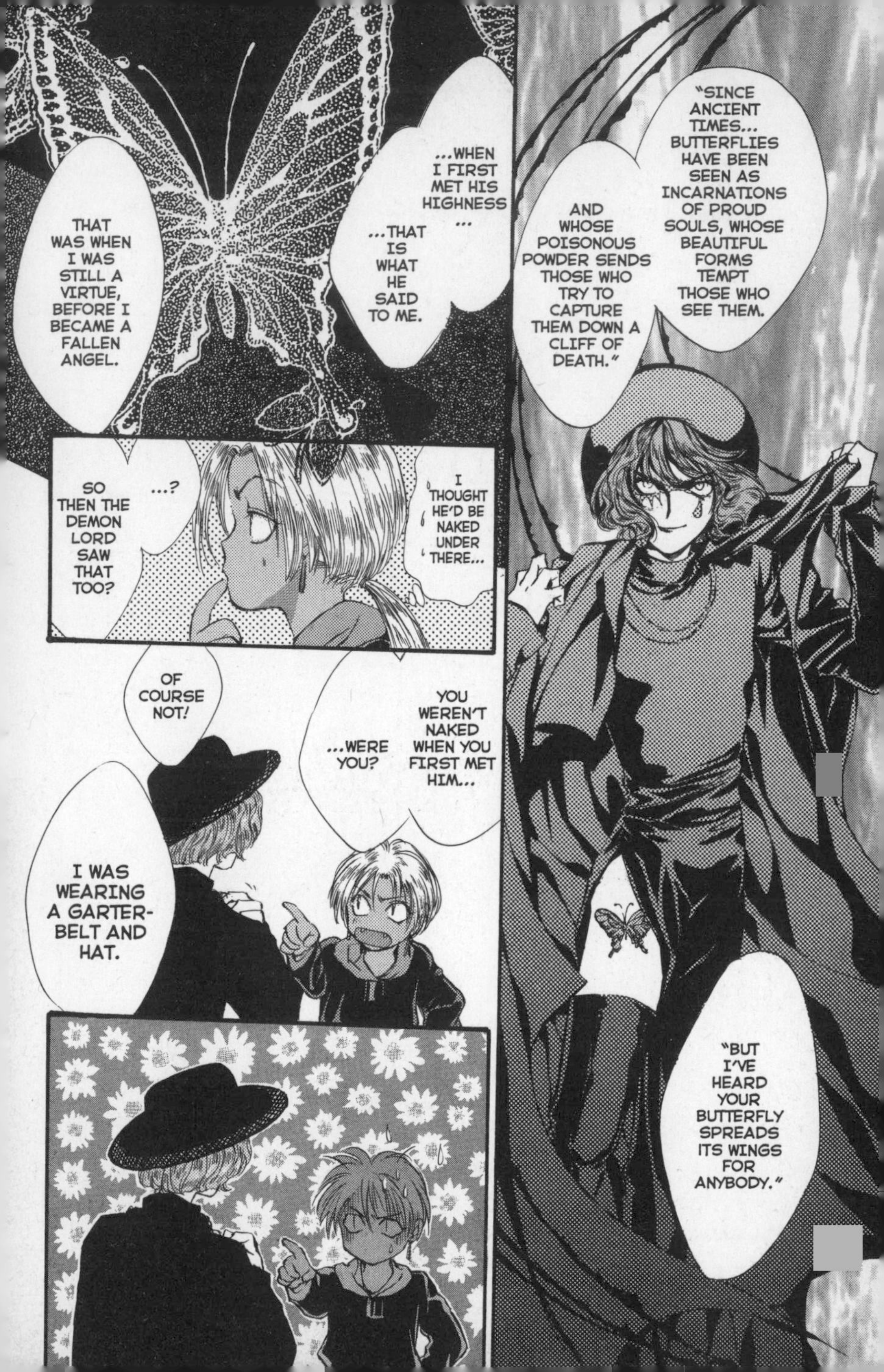
"SINCE ANCIENT TIMES... BUTTERFLIES HAVE BEEN SEEN AS INCARNATIONS OF PROUD SOULS, WHOSE BEAUTIFUL FORMS TEMPT THOSE WHO SEE THEM.
AND WHOSE POISONOUS POWDER SENDS THOSE WHO TRY TO CAPTURE THEM DOWN A CLIFF OF DEATH."
"BUT I'VE HEARD YOUR BUTTERFLY SPREADS ITS WINGS FOR ANYBODY."
...WHEN I FIRST MET HIS HIGHNESS...
...THAT IS WHAT HE SAID TO ME.
THAT WAS WHEN I WAS STILL A VIRTUE, BEFORE I BECAME A FALLEN ANGEL.
I THOUGHT HE'D BE NAKED UNDER THERE...
...?
SO THEN THE DEMON LORD SAW THAT TOO?
YOU WEREN'T NAKED WHEN YOU FIRST MET HIM...
...WERE YOU?
OF COURSE NOT!
I WAS WEARING A GARTER-BELT AND HAT.

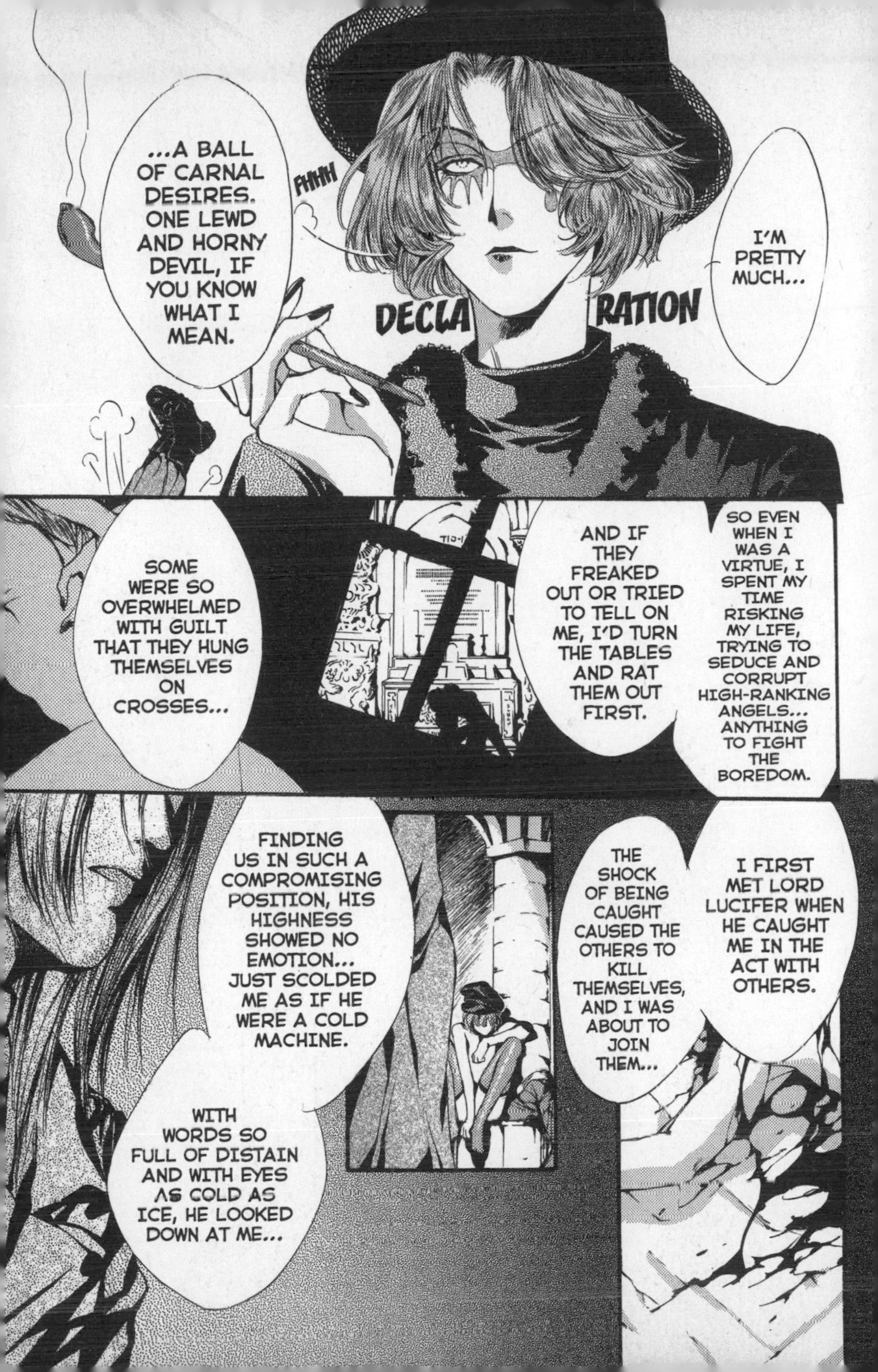
I'M PRETTY MUCH...
DECLARATION
FHHH
...A BALL OF CARNAL DESIRES. ONE LEWD AND HORNY DEVIL, IF YOU KNOW WHAT I MEAN.
SO EVEN WHEN I WAS A VIRTUE, I SPENT MY TIME RISKING MY LIFE, TRYING TO SEDUCE AND CORRUPT HIGH-RANKING ANGELS... ANYTHING TO FIGHT THE BOREDOM.
AND IF THEY FREAKED OUT OR TRIED TO TELL ON ME, I'D TURN THE TABLES AND RAT THEM OUT FIRST.
SOME WERE SO OVERWHELMED WITH GUILT THAT THEY HUNG THEMSELVES ON CROSSES...
I FIRST MET LORD LUCIFER WHEN HE CAUGHT ME IN THE ACT WITH OTHERS.
THE SHOCK OF BEING CAUGHT CAUSED THE OTHERS TO KILL THEMSELVES, AND I WAS ABOUT TO JOIN THEM...
FINDING US IN SUCH A COMPROMISING POSITION, HIS HIGHNESS SHOWED NO EMOTION... JUST SCOLDED ME AS IF HE WERE A COLD MACHINE.
WITH WORDS SO FULL OF DISTAIN AND WITH EYES AS COLD AS ICE, HE LOOKED DOWN AT ME...

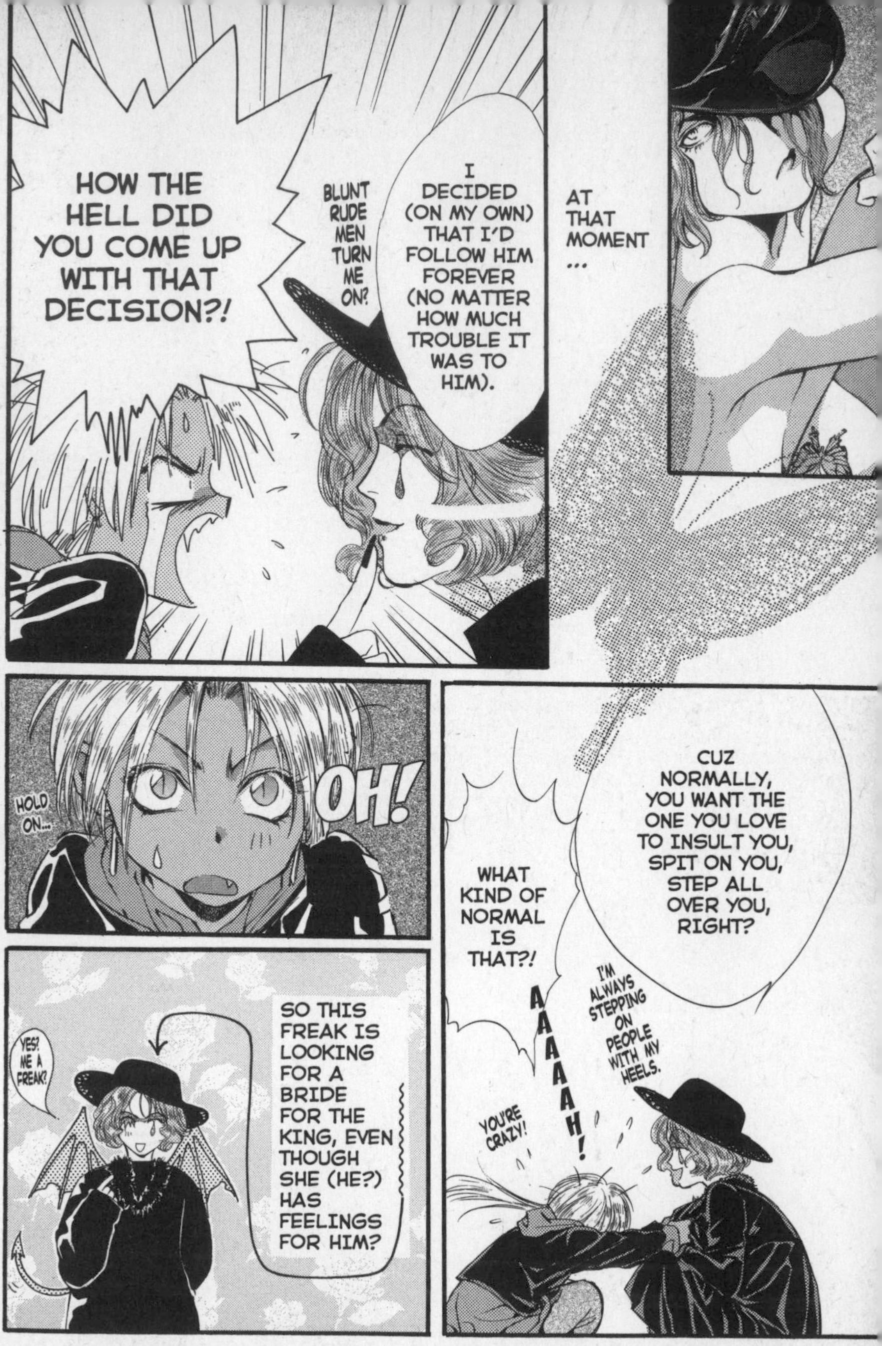

AT THAT MOMENT ...
I DECIDED (ON MY OWN) THAT I'D FOLLOW HIM FOREVER (NO MATTER HOW MUCH TROUBLE IT WAS TO HIM).
BLUNT RUDE MEN TURN ME ON?
HOW THE HELL DID YOU COME UP WITH THAT DECISION?!
CUZ NORMALLY, YOU WANT THE ONE YOU LOVE TO INSULT YOU, SPIT ON YOU, STEP ALL OVER YOU, RIGHT?
WHAT KIND OF NORMAL IS THAT?!
I'M ALWAYS STEPPING ON PEOPLE WITH MY HEELS.
AAAAAH!
YOU'RE CRAZY!
OH!
HOLD ON...
SO THIS FREAK IS LOOKING FOR A BRIDE FOR THE KING, EVEN THOUGH SHE (HE?) HAS FEELINGS FOR HIM?
YES? ME A FREAK?

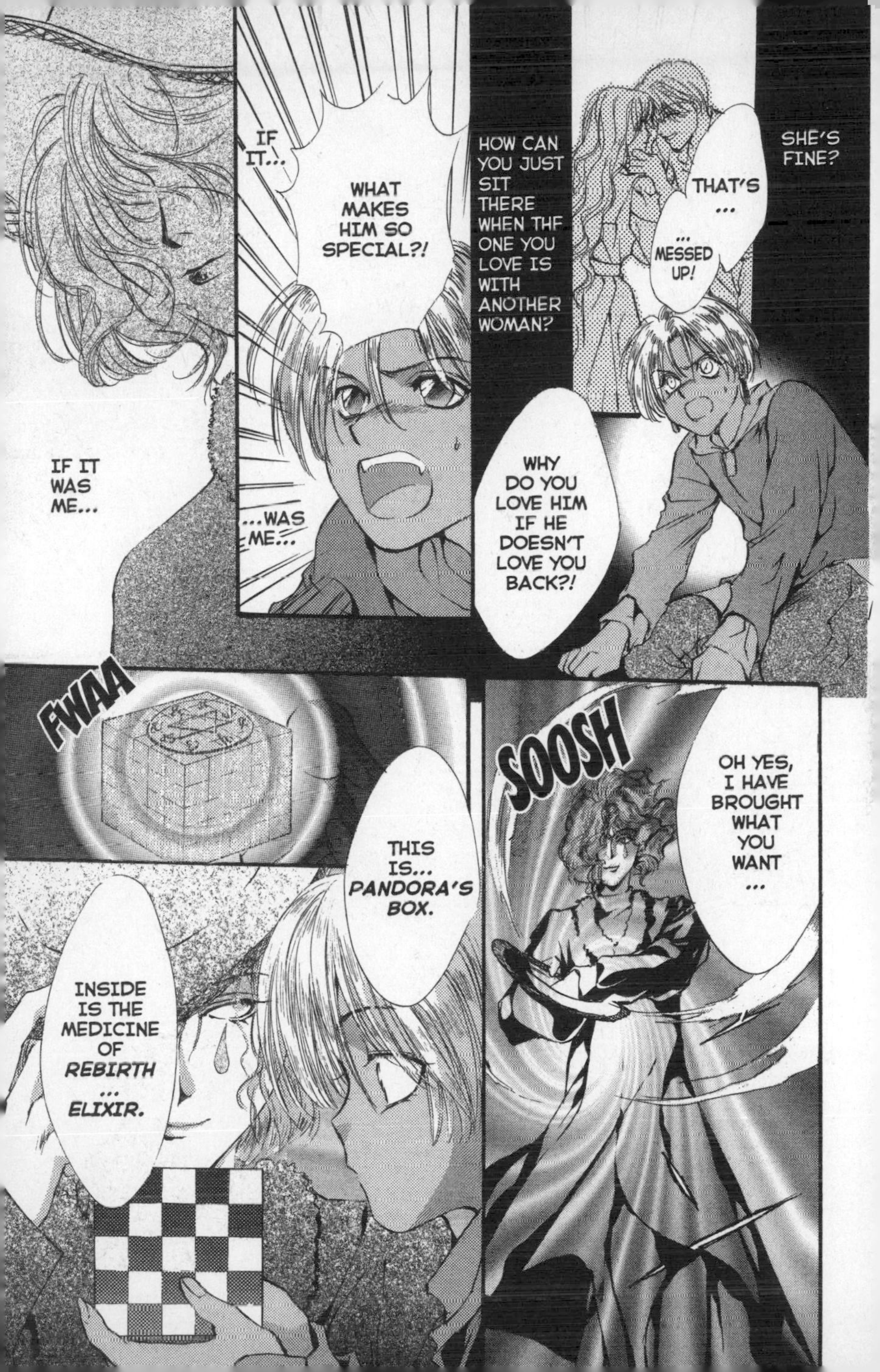
SHE'S FINE?
THAT'S ...
... MESSED UP!
HOW CAN YOU JUST SIT THERE WHEN THF ONE YOU LOVE IS WITH ANOTHER WOMAN?
WHY DO YOU LOVE HIM IF HE DOESN'T LOVE YOU BACK?!
WHAT MAKES HIM SO SPECIAL?!
IF IT...
...WAS ME...
IF IT WAS ME...
SOOSH
OH YES, I HAVE BROUGHT WHAT YOU WANT ...
FWAA
THIS IS... *PANDORA'S* BOX.
INSIDE IS THE MEDICINE OF *REBIRTH* ... *ELIXIR.*

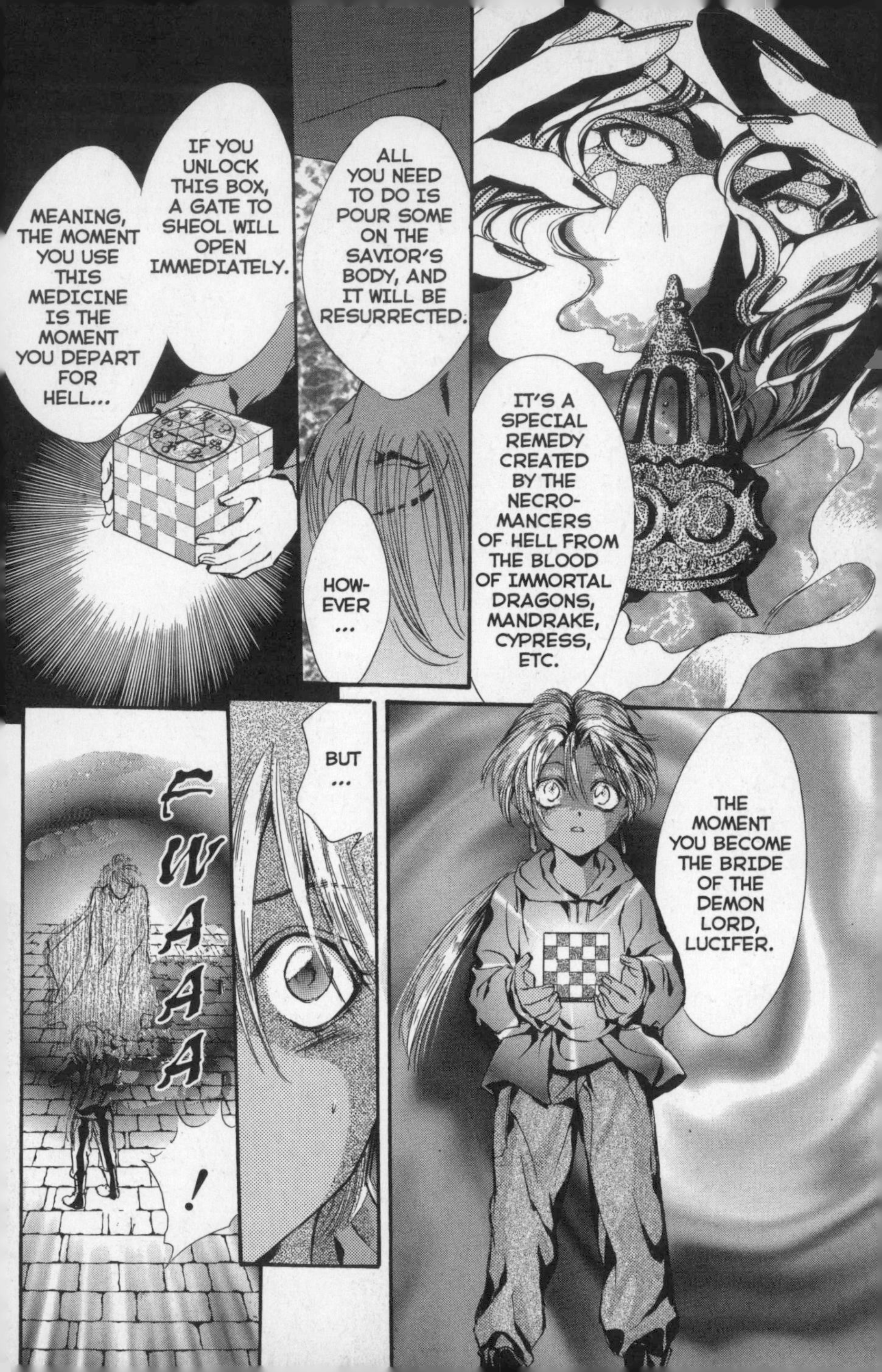
IT'S A SPECIAL REMEDY CREATED BY THE NECRO-MANCERS OF HELL FROM THE BLOOD OF IMMORTAL DRAGONS, MANDRAKE, CYPRESS, ETC.
ALL YOU NEED TO DO IS POUR SOME ON THE SAVIOR'S BODY, AND IT WILL BE RESURRECTED.
HOW-EVER ...
IF YOU UNLOCK THIS BOX, A GATE TO SHEOL WILL OPEN IMMEDIATELY.
MEANING, THE MOMENT YOU USE THIS MEDICINE IS THE MOMENT YOU DEPART FOR HELL...
THE MOMENT YOU BECOME THE BRIDE OF THE DEMON LORD, LUCIFER.
BUT ...
FWAAAA
!

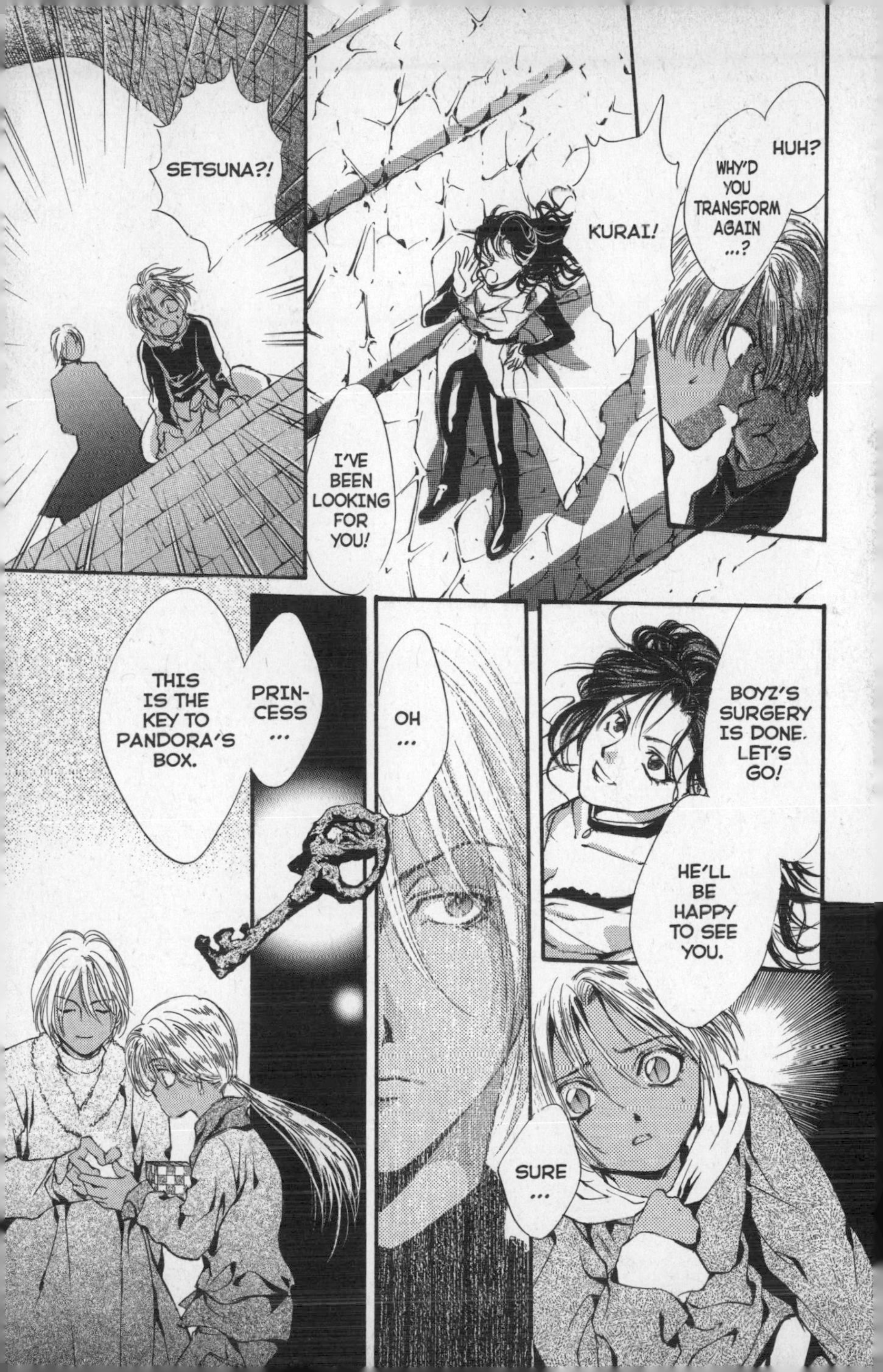
HUH?
WHY'D YOU TRANSFORM AGAIN ...?
KURAI!
I'VE BEEN LOOKING FOR YOU!
SETSUNA?!
BOYZ'S SURGERY IS DONE. LET'S GO!
HE'LL BE HAPPY TO SEE YOU.
SURE ...
OH ...
PRINCESS ...
THIS IS THE KEY TO PANDORA'S BOX.

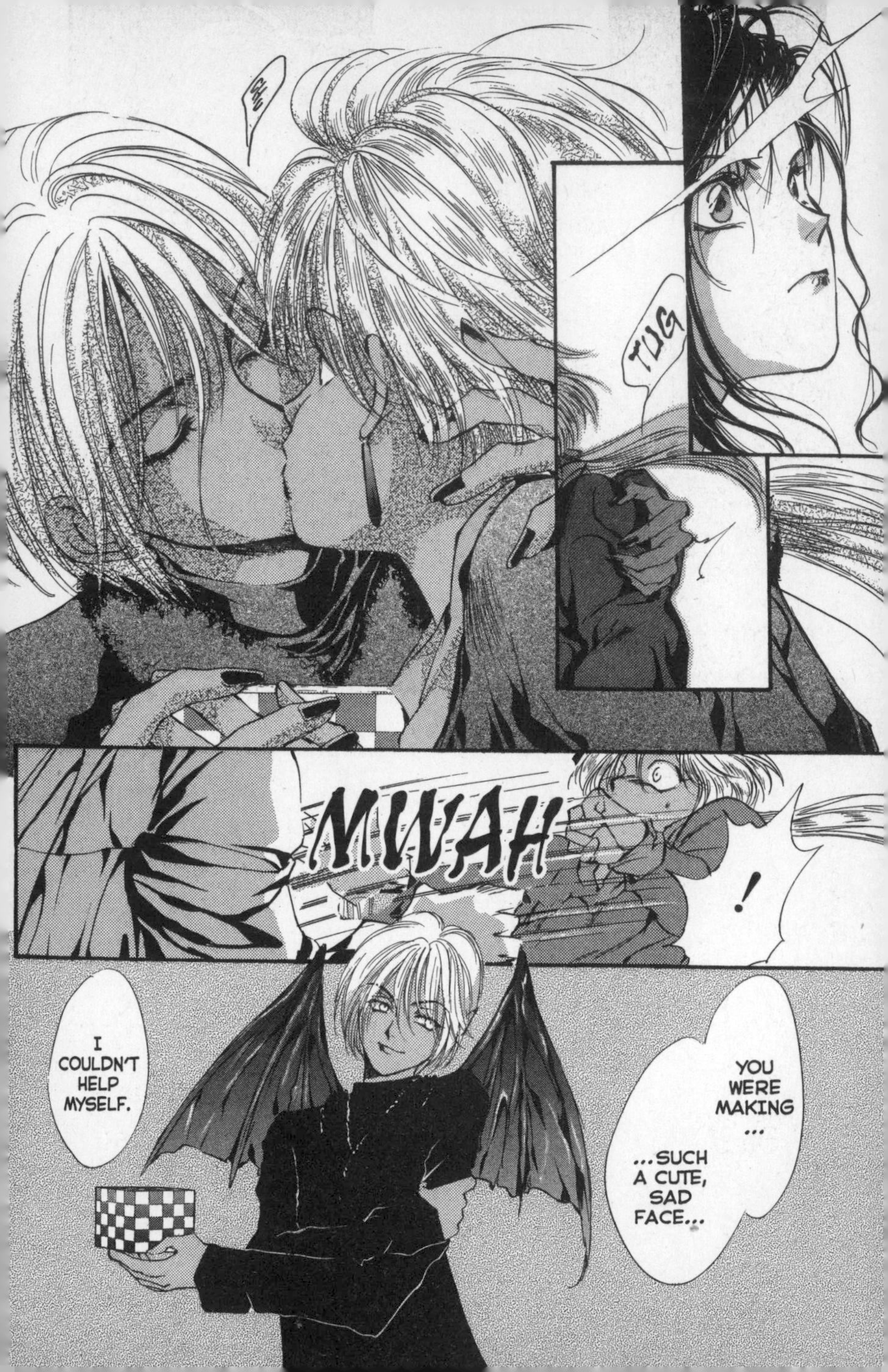
TUG
MWAH
!
YOU WERE MAKING... ...SUCH A CUTE, SAD FACE...
I COULDN'T HELP MYSELF.

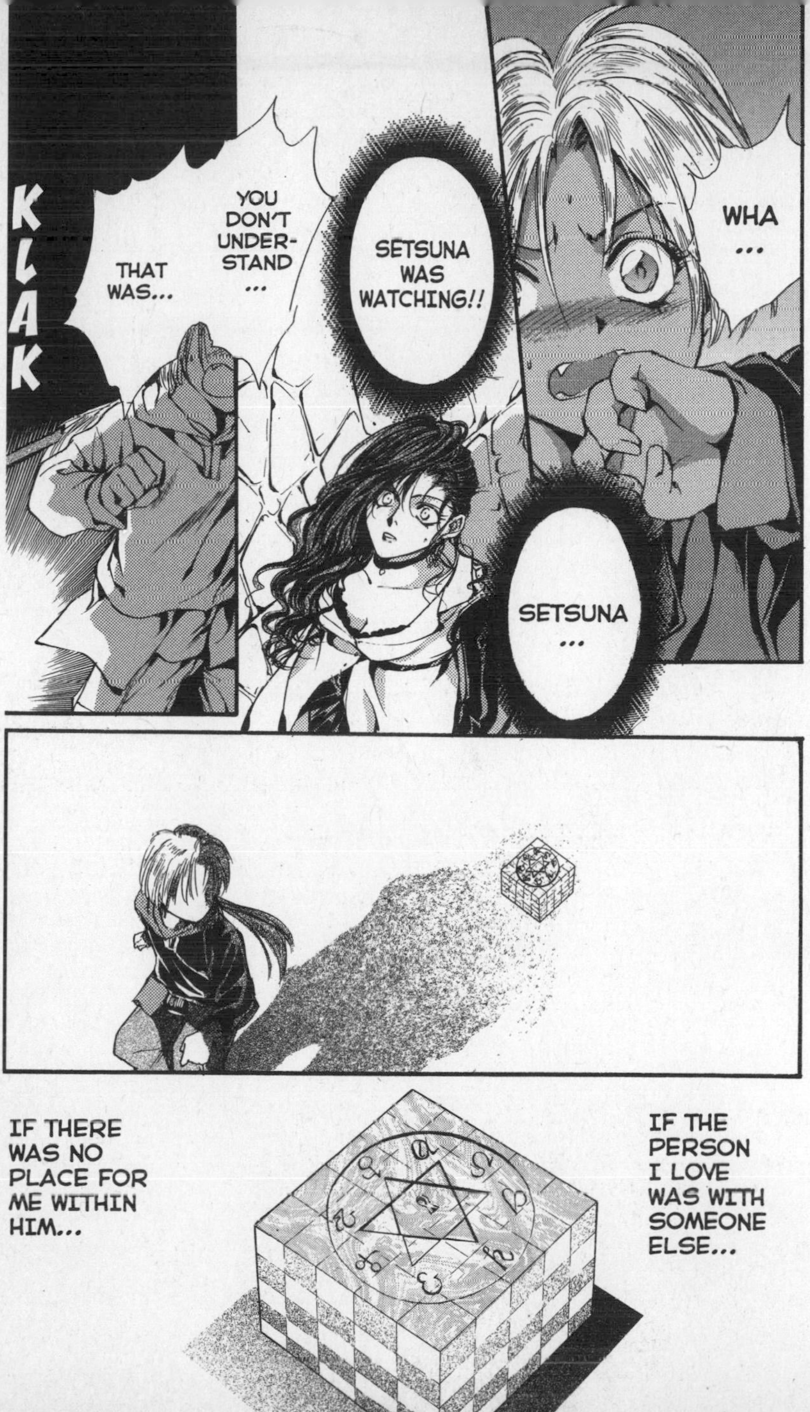
WHA ...
SETSUNA WAS WATCHING!!
YOU DON'T UNDER-STAND ...
THAT WAS...
SETSUNA ...
KLAK
IF THE PERSON I LOVE WAS WITH SOMEONE ELSE...
IF THERE WAS NO PLACE FOR ME WITHIN HIM...

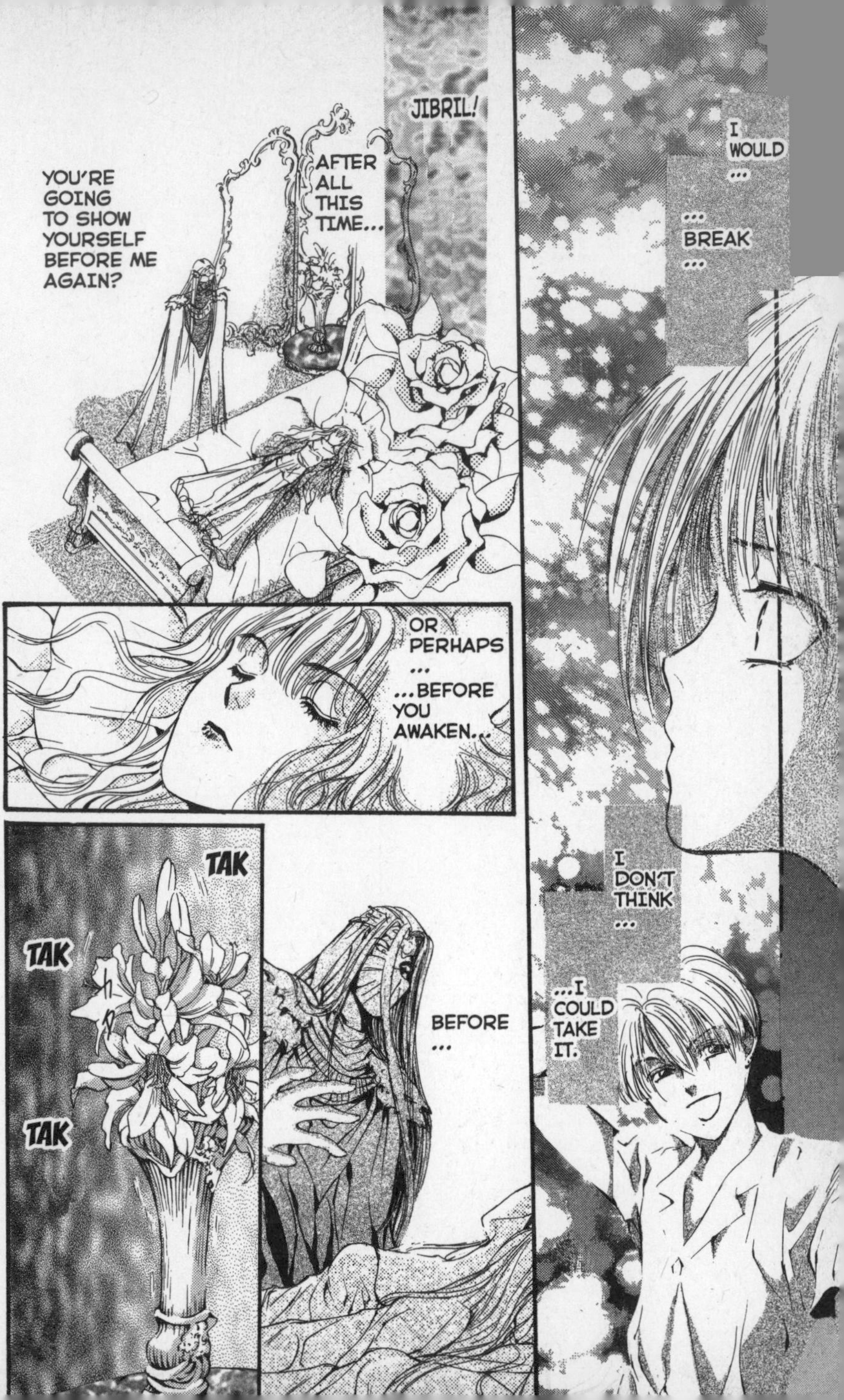
I WOULD ...
... BREAK ...
I DON'T THINK ...
...I COULD TAKE IT.
JIBRIL!
AFTER ALL THIS TIME...
YOU'RE GOING TO SHOW YOURSELF BEFORE ME AGAIN?
OR PERHAPS ...
...BEFORE YOU AWAKEN...
BEFORE ...
TAK
TAK
TAK

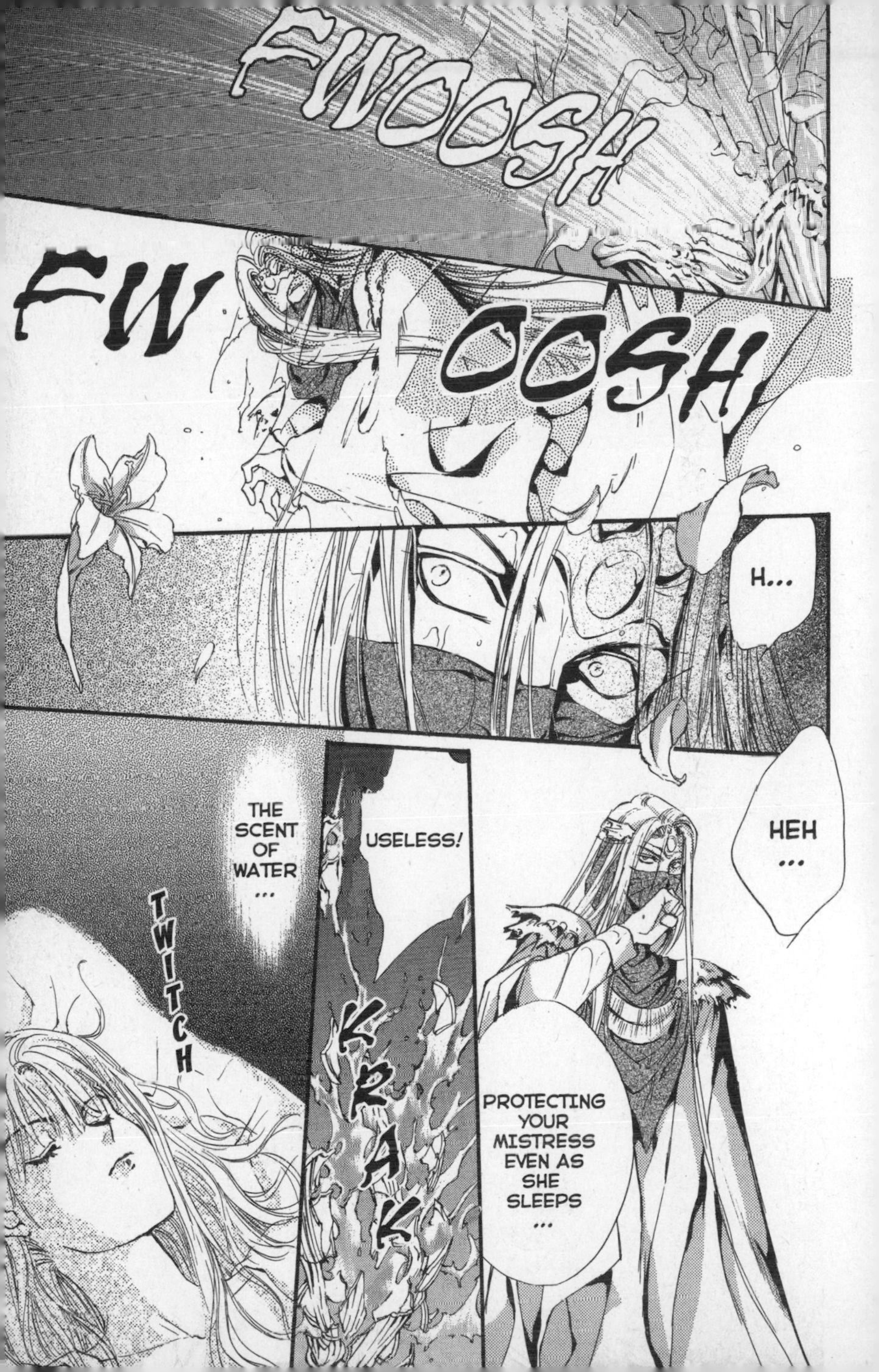
FWOOSH
FW OOSH
H...
HEH ...
PROTECTING YOUR MISTRESS EVEN AS SHE SLEEPS ...
USELESS!
KRAK
THE SCENT OF WATER ...
TWITCH

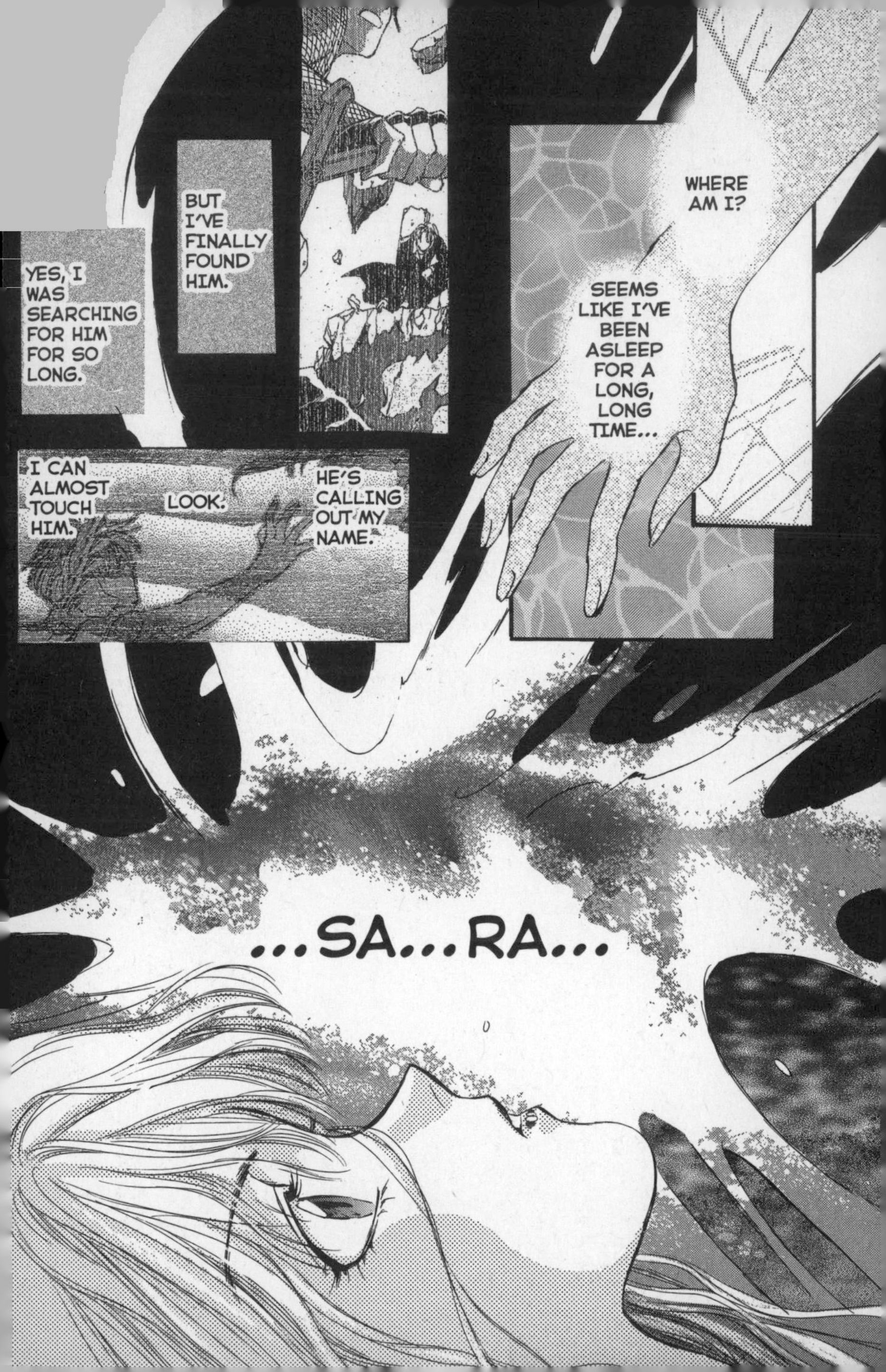
WHERE AM I?
SEEMS LIKE I'VE BEEN ASLEEP FOR A LONG, LONG TIME...
BUT I'VE FINALLY FOUND HIM.
YES, I WAS SEARCHING FOR HIM FOR SO LONG.
HE'S CALLING OUT MY NAME.
LOOK.
I CAN ALMOST TOUCH HIM.
...SA...RA...

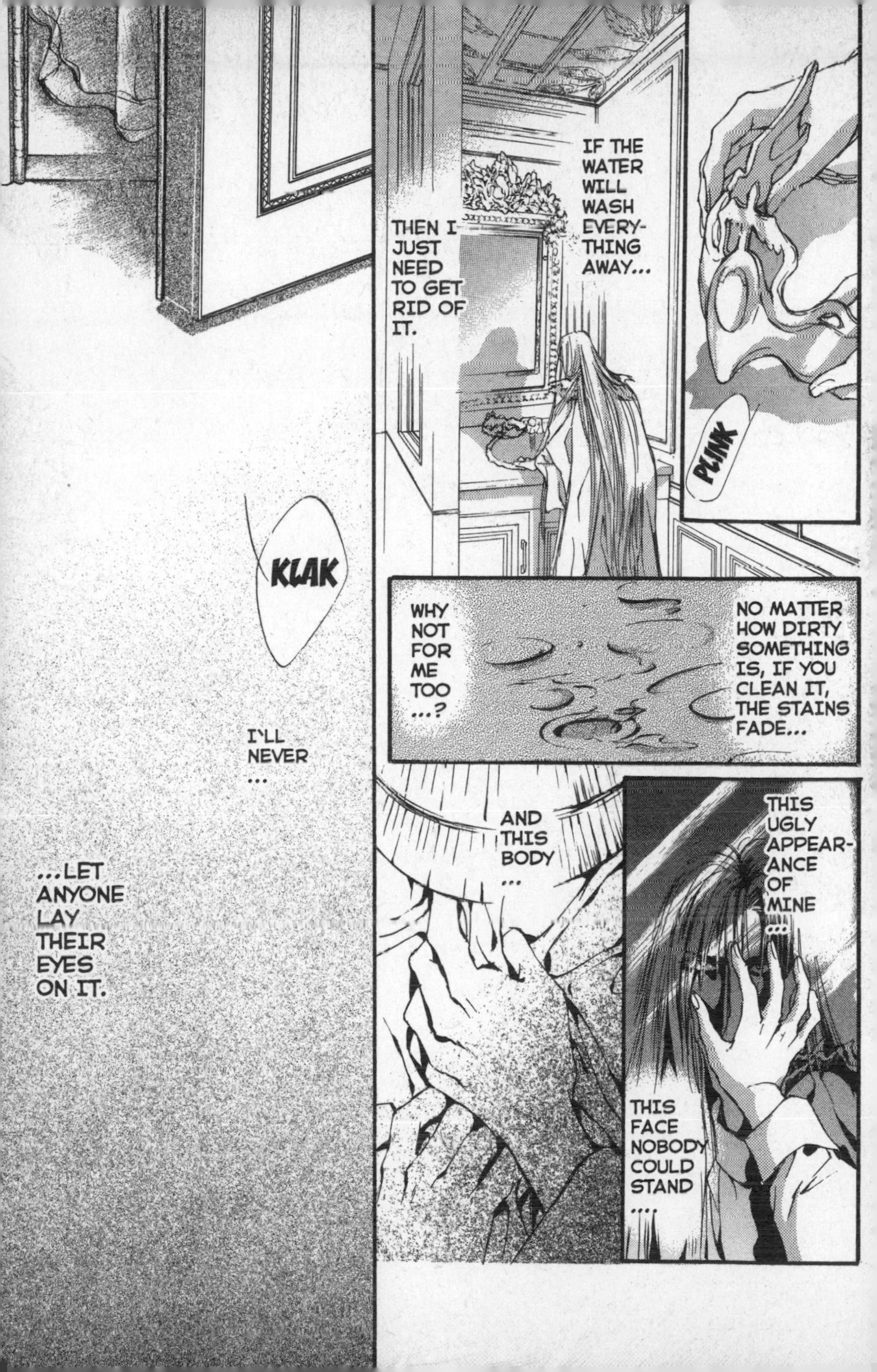
PLINK
IF THE WATER WILL WASH EVERYTHING AWAY...
THEN I JUST NEED TO GET RID OF IT.
NO MATTER HOW DIRTY SOMETHING IS, IF YOU CLEAN IT, THE STAINS FADE...
WHY NOT FOR ME TOO ...?
THIS UGLY APPEARANCE OF MINE ...
THIS FACE NOBODY COULD STAND ....
AND THIS BODY ...
KLAK
I'LL NEVER ...
...LET ANYONE LAY THEIR EYES ON IT.

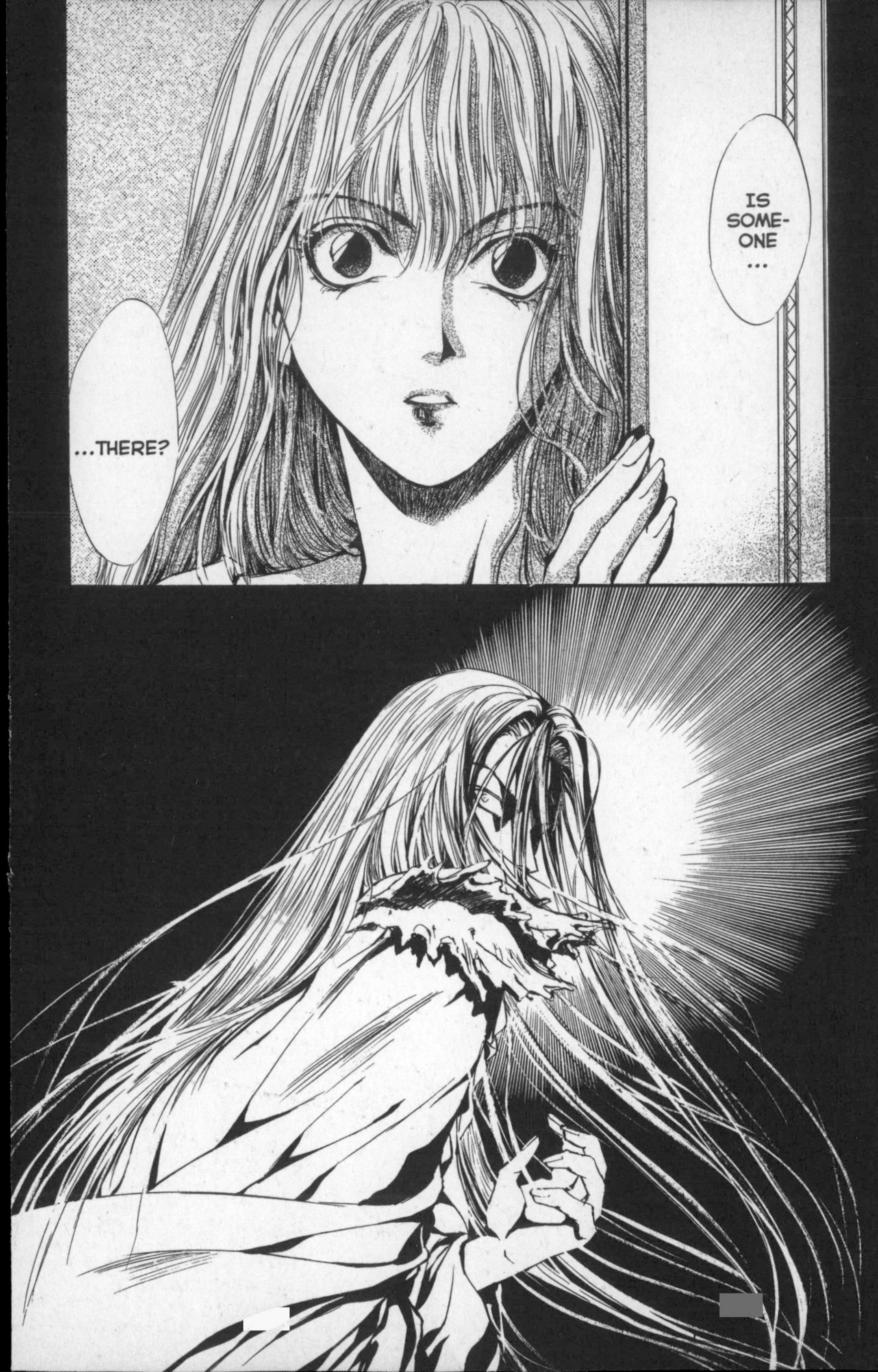
IS SOME-ONE ...
...THERE?

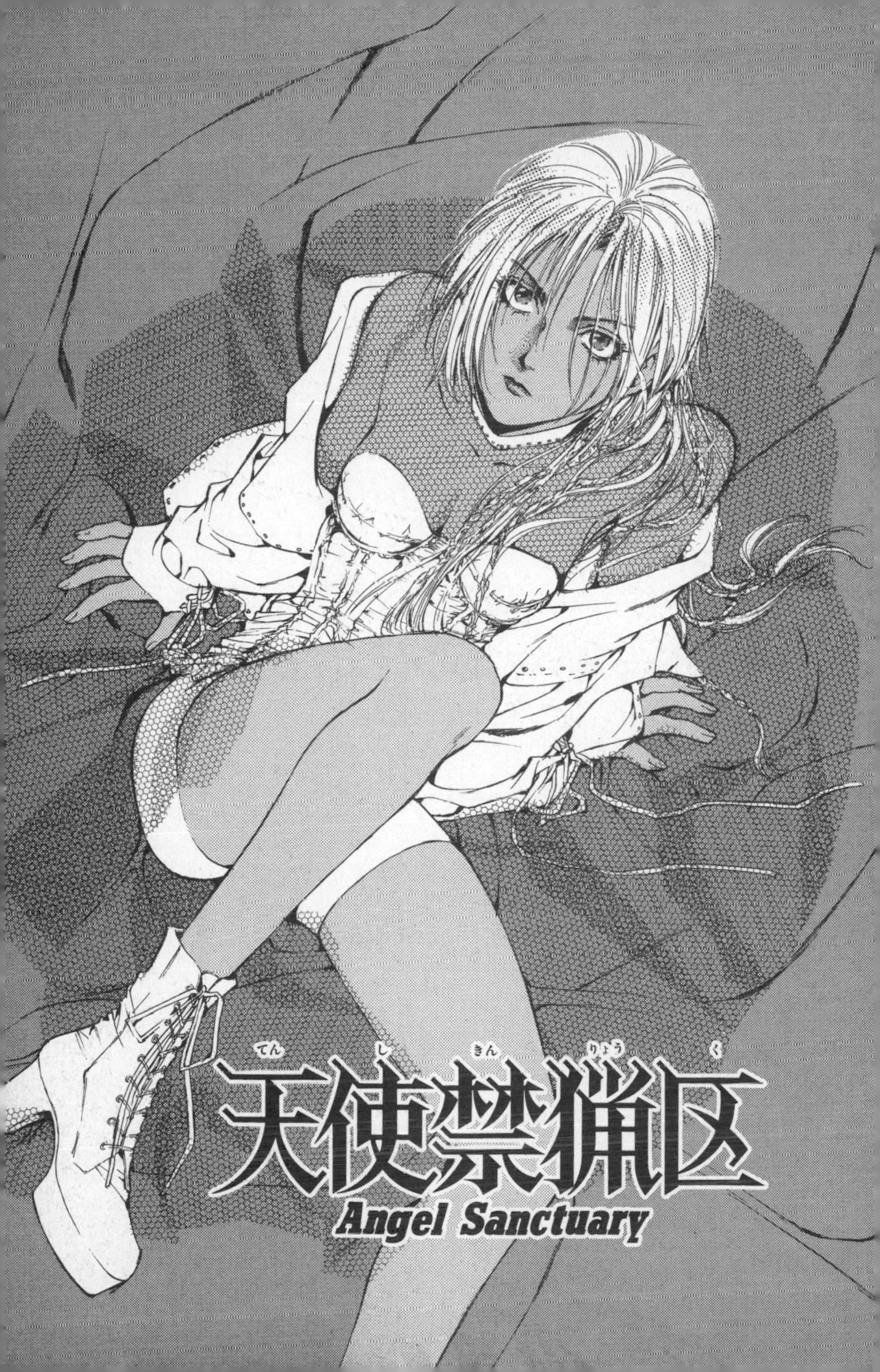
天使禁猟区
Angel Sanctuary

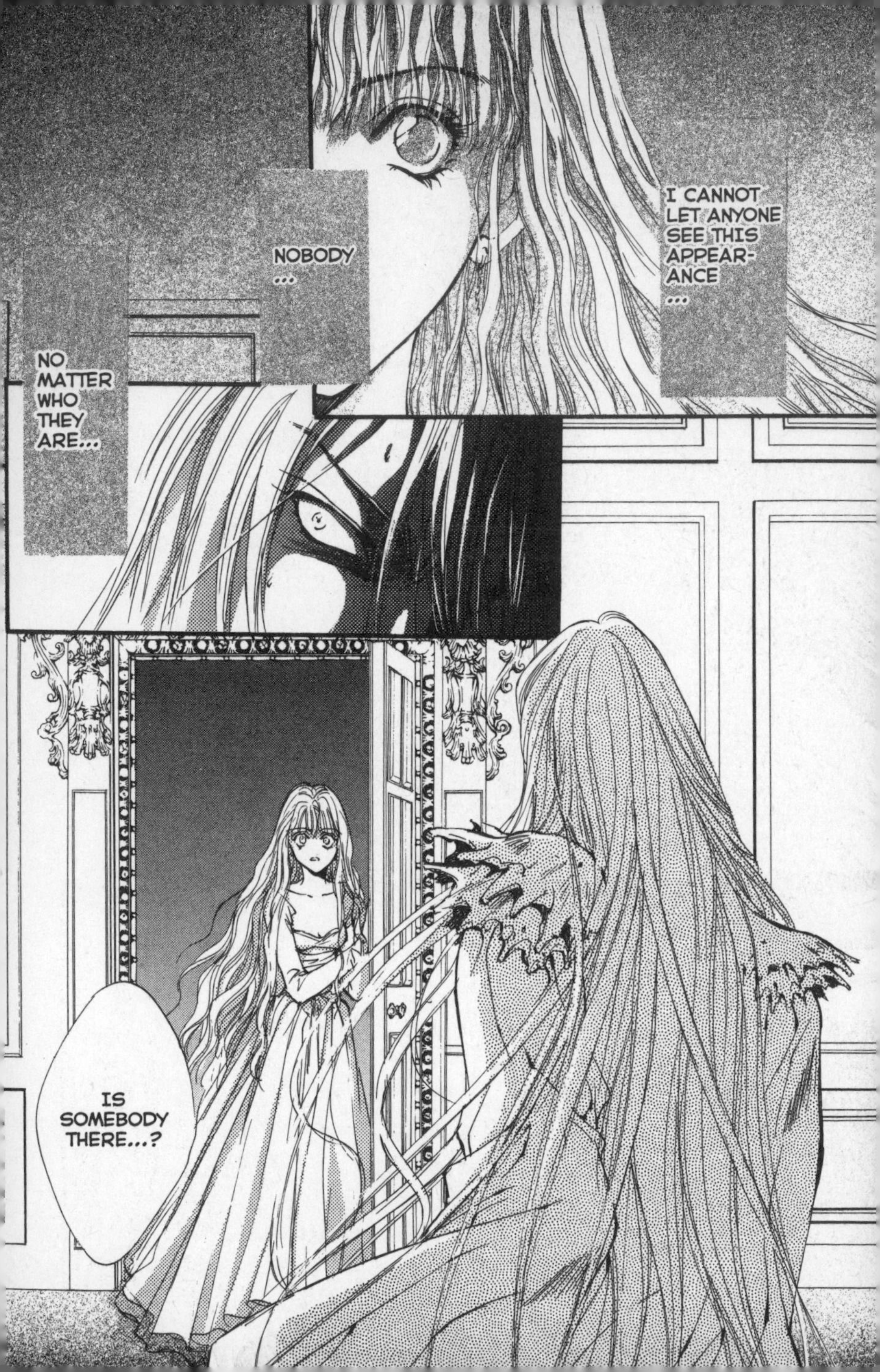
I CANNOT LET ANYONE SEE THIS APPEAR-ANCE ...
NOBODY ...
NO MATTER WHO THEY ARE...
IS SOMEBODY THERE...?

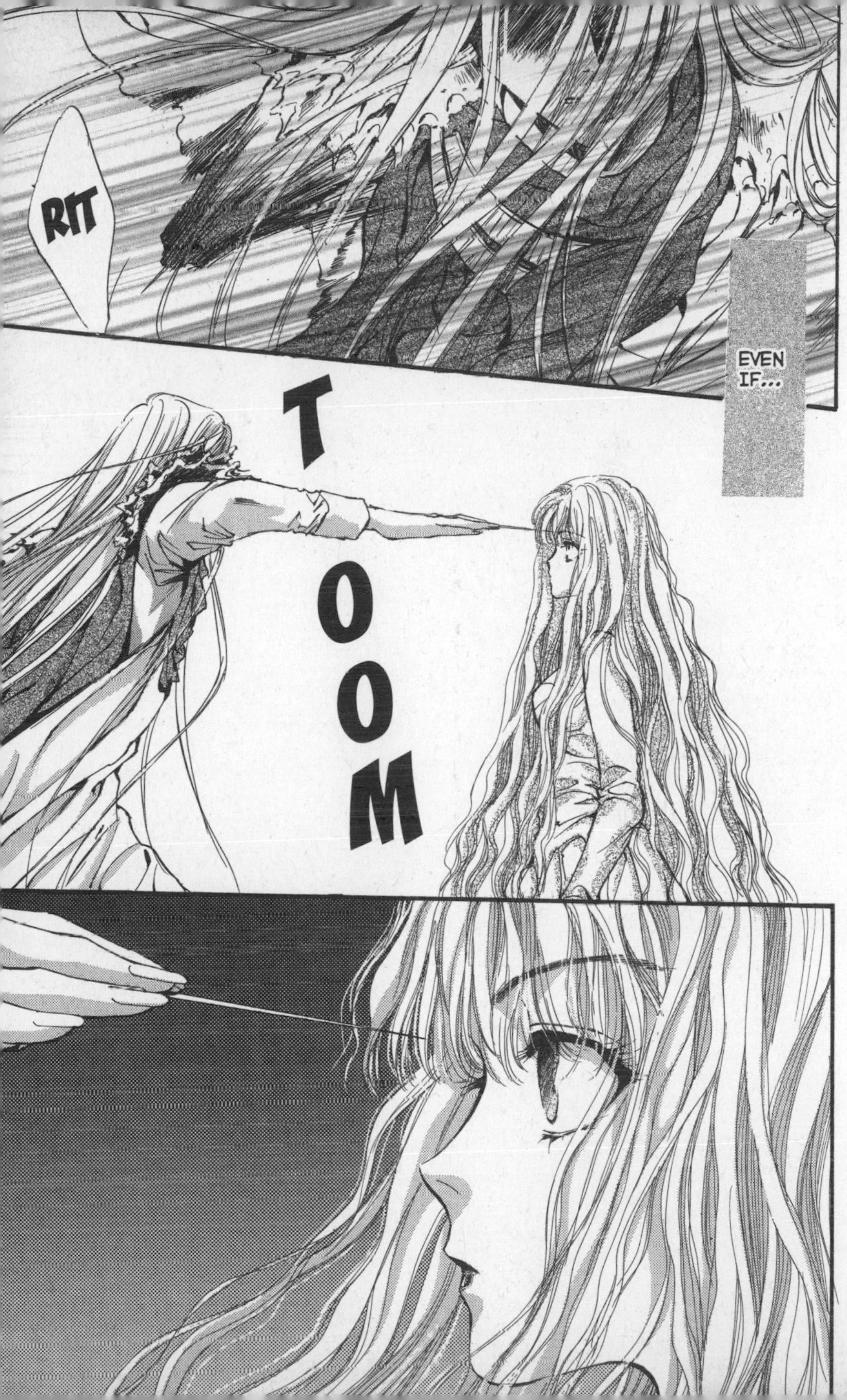
EVEN IF...
RIT
TOOM

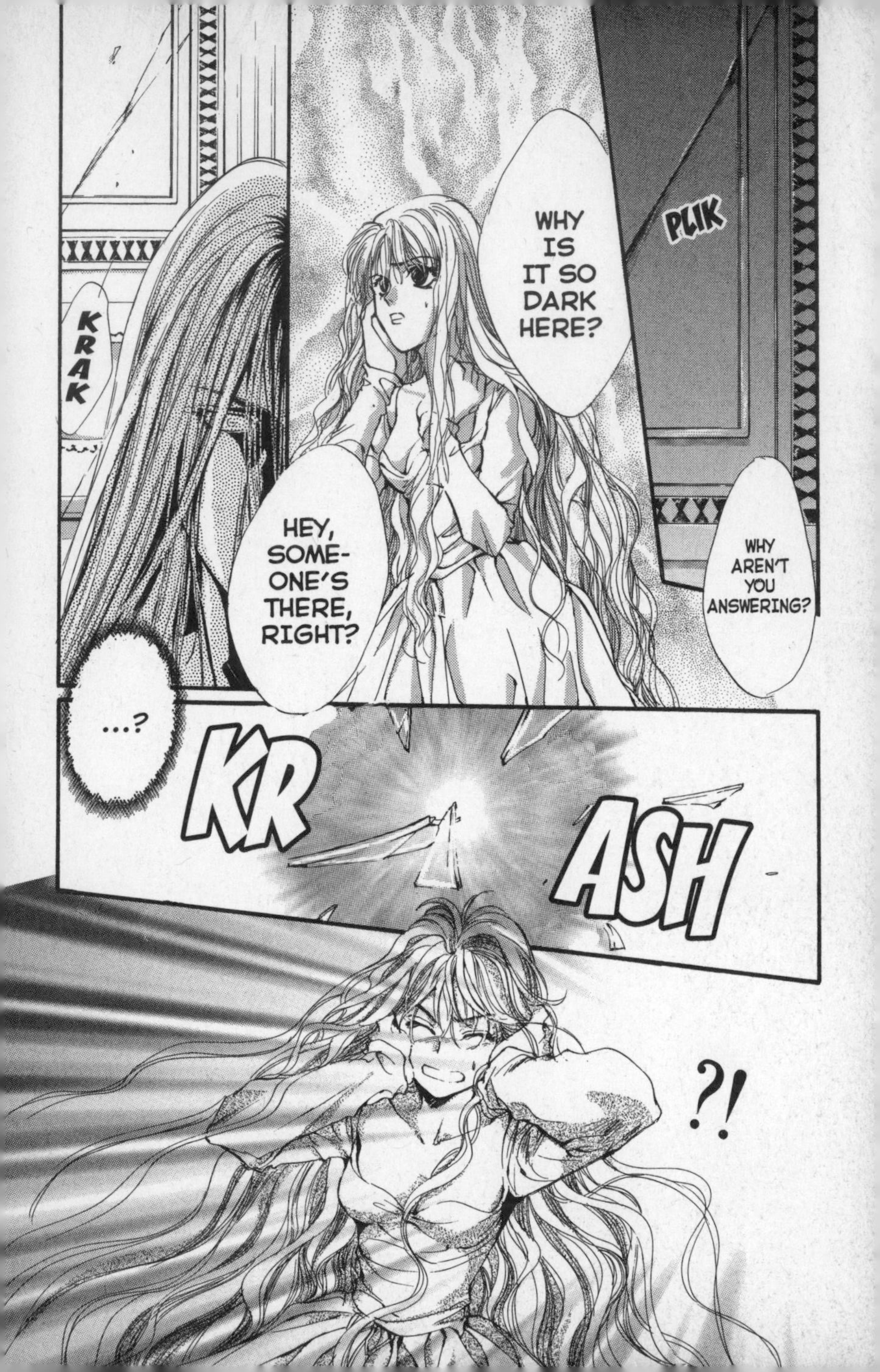
PLIK
WHY IS IT SO DARK HERE?
WHY AREN'T YOU ANSWERING?
HEY, SOME-ONE'S THERE, RIGHT?
KRAK
...?
KR ASH
?!

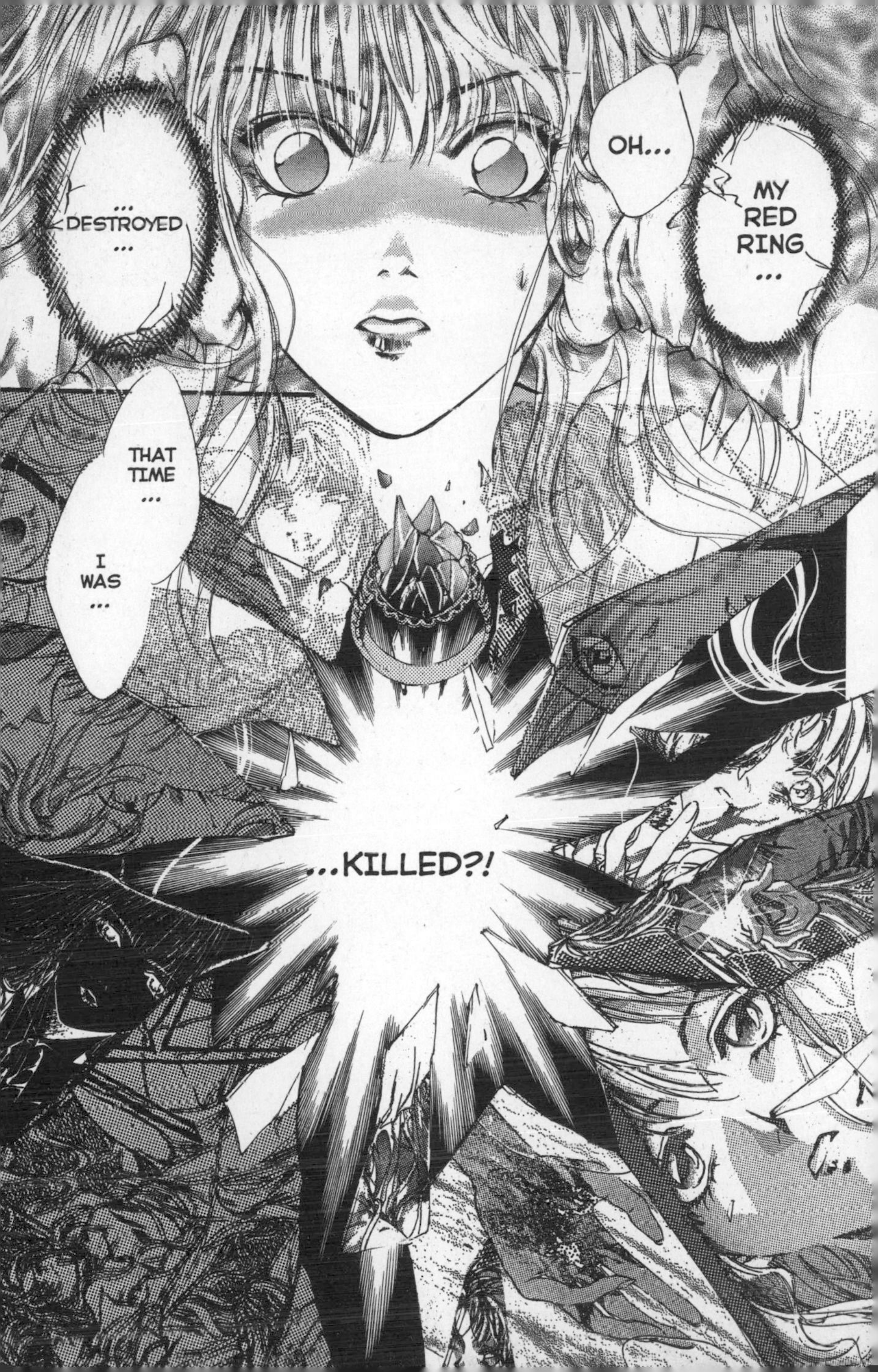
OH...
MY RED RING ...
... DESTROYED ...
THAT TIME ... I WAS ...
...KILLED?!

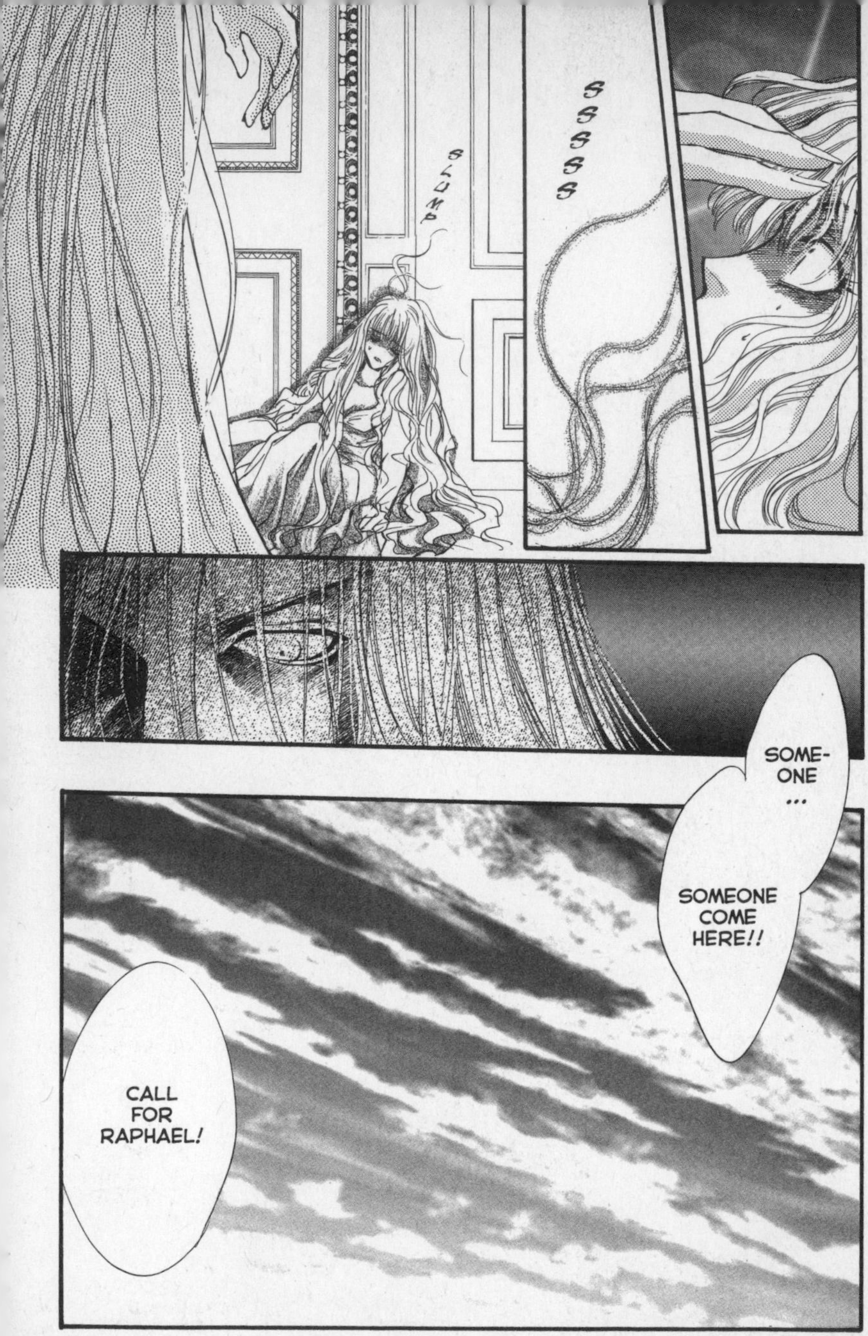
SSSSS
SLUMP
SOME-ONE ...
SOMEONE COME HERE!!
CALL FOR RAPHAEL!

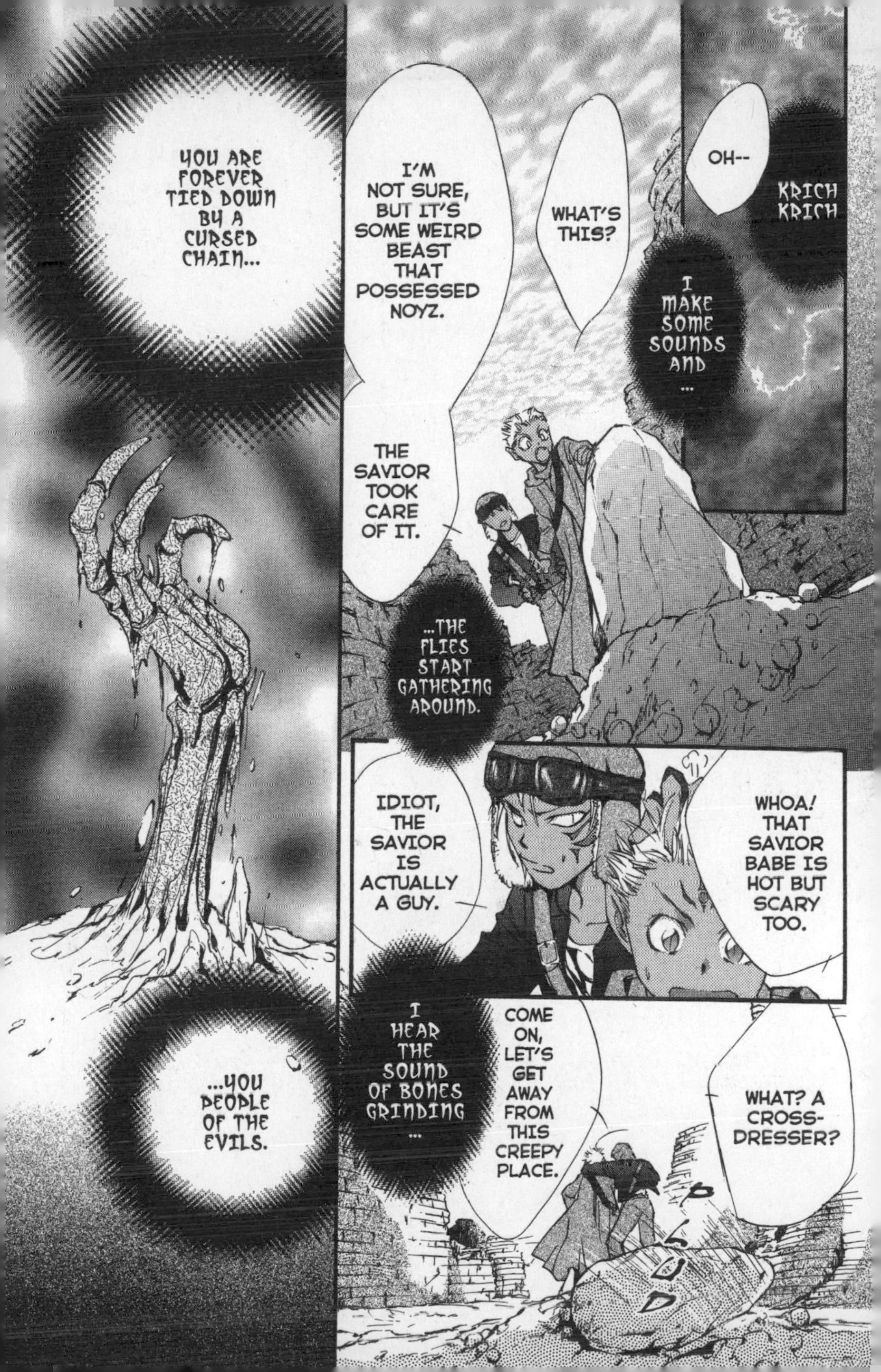
OH--
KRICH KRICH
I MAKE SOME SOUNDS AND ...
WHAT'S THIS?
I'M NOT SURE, BUT IT'S SOME WEIRD BEAST THAT POSSESSED NOYZ.
THE SAVIOR TOOK CARE OF IT.
...THE FLIES START GATHERING AROUND.
WHOA! THAT SAVIOR BABE IS HOT BUT SCARY TOO.
IDIOT, THE SAVIOR IS ACTUALLY A GUY.
WHAT? A CROSS-DRESSER?
COME ON, LET'S GET AWAY FROM THIS CREEPY PLACE.
I HEAR THE SOUND OF BONES GRINDING ...
YOU ARE FOREVER TIED DOWN BY A CURSED CHAIN...
...YOU PEOPLE OF THE EVILS.

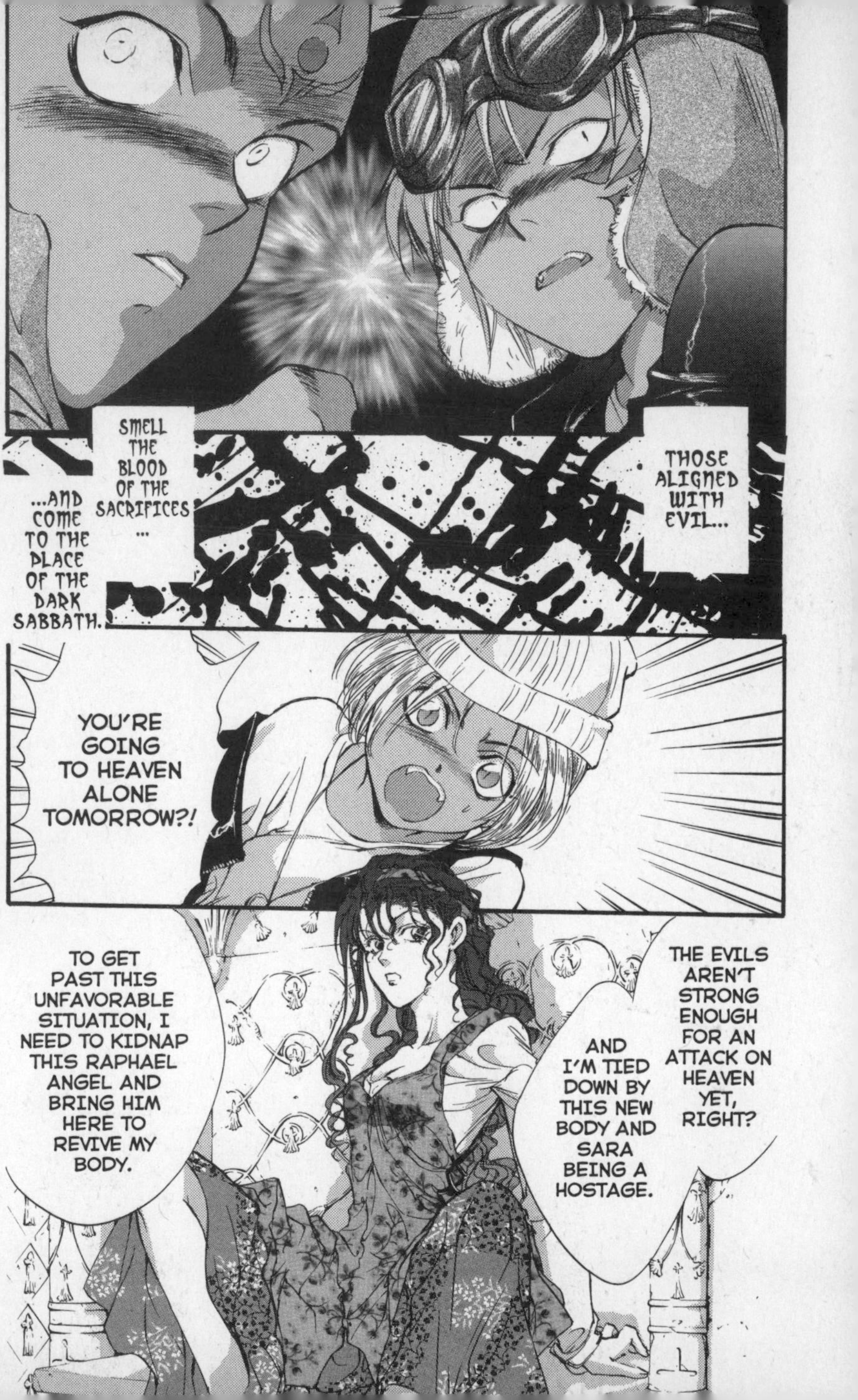
THOSE ALIGNED WITH EVIL...
SMELL THE BLOOD OF THE SACRIFICES...
...AND COME TO THE PLACE OF THE DARK SABBATH.
YOU'RE GOING TO HEAVEN ALONE TOMORROW?!
THE EVILS AREN'T STRONG ENOUGH FOR AN ATTACK ON HEAVEN YET, RIGHT?
AND I'M TIED DOWN BY THIS NEW BODY AND SARA BEING A HOSTAGE.
TO GET PAST THIS UNFAVORABLE SITUATION, I NEED TO KIDNAP THIS RAPHAEL ANGEL AND BRING HIM HERE TO REVIVE MY BODY.

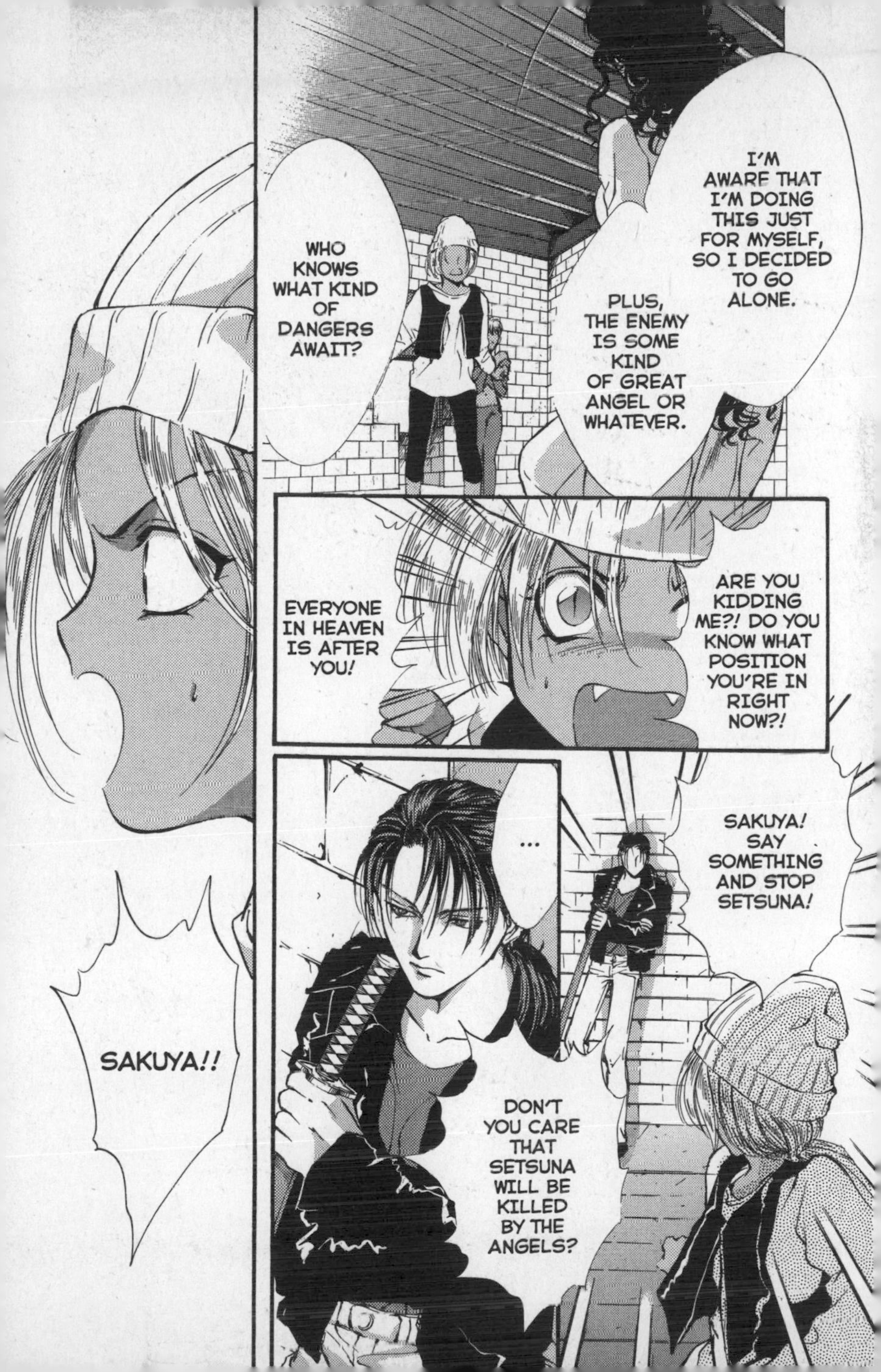
I'M AWARE THAT I'M DOING THIS JUST FOR MYSELF, SO I DECIDED TO GO ALONE.
PLUS, THE ENEMY IS SOME KIND OF GREAT ANGEL OR WHATEVER.
WHO KNOWS WHAT KIND OF DANGERS AWAIT?
ARE YOU KIDDING ME?! DO YOU KNOW WHAT POSITION YOU'RE IN RIGHT NOW?!
EVERYONE IN HEAVEN IS AFTER YOU!
SAKUYA! SAY SOMETHING AND STOP SETSUNA!
...
DON'T YOU CARE THAT SETSUNA WILL BE KILLED BY THE ANGELS?
SAKUYA!!

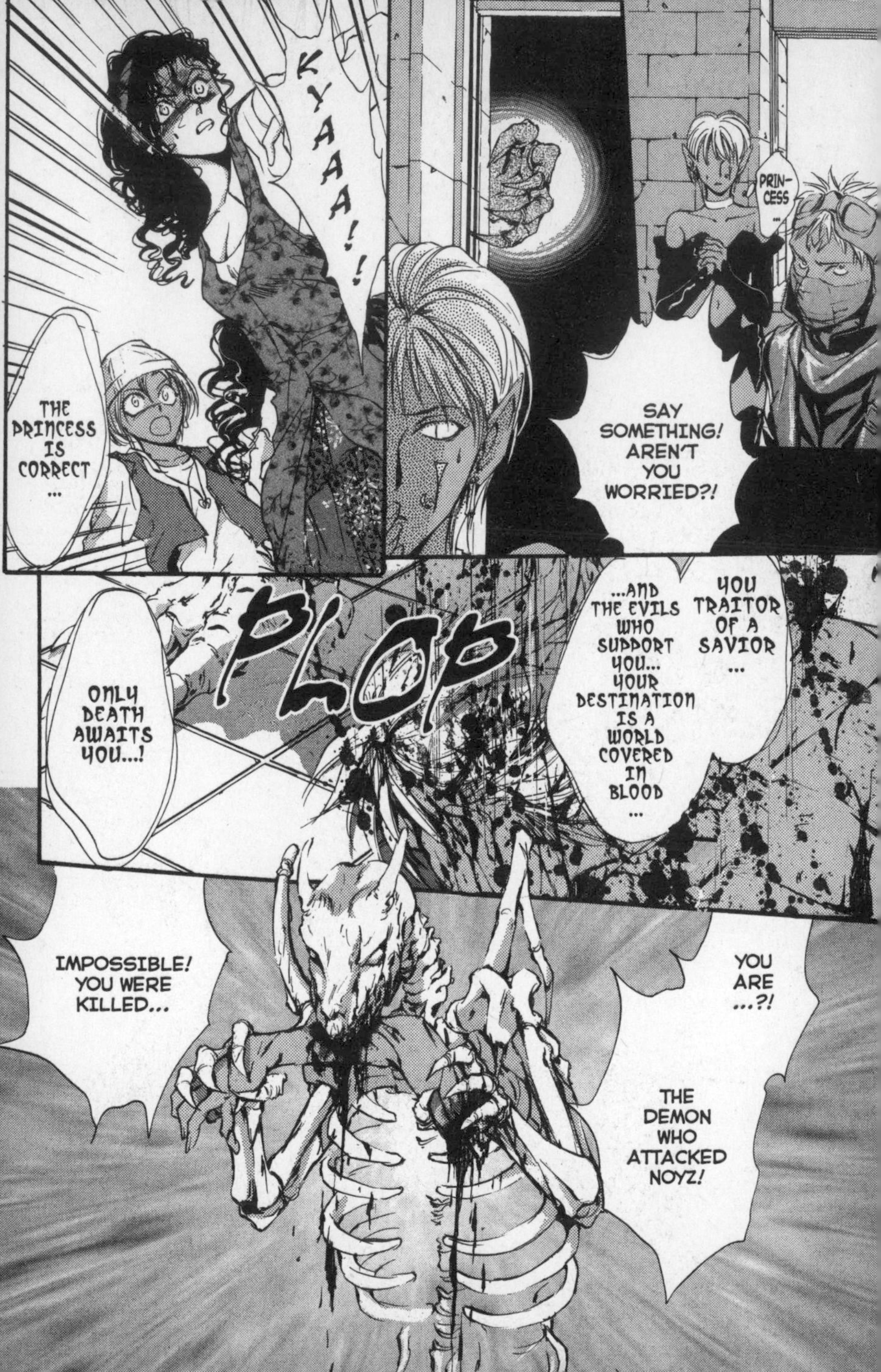
PRIN-CESS ...
SAY SOMETHING! AREN'T YOU WORRIED?!
KYAAA!!
THE PRINCESS IS CORRECT ...
YOU TRAITOR OF A SAVIOR ...
...AND THE EVILS WHO SUPPORT YOU... YOUR DESTINATION IS A WORLD COVERED IN BLOOD ...
PLOP
ONLY DEATH AWAITS YOU...!
YOU ARE ...?!
THE DEMON WHO ATTACKED NOYZ!
IMPOSSIBLE! YOU WERE KILLED...

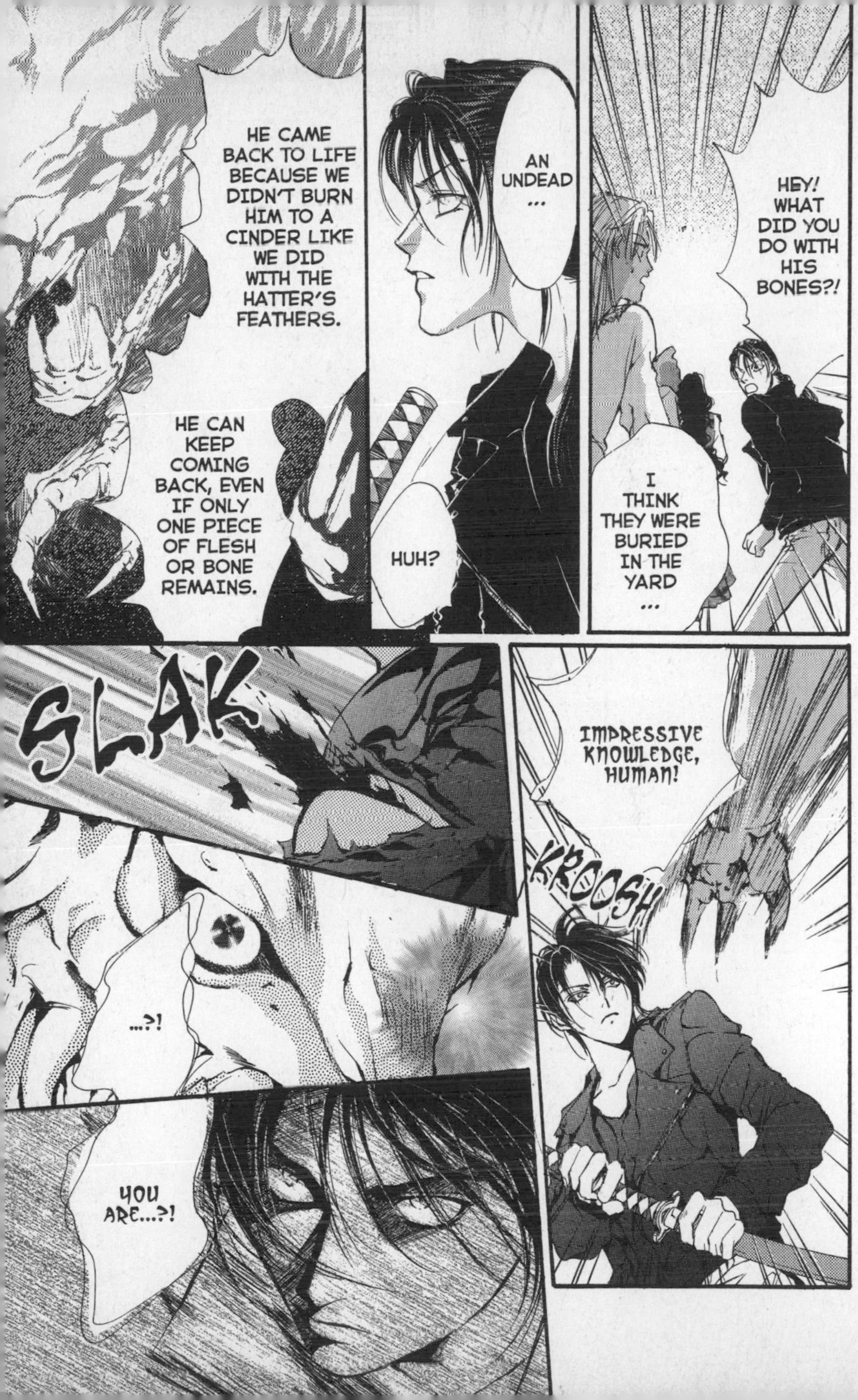
HEY! WHAT DID YOU DO WITH HIS BONES?!
I THINK THEY WERE BURIED IN THE YARD ...
AN UNDEAD ...
HUH?
HE CAME BACK TO LIFE BECAUSE WE DIDN'T BURN HIM TO A CINDER LIKE WE DID WITH THE HATTER'S FEATHERS.
HE CAN KEEP COMING BACK, EVEN IF ONLY ONE PIECE OF FLESH OR BONE REMAINS.
IMPRESSIVE KNOWLEDGE, HUMAN!
KROOSH
SLAK
...?!
YOU ARE...?!

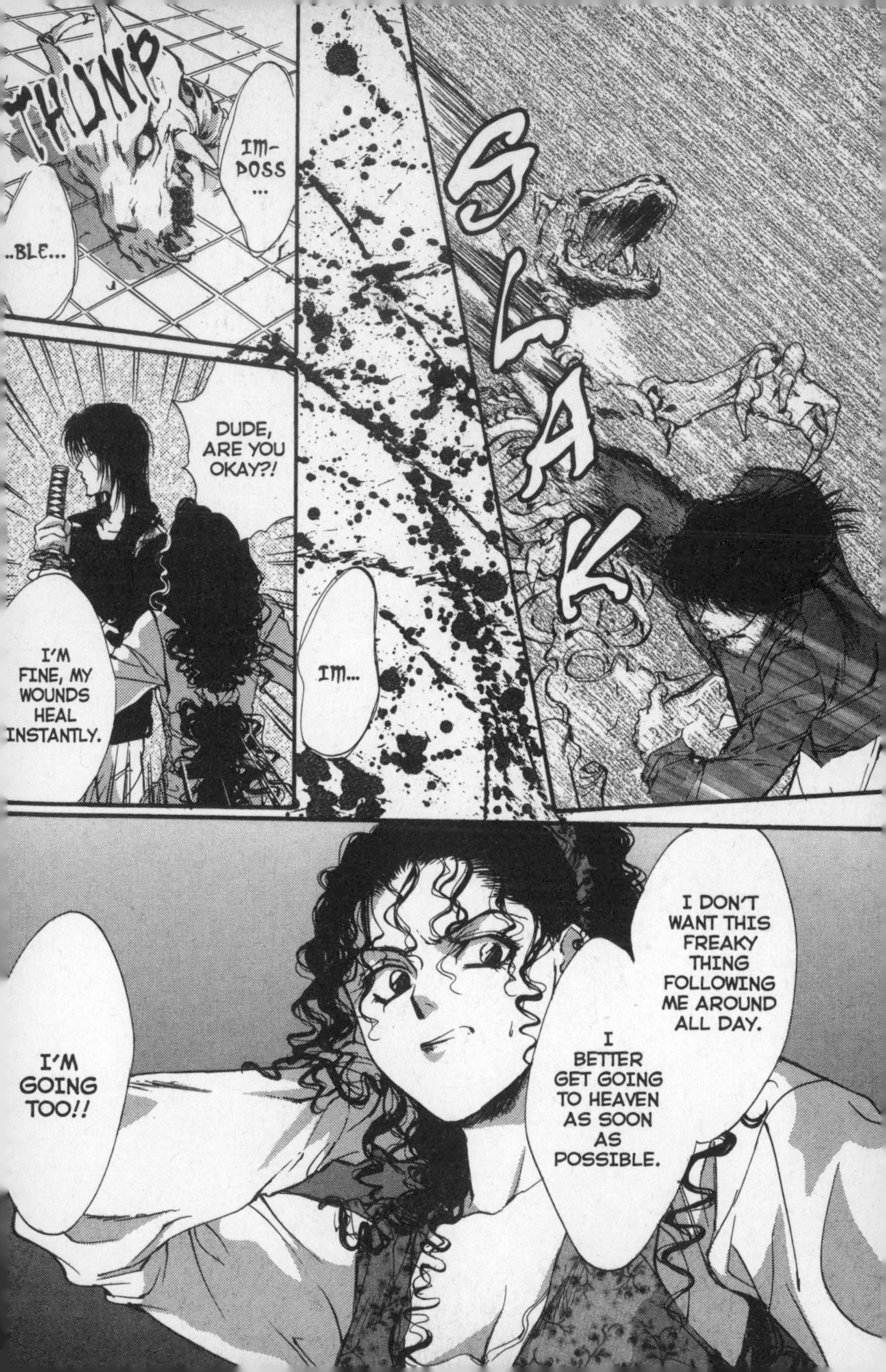
SLAK
IM...
THUMP
IM-POSS...
..BLE...
DUDE, ARE YOU OKAY?!
I'M FINE, MY WOUNDS HEAL INSTANTLY.
I DON'T WANT THIS FREAKY THING FOLLOWING ME AROUND ALL DAY.
I BETTER GET GOING TO HEAVEN AS SOON AS POSSIBLE.
I'M GOING TOO!!

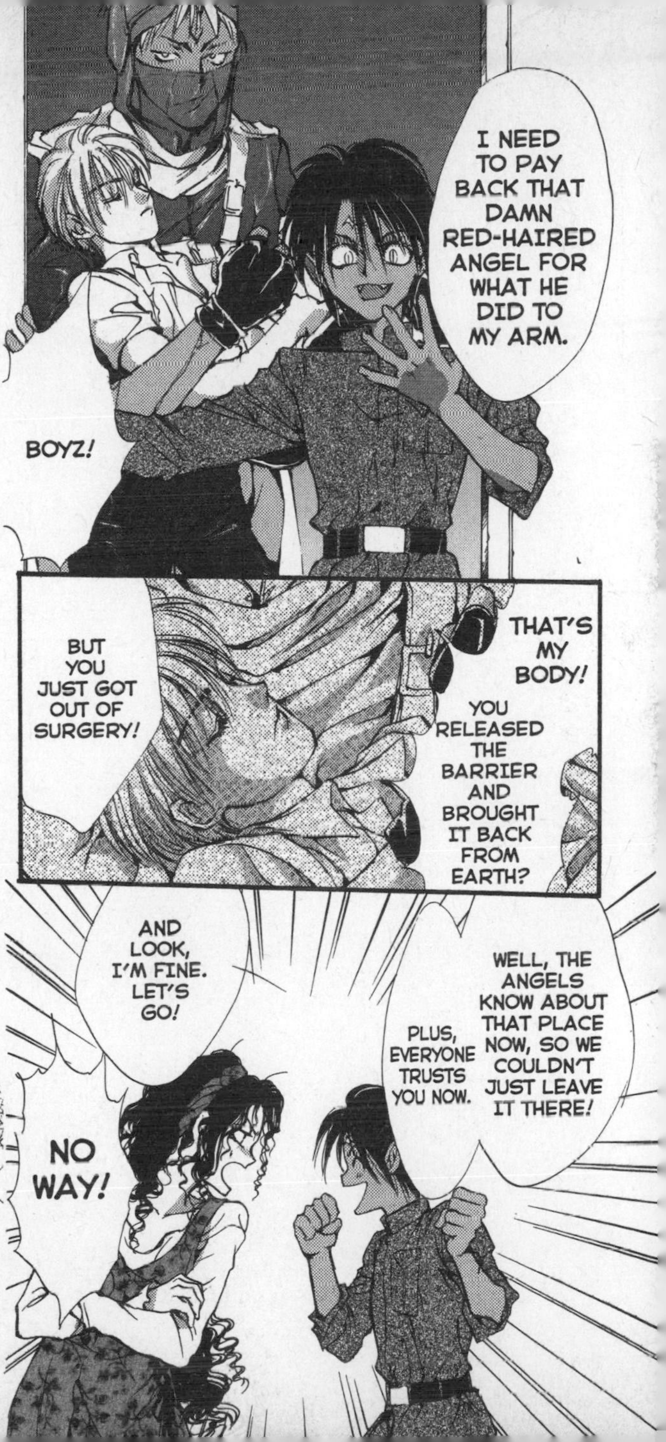
I NEED TO PAY BACK THAT DAMN RED-HAIRED ANGEL FOR WHAT HE DID TO MY ARM.
BOYZ!
THAT'S MY BODY!
YOU RELEASED THE BARRIER AND BROUGHT IT BACK FROM EARTH?
BUT YOU JUST GOT OUT OF SURGERY!
WELL, THE ANGELS KNOW ABOUT THAT PLACE NOW, SO WE COULDN'T JUST LEAVE IT THERE!
PLUS, EVERYONE TRUSTS YOU NOW.
AND LOOK, I'M FINE. LET'S GO!
NO WAY!

I bought a box similar to the Pandora's Box that appears in the manga. My room is much bigger now, so I keep buying weird things. I'm doing all this expensive impulse buying now (even from catalogs, too.) So much stuff that I don't really need. Silver boxes, lamps, these really green glasses, pins. I bought a crystal ball and put it in my cabinet. The absolute dumbest thing I bought was an antique black birdcage. But it looked cool! I put a fake white rose in it.

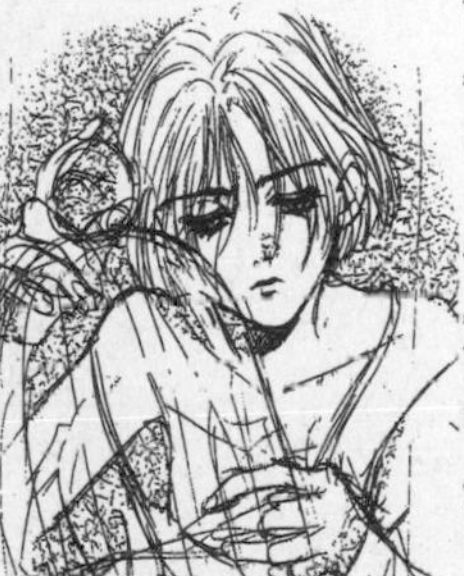

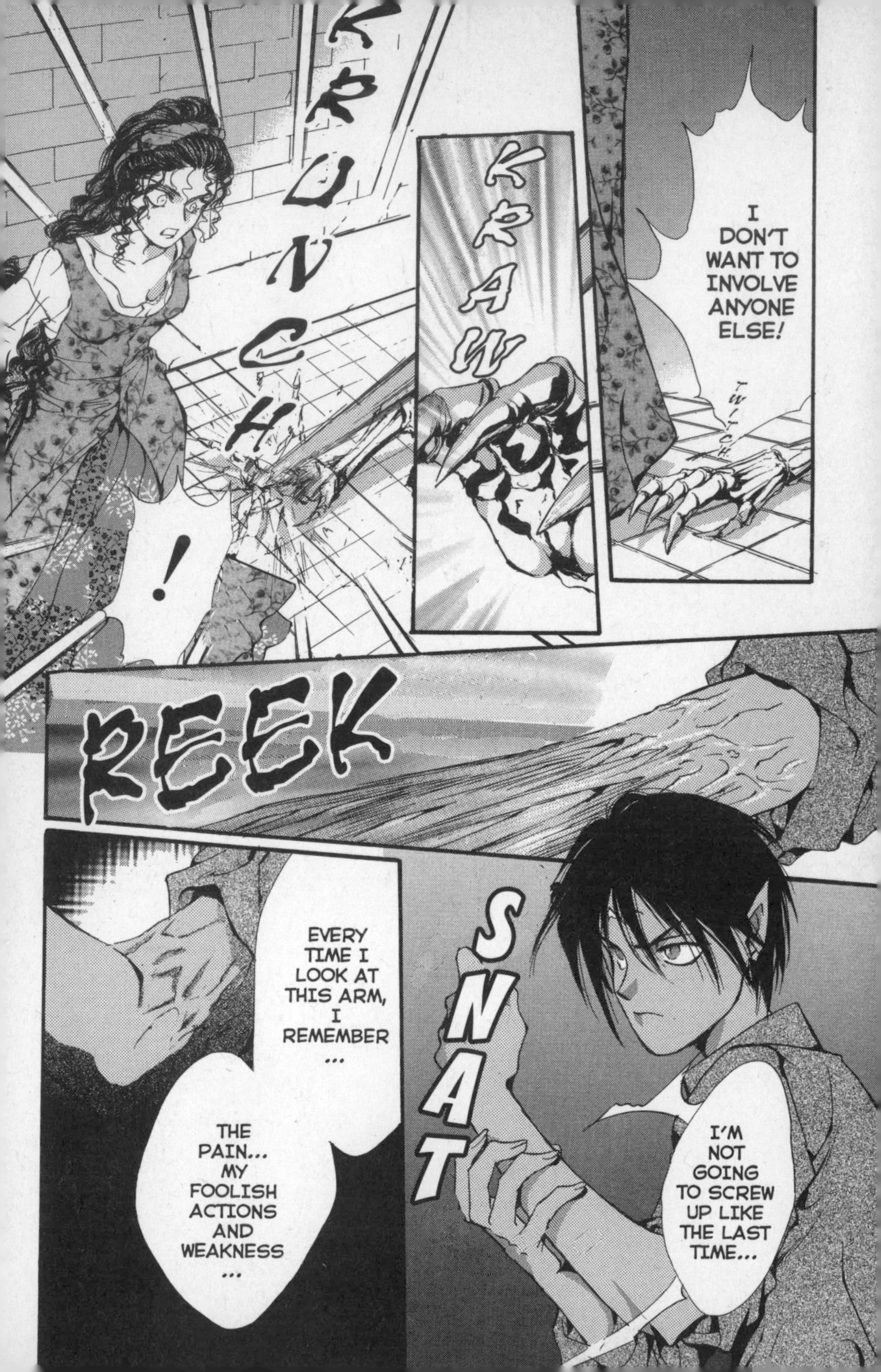
I DON'T WANT TO INVOLVE ANYONE ELSE!
TWITCH
KRAW
KRUNCH
!
REEK
SNAT
I'M NOT GOING TO SCREW UP LIKE THE LAST TIME...
EVERY TIME I LOOK AT THIS ARM, I REMEMBER...
THE PAIN... MY FOOLISH ACTIONS AND WEAKNESS...

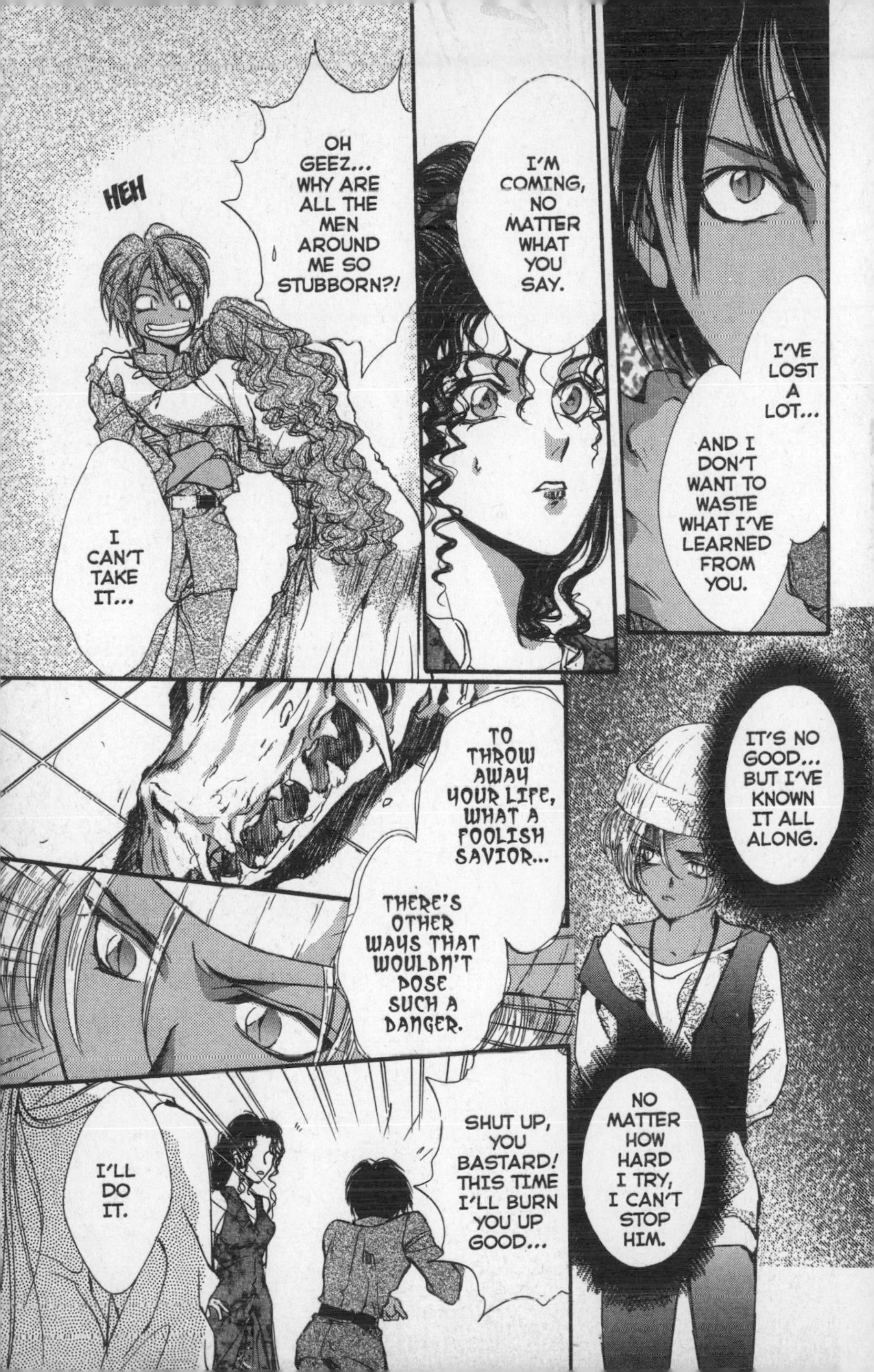
I'VE LOST A LOT...
AND I DON'T WANT TO WASTE WHAT I'VE LEARNED FROM YOU.
I'M COMING, NO MATTER WHAT YOU SAY.
OH GEEZ... WHY ARE ALL THE MEN AROUND ME SO STUBBORN?!
HEH
I CAN'T TAKE IT...
IT'S NO GOOD... BUT I'VE KNOWN IT ALL ALONG.
NO MATTER HOW HARD I TRY, I CAN'T STOP HIM.
TO THROW AWAY YOUR LIFE, WHAT A FOOLISH SAVIOR...
THERE'S OTHER WAYS THAT WOULDN'T POSE SUCH A DANGER.
SHUT UP, YOU BASTARD! THIS TIME I'LL BURN YOU UP GOOD...
I'LL DO IT.

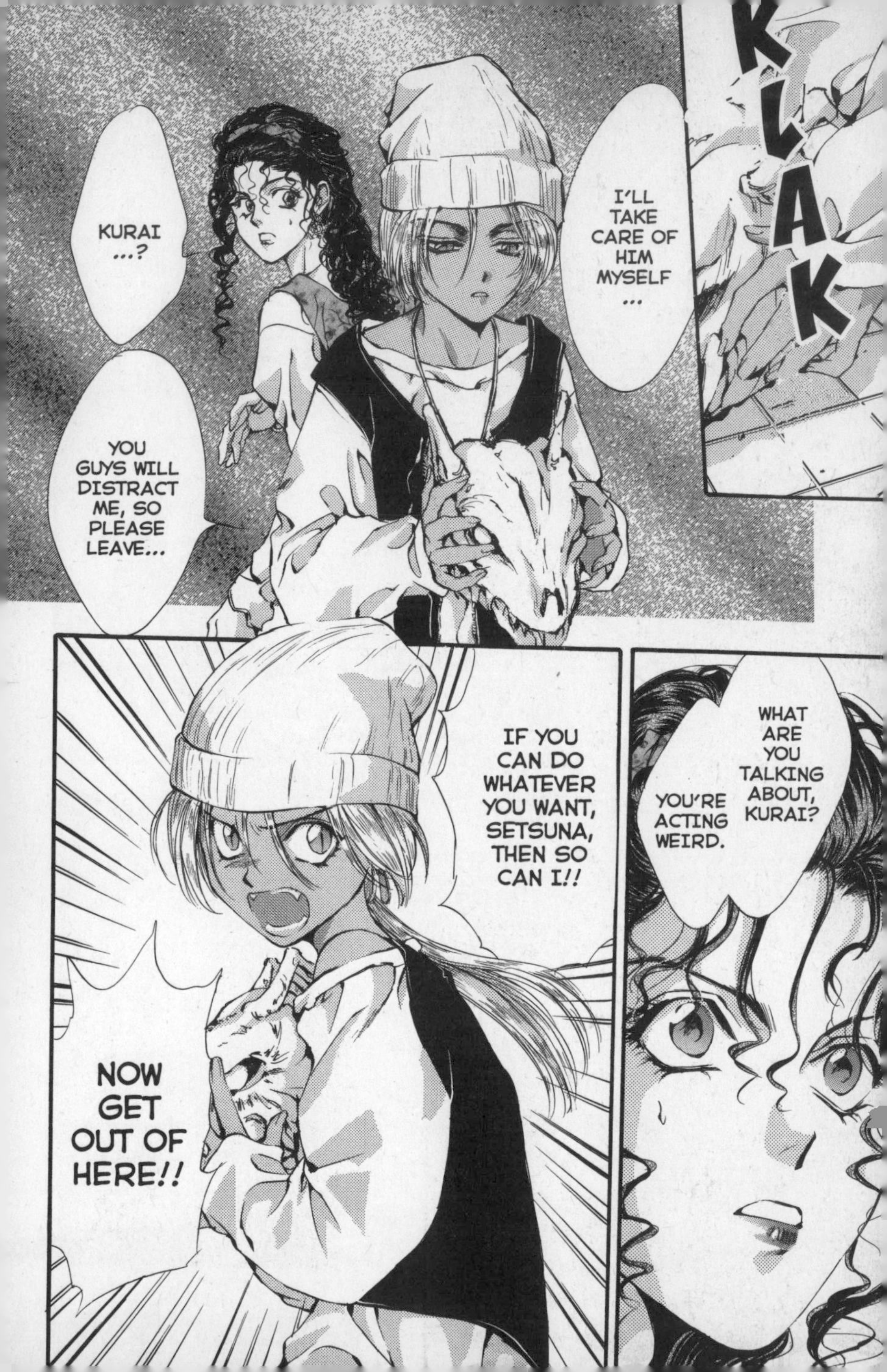
KLAK
I'LL TAKE CARE OF HIM MYSELF ...
KURAI ...?
YOU GUYS WILL DISTRACT ME, SO PLEASE LEAVE...
WHAT ARE YOU TALKING ABOUT, KURAI?
YOU'RE ACTING WEIRD.
IF YOU CAN DO WHATEVER YOU WANT, SETSUNA, THEN SO CAN I!!
NOW GET OUT OF HERE!!

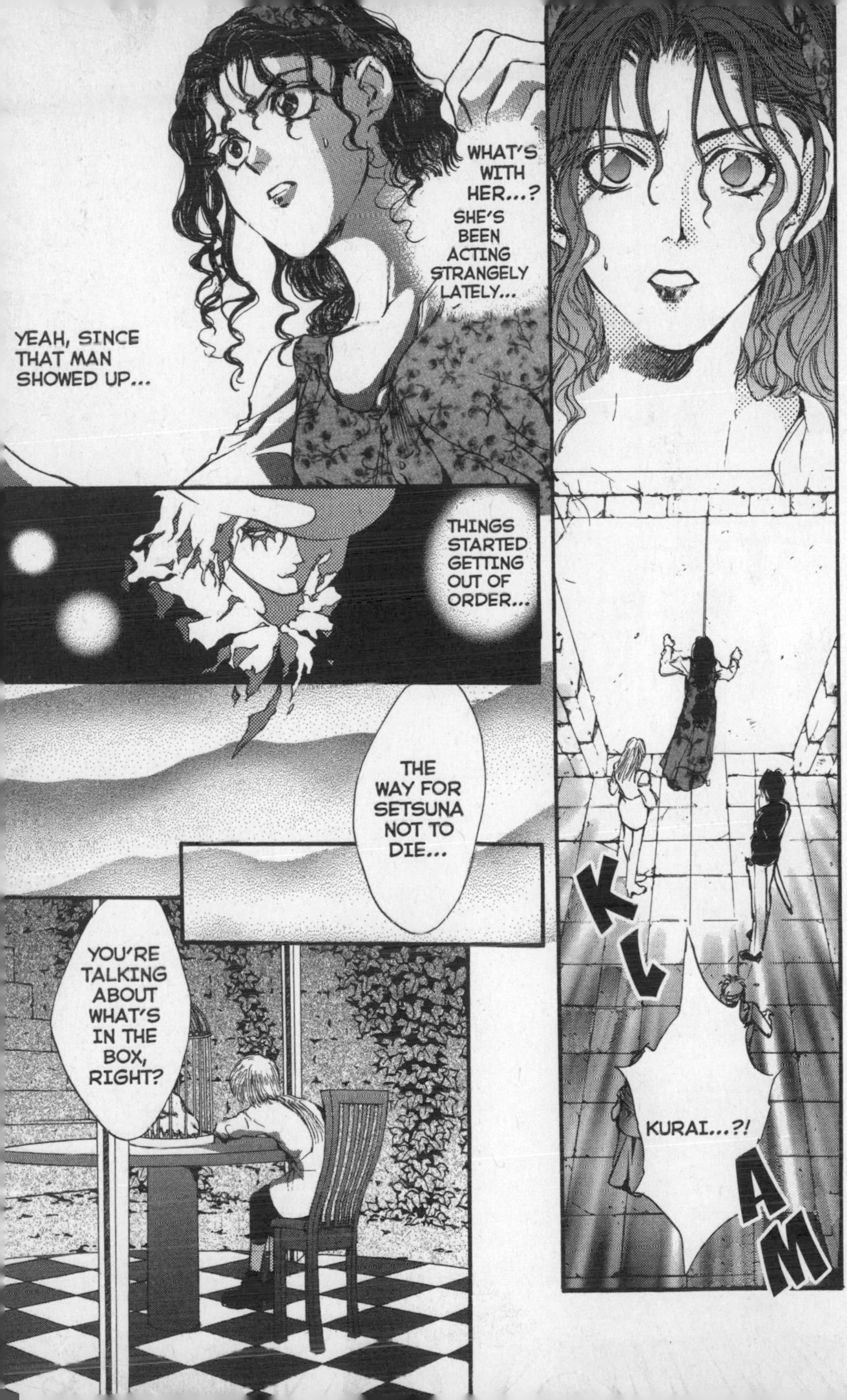
WHAT'S WITH HER...?
SHE'S BEEN ACTING STRANGELY LATELY...
YEAH, SINCE THAT MAN SHOWED UP...
THINGS STARTED GETTING OUT OF ORDER...
THE WAY FOR SETSUNA NOT TO DIE...
YOU'RE TALKING ABOUT WHAT'S IN THE BOX, RIGHT?
KLAM
KURAI...?!

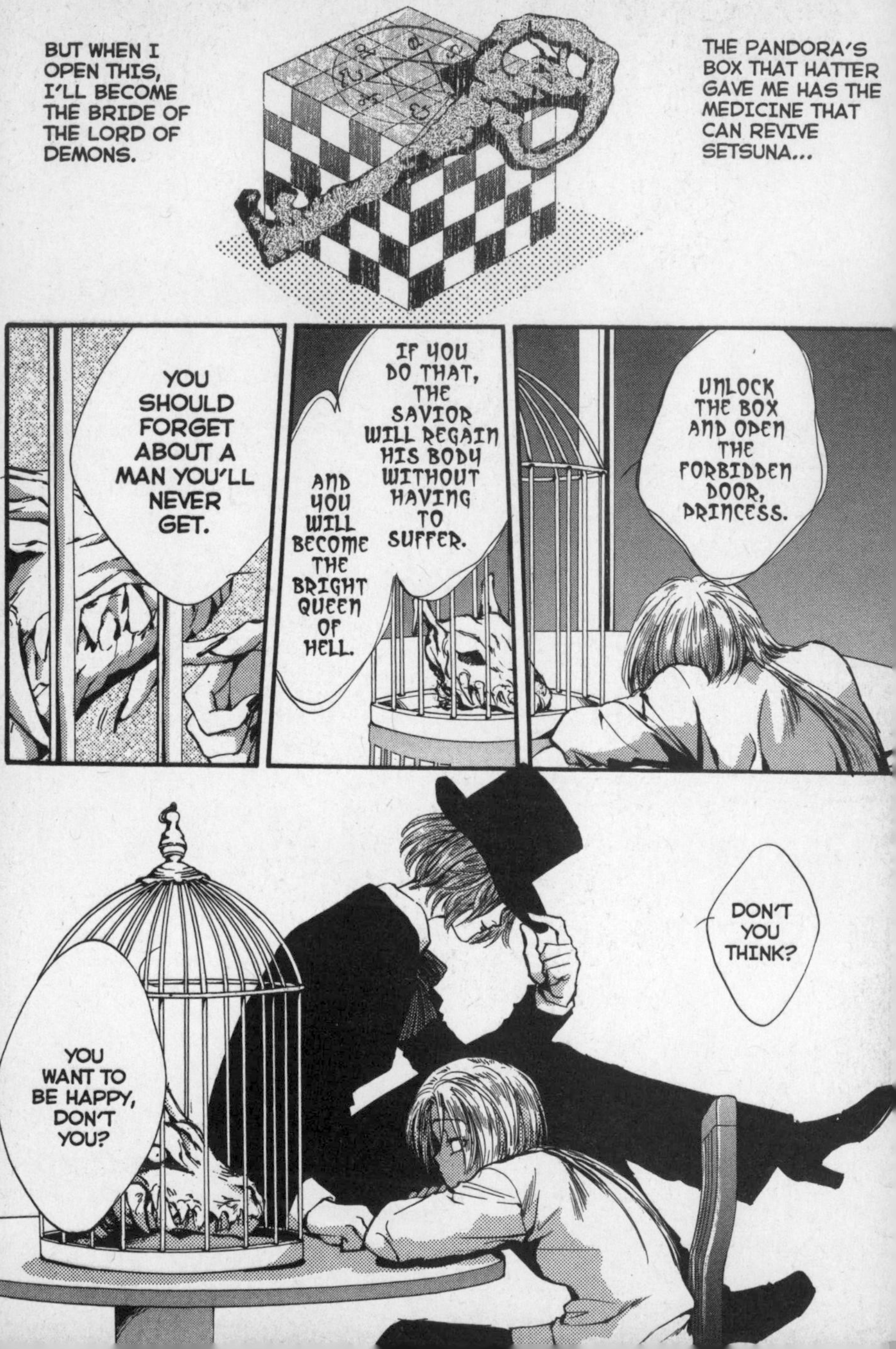
THE PANDORA'S BOX THAT HATTER GAVE ME HAS THE MEDICINE THAT CAN REVIVE SETSUNA...
BUT WHEN I OPEN THIS, I'LL BECOME THE BRIDE OF THE LORD OF DEMONS.
UNLOCK THE BOX AND OPEN THE FORBIDDEN DOOR, PRINCESS.
IF YOU DO THAT, THE SAVIOR WILL REGAIN HIS BODY WITHOUT HAVING TO SUFFER.
AND YOU WILL BECOME THE BRIGHT QUEEN OF HELL.
YOU SHOULD FORGET ABOUT A MAN YOU'LL NEVER GET.
DON'T YOU THINK?
YOU WANT TO BE HAPPY, DON'T YOU?

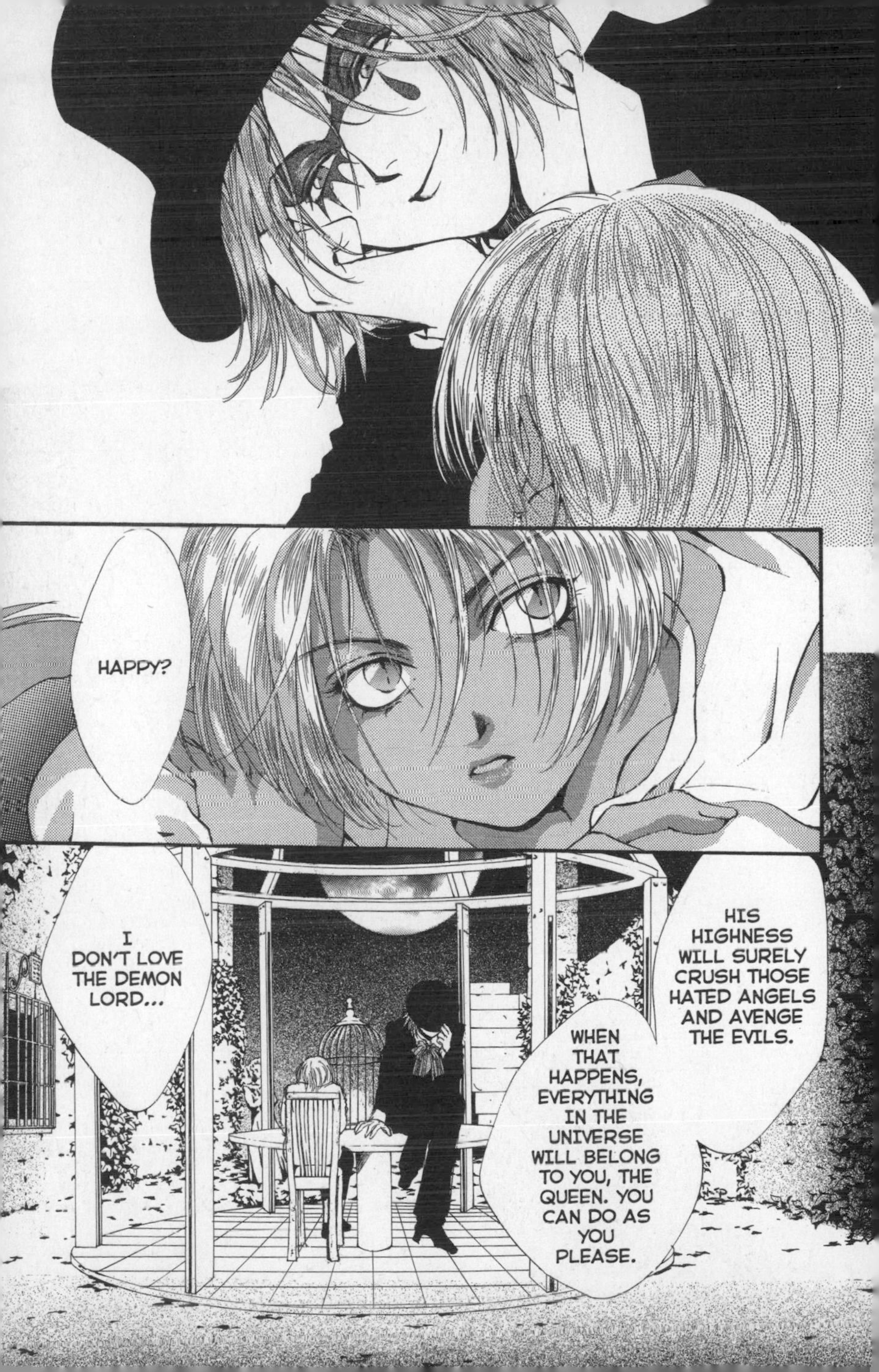
HAPPY?
HIS HIGHNESS WILL SURELY CRUSH THOSE HATED ANGELS AND AVENGE THE EVILS.
WHEN THAT HAPPENS, EVERYTHING IN THE UNIVERSE WILL BELONG TO YOU, THE QUEEN. YOU CAN DO AS YOU PLEASE.
I DON'T LOVE THE DEMON LORD...

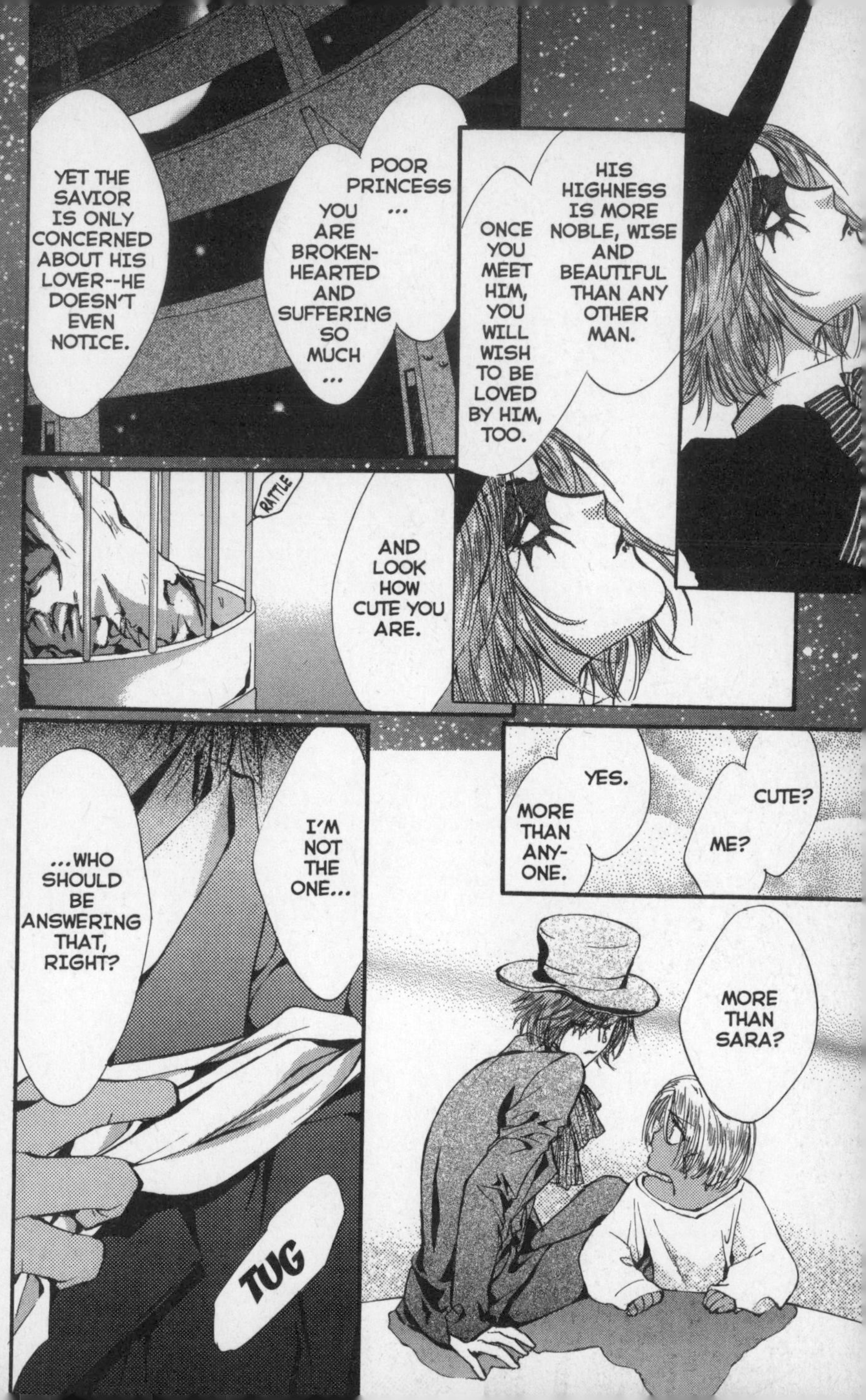
HIS HIGHNESS IS MORE NOBLE, WISE AND BEAUTIFUL THAN ANY OTHER MAN.
ONCE YOU MEET HIM, YOU WILL WISH TO BE LOVED BY HIM, TOO.
POOR PRINCESS ... YOU ARE BROKEN-HEARTED AND SUFFERING SO MUCH ...
YET THE SAVIOR IS ONLY CONCERNED ABOUT HIS LOVER--HE DOESN'T EVEN NOTICE.
AND LOOK HOW CUTE YOU ARE.
RATTLE
CUTE? ME?
YES. MORE THAN ANY-ONE.
MORE THAN SARA?
I'M NOT THE ONE...
...WHO SHOULD BE ANSWERING THAT, RIGHT?
TUG

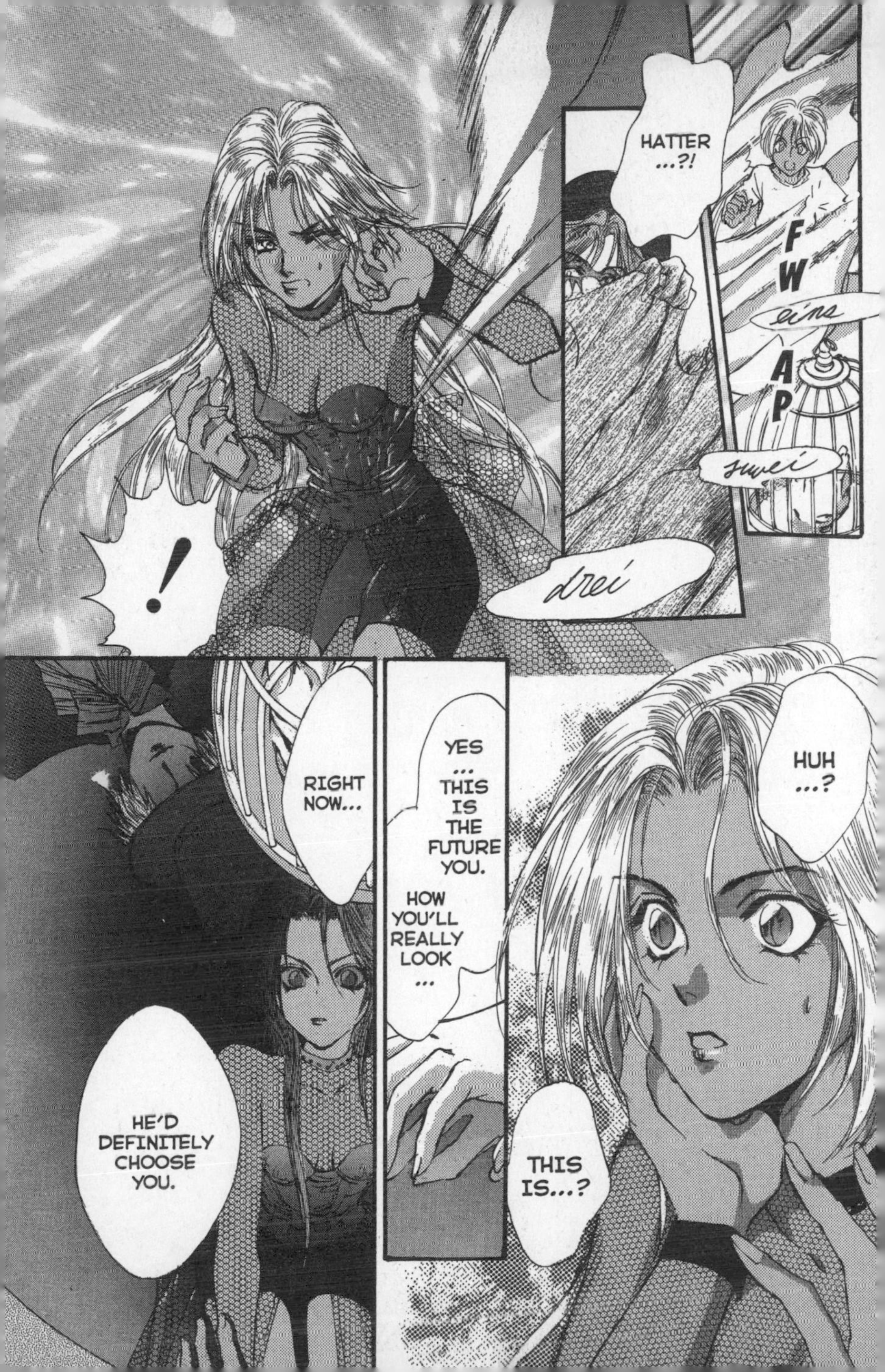
HATTER ...?!
FWAP
eins
zwei
drei
!
HUH ...?
THIS IS...?
YES ... THIS IS THE FUTURE YOU.
HOW YOU'LL REALLY LOOK ...
RIGHT NOW...
HE'D DEFINITELY CHOOSE YOU.

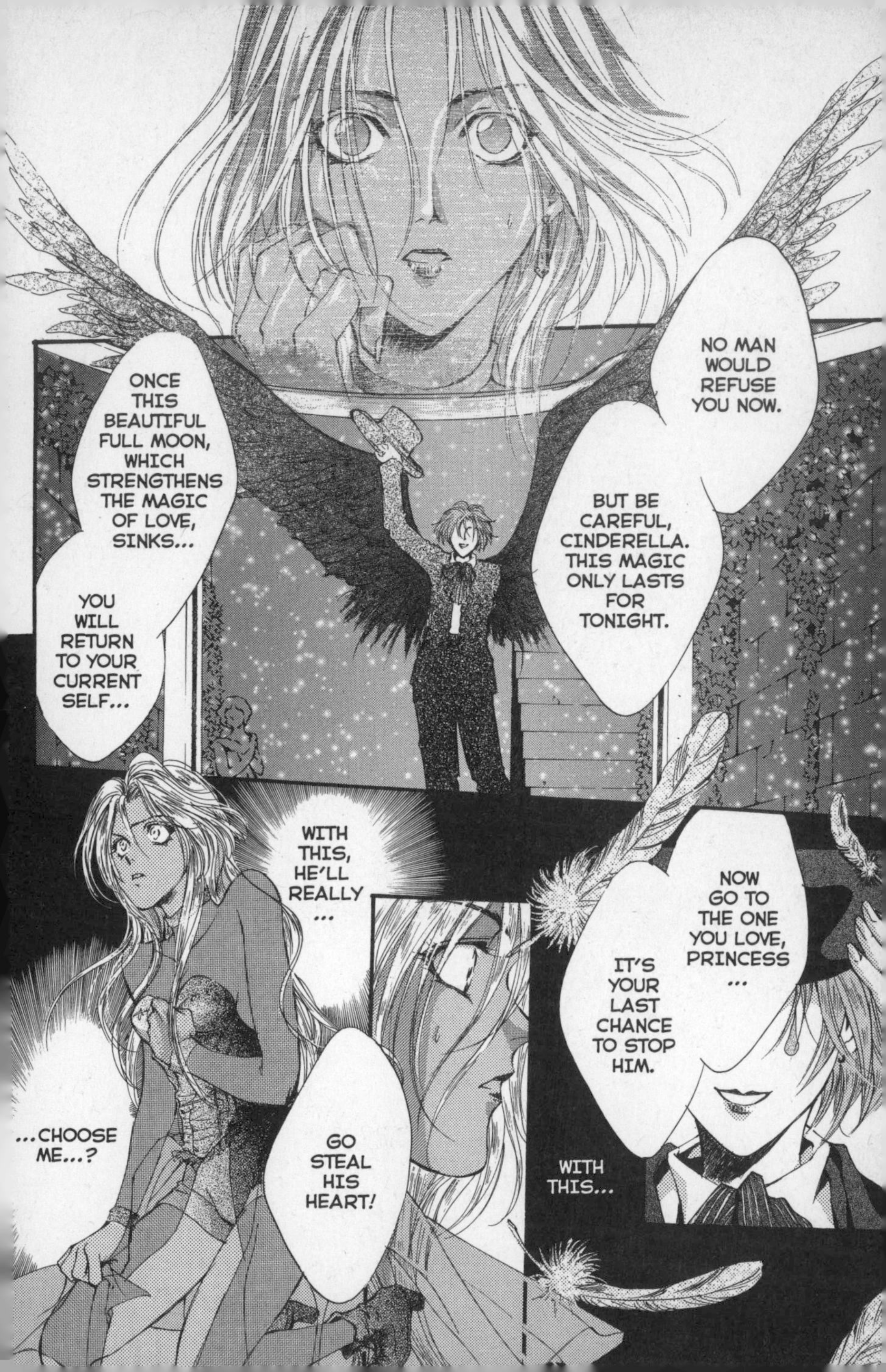
NO MAN WOULD REFUSE YOU NOW.
BUT BE CAREFUL, CINDERELLA. THIS MAGIC ONLY LASTS FOR TONIGHT.
ONCE THIS BEAUTIFUL FULL MOON, WHICH STRENGTHENS THE MAGIC OF LOVE, SINKS...
YOU WILL RETURN TO YOUR CURRENT SELF...
NOW GO TO THE ONE YOU LOVE, PRINCESS...
IT'S YOUR LAST CHANCE TO STOP HIM.
WITH THIS...
GO STEAL HIS HEART!
WITH THIS, HE'LL REALLY...
...CHOOSE ME...?

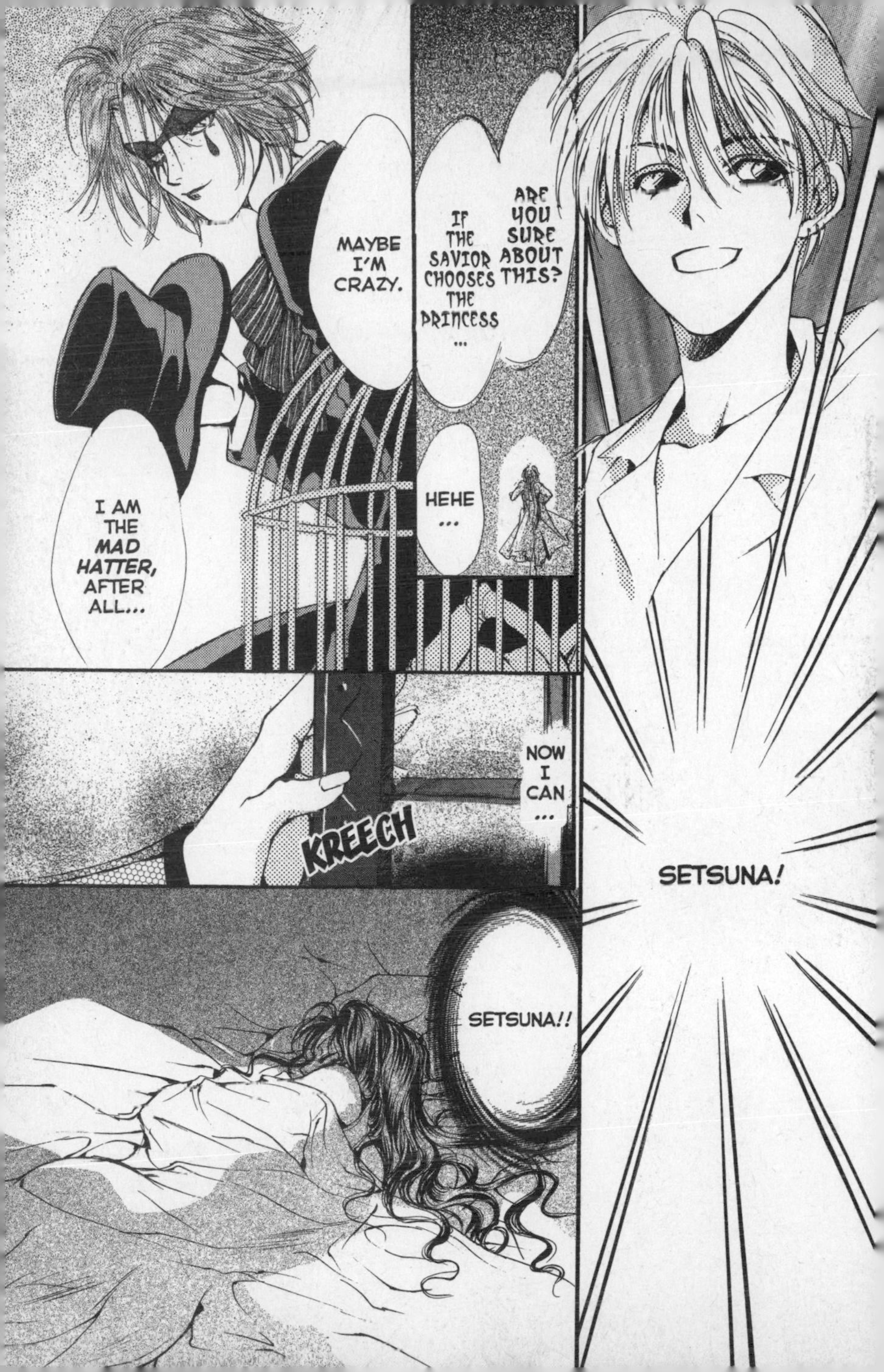
SETSUNA!
ARE YOU SURE ABOUT THIS?
IF THE SAVIOR CHOOSES THE PRINCESS ...
HEHE ...
MAYBE I'M CRAZY.
I AM THE *MAD HATTER*, AFTER ALL...
NOW I CAN ...
KREECH
SETSUNA!!

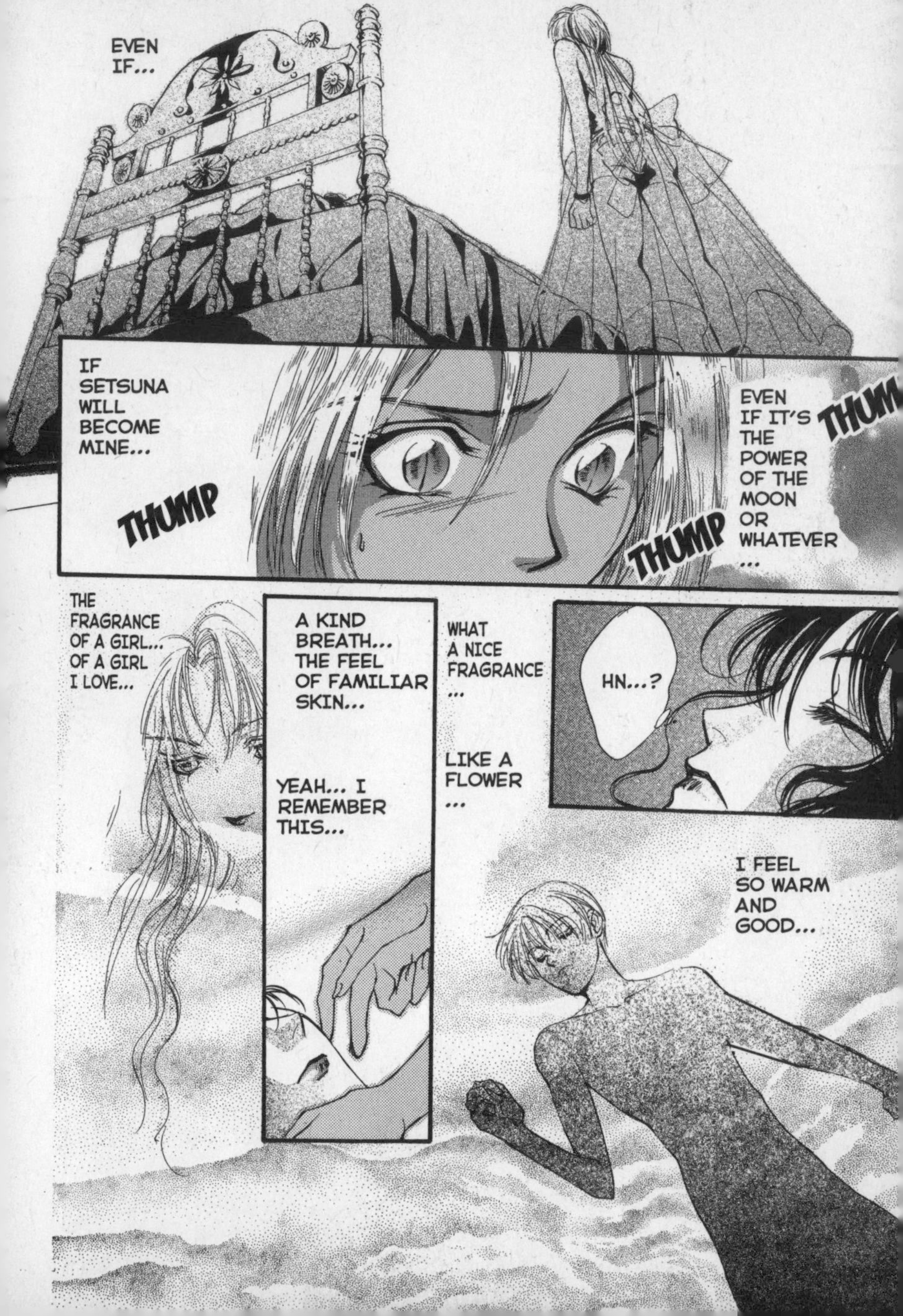
EVEN IF...
EVEN IF IT'S THE POWER OF THE MOON OR WHATEVER...
THUMP
THUMP
THUMP
IF SETSUNA WILL BECOME MINE...
HN...?
WHAT A NICE FRAGRANCE...
LIKE A FLOWER...
A KIND BREATH... THE FEEL OF FAMILIAR SKIN...
YEAH... I REMEMBER THIS...
THE FRAGRANCE OF A GIRL... OF A GIRL I LOVE...
I FEEL SO WARM AND GOOD...

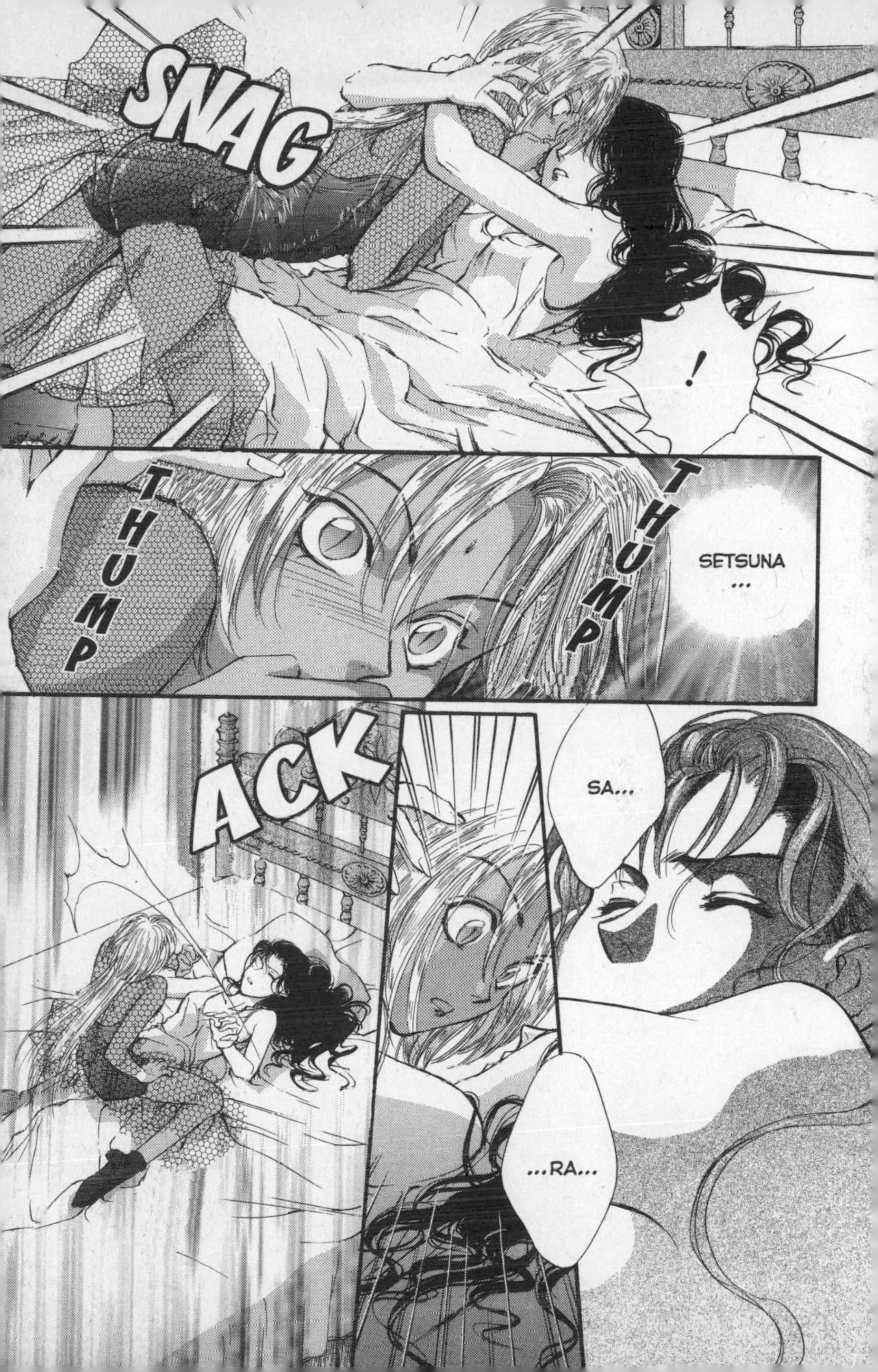
SNAG
!
THUMP
THUMP
SETSUNA ...
SA...
...RA...
ACK

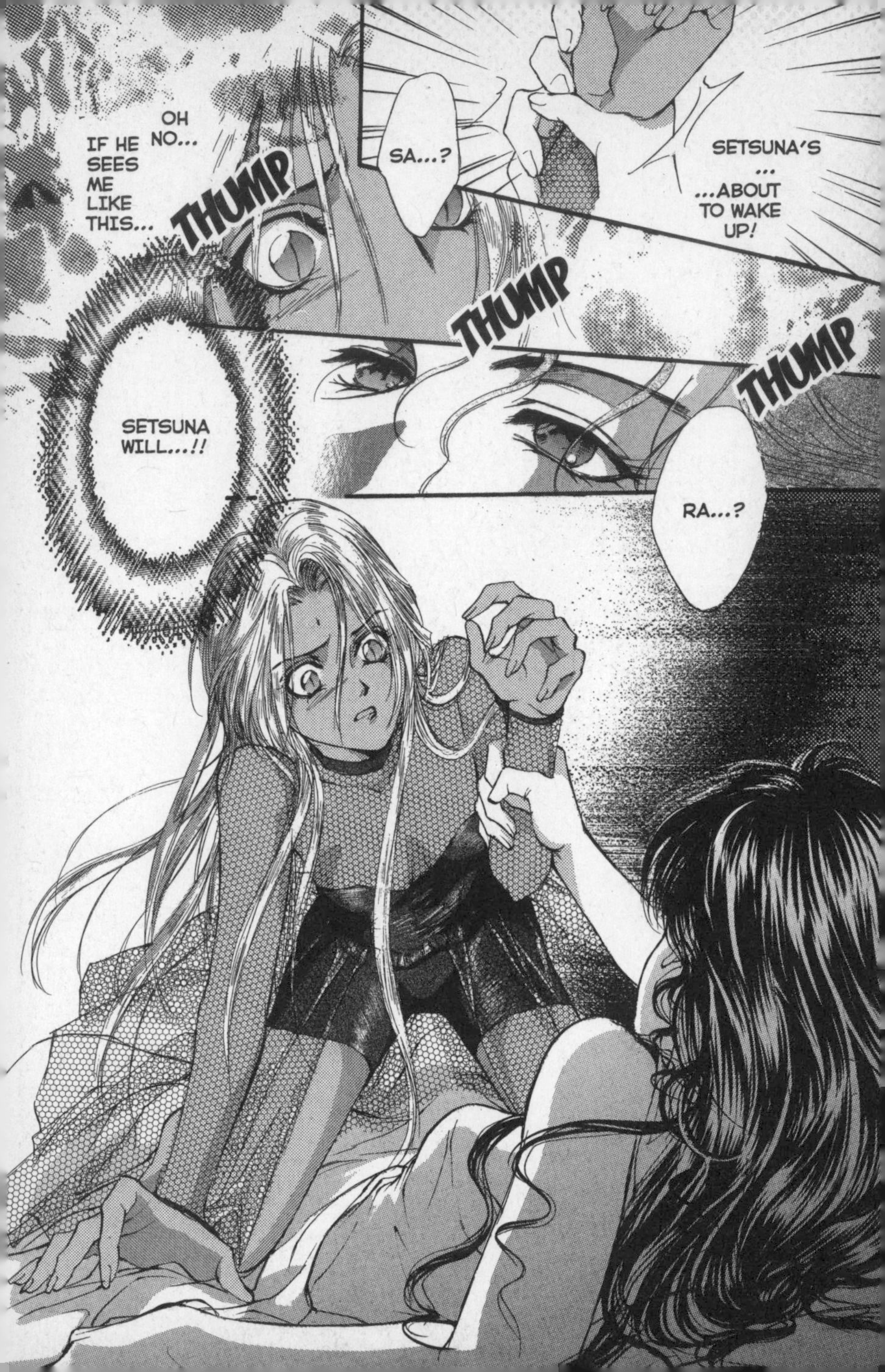
SETSUNA'S ... ...ABOUT TO WAKE UP!
SA...?
THUMP
OH NO... IF HE SEES ME LIKE THIS...
THUMP
THUMP
RA...?
SETSUNA WILL...!!

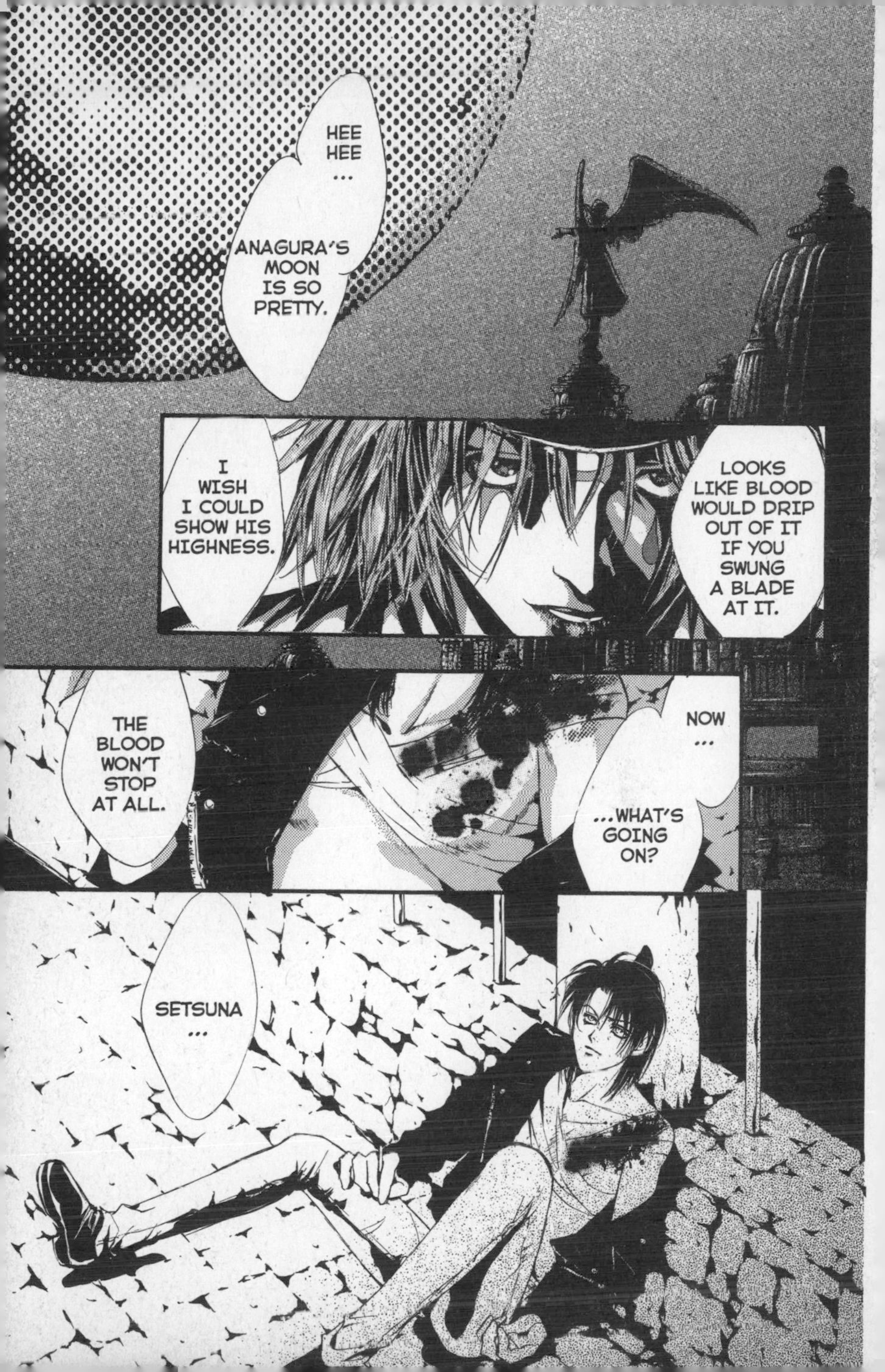
HEE HEE ...
ANAGURA'S MOON IS SO PRETTY.
LOOKS LIKE BLOOD WOULD DRIP OUT OF IT IF YOU SWUNG A BLADE AT IT.
I WISH I COULD SHOW HIS HIGHNESS.
NOW ...
...WHAT'S GOING ON?
THE BLOOD WON'T STOP AT ALL.
SETSUNA ...

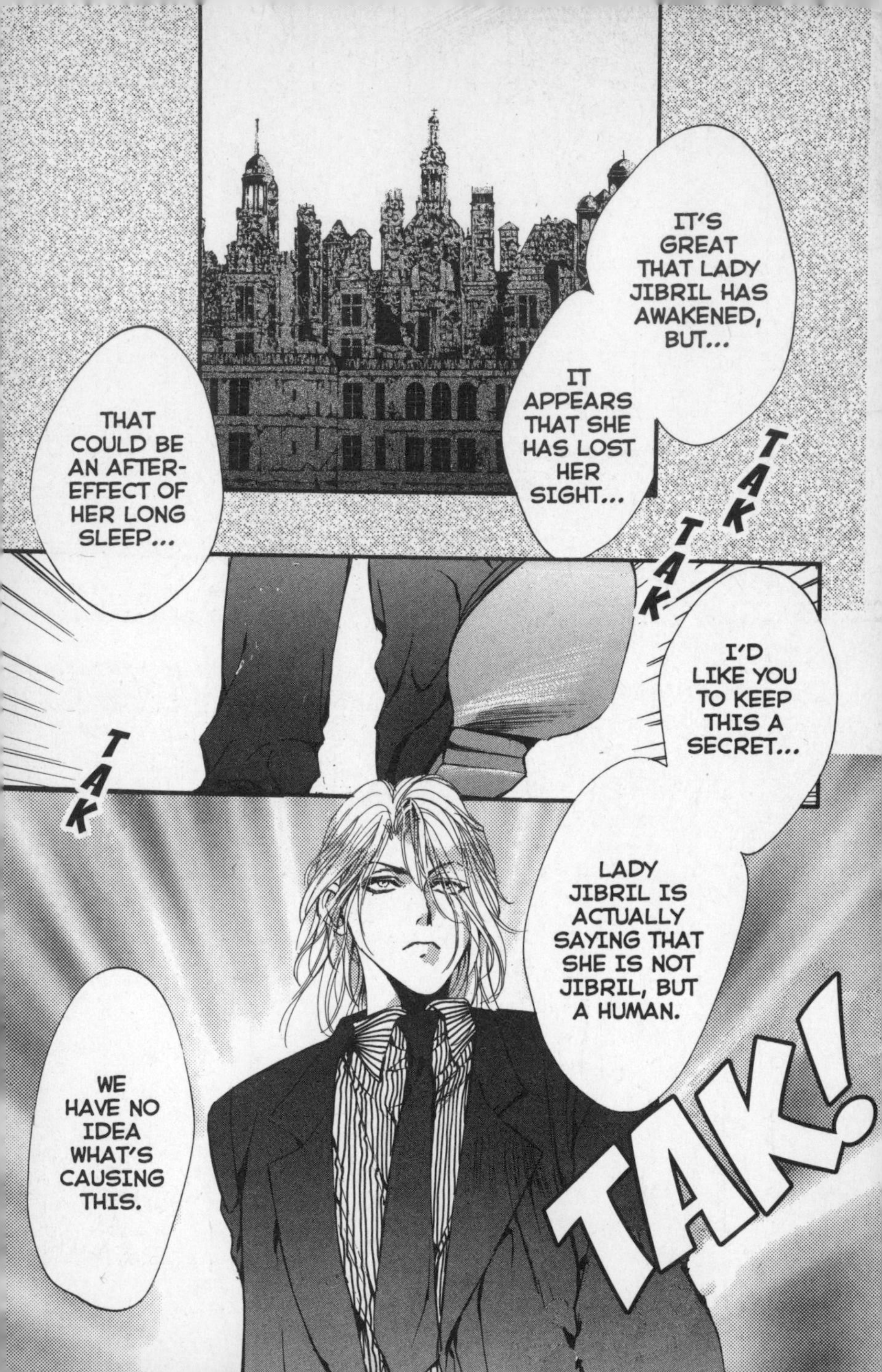
IT'S GREAT THAT LADY JIBRIL HAS AWAKENED, BUT...
IT APPEARS THAT SHE HAS LOST HER SIGHT...
THAT COULD BE AN AFTER-EFFECT OF HER LONG SLEEP...
TAK
TAK
I'D LIKE YOU TO KEEP THIS A SECRET...
TAK
LADY JIBRIL IS ACTUALLY SAYING THAT SHE IS NOT JIBRIL, BUT A HUMAN.
TAK!
WE HAVE NO IDEA WHAT'S CAUSING THIS.

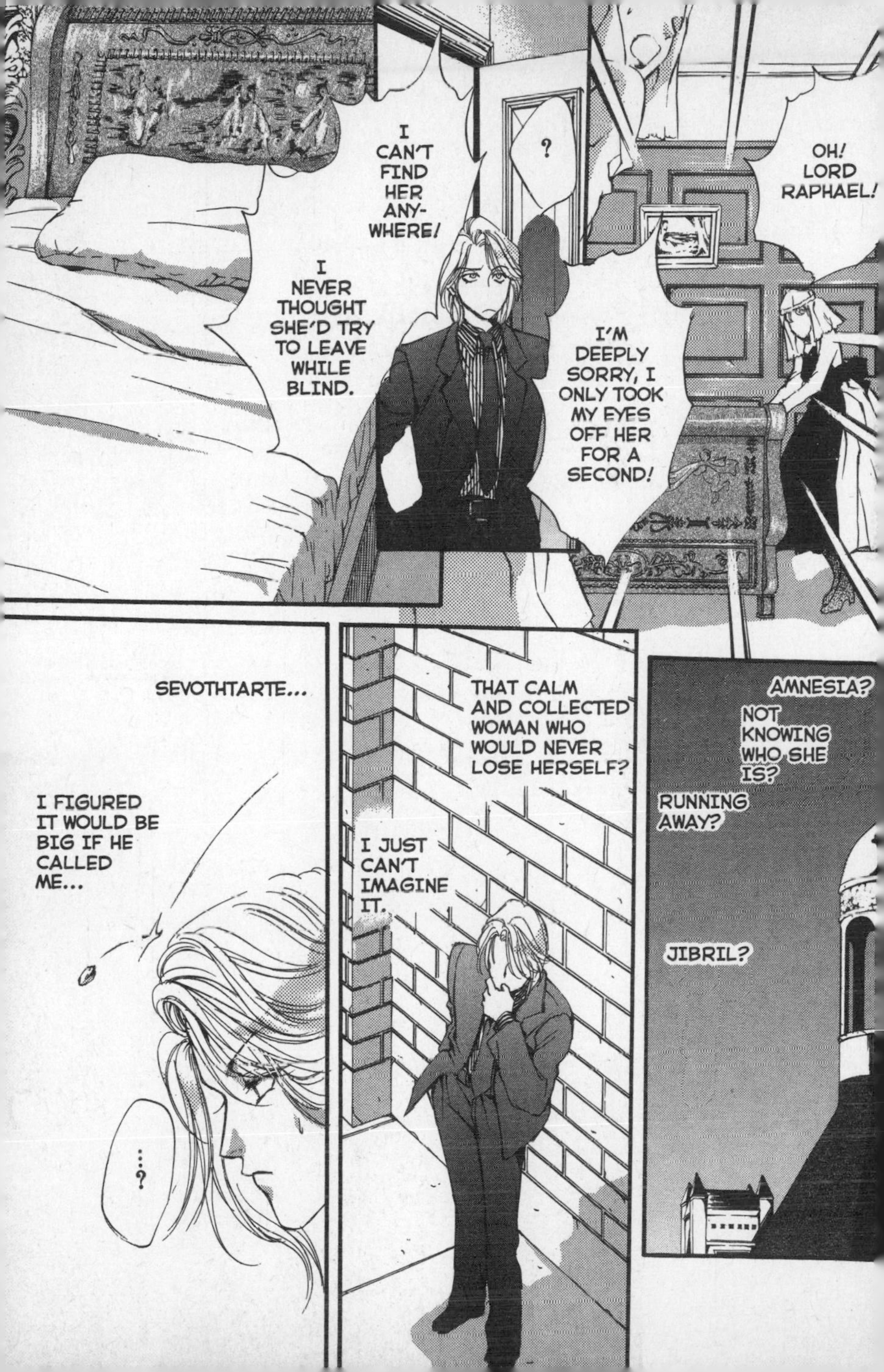
OH! LORD RAPHAEL!
I'M DEEPLY SORRY, I ONLY TOOK MY EYES OFF HER FOR A SECOND!
?
I CAN'T FIND HER ANY-WHERE!
I NEVER THOUGHT SHE'D TRY TO LEAVE WHILE BLIND.
AMNESIA?
NOT KNOWING WHO SHE IS?
RUNNING AWAY?
JIBRIL?
THAT CALM AND COLLECTED WOMAN WHO WOULD NEVER LOSE HERSELF?
I JUST CAN'T IMAGINE IT.
SEVOTHTARTE...
I FIGURED IT WOULD BE BIG IF HE CALLED ME...
...?

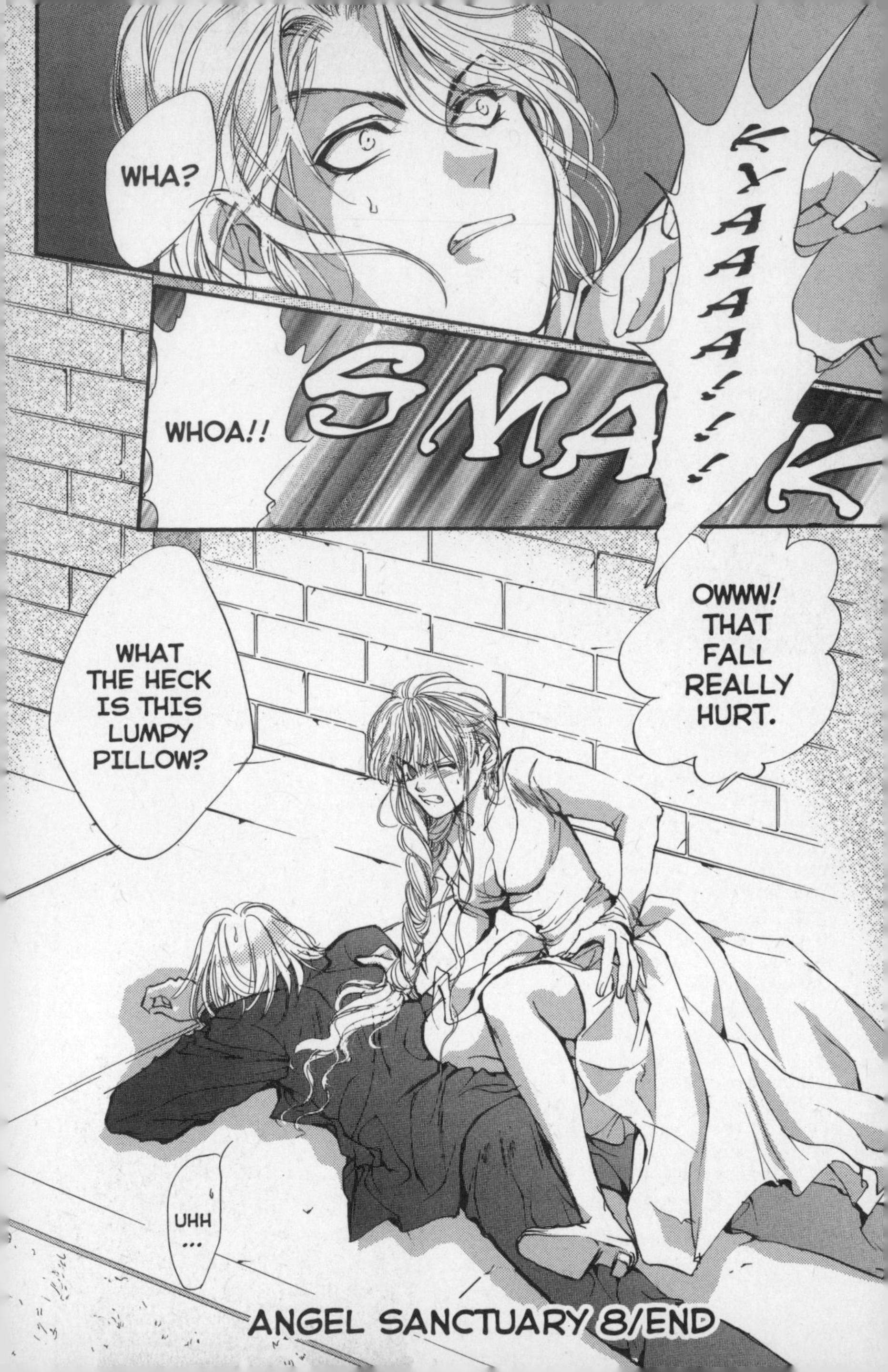
KYAAAA!!!
WHA?
SMA K
WHOA!!
OWWW! THAT FALL REALLY HURT.
WHAT THE HECK IS THIS LUMPY PILLOW?
UHH...
ANGEL SANCTUARY 8/END

Angel Lies and Devil Flattery

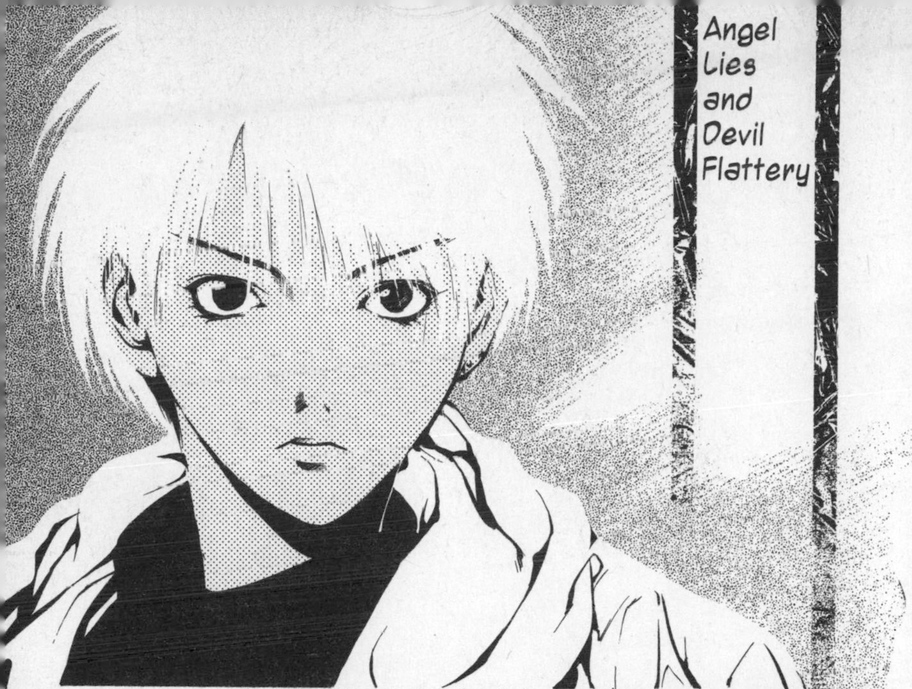

No more Alexiel... Drawing Setsuna's face is so much easier...!

Something that happened recently that I found very funny was seeing pictures of A.S. cosplayers. I've heard stories but... So it was true. Plus males were actually dressed as the male characters. (what a strange thing to say...) It's too bad that the picture I saw had the top part cut off. Doll and Sara were played by some really cute girls. The clothes were done so well. And whether it was Kato-kun or Kira, they had the poses down pat. This is a weird feeling... I'd like to see some better pictures next time. As a summer recommendation, how about the cool Mika? Only a boy could pull it off, but just have someone draw a tattoo on you! Oh yeah, the Hatter cosplayer even had make-up on her face. I heard there was also a Kurai. You'd need someone with big breasts to play Alexiel... But if her bust is really 87 cm (34 in), then that's not that large.

It's still big though.

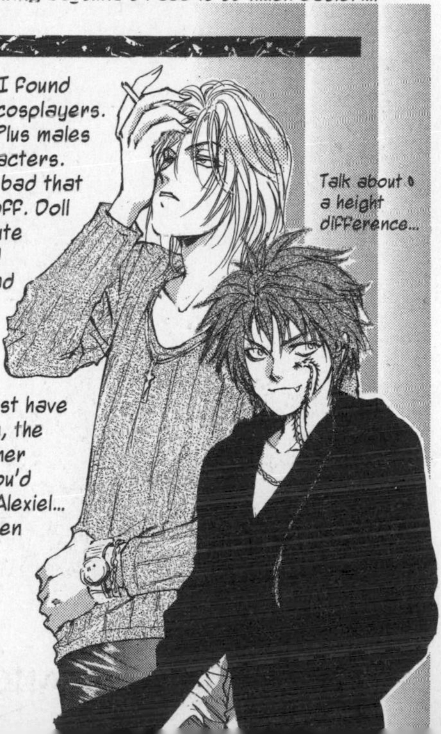
Talk about a height difference...

music and the man~gaka

It's back

Have you ever seen a broken CD?!!
I have! It really surprised me! I received
a letter and noticed it had a CD in it, but
when I pulled it out it was in two pieces!
Ever since I wrote about the cracked
tape I got, this kind of thing didn't happen,
but...This was thoughtless. If you don't wrap
the up then they will get damaged. What a
waste. By the way, the CD was "Lies and
Truth." Next time please protect before sending.
The cassettes were fine though. Thanks a lot,
I listen to them a lot. That blue CD was good too.
The other day an assistant took me to
a live music house for the first time in my
life. (The one who has to draw Mika's tattoo.
BTW, she has red hair right now.) Though it
was Aka--- Blitz, so it's a big place. But I
am only used to going to large concerts
where the artists on stage look like ants, so
it was great to be so close to the action.
All the pushing and shoving got me really
tired though. (I have no stamina...) It sucks
when the person in front of you is really
tall. And the second time I went was on
Valentine's day, and they were throwing
chocolate into the crowd, but the girls
(and guys) were getting so violent trying
to grab all the chocolate. We just stared
at them while stunned. It was scary! But one piece
of chocolate happened to drop in my hands somehow, and
I still have it.

Will it rot? Should   Yeah... I'm wasting it...
I eat it? (It's 3/12 now).

I'm hoping I can go to a lot of live
performances this year. It's tough that I
don't have much time off...   Come on...

I want to go to Guniw, and of course THAT one that was
postponed.

↖This is Lord Rosiel.

(Assistant A) "Yuki-san, Lord Rosiel hasn't appeared lately at all, what has he been doing?"

(Yuki) "Who knows? I haven't thought about that."

(Assistant B) "Dummy, isn't it obvious?! He's in a rose-petal bath! And Katan is scrubbing his back!"

(Yuki) "This whole time...?" he'd be all wrinkly...

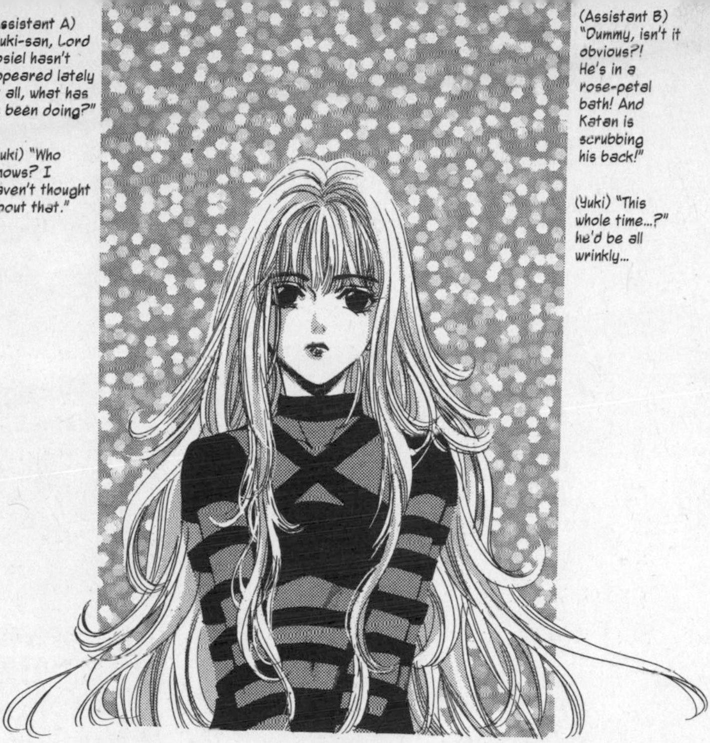

This manga is created from a fun work environment where conversations like the one above take place. And I have received a few letters asking what Rosiel has been up to. Let me answer... I don't know! The end. Well, eventually (in a long, long time) he'll appear a lot again. The Heaven arc can't begin until the Hell arc concludes. But 1999 is so close...

And also, I get a lot of letters expressing opinions like "This is different from how I imagine angels," "The hierarchy is wrong" and "There's no such angel in the books I have." That's because... This is a fictitious story I created using many different materials as a basis. Of course some things will be different. I mean, there's differences based on which of the various books you read. There's more than one story. It's all right if there's different interpretations. But there really is a Sevothtarte. Alexiel, Katan, and Kirie were created by me, but most of the rest of the characters are based on actual names. But the story is totally that of "A.S. World," okay?

And finally, thank you so much to my editor, I-san, who has helped me with my manga for over 5 years now. I would never exist as I do now without the help of I-san. Thank you so much for helping out with AS for so long! Goodbye♥

1997. 3/12

And now I will be causing countless amounts of suffering to my new editor! Yeah...

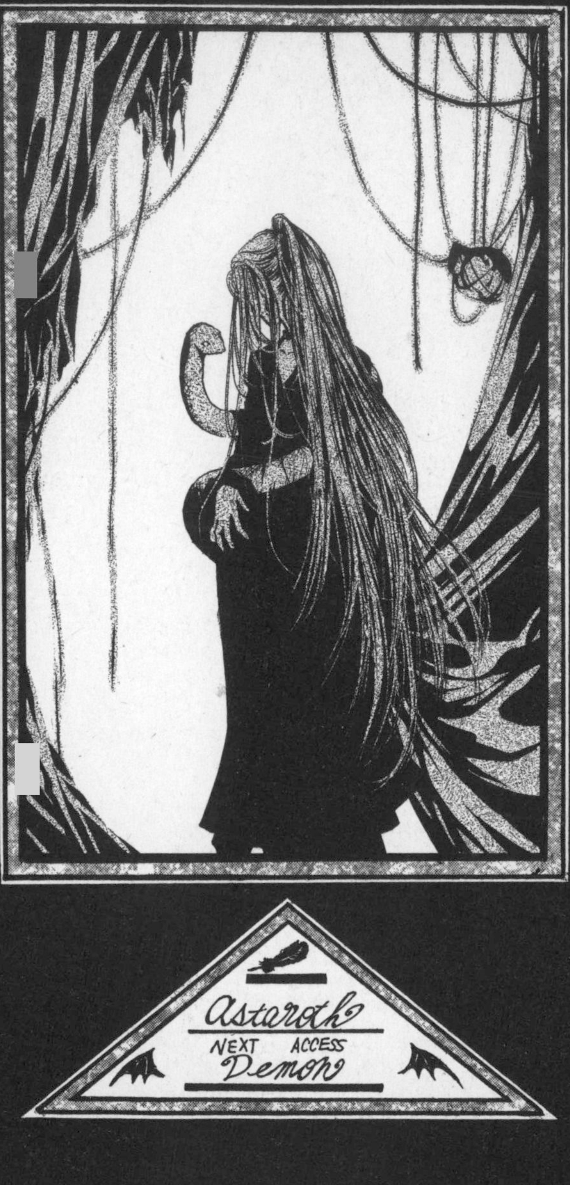
Astaroth
NEXT ACCESS
Demon

...TO BE CONTINUED

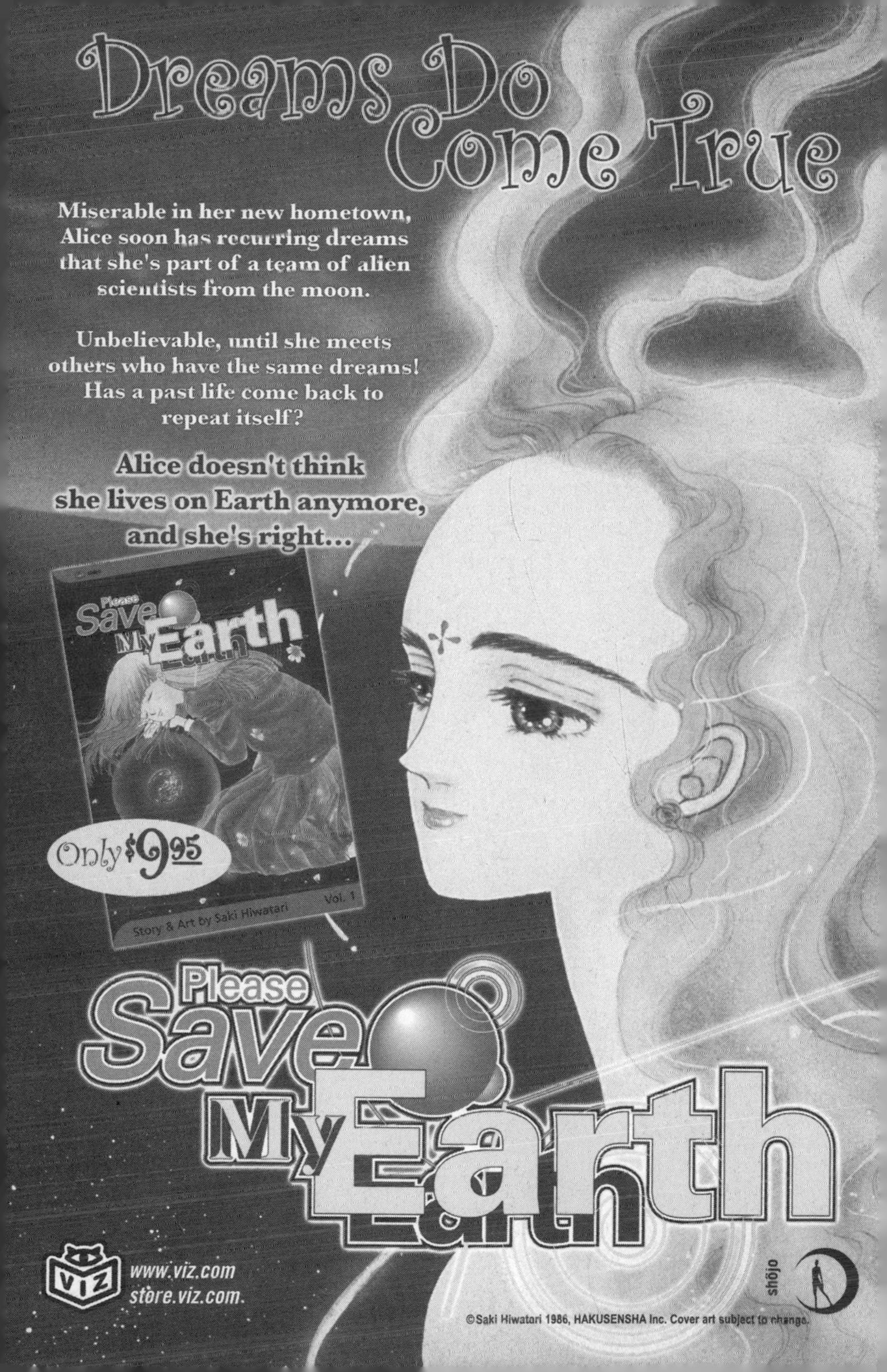
Dreams Do Come True
Miserable in her new hometown, Alice soon has recurring dreams that she's part of a team of alien scientists from the moon.
Unbelievable, until she meets others who have the same dreams! Has a past life come back to repeat itself?
Alice doesn't think she lives on Earth anymore, and she's right...
Please Save My Earth
Story & Art by Saki Hiwatari
Vol. 1
Only $9.95
Please Save My Earth
www.viz.com
store.viz.com.
shōjo
©Saki Hiwatari 1986, HAKUSENSHA Inc. Cover art subject to change.

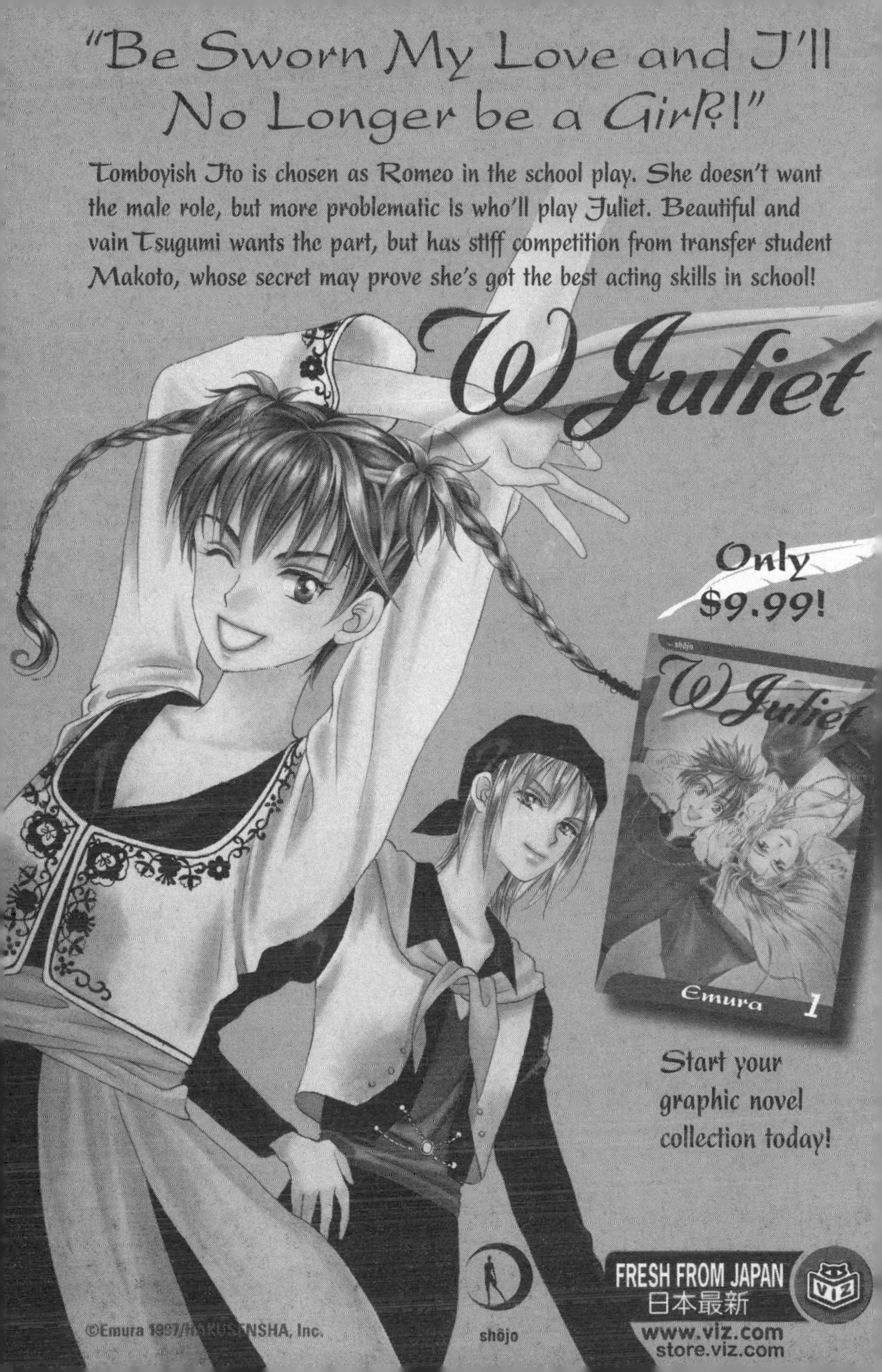
"Be Sworn My Love and I'll No Longer be a Girl?!"
Tomboyish Ito is chosen as Romeo in the school play. She doesn't want the male role, but more problematic is who'll play Juliet. Beautiful and vain Tsugumi wants the part, but has stiff competition from transfer student Makoto, whose secret may prove she's got the best acting skills in school!
W Juliet
Only $9.99!
W Juliet
Emura 1
Start your graphic novel collection today!
FRESH FROM JAPAN
日本最新
VIZ
www.viz.com
store.viz.com
shōjo
©Emura 1997/HAKUSENSHA, Inc.

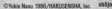

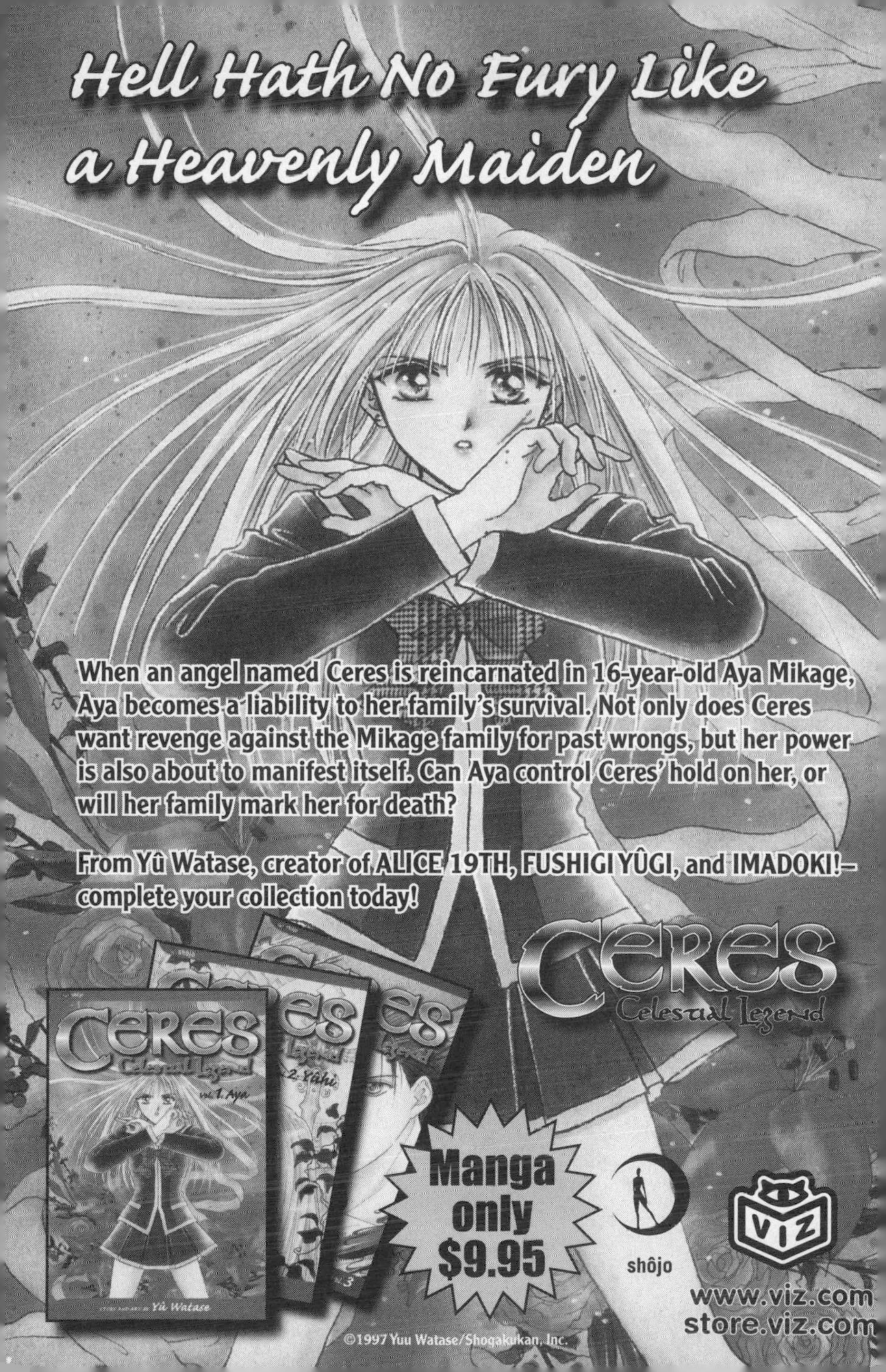
Hell Hath No Fury Like a Heavenly Maiden
When an angel named Ceres is reincarnated in 16-year-old Aya Mikage, Aya becomes a liability to her family's survival. Not only does Ceres want revenge against the Mikage family for past wrongs, but her power is also about to manifest itself. Can Aya control Ceres' hold on her, or will her family mark her for death?
From Yû Watase, creator of ALICE 19TH, FUSHIGI YÛGI, and IMADOKI!—complete your collection today!
Ceres
Celestial Legend
Manga only $9.95
shôjo
VIZ
www.viz.com
store.viz.com
©1997 Yuu Watase/Shogakukan, Inc.

COMPLETE OUR SURVEY AND LET US KNOW WHAT YOU THINK!

☐ Please do NOT send me information about VIZ products, news and events, special offers, or other information.

☐ Please do NOT send me information from VIZ's trusted business partners.

Name: _____

Address: _____

City: _____ **State:** _____ **Zip:** _____

E-mail: _____

☐ Male ☐ Female **Date of Birth** (mm/dd/yyyy): ___/___/_____ (Under 13? Parental consent required)

What race/ethnicity do you consider yourself? (please check one)

☐ Asian/Pacific Islander   ☐ Black/African American   ☐ Hispanic/Latino

☐ Native American/Alaskan Native   ☐ White/Caucasian   ☐ Other: _____

What VIZ product did you purchase? (check all that apply and indicate title purchased)

☐ DVD/VHS _____

☐ Graphic Novel _____

☐ Magazines _____

☐ Merchandise _____

Reason for purchase: (check all that apply)

☐ Special offer   ☐ Favorite title   ☐ Gift

☐ Recommendation   ☐ Other _____

Where did you make your purchase? (please check one)

☐ Comic store   ☐ Bookstore   ☐ Mass/Grocery Store

☐ Newsstand   ☐ Video/Video Game Store   ☐ Other: _____

☐ Online (site: _____)

What other VIZ properties have you purchased/own? _____

_____

How many anime and/or manga titles have you purchased in the last year? How many were VIZ titles? (please check one from each column)

ANIME	MANGA	VIZ
☐ None	☐ None	☐ None
☐ 1-4	☐ 1-4	☐ 1-4
☐ 5-10	☐ 5-10	☐ 5-10
☐ 11+	☐ 11+	☐ 11+

I find the pricing of VIZ products to be: (please check one)

☐ Cheap ☐ Reasonable ☐ Expensive

What genre of manga and anime would you like to see from VIZ? (please check two)

☐ Adventure ☐ Comic Strip ☐ Science Fiction ☐ Fighting

☐ Horror ☐ Romance ☐ Fantasy ☐ Sports

What do you think of VIZ's new look?

☐ Love It ☐ It's OK ☐ Hate It ☐ Didn't Notice ☐ No Opinion

Which do you prefer? (please check one)

☐ Reading right-to-left

☐ Reading left-to-right

Which do you prefer? (please check one)

☐ Sound effects in English

☐ Sound effects in Japanese with English captions

☐ Sound effects in Japanese only with a glossary at the back

THANK YOU! Please send the completed form to:

NJW Research
42 Catharine St.
Poughkeepsie, NY 12601

All information provided will be used for internal purposes only. We promise not to sell or otherwise divulge your information.